THE ITALIAN IDEA

From 1815 to 1823 the Italian influence on English literature was at its zenith. While English tourists flocked to Italy, a pervasive Italianism coloured many facets of London life, including poetry, periodicals, translation, and even the Queen's trial of 1820. In this engaging study Will Bowers considers this radical interaction by pursuing two interrelated analyses. The first examines the Italian literary and political ideas absorbed by Romantic poets, particularly Lord Byron, Leigh Hunt, and Percy Bysshe Shelley. The second uncovers the ambassadorial role played in London by Italians, such as Serafino Buonaiuti and Ugo Foscolo, who promoted a revolutionary idea of their homeland and its literature, particularly Dante's *Commedia*. This dual-perspective study reveals that radical poetic engagement with Italy operated alongside the writings of Italian literary exiles in London to form a cosmopolitan challenge to Regency mores.

WILL BOWERS is Lecturer in Eighteenth-Century Literature and Thought at Queen Mary, University of London. He is the co-editor of *Re-evaluating the Literary Coterie 1580–1830* (2016) and has published widely on Leigh Hunt, Percy Bysshe Shelley, Mary Wollstonecraft Shelley, and Lord Byron in journals such as *Essays in Criticism*, *Review of English Studies*, and *Romanticism on Net*.

CAMBRIDGE STUDIES IN ROMANTICISM

This series aims to foster the best new work in one of the most challenging fields within English literary studies. From the early 1780s to the early 1830s, a formidable array of talented men and women took to literary composition, not just in poetry, which some of them famously transformed, but in many modes of writing. The expansion of publishing created new opportunities for writers, and the political stakes of what they wrote were raised again by what Wordsworth called those 'great national events' that were 'almost daily taking place': the French Revolution, the Napoleonic and American wars, urbanization, industrialization, religious revival, an expanded empire abroad, and the reform movement at home. This was an enormous ambition, even when it pretended otherwise. The relations between science, philosophy, religion, and literature were reworked in texts such as *Frankenstein* and *Biographia Literaria*; gender relations in *A Vindication of the Rights of Woman* and *Don Juan*; journalism by Cobbett and Hazlitt; and poetic form, content, and style by the Lake School and the Cockney School. Outside Shakespeare studies, probably no body of writing has produced such a wealth of commentary or done so much to shape the responses of modern criticism. This indeed is the period that saw the emergence of those notions of literature and of literary history, especially national literary history, on which modern scholarship in English has been founded.

The categories produced by Romanticism have also been challenged by recent historicist arguments. The task of the series is to engage both with a challenging corpus of Romantic writings and with the changing field of criticism they have helped to shape. As with other literary series published by Cambridge University Press, this one will represent the work of both younger and more established scholars on either side of the Atlantic and elsewhere.

THE ITALIAN IDEA

Anglo-Italian Radical Literary Culture, 1815–1823

WILL BOWERS

Queen Mary, University of London

CAMBRIDGE
UNIVERSITY PRESS

University Printing House, Cambridge CB2 8BS, United Kingdom

One Liberty Plaza, 20th Floor, New York, NY 10006, USA

477 Williamstown Road, Port Melbourne, VIC 3207, Australia

314–321, 3rd Floor, Plot 3, Splendor Forum, Jasola District Centre, New Delhi – 110025, India

79 Anson Road, #06–04/06, Singapore 079906

Cambridge University Press is part of the University of Cambridge.

It furthers the University's mission by disseminating knowledge in the pursuit of education, learning, and research at the highest international levels of excellence.

www.cambridge.org
Information on this title: www.cambridge.org/9781108491969
DOI: 10.1017/9781108590228

First published 2020

Printed in the United Kingdom by TJ International Ltd, Padstow Cornwall

A catalogue record for this publication is available from the British Library.

Library of Congress Cataloging-in-Publication Data

NAMES: Bowers, Will, author.
TITLE: The Italian idea : Anglo-Italian radical literary culture, 1815-23 / Will Bowers, Queen Mary University of London.
OTHER TITLES: Anglo–Italian radical literary culture, 1815-23
DESCRIPTION: Cambridge, United Kingdom ; New York, NY : Cambridge University Press, 2020. | Series: Cambridge studies in romanticism | Includes bibliographical references and index.
IDENTIFIERS: LCCN 2019040875 (print) | LCCN 2019040876 (ebook) | ISBN 9781108491969 (hardback) | ISBN 9781108741378 (paperback) | ISBN 9781108590228 (epub)
SUBJECTS: LCSH: English literature–Italian influences. | English literature–19th century–History and criticism. | Romanticism–Great Britain. | Italy–In literature. | Dante Alighieri, 1265-1321–Influence. | Italy–Relations–Great Britain. | Great Britain–Relations–Italy. | Italy–Foreign public opinion, British.
CLASSIFICATION: LCC PR129.I8 B69 2020 (print) | LCC PR129.I8 (ebook) | DDC 820.9/3245–dc23
LC record available at https://lccn.loc.gov/2019040875
LC ebook record available at https://lccn.loc.gov/2019040876

ISBN 978-1-108-49196-9 Hardback

for Hazel,
Something there is about you that strikes a match in me

Cosi amor meco insù la lingua snella
Desta il fior novo di strania favella,
Mentre io di te, vezzosamente altera,
Canto, dal mio buon popol non inteso
E'l bel Tamigi cangio col bel Arno.
—John Milton, 'Sonnet III'

Contents

Preface

From 1815 to 1823, the influence of Italy on English literary culture was at its zenith. A pervasive Italianism characterised many facets of London life: poetry, periodicals, translations, the opera, and even the trial of Queen Caroline. Peace in continental Europe enabled tourists to cross the Simplon Pass to a culture they had been deprived of for twenty years. Those who stayed at home but felt 'a languishment / For skies Italian', as Keats put it, had on the banks of the Thames an increasingly Italianate metropolis.[1] There is plently of evidence to suggest that English readers were fascinated with Italian culture: Anne Elliot and Marionetta O'Carroll read and sang opera arias, for instance, and Dante Alighieri and Torquato Tasso were translated into English.[2] In poetic composition, the Italian tradition was put to radical use by poets who experimented with its forms and themes to produce some of the most enduring works of the Romantic period. The production of these texts was excited by the growth of an Italian migrant community in London, which included poets, musicians, and booksellers. The Italianism of the poets and the interest kindled by Italian exiles accumulated over the period, and it produced poetry and criticism that engaged in increasingly complex ways with Italian ideas.

It is my contention that some cosmopolitan Londoners conceived of supporting Italian culture, the British poetry influenced by it, and Italian independence movements, as part of a larger questioning of Britishness after the Battle of Waterloo. At the opening of her landmark study *The German Idea*, Rosemary Ashton writes of examining 'with an equal eye' the ideas English authors formed with reference to Germany and the idea of Germany that existed in England.[3] Like Ashton, I pursue two separate but interrelated objectives in my analysis of English interaction with Italian ideas. The first is to examine the Italian literary and political ideas absorbed by second-generation Romantic authors, particularly Leigh Hunt, Lord Byron, and Percy Bysshe Shelley. The second is to reveal the ambassadorial role played by Italian arrivals in London, such as Giuseppe

Binda and Ugo Foscolo, who promoted a historically informed idea of their homeland and its literature. I argue that we cannot understand the Italianate poetry of the period until we pay attention to the public reception of Italian exiles in Britain: Italianate poetry and Italian immigrants were viewed as part of the same threat. My subtitle refers to 'Radical Literary Culture', using 'radical' in its broadest sense to describe literature 'characterized by independence of or departure from what is usual or traditional; progressive, unorthodox, or innovative in outlook, conception, design', and for its early nineteenth-century associations with political reform.[4] After victory at Waterloo, the British state maintained cultural hegemony at home and abroad by legislating against the threat of revolutions from Europe, the external threat of immigration to Britain, and the internal danger of radical literature. There is a relationship between literary culture and a defence of the 'public mind', and one of my aims is to show how Regency mores were troubled by alien people, ideas, and literature. An idea of Italy as a dangerous place was partly a hangover from anti-Grand Tour discourse that criticised the femininity and rakishness of travellers to Rome, Venice, and Naples. These preconceptions intensified in post-war London, as the existential fear of foreign, and often Jacobin, corruption could be read into things as diverse as the decoration of Leigh Hunt's prison cell, the Italian staff at Holland House, or the digressive quality of Byron's poetry. Although the words 'Italy' and 'Italian' were commonly used in the period, what they meant is the subject of considerable debate.[5] That foreigners thought of Italy as culturally unified before political unification is apparent from the famous travelogues and histories published across Europe in the early nineteenth century, and in this study I use the term 'Italian' to describe the work of authors who were born in the various independent states that made up the Italian peninsula. While many of these Italians did not share a flag, or a legal system, they did share customs, history, and perhaps most importantly a literature and a literary language. Indeed, Giulio Bollati has argued that cultural products were a homogenizing force in the period, and that Italian writers aimed at 'rivendicare la tradizione di grandezza e di primato dell'Italia e di insegnare ai ciechi e distratti visitatori come si possa scorgerne una continuità attuale almeno nell'agone glorioso delle lettere e delle arti'.[6]

The Italian Idea is concerned with mapping and analysing the second of three waves of Anglo–Italianism from 1780 to 1860, which took place between the earlier engagement of the so-called Della Cruscan poets and the later literary engagement in the years leading up to the *Risorgimento*. This study spans what Claude Lévi-Strauss terms a 'hot-chronology', which contains many of the most important literary works and social events of the nineteenth century.[7] At Genoa in 1822, Byron wrote in a reflective mood,

> Talk not of seventy years as age! in seven
>   I have seen more changes, down from monarchs to
> The humblest individuals under heaven,
>   Than might suffice a moderate century through.[8]

He had witnessed from 1815 to 1822, a tenth of the biblical three-score and ten, more changes in kings and peasants than occur in many an 'age'. I argue that it is the reawakening of an Italian influence on English radical poetry, and the increase in Italian immigration, that made these eight years so immoderate. The advent of this influence at the European peace of 1815 makes for an appropriate starting point. For a terminus, 1823 has been chosen because Foscolo's growing seclusion from literary life and Byron's journey to Greece, a year after the death of Shelley, removed the key proponents of radical Italian ideas from literary culture. Internationally, the quelling of European revolution at the Congress of Laibach (1821) changed the role that Italy and Italian culture played in British life. The impossibility of Italian independence in the short term led to fewer calls for liberation in radical pamphlets and parliamentary debates, and literary–political discourse about Italy became increasingly academic, reflected in articles in the *Foreign Quarterly Review* and Antonio Panizzi's studies of Italian romance.

The study has six chapters that proceed chronologically. Chapters 2 to 6 each cover a juncture in Anglo–Italian cultural relations between 1815 and 1823. These chapters chart the short but brilliant transit of radical Italian ideas across Romantic literary culture, a transit that allowed Italy and its culture to move from relative obscurity to the centre of London life, before returning to the periphery eight years later. The Introduction lays out the previous critical approaches that have been brought to bear on the role of Italy in British Romanticism, before establishing the approach of *The Italian Idea*. Chapter 1 considers how Italian people and literature were viewed in the latter half of the eighteenth century, and then looks in detail at three Anglo–Italian interactions in London during the two decades before 1815. Chapters 2 and 3 contain a discussion of the rise of Italian literature in London. I argue that Italy and its poetic canon gave a model for the radical romances of Hunt and Byron, and show how English readers increased their knowledge of this literature through the periodical writings of Foscolo and Serafino Buonaiuti. The second half of Chapter 3 examines the Whigs who befriended Italian exiles at Holland House, and specifically the shared opposition to British foreign policy of Foscolo, John Cam Hobhouse, and Henry Richard Vassall Fox (Lord Holland). Byron and Shelley's opposition to the cant of British culture made them leave England permanently in 1816 and 1818, respectively. In Chapter 4, I discuss the two poets' time in Venice through a reading of 'Lines written among the Euganean Hills' and *Beppo*, to argue that their new environment engendered formal and moral freedom.

The growing dissent of Byron and Shelley is a prelude to the discussion of protest and revolution at London and Naples in Chapter 5. Queen Caroline's trial of 1820 complicated public views of Italy and its literature: to many Britons, Italians were a scurrilous people who were instrumental in the persecution of a much-loved Queen, but there was also a swell of British support for the Neapolitans in their fight against Austrian tyranny. The texts discussed in this chapter include caricatures, poems, and broadsides published by the burgeoning radical press. These works provided a bulwark for the Queen, allowing her to be defended by a radical counter hegemony before she was judged by the state. The situation at London and Naples from 1820 to 1822 was the closest that radicals and liberals in both countries came to successfully challenging state hegemony. The failure of these years of protest and revolution is reflected in the melancholy cast of the Pisan circle discussed in Chapter 6. The greatest product of this literary circle was Shelley's 'The Triumph of Life', a poem that I contend is the high point of the radical interaction with Italy and its poetry, but that is thematically concerned with failure and disappointment. In the Coda, I examine the relatively swift decline of the radical idea of Italy. The death of Shelley and the failure of *The Liberal* (a journal founded by Byron, Shelley, and Hunt), alongside the financial problems of Foscolo, and the diminished role of opposition politics in England, caused the importance of Italian culture to be diminished. German literature and philosophy was in the ascendant by the mid-1820s, and the book ends by assessing the brief but potent impact of radical Anglo–Italian interaction on Romantic literary culture.

Not all things Italian between 1815 and 1823 will be considered. There must be some awareness of the difference 'between the task of combining and the luxury of confusing'.[9] The largest literary omission is the influence and reception of Giovanni Boccaccio's *Decamerone* (1351), which was read and reread by the poets discussed in this work. Byron called Boccaccio the 'Bard of Prose' and the bucolic potential of Italy was often associated with his work, particularly by Walter Savage Landor and Hunt.[10] I have chosen not to discuss Boccaccio in order to restrict my study of Italian literature to poetry and the particular effect it produced on English literature.[11] To confine the study geographically, I will not consider, except in passing, the works of the Liverpudlian Italianist William Roscoe and his circle. London was home to the largest group of Italian writers and Italian language publishers, as well as being the centre of English poetry, fiction, and newspaper publication: those who published, read, discussed, and policed literary culture in the metropolis made up the core of the Romantic reading public. To move my study away from this and look at Anglo–Italian engagement in the northwest of England would detract from my analysis of the opposition I propose between a literary establishment and radical Anglo-Italian literature. I will also not give sustained attention to English or Italian professional translators of the period. These translators are not a central part of my argument: much good work has already been done on translation in the period, and the writers I give extended consideration to were proficient in Italian.[12]

Furthermore, the study attempts to make a distinction between an innovative Anglo-Italian cultural phenomenon across borders, texts, and forms, and English literature about Italy that was popular in the same timeline. C. P. Brand claims Regency Britons would consume 'almost anything Italian' and he does not distinguish between these many forms of expression.[13] My study will look at an influence that grows out of Italy and its literature, kindled by exiles in both countries, which catalysed poetry and criticism that questioned the status quo. I will only consider the concurrent Italian fashion in travel writing, the novel, and poetry, as a counterpoint to a radical idea of Italy. Joseph Luzzi has discussed how this manner of cultural interaction with Italy meant that the 'magnificent cultural residue from antiquity and the Renaissance overwhelmed any signs of cultural activity'.[14] It was an attitude that allowed visitors to engage with Italy without the investment in its contemporary state that preoccupied circles at Holland House and Pisa.

The Italian fashion can be seen in works like Felicia Hemans's *The Restoration of the Works of Art to Italy* (1816), Elizabeth Batty's *Italian Scenery* (1820), and Samuel Rogers's *Italy* (1822). Hemans's contemporary anti-Napoleonic poem considers Italy in the past tense; the 'Home of the Arts' has 'given' much, but has little left.[15] The language of decay is everywhere in her description of 'Fallen Italy' which is 'faded', 'mould'ring', 'dimm'd', and a 'wreck'.[16] Even the return of its plundered art offers little hope; it is only a chance 'to gaze, / On the rich relics of sublimer days'.[17] Its register is typical of a fashion that viewed Italy as a *temenos* for the English writer, and this literature has little interest in Italian forms, preferring instead the Spenserian stanza, blank verse, or the regular couplet. Italy's current state is remarkably absent in works that mediate to English readers the sense of wonder felt by English eyes, and its idea of Italy has none of the 'continuità attuale' that binds past glories with future potential.[18] Some overlap does occur between the Italian fashion in English literature and the radical Anglo-Italianism I intend to analyse. The fourth canto of Byron's *Childe Harold's Pilgrimage* was a touchstone for English travellers in Italy and contains many dirgeful stanzas, but the ruined Italy seen by Harold is what Byron himself railed against in his later poetry.

The modern conception of the Romantic poet in Italy has been formed with much more of *Childe Harold* in mind, than of *Beppo,* 'Euganean Hills', or 'The Triumph of Life'. In the BBC historical comedy *Blackadder the Third,* the protagonist tells the owner of a Regency coffee-house, within earshot of some stereotypically 'Romantic' poets, 'Mrs. Miggins, there's nothing intellectual about wandering around Italy in a big shirt, trying to get laid'.[19] Blackadder is quite right to see nothing inherently intellectual, authentic, or original about those who visited, or dreamed of visiting, Italy. Nor should there necessarily be anything innovative about the travelogues, poems, and prints that this produced. The established stereotype of a lark to the continent should not be confused with the subject of the following chapters: the engaged questioning of poetic and political values which occurred between English and Italian literary culture from 1815 to 1823.

Acknowledgements

I am grateful for funding received from the Arts and Humanities Research Council, the UCL Graduate School, and the Keats–Shelley Association of America. Further thanks are due to the fellows of Merton College, Oxford, who elected me to a Junior Research Fellowship that gave me the time and means to write this book. I would also like to acknowledge the librarians and archivists who made this book possible: Bruce Barker-Benfield at the Bodleian, Alyson Price at the British Institute of Florence, Alexandra Ault at the British Library, Caterina del Vivo at the Gabinetto Vieusseux, Elizabeth Denlinger and Charles Carter at the Pforzheimer Collection, and David McClay. Thanks also to the editors of *Romanticism on the Net*, who published an early version of a section in Chapter 2 as 'Hunt, Byron, and The Story of Rimini – A Literary Challenge to "the Public Mind"', 59 (2011), and to the editors of *Litteraria Pragensia*, who published my first thoughts on part of Chapter 4 as 'Italian Travel, English Tourism, and Byron's Poetry of Exile', 46 (2013), 86–102.

In the pub, on the fells, and in the classroom, Oliver Clarkson has provided good company and better talk throughout the writing of this book. A number of other people were generous in conversation, argument, and suggestion, particularly Peter Cochran, Nora Crook, Jack Donovan, Kelvin Everest, Jonathan González, Nick Havely, Zoe Hawkins, Roberta Klimt, David Laven, Richard McCabe, Michael McCluskey, Mathelinda Nabugodi, Michael O'Neill, Seamus Perry, Tom Phillips, Will Poole, Alan Rawes, Diego Saglia, Fiona Stafford, Kathryn Sutherland, Julia Tejblum, Valentina Varinelli, Michael Whitworth, and Christopher Wright. David Bromwich, Gregory Dart, and John Took read and commented on chapters, and these comments were invaluable.

I am deeply indebted to the people who have read versions of this work in its entirety: my supervisors John Mullan (who insisted on showing the wood and not too many trees) and Peter Swaab (who pushed me towards better reading); and my examiners Ralph Pite (whose questions on the thesis's argument were the catalyst for this lengthier study) and Rosemary Ashton (who first kindled my interest in Romantic poetry and whose critical work has informed my own). In later stages, the acuity and generosity of Michael Rossington and the lightly worn but formidable knowledge of Francesco Rognoni kept a wayward project from faltering. At Cambridge University Press, Bethany Thomas has been brilliant in seeing the book through the press, and James Chandler has offered valuable advice. Likewise, the two anonymous readers deserve praise; the book is better for them.

Final and greatest thanks are due to my parents, whose love made this book possible: my mum's belief in me and my dad's wisdom remain unstinting. And to my wife, Hazel, to whom this book is dedicated.

W. B.

Note on the Text

Ellipses used in quotations are my own if given in square brackets.

Texts are referred to in footnotes by their short titles, which are given in full in the Bibliography. The publisher's name for works prior to 1900 is not given in the footnotes but is given in the Bibliography.

All translations are my own unless a translator's name is given.

Short Titles and Abbreviations

Beinecke	Beinecke Rare Book and Manuscript Library, Yale University, New Haven, CT.
BL	British Library, London.
BLJ	*Byron's Letters and Journals*, ed. Leslie Marchand, London: John Murray, 1973–1994, 13 vols.
Bodleian	The Bodleian Library, Oxford University, Oxford, UK.
ENUF	*Edizione Nazionale delle Opere di Ugo Foscolo*, ed. Mario Scotti et al., Firenze: Le Monnier, 1933–1985, 22 vols. to date.
Hansard	*Cobbett's Parliamentary Debates Series 1*, London, 1803–1820, 41 vols.; *Cobbett's Parliamentary Debates Series 2*, London, 1820–1830, 25 vols.; *Cobbett's Parliamentary Debates Series 3*, London, 1830–1891, 356 vols.
Inferno	Dante Alighieri, *The Divine Comedy*, volume I, part 1, ed. and trans. Charles S. Singleton, Princeton, NJ: Princeton University Press, 1977.
LBCPW	*Lord Byron: The Complete Poetical Works*, ed. Jerome J. McGann with Barry Weller, Oxford: Clarendon Press, 1980–1993, 7 vols.
LHSW	*The Selected Writings of Leigh Hunt*, ed. Robert Morrison, Michael Eberle-Sinatra, Jeffrey N. Cox et al., London: Pickering and Chatto, 2003, 6 vols.
LJM	*The Letters of John Murray to Lord Byron*, ed. Andrew Nicholson, Liverpool: Liverpool University Press, 2007.
LMWS	*The Letters of Mary Wollstonecraft Shelley*, ed. Betty T. Bennett, Baltimore, MD: Johns Hopkins University Press, 1980–1988, 3 vols.

LongmanPS	*The Poems of Shelley*, ed. Kelvin Everest, G. M. Matthews et al., London: Longman, 1989–2014, 4 vols. to date.
LPBS	*The Letters of Percy Bysshe Shelley*, ed. Frederick L. Jones, Oxford: Clarendon Press, 1964, 2 vols.
Morgante	Luigi Pulci, *Morgante*, ed. Franca Ageno, Milan: R. Ricciardi, 1955.
MSJ	*The Journal of Mary Shelley*, ed. Paula Feldman and Diana Scott-Kilvert, Oxford: Clarendon Press, 1987, 2 vols.
NLS	National Library of Scotland, Edinburgh.
OED	*Oxford English Dictionary Online*, Oxford: Oxford University Press, 2018.
Paradiso	Dante Alighieri, *The Divine Comedy*, volume III, part 1, ed. and trans. Charles S. Singleton, Princeton, NJ: Princeton University Press, 1977.
Pforzheimer	Carl H. Pforzheimer Collection of Shelley and His Circle, Astor, Lenox, and Tilden Foundations, New York Public Library, New York.
PL	John Milton, *Paradise Lost*, 2nd ed., Alistair Fowler, London: Longman, 1988.
PoAP	Alexander Pope, *The Poems of Alexander Pope*, ed. John Butt, London: Routledge, 1989.
Principe	Vittorio Alfieri, *Del principe e delle lettere*, Kehl, 1795. References are to book, chapter, and page.
Purgatorio	Dante Alighieri, *The Divine Comedy*, vol. II, part 1, ed. and trans. Charles S. Singleton, Princeton, NJ: Princeton University Press, 1977.
RIME	Francesco Petrarca, *Rime sparse*, ed. and trans. Robert M. Durling, Cambridge, MA: Harvard University Press, 1976.
SC	*Shelley and His Circle, 1773–1822*, ed. Kenneth Neill Cameron, Donald H. Reiman et al., Cambridge, MA: Harvard University Press, 1961–2002, 10 vols. to date.
SPP	*Shelley's Poetry and Prose*, 2nd ed., ed. Donald Reiman and Neil Fraistat, New York: Norton, 2002.
WWMW	William Wordsworth, *The Major Works*, ed. Stephen Gill, Oxford: Oxford University Press, 1984.

Introduction

On 1 August 1814, thousands watched the St. James's Park display in which John Nash turned the 'Castle of Discord' in to the 'Temple of Concord'. People also lined the streets for the formal Triumphs to celebrate victory in the Napoleonic Wars. These events formed the centrepiece of the Regent's Grand Jubilee to mark victory in Europe and a century of Hanoverian rule.[1] Events at Waterloo were cause for further celebration: church bells rang out on 18 June 1815. In August of the same year, Wordsworth climbed to the top of Skiddaw where he ate plum pudding, drank rum punch, sang the national anthem, and toasted British victory.[2] But despite the widespread jubilation at the end of twenty-two years of war, 1815 saw a renewed fervour in the radical voice against the state. That year has been chosen as the starting point of this study because it marks a new phase of public discontent with British hegemony, a discontent which informs and is informed by the second generation of Romantic poets. The riots over The Importation Act which greeted Robert Stewart, Lord Castlereagh, on his return from the Congress of Vienna, heralded a period in which a largely patriotic wartime populace changed to a reform-seeking, internationally aware public. In a *Quarterly Review* article of October 1816, the poet laureate Robert Southey, who had celebrated atop Skiddaw with Wordsworth, sensed the strengthening of a radical current, and observed that those writers who 'deceive the feelings of the multitude, have now laboured more wickedly and more successfully in corrupting them'.[3] A month after Southey's article appeared, one of its direct targets, William Cobbett, published a two-pence version of the *Political Register* to appeal to a wider readership, and in the next month the Spa Field riots brought the radical cause to the street. Dividing lines were marked more clearly in October 1817 when William Blackwood changed the *Edinburgh Monthly Magazine* to *Blackwood's Edinburgh Magazine*, and took editorial control over the periodical that would become the primary conservative voice against radical poetry. A war of ideas not seen since the 1790s meant the return of anti-radical legislation. By April 1817, 'the disturbed state of the country' required the suspension of habeas corpus and the return of the Seditious Meetings Act, and in 1819 the Six Acts increased newspaper duties and reduced the time of libel trials.[4] The international situation was equally fraught. The question of who would govern in the Italian peninsula after French withdrawal occupied the mind of the victors at Vienna, and in London it inspired liberals and radicals who were in favour of Italian independence.

The range of texts, authors, and locations outlined above are illustrative of the shift in Romantic literary criticism in the past thirty years. Critical attention has moved from a small 'visionary company' to the manifold productions of Regency culture, and has sought to prioritise the political resonances of literature in the period.[5] The second wave of Romantic literature has proved fertile ground for such work. What Nicholas Roe has called 'the new contextualism', which he associates with Cultural Materialist and New Historical approaches, has become critical orthodoxy.[6] Critics of this stripe aim to provide a contextual background to elaborate the cultural situation of literary production. This study seeks to analyse Anglo-Italian literature and culture in the context of the particular political situation in Italy and London, but it will not prioritize the political context over the literary work. The chapters that follow consider a number of relationships in a number of locales across multiple forms. It is hoped that the concentrated rather than extended chronological focus allows for both detailed contextualisation and close readings of texts. The narrow timeline also permits extended engagement with manuscripts, both of well-known poets such as Hunt and Shelley, and those of the numerous travellers who visited Italy after Waterloo. The blend of traditionally disparate approaches – close reading, historical writing, literary theory (of many stripes), manuscript study – paints a suitably complex picture of Regency literary culture.

A brief *tour d'horizon* of the criticism that has celebrated the European, and specifically Italian, dimension of British Romanticism is necessary before outlining what I intend to consider in *The Italian Idea*, and how I intend to consider it. Gregory Dart has traced the influence of Rousseau and Robespierre on British discourse; the impact of contemporary German thought on writers such as Coleridge and Carlyle has been explored by Nicholas Halmi and Rosemary Ashton; and recent transeuropean studies by Paul Hamilton and Diego Saglia have shown the importance of figures such as de Staël, Schlegel, and Leopardi to the political character of Romanticism, and considered how periodical journalism and professional translation brought European literature to Britain.[7] German and French culture were the two dominant European spheres of influence on British Romanticism, but Italian culture enjoyed a privileged position after the Battle of Waterloo. The appeal of Italy lay in the revival of an ignored source. Italian literature was disregarded in the main current of eighteenth-century letters and was not a formative influence on the poetry of the Lake School. The Italian reading of Byron, Hazlitt, Hunt, Shelley, and others moved against this dominant tradition and propagated an idea of Italy that brought with it thematic and formal license. Furthermore, the literature of Italy provided a link back to Milton, who had found inspiration there for his poetry and his republicanism. The revitalising power of past English and Italian authors was promoted in the literature published by recent Italian immigrants. In the introductions to their publications, these exiles often reminded readers that Italy – its language, literature, and people – played an integral part in the two great ages of English literature, those of Shakespeare and Chaucer.[8] This promotion also suited these authors politically: English and Italian writers felt the need to mediterraneanise literature, against the Gallomania of mid- and late eighteenth-century European culture, and away from the melodrama and mysticism of German thought, to a culture which was historically innovative and republican, but free from the stains of 1790s France.[9]

Criticism of the Anglo-Italian literary relationship in the eighteenth and nineteenth century has two foundational texts. Arturo Graf's *l'anglomania e l'influsso inglese in Italia nel secolo xviii* is a remarkable and dense study that ranges across the eighteenth century. Graf regularly switches his analysis between Italian authors who were influenced by, and who attempted to influence, British literary culture, and those Italians who attempted to use English literature to change Italian literature.[10] The classic work in English is C. P. Brand's *Italy and the English Romantics.* Brand is one of the few critics who considers the work of exiles in England and Italy in tandem, and the work's greatest strength is its scope. More recent work can be split into two areas: considerations of English writers and travellers in Italy, and single-author studies of a writer's influence on, or relationship with, Anglo-Italian Romanticism. In the first group, the political idea of Italy and its past for English visitors has been discussed by Maura O'Connor and Roderick Cavaliero, and in an essay collection edited by Lilla Maria Crisafulli.[11] Jane Stabler, in *The Artistry of Exile,* closely examines the formal and thematic expressions of exile by Romantic and Victorian writers, and Maria Schoina's *Romantic 'Anglo-Italians'* pays particular attention to the dynamics of the Pisan circle.[12] Byron and

Shelley were the leading poets of this circle, and their relationship with Italian literature is dealt with in single-author studies by Peter Vassallo and Alan Weinberg.[13] Of all the English Romantic interactions with Italian literature, it is the interest in Dante that has received the most attention, with a number of works covering Romantic poets' readings and borrowings from the *Commedia*, notably Ralph Pite's *The Circle of Our Vision*.[14]

The international relations mapped in recent criticism show the influence of foreign writers on British Romanticism. A study of Anglo–Italian interaction can usefully go beyond these examinations of a one-way influence, and beyond Crisafulli's claim that Italy provided travellers with '[l]ibertà e liberazione dai rigidi codici comportamentali e sociali'.[15] Travellers, as Crisafulli acknowledges, enjoyed a liberty outside social codes: at carnival in Venice, mingling with expatriates at the Gabinetto Vieusseux in Florence, and gazing at the sights of Rome. But this liberty was not materially different from that which Thomas Gray, Horace Walpole, or William Beckford, enjoyed on their Grand Tours; it was not a phenomenon exclusive to the Romantic period. These travellers were usually making their sole journey abroad and intended to return home in a year or less. I use the manuscript diaries of 1820s travellers to show the differences between their experience of Italy and that shared by long-term residents such as Byron and John Taaffe. The radical authors in question were domiciled in foreign lands and saw themselves, in Shelley's famous line, as exiles.[16] They sought refuge in Italy from the reprimand of the establishment for their political beliefs and from the attacks on their experimental verse in the periodical press.

As Edward Said and Jane Stabler have discussed, the condition of being in exile is not easy to define, and the degree to which one person feels the ostracising pressure to leave "home" varies.[17] That Foscolo and Augustus Bozzi were exiles, in the sense of being in danger should they return to their native country, seems beyond doubt, but questions could be raised over whether the Shelleys or Margaret Mason were truly exiled from Britain. A possible alternative term would be 'émigré', but this is a Romantic period neologism for French royalists escaping the Revolution; calling these Britons 'émigrés' would be politically and geographically misleading. To identify as an exile in Italy is to place one's self alongside Dante, Petrarch, Machiavelli, Lorenzo Da Ponte, and Foscolo, and this hinterland is part of what makes it a paradise. Their opponents also appreciated their condition: in its attack on the blasphemy and immorality of *The Liberal* (a journal founded by Byron, Shelley, and Hunt), the *John Bull* noted that 'other things than poverty can exile men'.[18] Shelley was conscious of being cast out of Britain and makes an apposite comparison, discussed in Chapter 6, with the exiled angels in Milton's Pandemonium: like Mammon, they prefer 'Hard liberty before the easy yoke / Of servile pomp', but by placing themselves in opposition to their home they must deal with the emotional rupture of displacement.[19] As the book's epigraph shows, those who leave home hope for 'il fior novo di strania favella'.[20] But exiles who felt themselves forced to remain in Italy longer than Milton's brief exchange of the Thames for the Arno suffered from homesickness, a suffering that was liable to increase upon realising the inherent difficulties of trying to change British culture from afar. The paradisal quality of this exile came in an escape from a hegemonic culture policed, in the case of English writers by conservative elements of the press, and in the case of the Italian writers by repressive and censorious foreign regimes. A less well-known expression of Shelley's casts Italy as 'the retreat of Pariahs', an expression which engages with the hardships of the exilic condition, and the triangle that it creates between the exile, their native land, and their reader.[21] The English exiles were not passing through; Italy was their home, and its literature informed their letters, poems, translations, and critical works. The Italian exiles who went to England were also there on a long-term basis. They went, like Dante's pilgrim, seeking liberty, and found it in predominantly Radical and Whig circles.

It is my contention, following the classic works of Graf and Brand, that a study trying to map interactions in this period can be most illuminating by considering multiple authors and locations. Where some periods have been restricted through nomenclature – the Age of Dryden, Pope, Johnson, and even Wordsworth – any attempt to do so in the 'hot-chronology' of 1815–1823 is an obstacle to analysis.[22] Said has noted that one of the few benefits for an exiled writer is that, 'Most people are principally aware of one culture, one setting, one home; exiles are aware of at least two, and this plurality of vision gives rise to an awareness of simultaneous dimensions'.[23] The critic should attempt to map the dual perspective of two groups living in foreign lands who are also looking back and engaging with, the situation they left behind. The single-author perspectives of Weinberg, Vassallo, and Pite allow the deep examination of a single interaction, but cannot give an account of the complexity of the many Anglo–Italian currents active over the period. The opening of perspective I propose is extended to location. Previous works by Schoina and Cavaliero look at an English idea of Italy, without discussing Italian exiles' promotion of their culture and cause in London. The various exchanges between England and Italy were not taken in isolation; as Jeffrey Cox has suggested, we should '(re-)place Second Generation Romanticism' to look at groups, and coteries, and the extra dimensions of influence that they facilitate.[24]

A broad analysis must consider what role a radical current in literature played in the movement against the existing social order. Since the 'return to history', critics have offered a number of ways of describing the boundaries enforced by official culture, and the challenges which literature makes upon them. Jerome McGann writes of 'conventions and enabling limits', Francis Mulhern examines 'injunctive social practices', and Alan Liu opts for the succinct 'regulated state'.[25] As Terry Eagleton has noted in the context of British control of Ireland in the long nineteenth century, 'the peculiar resilience of bourgeois rule' in this period is predicated on a control 'which operates more through the consensual life of civil society than through the coercive instruments of the state'.[26] With this in mind, I have chosen to approach the constrictions the modern state places on literature by seeing them as hegemonic, taking inspiration from the writings of Antonio Gramsci, and my way of tracing these constrictions and the radical challenges to them is informed by the work of J. G. A. Pocock. Gramsci's approach derives from Marx's statement that 'popular persuasion is often as strong as material force', and claims that non-violent 'persuasion' is the foundation of the state.[27] Vittorio Alfieri expressed a version of this long before Gramsci's birth, 'L'opinone è la innegabile signora del mondo. L'opinione è sempre figlia in origine di una tal qual persuasione, e non mai della forza'.[28] Alfieri grasps the two central tenets of hegemonic power: that it is the most powerful tool in society, and that it can only be implemented by persuasion and not by force. It is the consensual basis of an existing system, which along with the occasional use of domination (the means of violence provided by a standing army), upholds the status quo.

How did a historical bloc gain hegemonic control over the British 'public mind'?[29] As Pocock has argued, the ability of a growing middle class to control culture is a product of the shift in eighteenth-century political philosophy from a 'law-centered paradigm and into the paradigm of virtue and corruption'.[30] The consequence of this transformation was the ability to govern not just through Parliament but also through manners and convention. Dissidents and radicals, who were not necessarily breaking any laws, could still be controlled through criticism of their vice, effeminacy, and corruption. A movement into a politics of hegemonic, rather than legislative, control was helped by the advent of nationalism and nationalist literature. In Oliver Goldsmith's *The Traveller or a Prospect of*

Society (1764), characteristics are demarcated that were to be upheld as 'English', and later 'British', and readers are warned against the faults and dangers of other nations. Goldsmith's traveller is fulsome in his praise of European nations but he is firm in his belief in 'the patriot's boast, where'er we roam, / His first, best country ever is at home'.[31] 'Home' is not simply the land mass of the British isles but also a place free of the 'opulence' and 'sensual bliss' of Italy, and Goldsmith ends his poem warning that too many Britons follow 'pleasure's lordly call' in their love of travel.[32] The availability of travel to people beyond certain professions (merchants, soldiers, diplomats etc.) allowed Britons to feel they belonged to a national consciousness, and the ability of national traits to create common attitudes towards things as diverse as commerce, morality, and literature was heightened by the use of stereotypical figures of Britishness. John Bull is important not just for the stout, masculine, and proud Briton that he represents, and which he asks other Britons to identify with, but also for what he is not. His stature is a reminder that he is not the effeminate, lazy, and flamboyantly dressed Italian that he is often set against. If Britons, by virtue of their place of birth and their shared language, culture, and history, can see themselves as British, so too can they project unified stereotypes on to the states in the Mediterranean peninsula that they called Italy. Hegemonic control was exerted over manners, personal appearance, and cultural production to constitute a positive 'Britishness'; so by extension non-British forms of expression such as Italian music and poetry were castigated for their difference from these standards. It is this struggle, produced by what Pocock calls the inherent difficulty for foreign ideas to 'become domiciled in an environment', that underpins the reaction against radical Anglo-Italianism.[33]

Romantic-period attempts to control culture can be explored through the early nineteenth-century usage of the phrase 'the public mind'. Since the 1750s, the phrase referred to how a politician was judged by the populace, or a politician's sensitivity to the needs of the public, but later it was used to define the collective opinion of the United Kingdom.[34] Such articulations still exist: in the parlance of today's press, the 'British Taxpayer' is the animated and attacking public voice against external and internal threats. Although the 'public mind' and the 'British taxpayer' share a collective function, and often focus on the foreign, the former has none of the force of the latter. The British 'public mind' in the Romantic period rarely attacks and is often characterised by its vulnerability. During the war with France, the 'public mind' was increasingly invoked as a single moral force guided by the state and its supporters to maintain order, which negatively reacted to new and unorthodox media. The hegemonic appropriation of this term at a time of acute danger is a neat example of the state's constant adaptation, and chimes with Raymond Williams's claim that a 'lived hegemony is always a process [. . .] It has continually to be renewed, recreated, defended, and modified'.[35] The term is used by Pitt, during the proposal of the Unlawful Societies Act 1799, when he claims that the 'most important' effect of the legislation will be to 'prevent the press from becoming an engine of corruption and innovation [. . .] to circulate cheap publications, adapted to inflame and pervert the public mind'.[36] The quotation is typical of Romantic usage, as a public whole reacts against threats to hegemony. The threat often came from the continent, and the rhetoric used to stop these radical ideas has a marked similarity to that used against European immigrants. Advocates of the status quo told their reader of the dangers posed to the 'public mind': Arthur Young claimed, 'The public mind had been corrupted by France'; the *Monthly Meteor* chastised British radicals for 'deluding and inflaming the public mind', and for Coleridge an audience's lack of disgust during a production of Charles Maturin's *Bertram* (1816) showed 'the depravation of the public mind', and proved that the 'shocking spirit of jacobinism [*sic*] seemed no longer confined to politics'.[37]

In 1819, Shelley claimed in a letter to Hunt that 'every word a man has to say is valuable to the public now', and he was acutely aware that the style and form of these words was integral to their potential to 'awaken the minds of the people'.[38] Despite arguing for an approach that shows conservative culture defending its hegemonic control, I do not intend to reduce literature and contemporary criticism, in all its complexity, to an expression of national politics. Pocock has argued that a '"history of ideas" [. . .] gives way before a history of languages, vocabularies, ideologies, paradigms', and I extend this expansion to explore history of poetic forms.[39] Conservative periodicals promoted valued literary forms and genres; these had to be defended, and innovative works that were deemed subversive, likewise had to be attacked. As James Sacks has illustrated, the vigilance of these journalists goes far beyond twentieth-century suspicion of a biased or partisan press: the state was often funding these maintainers of hegemony, as it did when it gave £1500 to J. W. Croker to set up the *Guardian*.[40] The diction, themes, and forms of Italian-influenced poetry represented a threat to the 'public mind', and the literary establishment attempted to negatively portray this literature. This occurred principally through periodicals, particularly *Blackwood's* and to an extent in the *Quarterly*: if the pamphlet was the medium of anti-revolutionary literature of the 1790s, then reviews and periodicals were frequently that which 'conducted conservative political expression' after Waterloo.[41] The anonymity and regularity of this journalism, which was read by more than one hundred thousand Britons, meant they could claim to speak as organs of a public voice, not just as a subjective single author.[42] The maintainers of a conservative order did not applaud foreign ingenuity: the maintenance of hegemony occurred through a sense of collective authority that fell back on the twin pillars of tradition and present taste, which meant guarding strictness in form, and upholding suitable generic themes and locations. Conservative journals had their favourites; as is shown throughout this study, the works of Alexander Pope and Walter Scott were upheld as standards that much poetry was judged against.

From 1815–1823, radicals were not, except possibly for a few months during the trial of Queen Caroline, in a position to take control of British culture. They were instead concerned with how to challenge the values and strictures of the historical bloc through innovation and dissent. James Epstein has examined how post-Waterloo radicals offered counter-definitions for the meanings of concepts such as 'Liberty' and the 'Constitution'.[43] This also occurred in usage of the 'public mind', a phrase that had principally maintained hegemony began to be used to question and erode it. In 1815, Cobbett wrote,

> The mayor refuses to call a meeting, on account, as he says, of 'the unsettled state of the public mind'. Why, what is that to the purpose? The people's meeting, discussing the great subject of peace or war, and proposing a petition, is, one would suppose the best possible way of settling the public mind.[44]

Cobbett retorts that a 'people's meeting' is in itself a part of the public mind and exposes the inconsistency of an accepted term. Cobbett began a trend: Thomas Wooler could open an article titled 'March of the Public Mind' by writing, 'The progress of public opinion is now unimpeded' and claiming 'the death warrant of both whiggism and toryism is nearly signed in this borough', and Shelley could talk of princes 'who flow / Through public scorn' in 'England in 1819'.[45] These writers had the privilege of being second to a formulation; as Jon Klancher argues, 'the radical writer always claims the last word, laying bare the rhetorical stance which his middle-class interlocutors find intolerably fixed'.[46] To lay bare the meanings of terms like 'public mind' requires an awareness of the polyvalence of terms and their history. The 'public mind' was a complicated case in this process: it had earlier classical roots in terms such as *res publica*, which in conservative opinion mitigated its corruption by the French public revolt. Yet, for radicals like Cobbett and Wooler, the 'public mind' has a history before 1789, in the English commonwealth and its intellectual engagement with the republicanism of the Italian city states.[47]

Just as journalists challenged terms of authority, so literary critics began to question how periodicals maintained state hegemony. Hazlitt, an admirer of Cobbett, whom he described as a '*fourth estate* in the politics of this country', began to find counter-definitions for the 'public mind'.[48] He attacked the editor of the *Quarterly,* William Gifford, as a 'government spy', and went on, 'You "keep a corner in the public mind, for foul prejudice and corrupt power to knot and gender in."'[49] Hazlitt revises Othello's image of his heart as a fountain turned into 'a cistern for foul toads / To knot and gender in'.[50] As Othello hopes to show Desdemona's falsehood, so Hazlitt sought to expose Gifford's role in forming the 'public mind'. He replaces the original lines with the same diction of bodily disease that conservatives such as Gifford had used to attack radicals. Hazlitt's choice of diction is a reclamation of older republican discourse: talk of corruption was widespread in the writings of the English Revolution, especially in the work of James Harrington who took his inspiration from Machiavelli and Guiccardini; here Hazlitt is instigating a revolution in the sense of moving the usage back to an earlier starting point.[51] As Pocock has shown, the movement of ideas in language from Florentine thinkers, via the English Revolution, to the centre of Georgian cultural debate affected the opposition of 'Court' and 'Country', the castigation of a ministerial class, and the framing of patronage as 'corruption'.[52] Hazlitt's discussion of 'corrupt power' reminds his readers that this was an earlier term for panderers to a 'court party' in Medici Florence and Caroline England, people who 'overstepped the proper limits of royal favor and entered the sphere of bribery and venality'.[53] In a review of the *Christabel* volume, three years before his attack on Gifford, Hazlitt had used the idea of a corrupt court to criticise Coleridge as an author 'whose daily prose is understood to be dedicated to the support of all that courtiers think should be supported'.[54] Here Hazlitt appropriates the Florentine critique of hegemonic power, a critique that was the philosophical foundation for the brief English Commonwealth. It is fitting that Hazlitt goes to Italian discourse for his terms: after the 1790s and the failure of the French Revolution, Italy represented an earlier land, and landscape, of liberty and republicanism which were not sullied by the guillotine or Bonaparte. In post-Waterloo London, what it was to be a citizen, and how much control the government had over what you thought, read, and wrote, was the subject of fertile debate; Italian history – better known since the work of Pierre-Louis Ginguené, William Roscoe, and Jean Charles Léonard Simonde de Sismondi – provided historical ideas, and therefore historical vocabularies and forms, with which to have this debate.

The undercutting of privileged concepts, such as the 'public mind' and 'corruption', is an intrinsic feature of radical Anglo-Italian literature. Gramsci claims those who realise the existence of the hegemonic system can create a new ideological terrain; radical ideas of and from Italy were used to prompt this realisation.[55] The proponents of these ideas instigated a taking-up of foreign forms, and altered accepted genres such as the Romance and the Epic. As Stuart Curran has claimed, this innovation did not temper attitudes towards compositional rules; on the contrary, it reinforced them, 'reminding us sharply of the very aesthetic distances they subvert'.[56] So, when a poem in couplets appears which constantly enjambs and pauses unexpectedly, or a protagonist called 'Don Juan' is not the seducer but the seduced, writers are advertising their affronts to hegemony by clothing verse in forms they then abuse. Cox has examined this reversal in the context of Hunt's *The Descent of Liberty* (1815), claiming that in order to challenge their sentiments, Hunt 'echoed' the nationalist marches that celebrated British victory in Europe.[57] Shelley's Italian verse is committed in its effrontery to hegemonic control and offers illuminating examples of it at the level of the individual word or phrase. Kelvin Everest has argued that, in talking of 'legioned rooks' that 'hail the sun's uprise majestical', or appealing 'To the eternal years enthroned before us', Shelley calls into 'radical service the vocabulary of the very social structure that obstructs the realization of his ideals'.[58] The poetic interactions analysed in *The Italian Idea* share this refusal to be fenced in, and the writers considered herein were staging a deliberate challenge to hegemony by flouting those literary conventions and customs that were so often seen in national terms.

CHAPTER 1

Italians and the 'Public Mind' before 1815

> Recava infatti vergogna estrema ai nazionali Italiani, e gran stupore perfino ai culti stranieri il veder come circolassero per Londra tanti periodici fogli compilati in lingua alemanna, francese, spagnuola e portoghese, oltre una quantità immensa in oppositi sensi e varie fogge inglesi, mentre fra questi tanti *Giornali*, *Gazzette*, *Riviste* e *Magazini*, neppur un sol pubblico foglio ritrovavasi scritto nell'aurea lingua Italiana.[1]
>
> **Augustus Bozzi, *L'Italico* (1813)**

To examine the effect of, and the reaction to, radical Anglo-Italian literature in the public mind, it is necessary to consider British ideas of Italians and Italy in the generation before Waterloo. To Britons at the time, Italy signified two very different things: the historical Italy – the setting for Republican and Imperial Rome and the cradle of the Renaissance – and the modern Italy of the eighteenth and early nineteenth centuries. The former was enjoying something of a resurgence in the last quarter of the eighteenth century, caused in no small part by Edward Gibbon's *The History of the Decline and Fall of the Roman Empire* (1776–1789) and *Miscellaneous Works* (1796). In the revolutionary decade there was heightened demand for Renaissance Italian history, spurred on by its republican politics, which was met by the publication of William Roscoe's *Life of Lorenzo de' Medici* (1795), a work that claims not only to be concerned with 'mere historical events' but also with 'the progress of letters and arts'.[2] Roscoe is true to his word and offers brief literary sketches of Dante, Petrarch, and Boccaccio, and includes, as an appendix to his second volume, an anthology of the poetry produced by Lorenzo's court (including the works of Luigi Pulci that Byron would later study). Despite running to four editions by 1800, the *Life of Lorenzo* did not entirely satisfy public curiosity; as Roscoe himself points out, 'a compleat history of these times has long been a great desideratum in literature'.[3] Roscoe's desire was met by two Francophone scholars, Pierre-Louis Ginguené and

Jean Charles Léonard Simonde de Sismondi, whose multi-volume histories of Italy and its literature are an important but often contested point of reference for the radical idea of Italy.

In 1811, the first volume of Ginguené's *Histoire littéraire d'Italie* was published. It ran to nine volumes before his death in 1815. Ginguené's title page announces him as a 'Membre de l'Institut de France', and the study has the organised structure and detailed indexes of Enlightenment tomes.[4] The first volume covers the period from Constantine to the Provençal troubadours and the second opens with a long discussion of Dante. The range of Dante's works discussed – including the *Rime, Vita nuova,* and *De vulgari eloquentia* – is impressive, but Ginguené's view of the poet as someone who 'créa une nouvelle machine poétique, une poésie nouvelle' would be challenged by the later historical readings of Foscolo.[5] Released two years after the first volume of Ginguené's *Histoire*, Sismondi's *De la littérature du Midi de l'Europe* (1813) was a more concise literary history. Sismondi's fame as the author of *Histoire des républiques italiennes du moyen âge* (1807–1818), made *De la littérature du Midi de l'Europe* a bestseller across the continent. His second work eschews wider historical commentary, and Sismondi claims that his subjects are 'trois carrières de l'esprit qu'on croirait si dissemblables, en politique, en religion, en poésie'.[6] Like Ginguené, Sismondi casts Dante as the exceptional figure of the gloomy past, as 'le plus grand des Italiens' who made his poem from the 'matériaux grossiers' of his age.[7] These historical works were central to British ideas of Italian literary and political history before 1815, and they contributed to certain types of Italian nationalism; as Shelley observed in a note to *Hellas*, Sismondi had 'done much towards awakening the Italians to an imitation of their great ancestors'.[8] These Francophone works became the accepted authorities on Italian history: when Henry Hallam wrote his *View of the State of Europe during the Middle Ages* (1818), he used Sismondi as the 'substratum' to his chapter on Italy and claimed that a literary history of Italy is unnecessary, thanks to Ginguené.[9] As with many received notions – the 'public mind', corruption, harmony – the idea of Italy was contested after 1815, and the histories of Ginguené and Sismondi, which were often recapitulated in British writing, were scrutinised by the Italian exiles in London and British radicals in Italy. Although these histories created the informed reading public for the works considered in the following chapters, authors such as Hunt, Foscolo, and Shelley also nuanced, and sometimes fiercely opposed, their idea of Italy.

The reputation of contemporary Italian culture and of the modern inhabitants of Italy was quite separate from the historians' praise for the *stilnovisti*, the republic of Florence, and the court of Lorenzo. A number of mid eighteenth-century travelogues and novels display the contempt in which many Britons held modern Italians and their culture. Tobias Smollett's *Travels through France and Italy* (1766) has little complimentary to say about the Italian language, people, or faith, and this is perhaps to be expected from a writer whose novels had sought to expose the moral turpitude of foreigners.[10] A moment in *The Adventures of Peregrine Pickle* (1751) is of particular interest.[11] Peregrine and his painter friend Mr Pallet are in Paris in the company of an Italian count and a German baron:

> the count, tired with the eternal babble of the painter, reeled towards the sleeping baron, whom he viewed with rapture, repeating from the *Il Pastor Fido* of Guarini,
>
> *Come assetato infermo*
> *Che bramò lungamenté*
> *Il vietato licor –*
> *– Tal' Io! gran tempo infermo,*
> *E d'amorosa sete arso, e consunto.*
>
> Then boldly ravished a kiss, and began to tickle him under the ribs, with such expressions of tenderness, as scandalized the virtuous painter ... Peregrine who entertained a just detestation for all such abominable practices, was incensed at this information; and ... saw with his own eyes enough to convince him, that Pallet's complaint was not without foundation, and that the baron was not averse to the address of the count.[12]

The count's 'rapture' suggests his ecstasy and his urge towards violation, and his repetition of some redacted lines from *Il pastor fido* (1590) make him appear deranged at the prospect of fulfilling his lust. The selective quotation turns a complaint on the impossibility of quenching love's thirst by Guarini's doleful lover Mirtillo into an apothegm recited before lust's fulfilment. Peregrine is a moral weathervane who seeks to give to the Italian and German 'a disgrace suited to the grossness of their ideas': he convinces the landlady, by one of his many practical jokes, to enter the foreigners' room; she then marches them to the street in a state of undress, where a crowd gathers to witness her 'just invectives'.[13] Beneath the humour, sharp lines are drawn: the Italian is theatrical in his seduction, slippery in his quotation, and gross in his ideas, while the Englishman is the energetic policeman for British morality abroad, who contrives to try the sinners before the court of public opinion. Samuel Richardson's *Sir Charles Grandison* (1753) is less dramatic in its scorn, but it nevertheless begins with a list of 'Principal Persons' divided between 'Men', 'Women', and 'Italians'. This demarcation prefaces a narrative in which Pollexfen kidnaps Harriet at an Italian masquerade, and in which the Catholic Italian Porretta family constantly impede her union with Charles. More than a hundred years later, Richardson's portrayal still resonated with George Eliot, who describes the Italians in *Grandison* as 'the swine, apparently of some foreign breed'.[14]

These works focus on the religious and moral traits that separate Italians from English men and women, a trend that becomes more pronounced due to the growth in print caricature in the second half of the century.[15] A favourite subject for the burgeoning caricature industry was the so-called 'Macaroni man', who got his name from the foppish 'Marchese di Macaroni' in David Garrick's play *The Male Coquette* (1757).[16] 'Macaroni' was a term in everyday use from the 1760s onwards to castigate cosmopolitan men who had a penchant for ornate Italian textiles and fashions. The caricaturists used the glare of the 'Macaronis' ornate buttons and buckles, the opposition of macaroni pasta and good roast beef, and the feminising aspect of tighter frock coats, to cast these men as effeminate, weak, and morally dubious.[17] The term became particularly associated with the travelled Whig men who frequented the Almack's Club (which became Brooks's in 1778), a place and a group 'notorious for gaming, feasting, and carousing'.[18] Here Charles James Fox and Richard Brinsley Sheridan, the intellectual forefathers of the Holland House set, revelled in their classification as 'Macaroni men' and had pasta served at their dinners as a nod to their Italian heritage. The portrayal of Italians and their culture was not uniformly negative, but two events led these perceptions of immorality to become entrenched by the end of the century: the Gordon Riots and the French Revolution.[19] The Gordon Riots were a protest against the Papists Act of 1778, during which Catholics were attacked and their property burned; unlike the protests from 1815 to 1823, these riots were a conservative appeal for state control over religious practice. George Rudé has shown an anti-immigrant element to these attacks, which focused on the Irish and Italian district of Holborn, where the Sardinian Chapel on Duke Street, the centre of Italian Catholic worship, had many of its fittings and decorations removed and burnt in the street.[20]

Between the end of the Gordon Riots and the French Revolution's first days, the group of poets later known as the Della Cruscans – including Robert Merry, Hester Thrale Piozzi, Bertie Greatheed, and William Parsons – became resident in Tuscany. Aside from Piozzi, these poets were young men of the leisured, but not aristocratic, class, who, as Merry wrote in 'Il Viaggio', sought 'fair travel' to avoid the 'Dull scenes that Britain knows! / Which waste the sum of life, and daily bliss destroy'.[21] In some ways this group, in its cosmopolitanism, its engagement with the Italian canon, and the violent reaction against it from the establishment, anticipate the radical Anglo-Italian literature of the post-war years. But their poetry also has attributes that make them anathema to this literature: their pride in the ephemeral, their intensely English formal choices, and their (possibly ironic) saccharine sensibility. Their decorative style is made clear in the 'Dedication' to *The Florence Miscellany* (1785):

> But my thoughts neither beautiful are nor sublime,
> So I wrap them in metre, and tag them with rhime,
> Like theatrical dresses, if tinsel'd enough,
> The tinsel one stares at, nor thinks of the stuff.
>
> (3)

What may seem like stock modesty is not far from the truth: the small, mainly lyric, poems of the *Miscellany* appear as little gifts, aided by the decoration of the book itself, with its liberal use of fleurons and printer's ornaments. The idea of the poetry only being surface deep was extolled in Piozzi's preface, which claims that these poems have nothing to stay, but that they 'shall at least be allow'd to have glisten'd innocently in Italian Sunshine' (6). But the wish for readers to stare at the costume of this verse rather than its meaning had a strange fulfilment in that it was precisely its style that its most vociferous opponent, William Gifford, found most appalling. Gifford attacked the poets' ornamentation and prolixity, the 'lumbering line' with its 'gigantic bulk', which sparkles for too long.[22] Only a few years after conservatives had stripped the altars of Catholic churches in London, the 'flowery subject' and the 'sad variety' of Della Cruscan poetry was cast as a disease of poets who were 'unconscious of the critic's laws'.[23]

The opening poem of the volume, 'A Dream' by Greatheed, begins with a narrator who falls asleep 'beneath a cypress shade' where 'fairy visions charm'd [his] soul'; he goes on,

> A Poet trod the dewy lawn,
> With solitary steps, and slow,
> Where hoary Arno's waters flow.
> The Muse he sought whose song of yore
> Resounded on the Tuscan shore.
> At length his vagrant footsteps stray'd
> To Val-ombrosa's gloomy shade;
> Where, stretch'd upon the mossy ground,
> In death-like sleep the Maid he found
>
> (7)

The 'Maid' turns out to be the Muse, at whose awakening the narrator flees. In his absence the Muse calls upon Dante, Petrarch, and Boccaccio, and then in the 'thickest bow'r [. . .] Immortal Milton's shade she found' (9). The Muse mourns the absence of poetry in contemporary Italy, and calls upon Milton to provide some for her. Milton obliges and goes to 'Albion's chalky shore' where he gathers 'a genuine Band [. . .] To hither come and sing [her] praise' (11). Greatheed stages his encounter with abandon, in invoking the Muse and the *tre corone*, in casting the Muse in the pose of one of Satan's fallen angels, and in a narrator who mimics the walk of the expulsion from Eden. The abandon is matched by the poem's camp style: tripping regular couplets, stock phrasing, and nouns rarely spared an adjective; it is poetry that shows its working out, like a carriage clock in a glass case. The Della Cruscans did read and engage with Italy's literary history: 'Th' Italian Muse's rich poetic mine' (25) produced translations of Petrarch and Dante, and collaborations with living Italian poets like Ippolito Pindemonte and Giuseppe Parini. McGann has argued that this interaction goes further, and he views the poetic conversations of the Della Cruscans as a conscious attempt to mimic the *tenzone* of earlier Italian poets.[24] But despite the Della Cruscans' somewhat haphazard tour around the Italian canon, they remained formally English: when Parsons translates the terza rima of the Paolo and Francesca episode, he does so in couplets, and when Pindemonte's ottava rima 'Hymn of Calliope' is followed by an English translation by Piozzi, this is given in four-couplet stanzas with a terminal alexandrine. The Della Cruscans' political commitment is also something of a compromise: while they did collaborate with anti-government poets, their *Miscellany* opens by declaring, with a wink to the censors of the Tuscan Arch-Duke Leopold, that it is a work for 'OURSELVES and our FRIENDS', privately printed to cause little controversy (3). The sense of poets who were formally and politically mixed up, who didn't quite know what they wanted from England or Italy, has been a charge against the Della Cruscans since Gifford criticised their 'motley fustian'.[25] But perhaps this is the threat these poets pose, a kind of Italian chinoiserie that has little regard for ideas of authenticity or consistency, poetry characterised, as Michael Gamer has argued, by its 'experimental determination not to abide by existing conventions'.[26] In his brilliant study of these poets, W. N. Hargreaves-Mawdsley casts them as the ideal representatives of 'the last decade of the old world'; their stylistic heirs in the new world were Rogers and Hemans, but there is something in their attempts at cultural hybridity and refusal to observe the rules which anticipates radical Anglo-Italian poetry.[27]

The craze for Della Cruscan poetry and the establishment reaction against it occurred at a liminal moment for the English perspective on Italians, which moved from an eighteenth-century tourist or reader viewing an Italian in Italy, or the few Italians in London, to a public encountering a prominent migrant community. It was not only Macaroni men and verse with Italianate decoration, but real Italians who could be seen on London's streets, and their greater number lead to a change in their depiction in prints.[28] The rotund middle-aged John Bull laughing at the continent in his 1770s isolation becomes a young Spartan defending his country against the internal depravity of the high life and the external danger of outside influence. Foreigners become more strongly rendered as the opposite of the 'typical Englishman', with common motifs being malnourishment, uncleanliness, and animal comparisons; one caption identifies 'a chattering French baboon, an Italian ape'.[29] This immigration was a prominent topic in political debate: the Aliens Bill passed both Houses in 1793 and was the basis of British law until 1826. It initiated a centralised immigration system under the control of the Secretary of State, whose powers were limitless as long as he felt his actions were 'necessary to the safety of the state'.[30] The act was passed under the guise of 'emergency legislation', amid talk of 'extraordinary' and 'unprecedented' circumstances, but remained in place for more than thirty years.[31] The new system made entering Britain difficult, and there was no respite on arrival: Augustus Bozzi complained at length about the number of medical tests he underwent, the musician Giuseppe Naldi had part of his salary withheld due to his alien status, and the precarious legal position of aliens complicated the already dire financial position of Foscolo.[32] The default position of the state was to be antagonistic to foreigners abroad, on their arrival, and once they had settled in Britain. Just as the 'safety' of the Kingdom was the condition for the secretary's powers, so during debates members in favour talked of 'the safety of the state' which 'was not best sacrificed for hospitality', and the need 'to quiet the alarm that had been excited in the minds of the people'.[33] In these speeches it is hard to discern what precise threat foreigners posed, aside from not being British, and this lack of substantiation was admitted, and even argued, as necessary; its proposer, Henry Dundas (Lord Melville), was happy to clarify that the bill was 'grounded on suspicion'.[34] The vagueness of the threat meant that those attempting to maintain hegemonic control could be suspicious of everything about the foreigner, from their different fashions, accents, and sexual habits, to their literary and musical traditions. The Venetian Count Alvise Zenobio, who had written in favour of parliamentary reform and met with William Godwin, was deported in 1794.[35] The same punishment was given, without any public justification, to the Piedmontese violist Giovanni Battista Viotti, who was deported in 1798 due to what Warwick Lister has called the 'pervasive climate of suspicion in a country at war'.[36] These two represent only a fraction of the deportees: in the months following April 1797, ninety-five Italian pedlars and organ-grinders were removed from the country for 'either defrauding the people, or as in many instances dispersing seditious & improper publications'.[37]

The livelihood of Viotti and the organ-grinders was a common exile occupation: in its highest and lowest styles, Italian music was a popular and controversial part of Regency life. Due perhaps to their propensity for musical careers, particularly in the opera, song was also a cultural form in which Italians were satirised. Charles Dibdin was the most renowned songwriter and performer of the period, who had written his *British War Songs* (1803–1804) under a government commission. He also penned a range of anti-Semitic and xenophobic ditties, in which Italians are a regular target.[38] These include 'The Italian Music Master', where the Master is caught trying to take 'honest Jacky Bull's wife', and 'Jack at the Opera', where the English crowd have little time for 'the bad note Italiano'.[39] Dibdin also wrote songs in which the narrative voice was that of an Italian immigrant, designed to be sung in a mock-Italian accent, in which the 'moosic maestro' talks of how he 'teach de pretty laty de shak and de cadenza'.[40] The ballad 'In England Against Italy' is Dibdin's most concentrated articulation of John Bull's attack on the loose morals of Italians.[41] At the opening the Italian male is cast as controlled by 'the devil'; he then attempts to persuade women to bed with his charm. He is 'a squire of silk, a mandrake': soft and luxurious in appearance, but a pestilent thing, to be rooted up and removed, or deported. But this rake is unsuccessful; Dibdin's refrain reminds the listener that an English woman yields to 'not a monkey, but a man'.

The opposition to Italian immigration was not founded on the 'stealing our jobs' rhetoric of industrial society. Rather, Italians, in refined cultural forms like poetry and opera, and in prints and bawdy tavern songs, were viewed with suspicion because they posed a cultural danger. Their presence was a symptom of change and decline; a dilution of refined English manners and morals, by an extrovert and libidinous people. As the next chapter shows in detail, these views were extended to the Italian poetic canon, so that Dante was judged as rough and primitive, and Tasso as too full of glitter, when judged against 'French' standards of taste.[42] The classification of 'French' and 'Italian' schools of literature was common in eighteenth-century literary discourse. Pope sketched an English literary history based around foreign schools that Thomas Gray developed in a letter to Thomas Warton in 1770.[43] Gray's history begins with the first Italian school, 'Dante, Petrarch, Boccace'; then comes a second Italian school of 'Ariosto and Tasso [. . .] and this school ends in Milton'; followed by the 'School of France, introduced after the Restoration – Waller, Dryden, Addison, Prior, and Pope – which has continued to our own times'. The perceived correctness of Waller, Addison, and Pope was associated with the neoclassical strictures advocated by Nicolas Boileau and François Hédelin, the abbé d' Aubignac, so the terms refer to styles of expression that were thought to have been founded in Italy and France, but do not necessarily need to refer to literature from France or Italy. The formal purity and harmony of French neoclassicism was an aspect of the civilised life in *ancien régime* France, an idea of civility that had become the dominant cultural mode for most of Europe, while the Italian school was synonymous with the romance of Ludovico Ariosto and Tasso, and the visionary epics of Dante and Petrarch, but it was also associated with its geographical source: unstable and occasionally revolutionary city-states that were perceived to be in moral and economic decline. The Italian school of poetry was also associated with musicality and improvisation, based in part on the idea articulated by Voltaire in *Des effets de la poésie sur le génie des langues* (1746) that a greater number of rhymes were available to a poet in Italian, but also based on much quasi-scientific climate theory by the likes of Montesquieu, John Arbuthnot, and François-Ignace Espiard de la Borde, that argued for the greater musicality (and looser morality) of southern nations.[44] Just as being 'French' in style implied correctness in verse and in subject, so calling something 'Italian' goes beyond a purely literary judgement to engage with ideas of Italian cultural laxity. In this context, the Renaissance apothegm *Inglese Italianato, diavolo incarnato*, takes a broader meaning, and the binding of formal and moral judgements explains Southey's classification of Byron's poetry as both 'Italian' and 'Satanic'.[45]

An opposition to the supposed mechanical conservatism of Pope and his imitators (a regularity associated with the 'French' school) was a fundamental feature of English Romantic poetry. The first and second generation of Romantic poets chose different ways to counter the correctness of the 'French' school: Southey and Wordsworth promoted a native 'English' school, which they traced through Chaucer, Edmund Spenser, and Milton, while the later Romantics, in keeping with Gray, saw these three English poets as part of a larger inheritance from the

'Italian' school. The same associations between the English and Italian canon were made by Italian exiles such as Bozzi, Foscolo, and Buonaiuti. For Italians, the promotion of the literature of the Italian school was also an attempt to advertise their independent national cultural tradition whilst French and Austrian armies occupied their homeland. English poets who claimed to be part of the 'Italian school' were often ridiculed on the basis of 'French' standards of taste, but writers who engaged with Italy and its culture were then able to inhabit modes where these conceptions of moral and formal license were active, and access an intellectual culture in which figures such as Dante and Machiavelli were undergoing reassessment. A movement out of England, and away from the strictures of British correctness, allowed later Romantic poets a freedom in form and content which differentiated them from their immediate forebears. Byron's famous claim that he wished the Lakers would change their 'lakes for ocean' is not simply a desire for these poets to travel: Wordsworth, Coleridge, and Southey had all travelled extensively.[46] Rather, Byron's comment hits upon the perceived insularity of the later verse and prose of these authors.[47] William Christie has discussed how recent historicist critics have called Wordsworth 'to come down from the mountain and out of the counties and regions of the reclusive and sublimated self', but this call echoes a critique which began around 1815.[48] Said has argued that nationalism 'affirms the home created by a community of language, culture, and customs', and in this sense it can be seen in the opening of Southey's *Wat Tyler* (written 1794, published 1817), complete with maypole and morris dancing, and in his later work as laureate filled with expected praise of country, crown, and state. Wordsworth's patriotism when treading 'the grass / of England once again' while 'Europe is yet in bonds' in the sonnet 'Composed in the Valley near Dover, on the Day of Landing' (1802) is later given a nationalist tone in the hail to the state in Book VI of *The Excursion* (1814).[49] Whether the Lakers' turn from radicalism to conservatism was the simple *volte-face* that it is often made out to be, it was a swift and simple betrayal in the eyes of the later generation of writers – as Hazlitt claimed in 'On Court-Influence', Southey's position as laureate entailed 'accepting his place and discarding his principles'.[50] It was a betrayal that was felt keenly by those poets exiled in Italy, and finds its most obvious expression in 'Peter Bell the Third' and the 'Dedication' to *Don Juan*. This betrayal, in addition to providing opportunities for satire and rebuke, is also the impetus for the proudly esoteric, experimental, and radical pose that Italy gave these poets. Wordsworth claims at the end of the first verse-paragraph of 'Michael' to tell his tale, 'for the sake / Of youthful Poets, who among these Hills / Will be my second self when I am gone'.[51] But the 'youthful poets' did not produce their works in Lakeland ghylls, nor did they imitate Wordsworth to become his 'second self'; they chose to stay on the 'public way' by writing resolutely cosmopolitan literature cast by its detractors as 'Satanic', 'Cockney', and 'Italian'.

Al Risorgimento della Letteratura e della Poesia Italiana

As attitudes to Italy and its literature allowed radical English poets the space for licence and originality, they also provided Italian exiles with a task. The works of the first wave of Italian immigrants were motivated by the need to educate the public about their cultural and political situation, and explain the system of French and Austrian occupation and censorship in which many of the exiles were *personae non gratae.* Their motivation came from what they saw as a dominant 'French' style in literature and literary history, the slander of their moral character in print, and the misinformed discussion of Italy and its occupiers in Parliament. These exiles attempted to harness some of the enthusiasm for Italian Medieval and Renaissance history that had been drummed-up by Francophone scholars, and divert it towards the not altogether dissimilar present state of Italy. In literary publishing, to revive an interest in their native culture, the immigrants attempted to educate the English reader by printing Italian literature; apart from some language primers, poetry was the dominant medium of these works.

The prominent migration of Italians to London during the Romantic period, along with increased British tourism to Italy, enlivened British interest in Italian culture, which in turn caused a demand for Italian language instruction.[52] The importance of Italy as a cultural influence in the Regency was due in part to the fact that many Britons could read its literature.[53] Italian differed from other European literary languages: as far as an Italian language existed, it was principally a language of literature and opera based on the Tuscan dialect. This language was not spoken outside of Tuscany, where regional dialects were the common mode of conversation.[54] The literary nature of Italian had a profound effect on how it was learnt by the English: the language taught to students was aimed to help them read literature and not principally to aid communication abroad. The literary bias is illustrated in learning materials. Cesare Bruno's *Studio italiano* (1815) aimed to teach the language through the various forms and genres of Italian poetry, and includes a long vocabulary of phrases typical to romance and pastoral poetry.[55] An attempt at learning for conversation is offered in Antonio Montucci's *Italian Extracts* (1806) but only twenty-six of its 376 pages are given to phrases of practical use. It is perhaps unsurprising, given he had published fifteen plays of Alfieri for British readers in the same year, that Montucci devotes the rest of his primer to large selections from the Italian canon, including Dante, Boccaccio, and Metastasio.[56] Although the literary nature of Italian provided English poets with a reading public who were more attuned to their relationship with Italian culture, it posed a problem for Italian nationalists: as Benedict Anderson has shown in his analysis of the decline of Latin, a language that exists only in print or only in a verbal form is liable to be superseded by a language that can do both.[57] In the epigraph to this chapter, Bozzi calls for a periodical for Londoners in the 'aurea lingua Italiana', a call for linguistic unity with a particular urgency as French, and then Austrian, forces dominated Italy.[58]

Maria Schoina's notion of 'Anglo-Italianness', as a mode of cultural hybridity for English writers and travellers, is a useful method with which to look at 'Italo-Englishness', to show the ways in which Italian radicals were influenced by English literary and political debates.[59] In the Romantic period, foreign writers and artists often attempted to ingratiate themselves to their new national public. Luisa Calè has shown how Henry Fuseli's paintings from Milton in the 1780s and 1790s were designed to 'challenge the Swiss painter's foreign marginality' by 'pursuing the transfer of British cultural heritage from the field of poetry to that of painting'.[60] But the cultural transfer attempted by Italian exiles was of greater complexity: they had to convince the English reader to follow Dante's pilgrim, to leave a fascination with 'French' strictures and course over better waters. To this end, prefatory material to exile works would remind the reader of the historic links between Italy and England. This often involved a recollection of the Renaissance, and of Milton, who, the translator Gaetano Polidori was eager to tell his reader, played 'the Tuscan lyre on the banks of the Arno'.[61] Implicit in attempts to historically link these two traditions is the possibility of a return for Italy and England to a great age of culture and independence. These editors promised another renaissance if Italian literature surpassed what one anthologist called 'the many unbalanced and prattling works of certain *modern* French and Germans, that sprouts in many copies, like plants of bad health in a savage and broken land'.[62] The intended audience for the anthologies and periodicals published by Italian exiles has been debated. William Spaggiari claims that these works 'could represent a link with the abandoned homeland and, simultaneously, a form of spiritual support that would help the exile face the difficulties of a precarious life in an environment which was often seen as hostile', whereas Saglia suggests that these works 'contibuted in crucial ways to helping British readers familiarize themselves with authors and works from other European traditions'.[63] The statements of the works' editors and authors support Saglia's argument for their ambassadorial purpose. In his *Memorie* (1823), Da Ponte discusses the English clients who came to his bookshop, and the books they purchased, and sees himself fulfilling his 'favourite design of bringing back Italian literature to its earlier position' in London.[64] The Englishman Thomas Mathias addresses his anthology of Italian verse to 'Lettori Inglesi', and calls it a necessity 'to our nation'.[65] This was certainly how these works were received in the periodicals, with the *Edinburgh Review* claiming, 'this branch of literature, which has been too much neglected in Great Britain, may become very valuable to the public'.[66]

Mapping this literary community before 1815 means looking closely at some of its members. The three writers I consider are Lorenzo Da Ponte, Thomas Mathias, and Augustus Bozzi, who have been chosen because of the distinct forms they used to promote Italian culture and because their experiences resonate, overlap, and offer links with the Italians discussed later in this study. Lorenzo Da Ponte was born at Ceneda in the Veneto in 1749. In 1776, after securing a role as a master in a Treviso seminary, he wrote an epistle under the Rousseauian title 'Whether the happiness of mankind is increased within the social system, or whether he would be happier in a simple state of nature', for which he was banned from teaching.[67] In 1779 he was sent into exile and became the poet to the opera at Vienna. It was here that he became the professional rival of the Italian poet Giovanni Battista Casti, and, more importantly, where he wrote the libretti for *Le nozze di Figaro* (1786), *Don Giovanni* (1787), and *Così fan tutte* (1790). The death of Leopold II changed Da Ponte's fortunes, and precipitated a move to London. Da Ponte found a job at the Haymarket Opera writing and altering librettos. In 1797 he acquired premises and began selling Italian books, and publishing libretti and poetry on site. In his *Memorie* he talks of buying up Italian stock from an English bookseller:

> I asked the owner of the shop, if he had any Italian books.
> "Too many!" he replied.
> "I will come to see them," said I.
> "You will do me a favor in taking them off my hands!"
> In such discredit were Italian books in London, in the year 1800![68]

The bookseller treats Da Ponte's native literature as clutter and offers some 400 books for thirty guineas. Da Ponte's stated purpose was to 'revive the taste for our beautiful literature', and his publishing enterprise was the vehicle for this.[69] The endpapers to one of his published volumes claims his bookshop at 28 Haymarket has 'un copiosissimo catalogo di libri Italiani'.[70] Two versions of this catalogue still exist, one from 1800, and the other a sales catalogue from the shop's eventual closure in 1804; these documents provide useful information about Da Ponte as a bookseller and publisher. The 1804 catalogue lists 1883 items for sale, sold over a ten-day period, and contains all the classics of the Italian canon.[71] This catalogue differs in two ways from other Italian book sales in early nineteenth-century London: it features works by the modern Italian poets who had shown sympathy with the revolutionary ideals of the day, such as Pindemonte, Alfieri, and Casti; and it includes some editions of English literature, particularly the Italianate poets Milton and Gray.[72] The catalogue shows a bookseller who was not content with selling old editions of the classics; Da Ponte was keen to show an English readership the historic influence and current importance of Italian poetry.

Da Ponte was not just a bookseller, he also published Italian poetry, including the first British pressing of Tasso's *Aminta* (1573), a text Hunt would translate in 1820.[73] Da Ponte's most remarkable publication was an 1803 edition of his old rival Casti's mock-epic fabliau *Gli animali parlanti* (1802).[74] Casti had written the poem aged seventy-four in Paris, after he left his stipend at the court of Vienna partly inspired by revolutionary feeling and partly worried about the strain *Il poema tartaro* (1787) caused to Austro–Russian relations. In the preface Casti sets out the purpose of the work: 'si esponesse un'intera storia politica rilevando i vizi e i difetti dei politici sistemi'.[75] Da Ponte is printing an incendiary poem, only a year after its first publication, in which the digressive narrator rages against war, clerics, tyranny, and the suppression of freedom. To make the poem clearer for the English reader, Da Ponte includes a ten-page appendix of difficult words and an introduction which claims:

> Noi possiamo, senza timore d'incorrere la taccia d'esageratori, assicurare il pubblico, che quest' opera aggiunge nuovo splendore al secolo nostro, e nuova gloria al Parnaso Italiano.[76]

In a climate where many exiles feared incurring far worse than 'being accused of exaggerating', Da Ponte's introduction does not shy away from the current political situation. A stand against the structures of power articulated by Da Ponte and Casti is an obvious part of the idea of

Italy considered in this study, but Casti was also a poetic influence who was appraised in an essay by Foscolo and inspired British narrative poets.[77] Byron's recognition of the parodic potential of the ottava rima was partly due to Casti's early work – as an example of formal freedom, which Gabrielle Muresu calls the 'will, on the part of the poet, to move with independence on the inside of a codified tradition'.[78] *Gli animali parlanti* is not such a formal influence, but it did provide a model for the tone of Byron's later satires. The opening of the poem provides examples of this, in the mock invocation to the Zodiac and in the following stanza:

> Perciò quei prudentissimi animali,
> Legislator', filosofi, politici,
> Per porre alcun riparo a tanti mali,
> Esami fean sintetici e analitici
> Di qualunque governo, o buono o tristo,
> Repubblican, monarchico, oppur misto.[79]

Casti's fluid satirical voice has and wants none of the authority of the Popean tradition, and his lists, which bombard us into confusion, look forward to lines on famous soldiers in Canto I and the menu in Canto XV of *Don Juan.* Casti's subject is the mechanics of the political state – only one animal is silly enough to distinguish between synthetic or analytic decisions – but this technical register is undermined by its use to describe cats and dogs. It is this incongruity that appears in Byron's rhyme, of revealing absurdity through linguistic excess, and in vacillating between terms as in Casti's final line where the bathetic 'oppur' exposes the futility of all three modes of government.

Da Ponte's promotion of Italian literature, and his need to solve some financial problems, led to a close friendship with Thomas Mathias. It was an unlikely friendship, given Da Ponte's revolutionary sympathies as a teacher and publisher. Mathias was a Tory – a friend of Pitt, and a satirist in the vein of Gifford – who would become the librarian of the Queen's household in 1813. His literary reputation rested on Popean anti-revolutionary satires and his anti-Catholic *Letter to the Lord Marquis of Buckingham* (1796). Mathias also had an apparently separate interest in Italy and its culture, which led to friendships with the exiles Romualdo Zotti and Da Ponte. His numerous contributions to Italian literature before 1815 are worthy of study for their own sake, but they also elucidate the difference between the dilettantish promotion of Italian literature before 1815, and the radical Anglo–Italian current from 1815 to 1823. Mathias's outstanding contribution to Italian literature in England was his three *Componimenti* of Italian poetry.[80] These anthologies were addressed to English readers, written entirely in Italian, and provided overviews of the Italian lyric beginning with Guittone D'Arezzo. The *Componimenti* anticipate the widespread publication of anthologies of foreign literatures in the 1810s and 1820s; Saglia has found that poetry was the most frequently excerpted medium in these anthologies, as it 'was commonly deemed to enshrine the soul and genius of a people in its purest state'.[81] The preface to Mathias's first anthology features long quotations from the Italian critical canon (Giovanni Mario Crescimbeni, Ludovico Antonio Muratori, Giovanni Vincenzo Gravina, etc.), but it also reflects on the current situation of Italian literature in England:

> perchè l'ignorazione o l'obblio di tanti Poeti è la sola o la primiera cagione della caligine nella quale tra noi si giacciono trascurati; invogliato anch'io di cooperare, per quanto le mie forze permettono, al Risorgimento della Letteratura e della Poesia Italiana in Inghilterra, nella loro antica e consueta possanza; [. . .] come nel secolo, sopra tutt'altro poetico, dell'augusta e real nostra Vergine Dominante, ELIZABETA, protettrice sovrana dell'armi, dell'arti, de' studi, e DE' POETI.[82]

As Da Ponte felt he could 'revive', so Mathias wishes to 'cooperate' in the promotion of Italian literature. Despite his establishment credentials, Mathias shows the position typically adopted by the literary exile: by accepting the current neglect of Italian poetry, while invoking the role of Italy in the glory of the Renaissance. At the close of his opening epistle to two friends, cast in the Italian arcadian style as 'ALCÈO ED ARISTIPPO', Mathias elevates his tone and moves into verse:

> così possa sentir di novo l'altissima melodìa dalle labbra de' Vati futuri con fiato bastante a riempir le sonore lor trombe.
>
> Così la morta Poesia *risurga*,
> E di salire al ciel diventi degna![83]

He ends his preface with a prophecy that poets in coming years will be influenced by the neglected melody of Italy. The poetry that follows is an adaptation from the proem to Dante's *Purgatorio*; the original lines are in the opposite order,

> e canterò di quel secondo regno
> dove l'umano spirito si purga
> e di salire al ciel diventa degno.
> Ma qui la morta poesì resurga,
> o sante Muse,[84]

Dante's first two lines, which end the tercet, refer to the ascent of the soul to Heaven after climbing through Purgatory. The next lines are Dante's invocation to Calliope, which alerts the reader to the movement from the *Inferno*, the poetry of the dead, to a new canticle. Mathias elides the theological line beginning with the later invocation, to take Dante's tone of salvation and make it refer to the resurgence of Italian literature in England. The choice of two altered lines from the *Commedia* is apposite: Dante, and the reinterpretation of his verse shown here in microcosm, was integral to later radical ideas of Italy. The anthology was well received, and the *British Critic* called it part of an Italian movement 'gaining ground amongst us'.[85] The reception may have spurred Mathias's production of the *Aggiunta* in 1809. Here, English readers received a further three volumes of lyrics and biographical notices of featured writers. After moving to Naples, Mathias began a concerted and successful effort to write verse in Italian, and continued the *Componimenti* project.[86] With the help of Agnello Nobile, who published Foscolo's *Poesie* in 1803, he produced a four-volume anthology, which combined the 1802 text, the *Aggiunta*, and an additional preface. It was in the preface to this 1819 work that he could claim victory, as the Italian poets 'che ora in ischiere trionfanti *risalutano* la loro augusta patria'.[87]

Da Ponte and Mathias focused their efforts on the production and distribution of texts; a third member of the Italian community, Augustus Bozzi, began a literary and political periodical that reviewed these works, and provided a forum for exiled writers.[88] Bozzi came to Britain after serving as a British Navy surgeon in the Mediterranean. His politics were radical: as a student at Pavia in 1799 he was imprisoned for his ardent republican writings in the *Giornale senza Titolo*; on his occasional trips back to Italy he disseminated literature to encourage anti-French uprisings; he preached unification on his travels in 1814, for which he was arrested and held by Austrian secret police; and he wrote a trilingual appeal to Alexander of Russia from London on behalf of the Italian 'patriotic insurgents'.[89] He had come to Britain to live in liberty and escape 'scosse convulsive e tremende che agitano il Continente'.[90] Bozzi used London, as Foscolo would only a few years later, as a place from which to influence events at home and recruit sympathetic Englishmen to the idea of a free Italy.[91] The Austrian authorities, already aggravated by the promotion of Italian independence by Whig peers, were enraged by Bozzi's attempts to influence British policy, and both Metternich and Castlereagh had him kept under surveillance.[92] In this political climate, Bozzi and Filippo Pananti began the London-based periodical *L'Italico* (1813–1814).[93] Their venture was a bold one, as Italian literature had received meagre attention in the English language press before 1815.[94] As is apparent from John Herman Merivale's 1806 *Monthly Magazine* articles on the poetry of Pulci, when Italian literature was considered it was often disparaged for its lack of polish and refinement. Merivale penned seven articles, including translated excerpts, on Pulci's *Morgante Maggiore* (1483).[95] His purpose was to excuse the roughness and vulgarity of the work, which he saw as typical of a culture 'struggling to break through the darkness of ignorance'.[96] In its nine-issue run, *L'Italico* attempted to dispel these misconceptions, and examine a variety of political, moral, and literary subjects. Its range created remarkable juxtapositions: an article on 'La verità nella Poesia' was followed by an article on conscription in Napoleonic Italy, and Italian translations of letters between the Duke of Wellington and Colonel Richard Bathurst were preceded by an article on the consolations of exile.[97]

The 'Introduzione' to the first number of *L'Italico*, used as the epigraph to this chapter, states the need for a publication 'in the golden Italian language 'among 'the foreign cultures which encircle all of London'.[98] Bozzi praises the publication in London of the Italian canon by Zotti and Polidori, and claims that the work of Mathias was 'of the greatest merit'.[99] But Bozzi, in parallel with Da Ponte's focus on modern Italian literature, was attempting more than a review of the classics. He claimed that although the Italian canon was important, as editors 'Non serve risposarsi sotto l'ombra degli allori dei nostri antichi padri'.[100] Bozzi wants to take English readers beyond Dante, Ariosto, and Tasso, and to the current state of Italian letters to the likes of Alfieri and Vincenzo Monti. Bozzi was looking for the next great Italian author in London, where the 'air of true liberty breathes, which could adorn our hope for the resurgence of the old nation to its glory'.[101] In one *L'Italico* article, Bozzi surveys the miserable state of Italian literary life under French and Austrian rule. He rages against the use of French as an official language in Lombardy and Piedmont, and compares the system of censorship to the Inquisition.[102] Bozzi's ire is pointed when he discusses the persecution of Alfieri:

> L'oggetto era di condannare, e proscrivere il nostro Tragico Alfieri, di cui dispiacevano i sentimenti liberi e fieri, e il carattere, e il linguaggio di una grand'anima, incompatabili con gli uomini bassi e corotti di questa età vergognosa.[103]

Alfieri, the author who, as the next chapter shows, was crucial in forming the Romantic view of a republican Dante, is used as a symbol of Italian resistance to foreign rule. Bozzi had the same 'fire' for 'liberal thought' as

Alfieri, and had a clear purpose in *L'Italico*. He implored fellow exiles to appreciate 'the effect of the efforts that we are making to bring comforting news to those in Italy where it is yet unknown'.[104] Just as the idea of Italy examined in this study combines the literary and political, so Bozzi intended *L'Italico* 'to seek to uplift pleasurably, and, in a word, to make ourselves useful to society in general'.[105]

The Italians who came to Britain were predominantly of a radical bent, and as is apparent in the publication of *Gli animali parlanti* and in the pages of *L'Italico*, they were involved in the promotion of radical literature and politics. Theirs was a generation that was entirely distinct from the earlier dilettantism of Giuseppe Baretti or the pretty poems of the Della Cruscans, and from the later gradualism of Antonio Panizzi, a generation put in motion by the French Revolution and the subsequent occupation of Italy; as Fabio Camiletti claims when describing the effects of the French crossing into Milan, 'the act of writing could no longer be the same: [. . .] if a different kind of literature had been possible in Italy – different, namely, from the occasional sonnets printed on handkerchiefs – the ultimate reason had to be found in the date of 15 May 1796, which has opened an irremediable fissure between a '"before": and an "after"'.[106] Mathias was in no way advocating the same politics; he promoted Italian literature as a British dilettante. Mathias's political outlook was shared by many British supporters of Italian literature before 1815: the subscribers' list *L'Italico* featured George Howard (Lord Morpeth), who had supported the most draconian bills of the 1790s, and the Prince Regent himself; Da Ponte's customers included Pittites such as the First Baron Douglas, Archibald James Edward Douglas, and the future Duke of Marlborough, George Spencer-Churchill.[107] The seeming incompatibility of political principles between exiles and English writers was less of an obstacle after 1815; radical English poets and essayists began to write work about, and be influenced by, Italy, which inaugurated an Anglo–Italian relationship that was a formal and thematic departure from that pursued by Mathias and Merivale.

This chapter began by outlining British attitudes to Italians, in England and Italy, from the mid eighteenth century to 1815. An understanding of these negative preconceptions and their permeation into legislation, music, and the novel is necessary to appreciate their catalytic role; they gave an opportunity for overt literary radicalism to poets, and an educative purpose to exiles. The marked similarity in the reaction of the state to both these groups is no coincidence. The idea of Italy they shared from 1815 – once Italian ideas had been taken up by Byron, Shelley, and Hunt – comprised a questioning of hegemony and its strictures; it was not an influence which would, in the words of Mathias, 'direct the vessel of the public mind, and of the national understanding, in a strait and undeviating course'.[108] Writers often labelled as deviants by the conservative press kindled an interest in British readers for this neglected tradition, one with links to questionable morality and past revolutions. Italian life and ideas, whether being promoted by English poets in Italy or Italians in England, offered a new freedom: not simply in the sense of being away from home, or outside a native tradition and mindset, but of being at liberty to question state-promoted forms, genres, themes, and even the nation itself. The decision to leave England was clearly not a purely literary one: the accusations of incest that preceded Byron's departure have been a focus for many biographers; the marital, custodial, and health pressures on Percy and Mary Shelley were immense; and the foundation of Hunt's journey to Italy was the financial security offered by Byron.[109] These problems precipitated their journeys, but Italy also provided a crucial change of perspective. Ralph Pite has said that Shelley 'continually revisited England in thought', and this is also true of Byron and Hunt: a life spent in Italy did not mean an imaginative or cultural disengagement with home.[110] The change of lakes for ocean which most of the second generation took allowed not only for distance from home, and a schism with the earlier Romantics, but also a new cultural perspective from which to scrutinise and satirise the nation they left behind.

CHAPTER 2

London 1816
The Genesis of an Italian Style

Mio piccolo orto,
Da te, ch'a me città, palazzo, e loggia,
A me sei vigna e campo, e selva, e prato.
Bernadino Baldi, *Celeo e L'orto* (1590)[1]

Leigh Hunt was the first of the second generation to be formally and thematically influenced by Italy, and the majority of this chapter is an examination of his Italian romance *The Story of Rimini*. Hunt's poem is a 1,700 line prequel to Dante's encounter with Paolo and Francesca, narrated over some seventy lines of *Inferno* V.[2] Timothy Webb has recently claimed that *Rimini* 'might very reasonably be recognised as one of the more significant narrative poems of the Romantic period but it has not yet been accorded the status it deserves, either as cultural phenomenon or literary text'.[3] This chapter aims to right this wrong, and to view Hunt, as Byron did, as a man at 'the *centre* of *circles*', specifically someone at the vanguard of romantic engagement with Italian literature and versification.[4] Byron's (sadly) neglected romance *Parisina* was written in the same period, and was influenced by *Rimini*.[5] It is an influence about which criticism is relatively quiet, preferring instead to devote time to Byron's 'Turkish' tales (1813–1816) and *Childe Harold's Pilgrimage* (1812–1818). The influence provides a reason for Byron's move from the successful tales to the more formally and thematically radical work of his Italian exile. After tracing this influence there will be a close reading of two confrontations with established, and establishment, literary modes: the metrical romance and the heroic couplet. The experimental quality of this verse will be analysed in the context of the debate over French and Italian schools, to show that Hunt's rejection of the Popean couplet was inspired by his reading of Dante. The final section examines the reaction of 'public opinion' to these works through their reception in periodicals. My analysis appreciates the poems themselves, rather than just their authors' politics, as a threat to what the *British Review* termed the 'public mind'.[6]

Hunt and Byron knew the language and literature of Italy before 1816. Hunt had a good grasp of Italian before his two-year incarceration in Surrey Gaol in 1813, and he was discussing Dante's Paolo and Francesca as early as 1809.[7] A month before his imprisonment, Hunt had written in the *Examiner* of his disappointment over 'the long and dead silence that has hung over the name of Italy' since French occupation, and called the country 'the shining Muse of Romance and Poetry' and 'the leader of the new in arts'.[8] Hunt entered prison hoping to leave with 'a fuller mastery of my Italian', and managed to decorate his cell in an Italian style, as he relates in his *Autobiography* (1850):

> I had the ceiling coloured with clouds and sky; the barred windows I screened with Venetian blinds; and when my bookcases were set up with their busts, and flowers and a pianoforte made their appearance, perhaps there was not a handsomer room on that side of the water.[9]

Hunt's cell might have been finest on the south of the Thames, but he is also pointing to its overseas inspiration: it is an amalgam of all things Italian, with a ceiling mural of a Renaissance church, Venetian blinds, and a pianoforte from which to play his favourite 'Italian', Mozart.[10] Of all the books in his cases the most important were the fifty-six volumes of the *Parnaso Italiano,* an anthology of Italian poetry edited by Andrea Rubbi, which Hunt described as 'truly a lump of sunshine on my shelves'.[11] The anthology illuminated Hunt's incarceration and provided the source material for *Rimini.*[12] The *Parnaso* was a comprehensive survey of Italian poetry, 'regarded as the most correct edition', with a first line index, and a clear spacious text.[13] The scholarly strength of the *Parnaso* is shown in its three volumes devoted to Dante, the poet who Rubbi saw in a Shelleyan vein as 'il fonte d'ogni nostra sapienza poetica'.[14] Rubbi's esteem is reflected in a 175-page appendix to each Dante volume, containing critical and historical notices, and explaining difficult vocabulary. The *Parnaso* was also part of a wider project that Hunt would have sympathised with: Rubbi was an anthologist, translator, and poet, who promoted Italian literature 'sempre col proposito di rintuzzare l'arroganza francese'.[15] Rubbi positioned himself against the gallomania of Italian literary culture, and his literary endeavours echoed Juvenal's complaint: 'omnia Graece: cum sit turpe magis nostris nescire Latine'.[16] Hunt's cell had a small garden where he would take volume twenty-three of his *Parnaso* and repeat the lines of Baldi which are the epigraph to this chapter; he confided to Mary Shelley in 1819 that this made 'him read with an antibilious transport'.[17]

When not reading, Hunt hosted the most prominent figures in liberal and radical culture in his Italian prison-parlour.[18] Thomas Moore took Byron to visit 'the Wit in the Dungeon' on the 20 May 1813, and Hunt gave the poets a tour of his garden.[19] Three days later Byron returned with books to assist Hunt with *Rimini*.[20] A friendship began that would flourish in subsequent visits and a lengthy correspondence. The letters between Hunt and Byron contain drafts of *Rimini* and an extended conversation on Italian literature, which at this early stage may have inspired Byron to choose three epigraphs from *Inferno* V for *The Corsair* (1814).[21] Byron also had earlier knowledge of Italian, and had read widely in its literature; in 1813 he was reproached for lending a copy of Dante to Lady Frances Webster, which he mockingly supposed was 'because, forsooth, it is a language which doth infinite damage!!'.[22] The sources for Byron's conception of Italy are diverse: De Staël's *Corinne* (1807) is important for *Childe Harold IV*, but Byron had also read Sismondi, Tasso, Gibbon, Dante, and Hunt's retelling of Dante.[23] By the end of the decade, Byron's literary interaction with the Italian tradition would include Pulci, Berni, and Casti, but he would still be concerned with the Dantean subject of *Rimini*.[24]

The Pleasure of Supplying

Parisina is a verse romance of around 600 lines, set in Italy, which explores a different kind of moral crisis from those Byron had engaged with in his 'Turkish' tales. The narrative is set in the palaces and forests of Emilia-Romagna and uses a courtly love triangle to question notions of family and national loyalty. Byron claims the poem is 'grounded on a circumstance mentioned in Gibbon'.[25] The small amount of criticism on the poem has not looked beyond Gibbon as the definitive source of *Parisina*, but the poem itself and many of the intricacies in it suggest a more complex root.[26] The similarities between *Rimini* and *Parisina* begin in the structures of their narratives, which are split between the lovers' comfort in the arboreal openings and their despair at public wedding, trial, and execution scenes. In plot, the poems share the same triangulation of older man, younger wife, and younger lover; the betrayal of a male blood relation; and a setting in Medieval Italy. In both poems the genetic link between the adulterous lover and the legitimate husband is probed, as when Hunt says of Paulo and Giovanni, 'For when you see the one, you know the other', and Byron's Hugo, who was 'too like a son' to Azo (l. 295).[27] It is this bond which Byron and Hunt sever through incest, which threatens to break a society where the marital bed is 'the chamber of [Azo's] state' (l. 133), and where a betrayal of lineage makes Paulo a 'traitor to the noble name / Of Malatesta' (IV 233–34). When these betrayals are revealed, the poets choose a suitably Catholic diction of sin and punishment, and use conflicted imagery to describe the psychological despair of their female protagonists.[28]

The reluctance to see the similarity between these poems is due in part to the stage of Byron's development in which *Parisina* is placed. Byron had eastern Mediterranean settings for his previous five works, the 'Turkish' tales: *Parisina* was published alongside *The Siege of Corinth* and is often placed in this group. The difference between *Parisina* and the tales has caused a critical void around the poem; it escapes analysis in the body of work on Byron and the 'East' and in later discussions of the Italian influence. The clearest distinction is in the setting: *The Siege of Corinth* is set in the Levant in the recent past (1710–1720), in keeping with *The Giaour, The Corsair,* and *The Bride of Abydos*, and shows an enemy power invading coastal terrain. The topography of this landscape is commented on, and coloured with foreign diction like '*Spahi*', '*Turcoman*' and '*Tophaike*'.[29] *Parisina* shares none of these features: it is set entirely in Medieval Italy, and is contained within the court and forests of Ferrara. They also have different heroes: Hugo is resigned to his fate in *Parisina*, whereas Alp, the protagonist of *The Siege of Corinth,* is the typical Byronic hero who 'stood alone – a renegade / Against the country he betrayed', and is, like the Giaour, defiant in death.[30] Furthermore, the love in the 'Turkish' tales is wrong for its cultural impropriety, the clash of occidental and oriental faiths and values, as opposed to the moral concerns that surround the incestuous romance of *Parisina.* Beyond plot and setting, *Parisina* is also narratologically distinct from the five tales that come before it. *Parisina* has none of the mysteries and lacunae that are essential to the intrigue of the 'Turkish' tales (why does Ezzelin burst into the banquet in *Lara*? What is the relationship between the Giaour and Hassan? How does Medora die in *The Corsair*?). Hugo's and Parisina's incestuous adultery and Azo's knowledge of it are all told to the reader. Byron does not ask us to speculate why these characters have been outcast or why they are tormented, he instead asks how, with all the facts before us, we can morally judge those who have sinned; Byron's method aims to 'dramatize the impossibility of judgment and say, in effect, that this is what life is'.[31]

Hunt's *Autobiography* is the easiest place to begin to show that it was *Rimini* and not the 'Turkish' tales that Byron had in mind when he was writing *Parisina.* He writes, 'I had the pleasure of supplying my friendly critic, Lord Byron, with a point for his *Parisina* (the incident of the

Heroine talking in her sleep)'.[32] Hunt claims that the origin of Parisina's revelation in sleep is Francesca's disclosure to Giovanni in *Rimini* (the device is not in Gibbon, where Niccolo finds out about the lovers through 'the testimony of a maid, and his own observation').[33] Hunt builds 'The pangs within' (IV 146) Francesca by constant reiteration of her emotional state, and creates tension through the flittering between waking and sleeping to produce her revelatory climax. Francesca's sense of 'the long lingering day' is an obstacle to 'sleep again', and diminished perceptions are caused by her 'distempered sight' blurred by tears and 'disease's visions' (IV. 118–142). Byron distils this oneiric state to these lines:

> But fevered in her sleep she seems,
> And red her cheek with troubled dreams,
> And mutters she in her unrest
> A name she dare not breathe by day [. . .]
> And whose that name? that o'er his pillow
> Sounds fearful as the breaking billow
> (ll. 69–72; 93–4)

Her muttering takes place between the conscious action of talking and the silence of fevered dreaming. She releases her 'pangs within' which 'she dare not breathe by day' with a cheek red from shame and tears. The catharsis of Parisina's revelation comes as an aqueous wave, echoing the weeping in *Rimini*. Byron and Hunt use the same conflicted sensory imagery, just as they consider the same transgressive repercussions of incest. If we take Hunt at his word, we have the first of Byron's borrowings.

To find further influence, the composition of *Parisina* must be scrutinised. In 1814, Byron began to write a poem which later became *Parisina*. Jerome McGann has claimed that Byron placed his 1814 material on to a narrative frame after he 'first saw and read' Gibbon in January 1815.[34] In the pre-1815 material the heroine was called Francesca, which McGann uses to suggest that this earlier material ended up making two poems: *Parisina* and *The Siege of Corinth* (which features a ghost called Francesca). McGann argues for a split into two poems around January 1815, but admits that this theory is speculative as 'it is impossible to give particular dates'.[35] At this juncture the *Siege* is taken from a body of work, from which the remaining lines become *Parisina*, in a theory of the text's genesis that fits neatly with the questionable critical practice of grouping *Parisina* and the *Siege* together as 'Turkish' tales.[36] There are a number of problems with McGann's chronology. First, his statement that Byron 'first saw and read' the story in Gibbon in January 1815 is questionable. Byron owned an earlier copy of Gibbon's *Miscellaneous Works* from 1796, which he could have read long before he received the 1815 Murray edition.[37] Second, McGann's theory that Byron created *Parisina* and the *Siege* out of the same pre-1815 materials does not work: *Parisina* and the *Siege* differ too greatly in setting and diction. Lines that appear in the final version of *Parisina,* written before the supposed separation, support this. In 1814 Byron sent Isaac Nathan two lyrics for *Hebrew Melodies* (1815) entitled 'It is the Hour' and 'Francisca'.[38] These became the opening of *Parisina*, in which 'the nightingale's high note is heard' with the 'gentle winds and waters near'. Francisca sits 'in her garden bower' as her lover tramps 'through the foliage thick' and 'rustling leaves' to meet for their clandestine tryst.[39] The diction of these lyrics gives no hints of a 'Turkish' tale; this is the verdant forest of medieval romance, and is remarkably similar to the 'coil / Of bubbling springs about the grassy soil' and the birds which 'to the delicious time are singing' in *Rimini* (I. 11–12, 16). Byron's 'Turkish' tales usually begin with a clear marker of place – in the address to Corinth that begins the *Siege*, or the opening of the *Bride of Abydos* on 'the clime of the east' – and these gestures at scene-setting are hardly surprising if we believe Andrew Rutherford's claim that Byron's 'recollections of Albania, Greece, and Asia Minor were the soil from which the verse tales sprang'.[40] But at this 'earliest stage' before McGann's 1815 division, the lines share the tone of the meeting between Paulo and Francesca in *Rimini.* My proposed alternative to the split of one Francesca of 'earlier materials' into Parisina and Francesca is that Byron wrote two separate female characters with the same name. Byron was not averse to changing the names of his female protagonists, and even specifically to changing the names of those called Francesca (he had originally had Francesca as the heroine of *The Corsair*).[41] At this stage Byron had read draft versions of *Rimini,* and wrote the opening lines of what was to become a story of incest, set in Italy, with a heroine named Francisca. This provides the 'different but similar' narrative that McGann is seeking: the Italian narrative of *Parisina*, its courtly setting, the name Francesca, and the mode of romance have plausible antecedents in *Rimini.*

That *Parisina* was a different type of poem from the previous tales was clear to John Murray, who wrote to Byron, 'These two tales form an invaluable contrast, and display the variety of your power. For myself, I am really more interested by the effect of the story of 'Parisina' than by either, I think, of the former tales'.[42] The 'contrast' and difference in 'effect' that Murray found in *Parisina* is from the same generic tradition as *Rimini:* the medieval romance. It is not possible that these similarities were a significant influence from Byron to Hunt. Byron did make lengthy comments and suggestions on a draft of *Rimini* Cantos II and III in October 1815.[43] In the manuscript Byron's high regard for *Rimini* is shown in marginal comments: 'very Good indeed', 'Very Very Good', 'Very good too – as a whole', 'The whole page is very fine and original', and 'Superlative'.[44] Webb has argued that 'Byron's connection with *The Story of Rimini* was undeniably intense and intimate', that he was 'meticulously sensitive to verbal detail' and that his 'involvement in the preparation of Hunt's text was much more detailed and extensive than Hunt admitted in public'.[45] Yet, despite Byron's unprecedented involvement in the revision of the text, only two of his seventeen extant proposed amendments were accepted; Hunt appears disinclined to submit to changes suggested by the most popular poet of the day.[46] *Parisina* could not have been a significant poetic influence on *Rimini* as Hunt was not aware of its existence until February 1816. But Nicholas Roe, one of the few critics to dwell on the 'creative exchange' between Byron and Hunt between 1814 and 1816, has noticed that Hunt may be acknowledging Byron with the appearance of the names Azo and Hugo in *Rimini* I. 88–89.[47] Although *Rimini* was nearly complete by this time, and preparations were being made for its publication, Hunt's inclusion of these names acts as a small signal of their shared interest.[48] Byron announced *Parisina* to Hunt in a letter of February 1816:

> I desired Murray to forward you a pamphlet with two things of mine in it [*Parisina*/*The Siege*] – the most part of both of them – & of one in particular – *written* before *others* of my composing – which have preceded them in *publication*: – they are neither of them of much pretension – nor intended for it – you will perhaps wonder at my dwelling so much and so frequently on former subjects & *scenes* – but the fact is that I found them fading fast from my memory[49]

Byron is insistent that these works are 'former', '*written* before *others*' and 'fading fast'; he then dismisses the literary pretensions of these 'frequently' wrought scenes, and calls the ninety-page volume merely 'a pamphlet'. If this letter were only referring to *The Siege,* it would be relatively mundane: in the context of *Parisina* it is not. The claim to be dwelling on former scenes in *Parisina* is false. Byron had been working on a medieval Italian tale of incest for some time, and yet had not mentioned this to Hunt, who was also working on a similar poem which Byron had read in manuscript. Byron informs Hunt only a month before publication. The atypically hesitant tone of this letter could suggest that Byron felt insecure about his debt to Hunt. In spite of the critical tendency to downplay or ignore Hunt's influence, evidence in manuscript, the poets' correspondence, and the poems themselves strongly suggest that Byron was taken by something he read in *Rimini*, which incited a change in his approach.

Chivalrous Rhymes

Contemporary reviewers noticed that *Parisina* was not like *The Siege*, or any 'Turkish' tale. The *British Review*, though, did notice the similarities between Hunt's poem and *Parisina* and reviewed the two together, while John Lockhart claimed in *Blackwood's*: 'To none of these poems, however, does the subject of *Rimini* bear so great a resemblance as to *Parisina*'.[50] The resemblance is based on genre: *Rimini* and *Parisina* are medieval romances, a generic status both poets seem self-consciously to promote. Hunt devotes a verse paragraph to the deeds of 'knightly fame' (III. 55–66) and the world of *Parisina* is one of 'damsels' who live at a court where 'knightly spurs are worn', and in which men must honour the 'lineal throne' (ll. 124, 270, 262). *Parisina* and *Rimini* are new poetry couched within an old genre; these poems' divergence from contemporary practice can be seen in comparison with the bestselling romance poet of the era, Walter Scott. As William St. Clair has noted, 'the great poems of the romantic age were not those that feature in modern university courses but *The Lay of the Last Minstrel*, *Marmion*, *The Lady of the Lake*'.[51] The romance was the most successful genre of the age and Scott was its progenitor.[52] The Scottian verse romance carried political connotations and was 'underpinned by its deeply nationalistic character'; like its medieval predecessors, the subject of romance was the matter of the nation.[53] Scott's romances centre on champions who embody the conflict of whole nations, such as the rival deeds of Marmion and De Wilton in *Marmion* (1808), or the combat between Roderick Dhu and Fitz-James in *The Lady of the Lake* (1810). Although seldom taught today, the Scottian romance is the status quo that *Parisina* and *Rimini* pervert, and a proper understanding of its themes and techniques is necessary to understand why the romances of Hunt and Byron left reviewers so rattled.

Scott's romances were deeply concerned with current national politics. *Marmion* has two interrelated narratives, the romance based around the Battle of Flodden Field (1513) and the epistles that begin each canto addressed to present-day Tories. The first of these is addressed to the Tory Member of Parliament for Christ Church, William Stewart Rose, a dilettante Italianist who would befriend Foscolo a few years later. It begins in romantic fashion: an idealised winter setting at 'Glenkinnon's rill', couched in the archaic diction of 'sward', 'brier', and 'gambols'. It then moves into spring amongst the 'daisy flowers' and on into the 'summer bower'. After the seasonal progress, a change in tone occurs:

> But oh! my country's wintry state
> What second spring shall renovate?
> What powerful call shall bid arise
> The buried warlike and the wise;
> The mind that thought for Britain's weal,
> The hand that grasp'd the victor steel? [. . .]
> Where glory weeps o'er NELSON's shrine,
> And vainly pierce the solemn gloom
> That shrouds, O PITT, thy hallowed tomb![54]

Scott turns from the seasons of old romance to the political events of the early nineteenth century. Here Pitt and Nelson embody, like Scott's heroes, the political and military apparatus of a nation. Pitt is 'the mind that thought of Britain's weal [. . .] served his Albion for herself', and becomes, as Simon Bainbridge has suggested, the romance knight saving the damsel of the state.[55] Both men are elegised for their service to 'Britain', as Scott prefaces a tale of Anglo–Scottish conflict by reinforcing his Hanoverian loyalty. The epistle is filled with questions as to what, after the death of these men, will recover the spirits of the nation at war. Scott, in his most bardic mode, proposes his own nationalist romances, which combine verse and politics in their tales of 'heroes, patriots, bards, and kings', as the solution to the state's woes.[56] The blend of medieval romance and contemporary politics in the epistle, and the tactic of clothing these politicians in a romance garb, encourages the reader to find resonances between present and past. The feature occurs again in the next epistle, which shows the timelessness of hunting, a pursuit that uses the same hounds, birds, and arrows in Scott's day as it did in the fourteenth century. The reader is prodded into seeing now diffused in then. The technique continues in Scott's hugely popular novels. In the opening chapter of *Waverley* (1814), Scott sees his subject as those 'passions common to men' which have 'alike agitated the human heart, whether it throbbed under the steel corslet of the fifteenth century, the brocaded coat of the eighteenth, or the blue frock and white dimity waistcoat of the present day'.[57] *Marmion* works on the level of the Flodden Field narrative with heroes in single combat defending a nation from a foreign invader, which has Scott as bard telling a national history, assisted by copious footnotes for factual authority. The epistles then gloss these for the reader, to reveal in apparently factual and British tales, support and encouragement for the international wars of the present.[58] The promotion of favoured forms and themes was justified by their use in folkloric tales and epic poetry, which acted as an historic precedent for preferred modes of expression and behaviour. Scott's poetry represents one of the crucial components in the formation of a British 'public mind': the creation of a national past.

The nationalist and conservative romance is the genre *Parisina* and *Rimini* contend with. These works are radical in their denial of what had made this genre the mode of the decade: its basis in domestic history and focus on war.[59] A switch in locale to Italy gives Hunt and Byron space for innovation within an established genre. They render the romance politically ambiguous by taking it to a country that readers of the novel over the past fifty years would associate with loose morals and Machiavels, and readers of history would associate with republican states and revolutionary thought. A sense of civil disorder in *Parisina* and *Rimini*, of polities not involved in a foreign war but internally discordant, is ingrained in the poems' conflicted descriptions. This extract from *Parisina* shows this technique:

> He plucked his poignard in its sheath,
> But sheathed it ere the point was bare –
> Howe'er unworthy now to breathe,
> He could not slay a thing so fair –
> At least, not smiling – sleeping – there –
> Nay, more: – he did not wake her then,
> But gazed upon her with a glance
> Which, had she roused her from her trance,
> Had frozen her sense to sleep again
> (ll. 107–115)

Parisina's revelation of incest forces Azo to confront the prospect of losing his wife, seeking revenge against his son, Hugo, and bringing scandal to his court. Byron mimetically enacts this torment through the confused quality of the verse. Azo's first reaction is murder, so he at once draws his sword. Upon consideration it is replaced, creating the hesitation in line openings from 'plucked' to 'sheathed'. The alliteratively paired 'gazed' and 'glance' are also in conflict; how can Azo be studying with a 'gaze' which has the temporary quality of a 'glance'? The opposite terms partner the central concern of the extract with the relationship between consciousness and sleep. Parisina's state in the fifth line is 'sleeping'. To complicate this, Byron moves into a hypothetical mode, 'had she', which provides a false waking and return to sleep in the final two lines. This return is carried by the act of freezing, of making the fluid static, in a confrontation of opposite states which he will return to at the end of the poem.[60] The tensions that characterise Byron's first Italian poem appear again in the romance world of Haidée in *Don Juan* II–III. The world of *Parisina* is in flux, 'with all its change of time and tide', just as Juan washed up on shore has 'senses dim' and knows 'nothing more of night nor day'.[61] The reader is asked to understand the conflicted emotions of these characters through the description of uncertain points between oppositional states. Hunt's world is similarly conflicted, as when Francesca is

> sitting now, calm from the gush of tears,
> With dreaming eye fixed down, and half-shut ears,
> Hearing, yet hearing not [. . .]
> And looking up again, half sigh, half stare,
> She lifts her veil, and feel the freshening air.
> (II 141–3; II 146–7)

Francesca is crying but dreaming, so overcome that she has blocked her aural capacity in her 'half-shut ears'. She then stares up, but only half, as she is also cast down with a sigh. It is then revealed that she is veiled, giving a tangible barrier to vision and smell, to accompany the emotional obstacles of her mental state. The veil, like the lattice that Parsina screams behind at Hugo's death (a barrier which Keats's Isabella will also smile through to signal her tryst) allows Hunt to offer little in the way of clarity; the reader is being led, within these images, to a place of internal confusion that enacts the moral conflicts at the centre of each tale. Scott's minstrel had tapped into a historically assured tradition, with the weight of copious footnotes behind him. He played the secure role of storyteller or bard, heightened by the reference to a listening audience in the introductions to each canto – this security is denied in the new Italian romance.[62] Scott's son-in-law John Lockhart saw this perversion and expressed disgust: 'Leigh Hunt's chivalrous rhymes are as unlike those of Walter Scott, as is the chivalry of a knighted cheesemonger to that of Archibald the Grim'.[63] Although Lockhart is mocking *Rimini* in class terms (perhaps alluding Hunt's Cockney rhymes, which have been discussed by Greg Kucich), his comparison identifies the distance between the works of Hunt and Scott: a reader expecting a poem of war and national myth is instead confronted with a courtly Italian romance.[64] Incestuous relationships bring scandal through moral transgression: unlike Scott's tacit support for a unified nation against foreign agitators, Byron and Hunt show internal conflicts by asking their readers to weigh the passion of two individuals against the health of the state.

The new romance presents a challenge to Scott's inviolable chain between then and now, as we can see at the moment Azo, knowing of the infidelity, brings a crying Parisina before his court:

> Then, – had her eye in sorrow wept,
> A thousand warriors forth had leapt,
> A thousand swords had sheathless shone,
> And made her quarrel all their own.
> Now, – what is she? and what are they?
> (ll. 156–160)

The swords of state sheath and unsheathe themselves as Azo's did when he heard of the infidelity; the rhyme and anaphora mark the expected progress from the Queen's sorrow to her defence, a progress ruptured by 'Now' to leave only empty questions. The obvious allusion is to Burke's remarks on Marie Antoinette – 'I thought ten thousand swords must have leaped from their scabbards to avenge even a look that threatened her with insult' – and with it Byron pricks the neat political certainties of the genre (would Burke expect the soldiers to defend Parisina?).[65] David Duff has discussed how Burke's 'romance imagery is so common as to constitute a kind of myth-making', and it is this mythology that underpins Scott's romances; in *Parisina,* Byron begins to probe, as he will more fluently in *Beppo* and *Don Juan,* these reigning moral orthodoxies over power, desire, and freedom.[66] Hunt was asking similar questions. While writing *Rimini,* he began 'The Round Table', a series of essays written with Hazlitt, loosely modelled on the *Spectator* (1711–1712). Hunt ends the first number with a turn to King Arthur, 'as our Round Table, to a certain degree is inevitably associated in our minds with his', and welcomes this association on poetical and then political grounds:

> for what have the most chivalrous persons been from the earliest ages, but so many moral reformers, who encountered error and corruption with various weapons, who brought down brute force, however gigantic, who carried light into darkness, and liberty among the imprisoned, and dissipated, with some charm or other about them, the illusions of pleasure?[67]

The answer for most readers would be anything but: since the Romantic revival, 'chivalrous persons' were associated far more frequently with the imprisoner than the imprisoned. As Duff has argued, this is one of a number of 'attempts to reclaim the idea of chivalry for the democratic cause', and Hunt does this with some bravado, closing an essay in which he identifies as Arthur with escalating clauses pronouncing his own chivalry.[68]

For an attempt to reclaim or radicalise a genre to be successful, for the poems to become 'conspicuous testing-grounds for the received generic paradigms', there must be continuity between the then and the now.[69] Hunt revels in writing the parts of *Rimini* that maintain rather than reform these paradigms. A fine example is the ordered procession of the men of Rimini into Ravenna. Hunt breaks from irregular verse paragraphs and gives four sestets, which begin:

First come the trumpeters, clad all in white
Except the breast, which wears a scutcheon bright.
By four and four they ride, on horses grey;
And as they sit along their easy way,
Stately, and heaving to the sway below,
Each plants his trumpet on his saddle-bow.

The heralds next appear, in vests attired
Of stiffening gold with radiant colours fired;
And then the pursuivants, who wait on these,
All dressed in painted richness to the knees:
Each rides a dappled horse, and bears a shield,
Charged with three heads upon a golden field.

(I. 147–158)

After the heralds come twelve ranks of twelve squires, and after the squires come the knights, who appear like the sestets 'six in a row'. The marks of chivalry are present and correct: scutcheons, saddle-bows, and the attendants' 'painted richness'. But these lines are also formally appropriate: Hunt's irregular couplets stand to attention, and produce a clear style through frequent punctuation and little enjambment. The detailed heraldry on the pursuivants' shields is matched by the precise 'First come', 'by four and four they ride', 'each plants', 'every squire', 'next appear', 'each rides', so that lines describing men in heraldry use a regulating syntax to make them appear heraldic. Although Hunt is cleaving to the formality of the metrical romance, this sudden emphasis on order and hierarchy serves to expose the 'stately' routines of the genre.

Hunt relocates the romance to Italy and plays on the various standard locations of the genre, particularly the relationship between the static court, the enchanted forest, and, in keeping with earlier tensions, the garden in between. The manipulation of romance locations should be appreciated in the context of Hunt's Dantean source. The Paolo and Francesca episode takes place in *Inferno* V, and in the preceding canto there are notable similarities between Dante's treatment of romance settings and those in *Rimini*. Dante was writing in a period when the romance was enjoying an immense vogue, and in the preface to *Rimini* Hunt discusses the works of Chrétien de Troyes and the story of Amadís de Gaula that informed Dante's idea of romance.[70] Critics have been reluctant to see *Rimini* as offering a close reading of its Dantescan source, and few critics have considered parallel passages from the poems. Cox's claim that Hunt taught 'a generation of poets how to raid the Italian cultural archive' is right to place him as the first mover in the uptake of Italian literature, but talk of raiding devalues his considered engagement.[71] Webb has paid closer attention to the relationship between the poets, but argued that Hunt 'found it difficult to accept Dante' for theological reasons, which led Hunt to misread 'Dante's rigorous system of rewards and punishments'.[72] Hunt may not have been a careful reader of Dante's theology, but he was a highly sensitive reader of the literary elements of the *Commedia,* and the poetic focus of his reading was in keeping with European critical trends. Writings on Dante, both in the Romantic period and now, have suggested seeing the *Commedia* as a romance.[73] But, as Schelling found, this generic distinction is unsatisfactory: the *Commedia* is in 'a separate class', which 'consecrates all modern art to its vocation'. Schelling's focus on originality, and his comments on the poem as a work forged 'out of materials of his [Dante's] time', are in keeping with late eighteenth-century approaches to the *Commedia*. Knowledge of how the late-eighteenth and early-nineteenth centuries viewed the *Commedia*, is essential to Hunt's understanding of Dante. For much of the eighteenth century the *Commedia* was unread and viewed as unreadable, and Voltaire popularised the attitude that Dante had little relevance in an enlightened age.[74] In Britain, Thomas Warton judged the *Commedia* as having 'the want of art and method', as 'rude' and 'obscene', and claimed that Dante failed to understand Homer and Virgil.[75] A change in this reception can be traced to Italian criticism in the years after Warton. This began with the publishing efforts of Rubbi and with Alfieri, the man Bozzi saw as a symbol of liberal fire in *L'Italico,* and to whom Byron refers, in the preface to *Parisina,* as a writer unafraid of challenging 'delicacy' and 'fastidiousness'.[76] Alfieri saw Dante as the archetypal *libero scrittore*: a poet without patronage, who was free to write a poem 'che comportavano i tempi suoi', as opposed to Virgil and Horace who were compelled under Augustus to write 'contaminati di tante vili adulazioni e falsità'.[77] In 1806, Francesco Torti placed the *Commedia* ahead of the epics of Virgil, Ariosto, and Tasso because Dante wrote it 'senza seguire alcun modello' and the new mode he created allowed him to 'considerare la natura in un aspetto tutto nuovo'.[78]

These critics aimed to prove that Dante was both an original poet and an independent spirit, who freely condemned the Italian states in which he lived.[79] Now Dante was neither a poor imitator of the ancients, nor a medieval theologian, but a poetic original deeply involved in the political and literary current of his times. The revival of Italian poetry brought about by these works, and by Ginguené and Sismondi, meant that the idea of Dante as politically engaged experimenter was part of Hunt's and Byron's English perspective.[80] The three-fold view in continental criticism of Dante as a man of his times, a poetic experimenter, and a political radical is thought to have permeated British literary culture as part of a wider resurgence of interest in the *Commedia* in 1818 and 1819. Diego Saglia has called 1819 'the Dantean year', Michael Caesar gives prominence to 'the single year 1818', and Ralph Pite calls these the years in which 'Dante turned from a specialist interest into a necessary acquisition for the cultivated person'.[81] Foscolo's essays for the *Edinburgh* of 1818, Coleridge's public lectures from 1818 to 1819, and the reprinting of Cary's translation in 1819 all increased Dante's prominence in Britain, but calling these years the *terminus a quo* of an English Dante revival would be to neglect the period 1815–1816.

Hunt's reading of *Inferno* IV and V shows an appreciation of Dante as a poet engaged in the literature of his own time, a reading that influenced the interrogation of locations in *Rimini*.[82] Canto III begins with Hunt reflecting on his 'caged hours' at Horsemonger Lane, and the claims that his 'leafy dreams' of Italy are his only solace. Hunt then describes in detail the lush world, both natural and pruned, where Francesca commits her transgression. Its verdant qualities are constantly on display,

> Indeed the whole thing was leafy [. . .]
> With spots of sunny opening, and with nooks,
> To lie and read in, sloping into brooks.
> (III. 384, 418–419)

Dappled sunlight, undulating land, and multiple rivers characterise the natural idyll, and the nooks provide the secrecy essential for Paulo and Francesca to be alone.[83] The forthcoming danger of reading in the garden is alluded to in the second pun on 'leafy', and the rhymed 'nooks' and 'brooks' are close to the 'books' which will be the agents of the couple's fall. This play on the literary abounds in *Rimini* and *Parisina*: Parisina listens 'not for the nightingale' but 'her ear expects as soft a tale' (ll. 21–22), Azo confirms the betrayal from 'many a tale from those around' (l. 121), Paulo's expression is 'readable as open book' (I. 297), and his marriage 'seemed to realize the dreams of books' (II. 77). *Rimini* proudly decks itself in the garb of romance, but it seems self-conscious of the genre's dangers. The 'whole thing' is not quite as natural as Hunt claims: the nook that Francesca reads in is entirely of man's making. It is 'midst the flowers and trees', yet also in an enclosure complete with a bookshelf, that Francesca reads 'a bright romance' and lets Paulo cross the boundary from outdoor to indoor, and where the two kiss 'mouth to mouth, all in a tremble' (III. 520, 535, 604).

Hunt's construction of Canto III is a product of a careful reading of *Inferno* IV–V. *Inferno* IV can be read as a romance in miniature, of the pilgrim's quest from 'la selva' to 'al piè d'un nobile castello, / sette volte cerchiato d'alte mura, / difeso intorno d'un bel fiumicello'.[84] Once inside the castle, Dante and Virgil enter a 'prato di fresca verdura' where they meet souls from the classical world.[85] In this garden, the pilgrim meets the great poets of the past (Homer, Horace, Ovid, and Lucan) and is accepted by 'la bella scola', which leads to him being in 'la sesta compagnia' of poets.[86] It is these men, as the repeated first-person plurals suggest, who escort Dante through a meadow where they talk among each other as equals. Their conversations are not relayed to the reader, as Dante judges them 'cose che 'l tacere è bello, / sì com'era 'l parlar colà dov'era'.[87] The narrative mode of the *Commedia* – particularly its most famous episodes with Paolo and Francesca, Farinata, Ugolino, and Pia – relies on the pilgrim relaying discussion to the reader, so why is the reader not given the conversation between the pilgrim and the classical tradition? The answer lies in the location: a garden of a romance castle where 'sì mi fecer de la loro schiera'.[88] The pilgrim's mind is not devoted to God as he relaxes and forgets his pilgrimage amongst these men. But this acceptance is not extended to the reader: this is an exclusive company and the event gives the reader the first glimpse of the pilgrim's hubris. He has been charmed in the garden, like many a knight-errant, by the pagans who lived outside the Christian dispensation.

Inferno IV is Dante's taking into account of the French romance, of a garden where a hero disarms, is vulnerable, and succumbs. The pilgrim's hubris should be remembered during his meeting with Francesca da Rimini. In the next canto Dante enters the *bufera infernal* where Virgil, as he had done in the garden of Canto IV, lists the occupants in an epic enumeration. The cast is classical, except for the final sufferer: Tristan. The reference to the medieval tale of Tristan and Isolde moves the canto to the popular world of romance, and a forbidden love triangle within it. Dante then summarises Virgil's list of sufferers as 'le donne antiche e' cavalieri', twisting the predominantly classical cast towards the language of romance.[89] Dante's interpretation of Virgil's catalogue, alongside the interrogation of the garden and castle in Canto IV, asks us to read Francesca's narrative in the light of Romance. Francesca, like Dante, is a great reader, steeped in the courtly poetry of Guido Guinizelli and Guido Cavalcanti.[90] It is during her narrative that she divulges her illegitimate love for Paolo, the blame for which is laid on a romance text: 'Galeotto fu 'l libro e chi lo scrisse'.[91] In the typical manoeuvre of the infernal sinner, Francesca fails to take responsibility for her actions and, in keeping with the literary dimension of Virgil's list, blames the romance that she and Paolo read. The sin of this reading, and its clear basis in romance, is developed from *Inferno* IV. Francesca's desire to read and be taken in by literature leads to a suppression of reason – typical of those 'che la ragion sommettono al talento' – which precipitates her vice, as it had earlier brought about Dante's hubris.[92]

The problem that had been at the centre of Dante's garden, of the pilgrim relaxing in an apparently natural, but really manufactured and dangerous environment, is heightened by Hunt. The detailed retelling in *Rimini* exaggerates the division that already exists in Dante. We learn that Francesca's married life in Rimini has her deep in 'her books' (III. 185), and Hunt goes further than Dante by making her a *trobairitz* who sings to her warrior husband an 'old fiery lay / Of fierce Orlando, or of Ferumbras, / Or Ryan's cloak' (III 189–91). Hunt also develops the Dantescan play on locations to one of indoor and outdoor, as his Paulo and Francesca sin in a garden summerhouse "twixt the wood and flowery walks, halfway, / And formed of both' (III. 433–34). The preface hints at this use of the garden to confuse boundaries: 'let me take them with me a while, whether in doors or out of doors, whether in the room or the green fields'.[93] The 'green fields' recall Dante's own 'prato di fresca verdura'; what seems like an innocuous prefatory comment allows Hunt to acknowledge his source and allude to the tension between indoor and outdoor, room and field, which will be important to the narrative.[94] Hunt had read of another '*prato*' during the composition of *Rimini,* which occur in some lines he remembers from prison:

> I bought the 'Parnaso Italiano' while in prison, and used often to think of a passage in it, while looking at this miniature piece of horticulture: –
>
> ———Mio picciol orto,
> A me sei vigna, e campo, e selva, e prato.—Baldi.
>
> ———My little garden,
> To me thou 'rt vineyard, field, and meadow, and wood
>
> Here I wrote and read in fine weather, sometimes under an awning.[95]

Hunt misses the middle line from his *Parnaso*, 'Da te, ch'a me città, palazzo, e loggia', and invokes Baldi to describe the garden in which he read Dante and composed his romance under his own pavilion.[96] The full quotation shows the medicinal benefit of the 'little garden' to the prisoner, when the pleasures of the city were forbidden, but also reveals Hunt's awareness of the intermediary position of the garden. The central transgression of *Rimini* occurs in a fictional version of his prison pavilion, recalling Dante's use of the garden as a place to test romance. For Elizabeth Jones, the 'quasi-natural space' of the liaison is conflicted in Hunt's description of it as both 'bower' and 'the same marble pavilion referred to in the preceding gardenesque catalogue', which she links to the building of Nash's Regent's Park.[97] But this reading demotes the poetic precedent; the garden is the place where the hero disarms, and becomes vulnerable in Homer, Spenser, and most importantly in Hunt's source. Dante knew the tricks of romance, and so did Hunt, but what this analysis has shown is that Hunt seems to have learnt them from the Italian poet. *Rimini* is not just an Italian romance that questions established ideas of the genre through its themes; it is also an expression of Hunt's engagement with Dante, and with the new Italian criticism that saw him as both a poetic innovator and a man engaged in the political reform of his age. Hunt source is the *Inferno*, but the play on romance in *Rimini* is also the first expression of a nascent group of writers who saw the poets of the Italian canon as 'the *only* poetical *moderns*'.[98]

A Lax and Lawless Versification

Hunt thought the poetic legacy of *Rimini* was its reformation of the couplet, and this departure from formal standards was also bound up in things Italian.[99] The heroic couplet was the dominant form of eighteenth-century verse, finding its most famous proponent in Pope, continued through the century by Goldsmith, and sustained in the Romantic period by Samuel Rogers and Thomas Campbell. After Pope's death, his poetry was read as representing certain social mores through its metrical regularity, as when Samuel Johnson claimed that the 'fundamental principle' of Pope's verse 'was Good Sense, a prompt and intuitive perception of consonance and propriety', and the *Gentleman's Magazine* praised Pope for 'the chastity of the heroic couplet'.[100] More recently, William Bowman Piper has argued that Pope's use of the couplet 'put into harmonious definition a system of social practices and into harmonious agreement a set of social attitudes', and Earl Wasserman has called the form 'the very sanctum of the conservatives'.[101] Critics have seen regularity as integral to

Pope's couplet, and this was one of the central themes of Joseph Warton's *Essay on the Genius and Writings of Pope* (1756). Warton's *Essay,* which Hunt read before his imprisonment, established the idea for later generations of poets that Pope was tied to the formality of French neo-classicism and that there was a difference between 'a MAN OF WIT, a MAN OF SENSE, and a TRUE POET'.[102] A number of reasons have been offered for the turn against Pope begun by Warton, which was carried on by Cowper, Wordsworth, Bowles, and Hunt. Walter Jackson Bate has argued that the Romantics' rejection of couplet verse for its 'correctness' was not simply an aesthetic preference, but also a necessary decision to abandon a style that Pope had perfected.[103] Robert Griffin has argued that the overly regular reading of Pope by the Romantics (and their modern critics) is necessary to create the rupture that makes Romanticism a definable literary period, and claims that the 'unity of Romanticism as an ideology [. . .] is discovered in agreement over what it rejects'.[104]

The over-emphasis on Pope's regularity in the second half of the eighteenth century made room for a new poetry, one that looked to revive English poetry before the taint of the French school.[105] Among other things, there was a reassessment of Milton, especially his Italianate *Poems* (1645), which led Hazlitt to conclude in his fourth *Lectures on the English Poets* (1818) that Pope did not bear the original genius of Milton, but rather that he was a poet of 'propriety of thought and manners as established by the forms and customs of society'.[106] To mark their departure from Pope, the earlier Romantic poets often made clear their preferences for pre-Reformation poetry, a habit the later Romantics shared while also advertising the Italian roots of much of this older verse.[107] Many writers for the periodical press, although keen on a reassessment of Elizabethan verse, did not condone the turn away from the regular couplet. The monthlies and quarterlies seldom criticised Pope and often entrenched the conventions around the couplet and its social effect; Hazlitt called these men 'bigoted idolisers of our author, chiefly on the score of his correctness'.[108] Campbell, who was still loyal to closed couplets, defended Pope against Bowles in the *Edinburgh* in 1808, a defence taken further by William Gifford, who deleted whole paragraphs of Southey's negative critique of Pope in an article for the *Quarterly*.[109] The prevalent attitude of the major journals can be summarised by the editors of the other two great periodicals of the age: Francis Jeffrey, who commented that the standards of poetry 'were fixed long ago, by certain inspired writers, whose authority it is no longer lawful to call in question', and Lockhart, who claimed that 'to deny [Pope's] genius, is just as absurd as to dispute that of Wordsworth, or to believe in that of Hunt'.[110] The editors convey Pope's centrality to the rigid formal precepts of the period, and are a prelude to the 'Pope controversy' that engulfed Romantic literary culture from 1819 to 1822.[111]

The opprobrium Hunt received for meddling with the couplet can be understood in the context of these prevalent attitudes, but Lockhart's praise of Wordsworth reveals an incongruity. Wordsworth, whose genius *Blackwood's*, but not the *Edinburgh*, saw as 'absurd' to challenge, was also critical of Pope and other 'metrical writers utterly worthless and useless' and claimed to prefer those poets who had confided more in their 'native genius' such as Chaucer, Sidney, and Spenser.[112] In the preface to *Rimini*, Hunt states the reasons for his attack on the established conventions of the couplet. At the outset Hunt's divergence from Pope has much in common with that of Wordsworth and Southey:

> I do not hesitate to say however, that Pope and the French school of versification have known the least on the subject, of any poets perhaps that ever wrote. They have mistaken mere smoothness for harmony; and, in fact, wrote as they did, because their ears were only sensible of a marked and uniform regularity.[113]

Hunt directly castigates Pope and the 'French school' for their monotony, the 'marked and uniform regularity' of verse; his aim is to move 'towards the revival of what seems to be proper English versification', for which he finds precedents in earlier poets and, crucially, in Pulci and Ariosto.[114] Pitting Italian examples in opposition to 'French' verse is a common trait in poetically radical work of the period, but Wordsworth and Southey did not promote an 'Italian' school. Southey contended that pre-Reformation poetry was not Italian, but Hunt believed that poetry that confronted the 'French school' by turning to Milton and Chaucer must necessarily have an Italian root.[115] The opposition to the 'French' school taken by the Lakers corroborates Pascale Casanova's writing on literary nationalism, that support of a native school 'draws a large part of its self-definition from its direct rivalry, often ancestral, with other national spaces'.[116] So a native school can define itself by not being 'French' as much as it can by being English, a stance with added patriotic cachet during or immediately following the Napoleonic Wars. The appropriation of an Italian style is a different matter entirely: it is still a movement away from regular neoclassical verse, but it is one that remains abroad for its source of inspiration.

In *The Feast of the Poets* (1814) Hunt had argued for 'the great superiority of the Italian school over the French', and the opposition of 'French' and 'Italian' schools was something that Hunt and Byron discussed.[117] In a letter of February 1814, Byron commends Hunt for his knowledge of the Italian poets, and then goes on to claim: 'I have always thought the Italians the *only* poetical *moderns*: – our Milton & Spenser & Shakespeare (the last through translations of their tales) are very Tuscan and surely it is far superior to the French School'.[118] Hunt responds the next day praising Byron's 'congeniality of opinion with regard to my old friends the Italians'.[119] Byron's avid defence of Pope complicates his preference for the 'Italian' over the 'French', especially, as Johnson pointed out, because Pope had little interest in things Italian.[120] In correspondence, Byron consistently preferred Pope to contemporary poets and his first published work was heavily Popean in form and style.[121] The early Byron, who in *English Bards* is full of praise for Pope, and his heirs Campbell and Rogers, can be reconciled with the Byron of 1815 who backs *Rimini* and its Italianate perversion of the couplet.[122] A persuasive rationale for Byron's move away from Pope as a model, whilst retaining his defence of Pope's position within the tradition, is offered by James Chandler when he claims, 'Byron saves Pope not for the history of the future, but only for the history of the past'.[123] Byron defended Pope's reputation, but around the time of *Parisina*'s composition he was beginning to think differently. The heroic couplet was no longer his standard form for narrative verse, as the Spenserians of *Childe Harold* and the irregular hexameters that open the *Bride of Abydos* show, and the renunciation of the 'Tales' in *Beppo* as 'those pretty poems never known to fail' marks a clear turn against regularity.[124] Byron was propelled by Hunt into his decade-long relationship with Italian verse and culture, but his rejection of Popean methods left him torn. Byron commented on five lines of Canto III 'this sounds like a concetto, but yet is too good to part with'; Byron knew this style was improvised, Italian, and nothing like Pope, but felt it 'too good' to change.[125]

The couplets of *Rimini* are entirely distinct from the end-stopped regularity associated with Pope. The verse paragraph beginning 'These for a princely present' shows this digression from established form:

> The princess, from a distance, scarcely knows
> Which way to look; her colour comes and goes;
> And with an impulse and affection free
> She lays her hand upon her father's knee,
> Who looks upon her with a laboured smile,
> Gathering it up into his own the while,
> When some one's voice, as if it knew not how
> To check itself, exclaims, "the prince! now – now!"

And on a milk-white courser, like the air,
A glorious figure springs into the square;
Up, with a burst of thunder, goes the shout,
And rolls the trembling walls and peopled roofs about.
(I. 253–264)

The first line has neither the middle pause nor the end-stopped finality of the closed couplet; Hunt's enjambment causes constraint, as the reader cannot pause at the rhyming 'knows' but instead moves over the line break to find its sense three words later, a process continued as 'The princess', who was the subject of the first phrase, does not meet her corresponding action until 'She lays her hand' three lines later. The syntax stumbles, enacting the princess' confusion and embarrassment as 'her colour comes and goes'. The couplets are not self-contained in form or meaning, as Johnsonian 'good sense' gives way to a more conversational tone and a syntax more expressive of complex feelings. The internal confusion is a prelude to the climax at the end of the extract. To build suspense Hunt calms the reader with two lines of regular pentameter, but even these linger on 'laboured' and 'Gathering'. The sense of the next couplet is again extended over the line end to see what the unknown voice shouted, which is still not found as the line checks itself with 'exclaims'. Finally the voice is heard, which Hunt has delayed since the opening of the couplet, and the Prince arrives on the percussive 'now – now!' The final tableau brings the narrative away from Francesca's inner thoughts, to a view of one man, and finally to the outpouring of the masses. The penultimate line pauses three times before the alexandrine, and the section finishes its move from singular mind to the people's expression of collective approval in a final non-punctuated line. None of Pope's concision or aphorism remains in these couplets; the formal variety allows syntax and metre to reinforce the suspense, confusion, and joy of the scene. The couplet become a vehicle for immediacy and reveals the 'fascination with the quick of writing' that Michael O'Neill has seen as typically Huntian.[126]

Dante is a specific Italian precursor for Hunt's riposte to the neoclassical rules of the 'French school'. An 1803 a review of Henry Boyd's translation of the *Commedia* opened with the following statement:

> The rude poetry of early ages possesses some high excellencies, which can never be attained to an equal degree in the more polished state of the art. That energy and simplicity, which are then its characteristics, are apt to be weakened and effaced, as men advance in the refinements of society, and in the arts of composition. True genius, indeed, will always be distinguished by vigour and animation.[127]

While *Rimini* was being composed, Dante's stylistic vigour – and the idea of his style as anathema to refinement and polish – were discussed at greater length by Hazlitt in a review essay of Sismondi's *De la Litterature*. Hazlitt opens by chiding Sismondi for his criticisms of Italian literature, for which he 'too often borrows French rules and German systems', and for paying too little attention to Dante and Petrarch.[128] An examination of the *Commedia* then begins by claiming 'the invention is in the style' and then quotes a passage from Sismondi in translation. Sismondi describes the poetic norm of Dante's time:

> of madrigals, full of cold conceits, – of sonnets painfully harmonious, – or allegories false and forced, the only models which Dante had before his eyes in any modern tongue[. . .]Dante himself, as well as his commentators, attaches his excellence to purity and correctness: yet he is neither pure nor correct; but he is *a creator*.[129]

Hazlitt is full of praise for Sismondi's characterisation of the late Duecento and early Trecento as formally rigid with 'cold' and 'painful' observance of harmony. Dante is judged as stylistically 'neither pure nor correct', as a poet who did not follow the tradition he was born into. Hazlitt sees Dante as an experimental poet, one whom it is not possible to criticise through the ideas of polish and elegance espoused by the 'French' school. Dante was recruited to British arguments of versification in 1815. Hazlitt sees Dante as a poet who wrote against the dominant strain of his day, a feature that he also saw in Hunt. Writing to Hunt in 1816, Hazlitt proclaimed of *Rimini*: '*This will do*', accepting this new style and reversing Jeffrey's crushing 'This will never do' on Wordsworth's *Excursion*.[130] Hazlitt also made this connection in his later review of *Rimini* in the *Edinburgh*: he claimed Hunt's poem was quite unlike any modern poetry, and suggested 'its more immediate prototypes, perhaps, are to be looked for rather in Italy than in England' and in a time 'much older than Shakespeare'.[131] There is a parallel to be drawn between Hazlitt's judgement of Dante and his compliments about *Rimini*. Hazlitt sees Dante as breaking the formal precepts of his age, as the creator of an irregular new style, just as Hunt chooses a Dantean source to confront the entrenched regularity of the Popean couplet. Hazlitt's article substantiates the earlier claim that Hunt, and writers he was in correspondence with, saw Dante at this early stage of Romantic appreciation as the archetypal confronter of established literary norms. Dante's interrogation of the romance mode, stylistic innovation, and identification with the 'Italian' school, made him an attractive source for Hunt. *Rimini* is a microcosm of the new idea of Italy that was now being developed in radical literary circles, an idea in which a new conception of Dante is integral.

Hunt inspired a number of contemporary poets to 'break up their own heroic couplets into freer modulation'.[132] The legacy of *Rimini* can be seen in the languid opening of 'Julian and Maddalo' (1819) – 'I rode one evening with Count Maddalo / Upon the bank of land which breaks the flow / Of Adria towards Venice' – and in the *Quarterly's* complaint that in *Endymion* (1818) 'there is hardly a complete couplet inclosing a complete idea in the whole book'.[133] Unsurprisingly, the literary establishment that cherished the Popean couplet did not applaud this ingenuity. The *British Review* accused Hunt of 'a lax and lawless versification, which seems to propose to itself something of lyric irregularity, in the simple neglect of metrical consonance and methodical structure'.[134] The rules governing the regular couplet, like that of many literary and political customs, are self-validating: 'its own existence and its own presumed longevity are the main reasons for presuming it to be good'.[135] The *British Review* scrutinizes the poem by comparing it to earlier works in couplets, but Hunt's is disobedient to these established laws of versification. The reader, and more importantly the reviewer, is presented with a 'lawless' formal approach; there is 'simple neglect' for expectations. When modern critics have considered Hunt's use of poetic form, it has usually been seen in connection with political opinions articulated in the *Examiner*. William Keach and Nicholas Roe illustrate this:

> Hunt's effort to reform the heroic couplet is an exact image of his reformist politics.[136]

> In this free-flowing impressionistic verse we can recognise a stylistic equivalent of his liberal politics, a lyrical rejoinder to the 'rage for barracks', the threat of land enclosure, and 'a field shut in'.[137]

> Hunt's poetry of sympathetic, natural justice in *The Story of Rimini* [. . .] was a lyrical expression of the *Examiner's* oppositional politics.[138]

For Keach, formal experimentation is 'an exact image' of political belief, and Roe recognises changes to the couplet for their equivalence to, as an 'expression' of, and as a 'lyrical rejoinder' to, 'politics'. Presuming challenges to established form are a proxy for national political activism is useful for situating *Rimini* among Hunt's wider journalistic output, but it also restricts the meanings of the poetic text. In the lengthy preface, Hunt does not espouse national political commentary; it is a document focused on poetry, specifically the new Italian sources for his style and genre. The poem itself avoids a direct narrative address to contemporary problems; it more subtly questions notions of transgression, privacy, identity, desire, and persuasion. These themes make one question Cox's suggestion that Hunt's Giovanni 'would have understood the tactics of Castlereagh and Metternich', on the grounds that it constructs too neat a relationship between politics and poetry.[139] The challenge presented by *Rimini* is political but, as critics such as Peter Manning and Susan Wolfson have found in other Romantic poems, it emanates from challenges to genre and form.[140] These are poetic provocations, which Keach and Roe correctly view as overturning politically conservative forms, and are relevant to the national political issues which Cox mentions. But this relevance can only begin in the Italian challenge to form and genre: *Rimini*, and the virulence of the attacks on it, must be seen as a literary confrontation.

The tendency has been to read *Rimini* as a sister project to Hunt's criticism of the state's use of domination, his 'reformist politics', but in peacetime London the control of culture via public opinion had predominance over domination. Hunt's and Byron's works offer a literary challenge to the 'public mind' and its defenders in periodical culture. Byron saw something new in *Rimini*. It is a novelty which Hunt parades in the preface and on which Byron had commented, 'you have 2 excellent points in that poem – originality – & Italianism – I will back you as a bard', and later claimed *Rimini* had 'the substratum of originality, and with poetry about it, that will stand the test'.[141] The central feature of *Rimini* for Byron was its originality, which he saw as Italian. Both *Rimini* and *Parisina* are deviations from the standards of the genre, and fail formally to comply with literary heritage. T. C. W. Blanning argues that the crucial feature in the rise of hegemony in the preceding century was that 'public opinion' came to be recognised as the ultimate arbiter in matters of taste.[142] How 'public' this was, as the discussion of the 'public mind' in the last chapter has shown, is debatable. As Blanning has observed, 'the liberal notion of a universal public sphere was a fiction. In reality it was particular, subjective, and contingent [. . .] the culture industry is just a prop for the status quo'.[143]

In literary terms, the status quo is represented by established forms and genres, and perpetuated by favoured writers. 'Public opinion' is the defender of this subjective culture, becoming both the creator and judge of social values, and creating what Byron calls the 'fastidiousness of the reader'.[144] The defence of the status quo pursued by the historical bloc is based on the perceived iconoclasm of breaking formal and generic orthodoxy. These standards are defended through the periodical press that appears to speak as 'public opinion'.[145] In a review of a Royal Academy exhibition, Hunt's brother Robert opens with the following lines:

> How difficult it is in the Arts, as in morals, to subdue old habits. They cling with almost as glutinous a tenacity as a vicious Ministry does to a corrupt system of politics.[146]

He opts for an analogy between politics and art; the arts are the central subject, with the national issues of the ministry as the term of comparison. It is the difficult 'tenacity' of literary traditions that *Rimini* confronts. A similarly politically focused approach has been taken to the negative contemporary reception of many works of second-generation Romanticism, which are often read as personal attacks on the poets' politics, rather than as attacks on the threat to hegemony entrenched in their work.[147] But the *Quarterly* article on *Rimini* is, aside from the first paragraph on Hunt's incarceration and the last on the dedication to Byron, concerned with the poem itself.[148] Croker and Gifford are methodical in their destruction of the work on literary grounds, moving from a thorough analysis of the perceived misuse of the couplet ('a negligent, and harsh style of versification') to chastising the experiments in diction ('which are the cant of ordinary discourse').[149] Even the 'Cockney School' articles, which have been viewed as the acme of the personal attacks on Hunt and Keats, maintain a literary focus.[150] They are based on the manner in which 'the work [*Rimini*] is executed', its 'indelicacy' in diction and form.[151] Lockhart does mount a comprehensive assault on Hunt's class and opinions, but this has its basis in the literary dimension. For the *British Review,* the problem was Hunt's 'levelling doctrines in poetic composition'.[152] National politics function as secondary, as in the earlier analogy, as a way to appraise 'poetic composition'. Hunt is aware of the political parallels to which his revisions lend themselves, as shown by the claim, in the preface to *The Feast of the Poets*, that he is pursing 'the various and legitimate harmony of the English heroic'.[153] Yes this is political, but any wider historical concern must be seen as part of the literary horizon; the alteration in *Rimini* of the couplet and romance is in itself an attack on the consensual basis of hegemony.

The periodicals saw a literary threat from *Rimini* and *Parisina.* They embodied a romance mode of transitional states centred on incestuous infidelities, which was irreconcilable with the nationalistic war-based romances of Scott. Lurking in the preface to *Rimini* is an awareness of the confrontation embodied by its comprehensive originality. Hunt justifies his decision not to adopt Scott's practice of including historical footnotes: 'I can be content that he [the reader] shall miss an occasional nicety or so in other matters, and not be quite sensible of the mighty extent of my information'.[154] Hunt's comment is casual but heavily ironic as he alludes to the incendiary features that may reveal themselves to the reader.

A sense is created of the complexities that abound in the 'mighty' text, which challenges the formal and thematic precepts of official culture. Reception of *Rimini* and *Parisina* was hostile, but was also precise in its perception of the transgressions they represented. Two reviews saw the danger of Hunt's and Byron's 'mighty information' and viewed it as a cultural threat. The *British Review* found in *Parisina*: 'some danger to public sentiment lurking in this new poetical character [. . .] We love the public mind, and feel tremblingly alive to its best interests'.[155] *Blackwood's* found that: 'Many a one reads *Rimini* as a pleasant romance, and closes it without having the least suspicion that he has been perusing a tale pregnant with all the horrors of the most unpardonable guilt'.[156] As Hunt's 'mighty information' implied, critics saw these poems as a 'danger to public sentiment' which would not be in the 'best interests' of the 'public mind'. It is specifically in its 'new poetical character' where this danger is 'lurking'. Lockhart warns his reader of a tale 'pregnant' with 'horrors': looking presciently to the birth of the experimental Italian vein in Shelley and Byron. The virulence of Lockhart's reaction proves Hunt's relevance before the coteries at Hampstead and Marlow, just as Dante is relevant to British Romanticism before the 'Dantean' year.[157] *Rimini* should be regarded, in its effrontery, experimentation, and engagement with an Italian locale, as the beginning of the Italian influence on the second generation of Romantic poets. Byron, the poet whom *Rimini* influenced, was about to leave Britain's shores and literary conservatism; he 'turned to Italy for added light'.[158] Shelley and Hunt would follow, and from Venice, Ravenna, and Pisa they would continue to engage with an idea of Italy that challenged Regency hegemony.

CHAPTER 3

London 1817–1819
Foscolo, Hobhouse, and Holland House

E mentre voi, giovinetto, ricalcando i vestigi di quel cittadino salirete animoso per le vie della vita, io stanco e privo di patria, andrò ripensando al sicuro riposo[1]

Ugo Foscolo, *Discorsi nel Parlamento in Morte di Francesco Horner* (1817)

To enhance the British appetite for Italian culture beyond Byron's and Hunt's engagement with their 'old friends the Italians', a figure with sufficient fame in Regency London was required, one who was able to write for the taste-forming medium of the age: the literary periodical. Ugo Foscolo arrived in London in September 1816, and died just outside the capital a decade later. He went to Britain in exile from Austrian-occupied Milan in the last of his many migrations. These began at the age of seven when his family moved from the Venetian protectorate of Zante to Venice, which he subsequently left after the cessation of the Republic in the Treaty of Campoformio (1797). He fled to the Euganean Hills, and then moved to Bologna where he worked as a journalist before spending two years in northern France, serving in Napoleon's army for the planned invasion of England from 1804 to 1806. Foscolo returned for a short and controversial tenure as the Master of Rhetoric at the University of Pavia, during which he produced the seminal oration *Dell'origine e dell'ufficio della letteratura* (1809). A relatively settled spell in Milan under the Cisalpine Republic was broken by Austrian occupation; this led to his exile, first in Zurich and then London. His literary works are similarly wide ranging: Foscolo began as a tragedian in the style of Alfieri, was then a novelist, and finally a poet famed particularly for his *Sonetti* (1803) and *Dei Sepolcri* (1807).

Foscolo published no fiction, drama, or poetry after his arrival in London; his work in England was literary criticism and translation.[2] In the preface to his first British translation, which is the epigraph to this chapter, Foscolo presents the central characteristic of his exile journalism: he 'will go looking back', showing a will to promote his national literature and history as a means to future Italian independence, balanced with a nostalgia for his occupied homeland and the works he had written there. Foscolo looked back in particular to *Le Ultime Lettere di Jacopo Ortis* (1801–1802) and the *Orazione* at Pavia, both of which reverberate in his later criticism. As Foscolo's finest critic has observed, his London exile was 'l'ultima fase dello svolgimento della sua personalità quale ci si è manifestata nei precedenti periodi della sua vita'.[3] The political convictions that inspired these works were adjusted on arrival in Britain; Foscolo looks back and complicates his earlier discussion of displacement, nationhood, and tyranny. Although changes occur, Foscolo's tendency to take oppositional stances and his willingness to challenge established thought remains constant in his engagement with British literary and political culture.

As varied as Foscolo's places of residence, and the literary forms in which he excelled, were the reactions to his character. As the two quotations below show, he was a man who divided opinion:

> Dear Foscolo, to thee my dedication's
> Address'd with reason. Who like thee is able
> To judge betwixt the theme and variations?
> To whom so well can I inscribe my fable,
> As thee? Since I, upon good proof, may sing thee
> *Doctum sermones utriusque linguae*.[4]

> Talking of strangers, London held, some four or five years since, one of those animals who are lions at first, but by transmutation of two seasons become in regular course Boars! – Ugo Foscolo by name, a haunter of Murray's shop and of literary parties. Ugly as a baboon, and intolerably conceited, he spluttered, blustered, and disputed without even knowing the principles upon which men of sense render a reason, and screamed all the while like a pig when they cut its throat.[5]

The first quotation is the Tory Member of Parliament and Italianist William Stewart Rose's dedication to Foscolo of his rendering of Casti's *Gli animali parlanti*. They met in Italy during the summer of 1814, corresponded regularly, and Foscolo stayed at Rose's house on the Dorset coast. Rose claims Foscolo's expertise in Italian verse is unmatched, and, as the refrain 'upon good proof' suggests, this was an aid to his translation. Rose reinforces this in the final line by adjusting the opening of Horace's ode to his benefactor Maecenas, to hint at the intellectual gifts he has received in Foscolo's company. The second quotation is from Walter Scott, who had dedicated the first epistle of *Marmion* to Rose, and records quite a different reaction to the Italian five years later. Foscolo's prominence in London literary circles was beginning to wane by 1821 (the period Scott's diary remembers), and this comment appears in biographies in conjunction with other anecdotes to prove Foscolo's failure to conform to the etiquette of British society.[6] But Scott's virulence and the presence of the familiar language of British xenophobia warrants further scrutiny. Scott's bestial imagery revives the conservative methods used to defend the 'public mind' during the Napoleonic Wars. Foscolo is a 'stranger' and 'haunter' at literary events: a disturbing foreign presence, with foreign ideas.

Although relatively neglected in English language criticism, Foscolo is a central figure of the Italian canon.[7] His fame was not posthumous like that of Shelley or Keats; Foscolo was known in literary circles when he arrived in London. Before meeting Foscolo, his future friend and collaborator John Cam Hobhouse described him as 'the Xenophon of his day', and observed that 'it requires a pen like Foscolo's to describe the present state of Italy'.[8] British readers would have known his novel *Jacopo Ortis*: the Italian text was published in London in 1811, twice in 1817, and again in 1818; it was also published in translation in 1814 and 1818. From 1812 it was widely reviewed and praised, and the frequency of publication after 1816 shows the growing interest of English readers in Foscolo specifically, and Italian literature generally. The *Monthly Meteor* claimed that *Ortis* was,

> sufficient to shew that Foscolo was no ordinary man, but one whose literary acquirements were an honour to his own, and would have raised him to a high rank in any other country.[9]

The Italianist William Roscoe agreed with this opinion, telling Lord Holland that he knew Foscolo's,

> 'Ultime Lettere di Jacopo Ortis' and his 'Discorso sulla Letteratura de . . . ' delivered at Pavia – the former displays great energy and warmth of imagination and character, the latter a deep and reflecting mind. The direction which such talents may take is of importance to the world[10]

Both judgements assume a cosmopolitan pose to press the international importance of Foscolo, worthy of praise in 'any other country' with work 'of importance to the world'. Through a reading of his early writing in exile, and an examination of manuscript sources relating to his friendships, this chapter aims to demonstrate Foscolo's importance to radical Anglo-Italianism. His promotion of Italian literature to the front pages of Regency periodicals was a collaborative project. I will also consider Giuseppe Binda, who acted as an unofficial diplomat between radicals in England and Italy, and Serafino Buonaiuti, who wrote about the history and politics of his native land to attract and engage British readers. These exiles were attempting to correct false perceptions surrounding Italian literature, people, and history – to create an idea of Italy that would appeal to elements of metropolitan literary culture, which would in turn increase support for their political and cultural struggle.

Foscolo's time in London is in need of reassessment. With the exception of work by John Lindon and Nick Havely, previous criticism has been restricted to two approaches. First, Foscolo has been discussed from a biographical perspective: his initial success, welcomed by the salon of the day at Holland House, followed by dire money troubles, marginalisation, and eventual disappearance, makes for an engaging narrative.[11] Although biographers acknowledge Foscolo's criticism, there is little engagement with the work, appreciation of its place in a growing Italian influence, or of its status as exile literature. The second approach has focused on Foscolo's 1818 collaboration with Hobhouse, the 'Essay on the Present State of Italian Literature', which appeared in the *Historical Illustrations of the Fourth Canto of Childe Harold* (1818).[12] The essay was controversial for its dismissal of the Italian 'Romantiche', which led to epistolary attacks and counterattacks between London and Milan.[13] Despite this attention, there has only been brief engagement with the work itself, with more time spent on the vitriol recorded in correspondence, its links to Byron, and Foscolo's money troubles.[14] Scrutiny of the 'Essay' is needed, and this must be part of a broader consideration of the output of Italian exiles in the period. My analysis will focus on the first two years of Foscolo's career in London. In the period 1817–1819, Foscolo translated the Parliamentary speeches of Francis Horner, authorised John Murray to publish an edition of *Jacopo Ortis*, and wrote essays on Dante, the present state of Italian literature, Italian narrative poetry, Pope Pius VI, and the Greek port of Parga.[15] The chronology has been chosen to reflect Foscolo's most financially comfortable and socially active period in London, rather than following the biographers in charting his rise and fall.[16] He dined with the reformist and cosmopolitan coterie at Holland House more than forty times from September 1816 to March 1819, and in these early years he was welcomed by other exiles.[17] (Due in part to his financial mismanagement, these aspects of Foscolo's social life would sour in the 1820s and he dined at Holland House only twice from 1820 to his death in 1827.) At the beginning of his exile Foscolo was also in favour with the *Edinburgh Review*, where his articles were given prime position and spread over multiple issues.[18]

Foscolo's early critical essays build on the educative work of Da Ponte and Bozzi, and provide a radical introduction to Italian culture for English readers, but the difference between the expression of exiles before and after the Congress of Vienna (1814–1815) was an increased candour in their political activism and the use of host-language sources to facilitate this. As Maurizio Isabella has observed, after the congress,

> the exiles relentlessly promoted their political programme and attacked the conservative order in the liberal press. Journals such as the *Revue encyclopédique* and the *Globe* in Paris, the liberal press in Brussels, and the *Edinburgh Review* in Great Britain hosted their writings.[19]

Foscolo began this 'political programme' in his promotion of liberty in the essays on Parga and Pius VI, but in a discussion of a 'political programme' we must be wary of classifying a foreign writer within the standard British categories of Radical, Whig, and Tory. Foscolo had friends across the national political spectrum: the Radical Westminster set around Hobhouse, Foxite Whigs such as Holland and Earl Grey, and Tories, namely Rose and John Hookham Frere. An appreciation of Foscolo's 'programme', which in many ways was an attack on 'conservative order', must be grounded in his literary output. As the last chapter demonstrated, the kind of literary acts and judgements Foscolo made – criticism of a 'French' school, promotion of Alfieri, and praise of Hunt's *Rimini* – were inherently political articulations.[20] When Foscolo promoted the 'Italian' school in his journalism, he knew well the political import of this position.

Like exiled journalists before him, Foscolo was at pains to make connections for his English readers between the cultures of his new home and his native land. He did this through frequent references to the links between the English canon, particularly Gray and Milton, and the Italian tradition.[21] His exile status also contributed to his important friendships, as his reputation as a political rebel made him alluring to Holland and Hobhouse. But, as Scott's diary entry reveals, even a man of Foscolo's renown experienced animosity; a reading of Foscolo's critical works must be aware of his difficult position within London society. Foscolo wrote an article criticising the British ceding of Parga to the Ottomans, and the reply in the *Quarterly* to this article shows how xenophobic attitudes shaped the reception of his journalism. The *Quarterly* attacked Foscolo as both a foreigner and as someone who was disturbing the 'public mind' because he provided the Whig Member of Parliament Sir Charles Monck with information for a speech on Parga.[22] The article reminds the reader three times that Foscolo is 'not a British subject', going on to twice call him an 'agent', and claim that he 'found means to infect the minds of the rest of the community with a distrust of the intentions of the British government'.[23] According to the *Quarterly*, the Greek and Italian roots of the Parganotes give them 'all the rude virtues and all the gross vices of these several people', a people renowned for their 'acuteness, low cunning and intrigue'.[24] These insults also apply to Foscolo: as the *Quarterly* reviewer was no doubt aware, he was of Greco-Italian descent. This heritage made him a contact for many Greek nationalists on visits to London, which led him to confide to Barbarina Brand, Lady Dacre, 'mon cousin en me portant ici des douzaines de lettres, veut que de toute manière je me mêle des affaires des grecs, et que je finisse par me faire renvoyer en vertu de l'Alien Bill'.[25] In spite of the prejudices of pro-state journals, and the very real threat of deportation for revolutionary 'agents', Foscolo's early exile is defined by his forthright intervention in cultural debate. Parga may seem like something of an outlier in Foscolo's English journalism, but the essay allowed him to show that his support for free states was not confined to the Italian Peninsula.

From a literary perspective, Foscolo was prepared for life as an alien: his earliest writings had consistently dealt with ideas of nationhood and the displacement of self. As the *Risorgimento* intellectual Carlo Cattaneo observed, Foscolo made exile an Italian institution.[26] The constant displacement of Foscolo's life meant this exilic current existed in his work before his arrival in England. It is a condition he explores at the outset of *Jacopo Ortis*. In the second sentence of the novel, after declaring the sacrifice of Italy complete, Jacopo tells Lorenzo, 'Il mio nome è nella lista di proscrizione'.[27] Jacopo is an enemy of the newly formed Austrian state; on the same list that Byron would find himself in 1821.[28] The proscription of Jacopo leads to his exile in order to avoid 'le prime persecuzioni, e le più feroci'.[29] In the next letter, two days later, Jacopo resigns himself to exile, which will offer, 'al più, breve e sterile compassione, solo conforto che nazioni incivilite offrono al profugo straniero'.[30] The resignation to the lamentations of exile is at its most concentrated in the opening 'A Zacinto':

> Né più mai toccherò le sacre sponde
> ove il mio corpo fanciulletto giacque[31]

The narrator's futile longing for *nostos* is neatly expressed in the comparison between the declarative monosyllables of the opening and the languid assonance then used describe the Greek idyll. These narrators wear the literary mask of exile as an oppressive and unfortunate weight in their lives, yet when Foscolo arrived in London he was not overly burdened by his condition. Havely has shown that before his arrival, Foscolo constructed a Dantean alter ego with which to articulate his exile.[32] Foscolo also took inspiration from his hero Plutarch, who in his essay 'On Exile' warned to 'not sit idle or lament'.[33] Foscolo was not idle: he used his exile status to his advantage: he stayed clear of what Plutarch calls the 'fools' who see 'exile', like 'foreigner' and 'immigrant', as 'a term of reproach', and instead admired and cultivated the 'good men' who saw his talent.[34] Foscolo used these connections, and his position as someone deeply absorbed in another culture, to begin the educative project that was the product of his displacement.

The Authentic Materials of History

As Lindon has argued, Foscolo's criticism builds on the foundations of the *Orazione* given at Pavia in 1809.[35] In a letter to Vincenzo Monti, Foscolo writes that the oration was intended to 'discorrere filosoficamente e eloquentemente su la storia letteraria di tutti li secoli e tutti i popoli'.[36] The project he began in Britain shares the two central features of this work: an emphasis on history, and a belief in the political importance of a literary education. Where it differs is in its range and subtlety; Foscolo's work in Regency periodicals was not aimed an entire nation, nor was it a call to *kulturkampf*. His work was tailored to a British readership and aimed to promote the Italian cause by elucidating its national history and literature, particularly Dante. Foscolo thought that his new audience misconceived Italy, its poets, and culture, because of poor writing in the British periodical press. His approach was designed to erode the view of Italians propagated by the defenders of the 'public mind'. He writes,

> Readers, especially foreign readers, believe on the faith of the commentators, that they have seen the whole; like the readers of modern travels, who fancy they know a country from the descriptions of those who have ran through it with a roadbook and a dictionary, and return home to publish their tour.[37]

The analogy between a misguided commentator on Dante and the hurried travel writer provides a clear counterpoint to what Foscolo can offer his readers – an opportunity to 'see the whole,' from a man with an authentic absorption in Italy and its history.[38] In a later essay, Foscolo accuses John Eustace, in a review of his *Classical Tour* (1815), of 'undermining the very foundation of Italian national consciousness, its cultural heritage'.[39] A focus on authenticity, whether in a discussion of travel literature or poetry, is at the centre of the historical conception of Italy that Foscolo proposes in his criticism.[40] The basis for this historicism, as well as Foscolo's belief in the social role of the writer, is in part VII and XV of the *Orazione*. The speech begins by claiming that the progress of civilisation is based on a veneration of history, that Xerxes and Alexander looked in awe at the Pyramids, the Romans adored the Greeks, and Michelangelo and Raphael perpetuated the glory of Phidias.[41] Foscolo twice exhorts his audience to return to history, to the Italian canon that he claims is 'la letteratura che illumina il vero'.[42] Foscolo believes this exhortation is necessary because of the failure of his countrymen to appreciate history: 'ma dov'é una storia d'Italia? [. . .] Come ricambierete le vigilie de' nostri padri se non profittate de' documenti che vi apprestarono?'[43] The failure to appreciate native history is not only a betrayal of the tradition that produced Vico and Machiavelli, but also a cause of Italy's current domination by foreign powers. The works of history Foscolo which wrote for English periodicals between 1817 and 1819 maintain this focus. The first of these concerns Pius VI, the pope during the French Revolution, and opens by criticising an earlier writer for not adding to 'the authentic materials of History'.[44] In contrast, Foscolo strives for authenticity through contextual background, detailed descriptions of the conclave, and, most importantly, quotation from sources.[45] He quotes the words of Cardinal Carlo Rezzonico, translates the Latin inscriptions on a sacristy built by Pius, and transcribes in full a letter from the pope to Joseph II of Austria.[46] The second historical essay on Parga has a similar focus on original sources. Foscolo presents a history of the port from 1401, replete with quotations from a treaty between Ali Pasha and Venice, debates in the Commons from 1798, extracts from letters of the French ambassador, and an entire speech by a Parganote elder.[47] Both Parga and Pius VI are articles on subjects about which the British reader had preconceptions, from the ferocity of Byron's 'Turkish' tales to reports of the infrastructural and moral decay of the Catholic Church. Foscolo's view on Parga was directly contrary to that of the British government and many Parliamentary Whigs, but he uses the 'authentic materials of History', in the shape of primary sources, to 'withdraw the veil' from the present situation.[48]

The fundamental historicism of Foscolo's writing on Parga and Pius VI is also apparent in his literary criticism.[49] From the first essay on Dante onwards, Foscolo emphasises the importance of educating the reader in the Italian historical situation that produced its poetry.[50] Criticism of Shakespeare is the congenial model Foscolo uses to make his point to a British audience, and he quotes from William Warburton's preface to his 1747 edition of Shakespeare on the role of the critic to 'correct the faulty text, to remark the peculiarities of language, to illustrate the obscure allusions, and to explain the beauty and defects of sentiment or composition'.[51] Foscolo claims that to follow Warburton is 'only half his task' in critiquing a work of Italian literature for a foreign reader. In the second essay on Dante, Foscolo remarks,

> To explain how he executed his vast design, it appears to us indispensable that we should give a slight sketch of the political and religious state of Italy at the period when he wrote.[52]

He later reinforces this claim:

> Hence, in order to appreciate the force or the value of their expressions, it is often necessary to have an accurate knowledge of the different systems of literary education, of manners, of revolutions, of governments.[53]

It is 'indispensable' and 'necessary' for an 'appreciation' of Dante – and later of Pulci, Ariosto, and Tasso – to understand the historical situation of their work. Foscolo upbraids one English historian who claims medieval Italians were 'people with slaves attached to the soil, who had no consolation but their religion'.[54] The depiction of Italy as a rural peasant society is related to the earlier discussion of Voltaire's and Warton's claims that the Italian canon was 'obscure' and 'primitive'. Foscolo uses his native status, with recourse to heavy quotation from sources, to correct the view of an undeveloped literature born out of a primitive society. His arguments for Italy's past development, as with his reinterpretation of Dante as a republican, are a sign of his hope for a free and united Italy in the future. He depicts the city-states of Milan and Florence as advanced mercantile societies, 'republics starting forth out of nothing', supported by and supporting a complex literary culture.[55]

Foscolo's discussion of heritage, history, and authenticity overturned contemporary thinking. This was a radical argument that interacted with the debate over history at the centre of Regency periodical culture. As the earlier discussion of Hunt and Byron showed, elements within the major conservative periodicals contested the radical idea of Italy. Foscolo outlined his view of history in articles for the *Edinburgh Review*, a journal that had challenged the status quo since its foundation. One of its earliest enemies, the *Anti-Jacobin Review*, called it 'a fortress of Jacobinism' and a production 'adverse to their country'.[56] John Ring claimed in 1807 that 'the Tongue of the *Edinburgh Review* is not the tongue of the wise. It is not the tongue of health, but a running sore'.[57] The worry that these apparently infectious ideas were being disseminated led to the foundation of the *Quarterly Review*. Its purpose was clear: Murray wrote to George Canning of the need 'to counteract' the 'dangerous tendencies' of the *Edinburgh*, whose principles were 'radically bad'.[58] The traditional view of the *Edinburgh* is as an organ of that disparate grouping known as 'Whigs', but the reactions above suggest more extreme opposition.[59] That is not to say that many of its articles did not chime with the opinion of Parliamentary Whigs: just as the *Edinburgh* did not wholly support innovation to the couplet, so too was much of its political writing only mildly reformist. But two reasons meant some of its material was of a more radical bent. First, the strong interest in foreign affairs in the *Edinburgh* led to articles that criticised the position of both political parties on, for example, the Peninsula Wars, Parga, Greek independence, and the Italian situation. Foreign nationals in London often wrote these works, using their comprehensive local knowledge to offer insights for British. Jennifer Mori has argued that by the end of the eighteenth century, Britons working or living abroad 'were drawing a clear distinction "between Foreign Service & Home Politicks"'.[60] This split is articulated in the way in which the *Edinburgh* juggles its mild support for domestic reform while pushing a more radical agenda abroad. The *Edinburgh* was openly critical of British foreign policy. In a controversial article on the works of Don Pedro Cevallos, co-written by Jeffrey and Henry Brougham in 1808, the *Edinburgh* expressed its disapproval over the war and went on to claim that Spanish patriotism might spur on political reform in Britain.[61] Conservatives, including the future laureate Southey, were incensed by the pacifism they saw expressed by Brougham and Jeffrey, and the article was a factor in Scott's decision to stop writing for the *Edinburgh* and move to the *Quarterly*.[62] The second reason for adjusting the perceived wisdom on the *Edinburgh*'s politics is the variety of voices which the journal was prepared to publish from across the spectrum of opposition; Jeffrey told Foscolo's friend Horner that the *Edinburgh* should welcome 'a considerable diversity' bound by a 'common tendency to repress servility, and diffuse a general spirit of independence in the body of the people'.[63] It published established Whig voices such as Brougham and Sir James Mackintosh, but it also hosted the opinions of the Benthamite James Mill, and the more radical views of Hunt, Hazlitt, and Foscolo. This was partly due to the absence of despotic editorial control at the *Edinburgh*: as Jeffrey admitted to Horner, he had 'limited power' over his contributors.[64] The freedom of the *Edinburgh* was quite different from the tight control that William Gifford had over articles in the *Anti-Jacobin* and *Quarterly,* and that John Lockhart would exercise when he took control of *Blackwood's* in 1818.

The arrival of *Blackwood's* and its acerbic conservatism was a further challenge to the *Edinburgh*.[65] According to a recent study by Mark Schoenfield, the 'foundational discourse' of *Blackwood's* was history and this made it exceptional; it differed from the quarterlies because they misconceived 'the relation between history and the present'.[66] Schoenfield supports the claim for *Blackwood's* interest in history, especially medieval history, by quoting what he claims is an article by Peter George Patmore on Dante, which sees the poet as someone who 'stands bewildered, but not appalled, on the dark shore which separates the ancient and modern world'.[67] The article is in fact a 'Notice of a course of lectures on English Poetry, now delivering at the Surrey Institution, London, by W. Hazlitt, esq.' and the quotation is from the first of Hazlitt's *Lectures on the English Poets* (1818). As discussed in the previous chapter, Hazlitt brought a radical historicised view of Dante to readers of the *Edinburgh* in 1815. This was nothing to do with *Blackwood's*, a periodical that attacked Hazlitt and his opinions. In fact, *Blackwood's* gives Dante no proper study from 1817 to 1819 apart from the occasional mention of his 'severe and simple manner'.[68] Hazlitt's lines are contrary to *Blackwood's* conservative view of medieval literature, as outlined in an article of 1819:

> With the exception of the great Chaucer, who stands in wonderful separation from his own, from the preceding and the following age, it shews us a dreary prospect of toilsome invention and compilation of which, the merits are any thing but those of a poet's mind.[69]

If the foundational discourse of *Blackwood's* is 'History', then two observations must be made. First, that the *Edinburgh* also put history on its front pages, as it did with the work of Foscolo and Hazlitt. And, secondly, if history was to be *Blackwood*'s 'foundational discourse', it was a certain type of history: one that saw the medieval period as dark, its culture as 'a dreary prospect of toilsome invention', and viewed Chaucer as the exceptional figure in a dull age. The conservative co-option of history, specifically literary history, meant certain authors of a dark age were approved by the logic of custom: they were acceptable because they always had been. But Foscolo had shown Dante's period as one of germinating republics, a time in which 'the imprudence of Popes, and the civil wars of the cities, and the consequent introduction of foreign arms' brought turmoil to the Mediterranean – a situation remarkably like the contemporary state of Italy that led to Foscolo's exile.[70] Just as Hunt and Byron had challenged expectations of the romance, so Foscolo was not content to rest on entrenched views of historical periods, and worked to counteract them from a study of primary sources and the social situation which produced them. *Blackwood's* foundational discourse was not 'History'; its real concern was strenuously to maintain the status quo, whether in the discipline of history, economics, or as the attacks on the Romantics show, literature.

So the medieval period is 'Dark', just as couplets are regular, and, as expressed in *Blackwood's* review of Schlegel, 'literature should have reference to an established centre, namely to religious faith, and to national history and character'.[71]

Foscolo positioned himself against the newly energised attempts by the conservative press to maintain control of the public mind. He sought to prove the erudition of Italian culture past and present through close readings of its poetry, paying particular attention to linguistic complexities missed by French and English critics. The essays on Dante often use Cary's *Vision* as an example of a generally good translation, but one that slips at the level of the individual word or phrase. Foscolo begins a long section in which he close-reads certain key episodes in the *Commedia* by taking issue with Cary's misreading of the pronoun '*voi*' as '*tu*' in the lines addressing Brunetto Latini in *Inferno* XV ('Siete voi qui, ser Brunetto?').[72] Foscolo shows this is an oversight; although the Pilgrim uses the familiar '*tu*' in his encounters up to this point, he uses the formal '*voi*' for the meeting with his mentor. Foscolo goes on to discuss the 'sweet harmony' of some lines in the *Purgatorio* when compared to Ariosto's reworking of them in the proem to the *Orlando Furioso* (1532); he then gives a reading of the meeting with Casella, with special attention given to the phrase 'amoroso canto' which Foscolo believes Cary mistranslates to destroy 'the beauty and delicacy of the poet's idea'; and ends with a long discussion of the Paolo and Francesca episode.[73] It is this manner of what Foscolo calls 'minute exposition [. . .] from verse to verse and sometimes from word to word', that reveals the complexity of the *Commedia*.[74] This high level of scrutiny and technical appraisal is also brought to bear on modern Italian poetry in the 'Present State' essay. He quotes from Angelo Mazza's odes showing 'those difficult rhymes which the Italians call *sdrucciole*, or slippery' where a movement from a hendecasyllable to an alexandrine shifts emphasis.[75] In his appraisal of Giuseppe Parini, Foscolo quotes a lengthy extract from *Il Giorno* in order to highlight 'the certain solemnity' of Parini's variety in tone and metre which make him 'entirely different from that of the other authors'.[76] Foscolo uses his knowledge as a native poet to illuminate the subtleties of Italian verse through close reading, in an attempt to broaden the horizon of the English reader. These readings, along with many historical elucidations and connections to the English tradition, work at a local level to complicate an idea of Italian literature as historically primitive and currently moribund. They also partake in a wider cosmopolitan project: Foscolo advertises the attributes of Italian culture that make it attractive to those attempting to challenge Regency hegemony.

Doctum sermones utriusque linguae

Foscolo's influence was not confined to periodical journalism, and he was not the only Italian promoting his native literature and cause. As the dedication to *The Court of the Beasts* shows, Rose relied on his friend's judgement as a lover of English literature and an expert in the Italian tradition, and so did Hobhouse: only five days after their first meeting, Hobhouse visited Foscolo in Kensington, where his diary records that the Italian poet offered to 'help me with facts for my memoir on the revolution'.[77] Critics have long seen Foscolo as the most important Italian exile in the period because of his fame, the length and prominence of his articles, and his friendships within British society. By only looking at Foscolo, we grant him the status of the exceptional Italian exile in the Regency, rather than seeming him as part of an active community. The reluctance to look more widely at the community may be due to the lack of accessible primary material. But the dinner attendance records at Holland House, and the correspondence of this circle, reveal the various roles played by Giuseppe Binda and Serafino Buonaiuti. Binda, although not an author, was a facilitator of literary and political activism, and Buonaiuti promoted his national literature and shared many of the same educative inclinations as Foscolo. Both of these men worked in secretarial and tutoring roles at Holland House, and were friends and correspondents with Foscolo. That these three Italians were part of the reformist cosmopolitan literary coterie at Holland House was not a coincidence. As well as being the meeting place for contributors to the *Edinburgh Review*, Holland House was also a locus for recently displaced Europeans.[78] John Whishaw, a contributor to the *Edinburgh*, recalls a trip to see the Hollands in November 1815. He calls the House 'a curious moving scene of all nations and languages', and records meeting a group of Spaniards 'all of them banished or proscribed' and the Italian Antonio Canova, the greatest sculptor in Europe.[79] The presence of Spaniards and Italians reflects Lord Holland's travels in Europe before and during the Napoleonic Wars: he toured Spain and Italy from 1793 to 1794; lived in Florence, where he met Alfieri, from 1794 to 1796; visited Spain on a tour with John Allen from 1802 to 1805; and travelled through Italy in 1814 to 1815, to assess Napoleon's impact on the peninsula.

Whishaw also mentions 'a young Italian by the name of Binda', and in the same year as this 'scene of all nations' Holland and Binda made a direct intervention in Italian politics. Whilst in Rome, Holland wrote a constitution for an independent Naples, which he sent to the Neapolitan government in the custody of Binda. Holland's intervention was timely: the Neapolitan King Joachim Murat had declared war on Austria on 15 March and made his proclamation for 'L'Indipendenza D'Italia' at Rimini on 30 March.[80] In a speech that has striking similarities with the end of Foscolo's *Orazione*, Murat opens with grand rhetoric: 'Italiani. L'ora è venuta che debbono compiersi gli alti vostri destini'.[81] Holland's actions were contrary to British policy and Leslie Mitchell has called them 'one of the oddest steps of his career'.[82] It has been claimed, based on one source (a letter by Lord Burgesh), that Holland drew up the constitution and then sent it to Naples in the custody of Binda in April 1815, but, so the story goes, Binda did not reach the Neapolitan government and was captured by the Austrians at Lucca on 20 April 1815.[83] However, two unpublished letters from Binda on paper marked 'Napoli Il Ministro degli Affari Esteri' were sent to Lord Holland in Rome on 29 March 1815, which suggest that Binda was active within Naples and in its government long before he was captured at Lucca.[84] He gives Holland political and military information from the Neapolitan base at Ancona, where Murat was planning his battle with the Austrians at Tolentino (2–3 May 1815). Binda had the ability to send these dispatches because of a temporary position he had taken in the Neapolitan forces, a role on which he comments, 'Io sono contentissimo della mia situazione e con eternal riconoscenza mi rammenterò sempre che lui la debbo'.[85] Binda thanks Holland for sending him to the Neapolitan camp in March, where he has stayed on to work, after he had given the constitution to the government of Naples. The letter is written to Holland at the crucial period between the declaration of war and Murat's call to arms at Rimini, long before his capture at Lucca when the constitution was sent to Vienna. The capture of Binda by Austrian forces can be explained without contradicting this new evidence. Binda left Naples, and, as the Burgesh letter suggests, was 'on his journey to Milan', which meant going through Lucca.[86] Binda was captured and the constitution went to Vienna, but it had already been delivered to the Neapolitans.

Holland's larger role in Naples can be gleaned in the opening of Binda's second letter.

> Mi lord
>
> Io avevo dato una lettera per lui al General Pignatelli, quando ha ricevuta in questo instante la sua del 23 di questo mese.[87]

First, this letter shows that Lord Holland, a peer of the realm, was in correspondence with a general of an enemy army who was a known Jacobin.[88] This suggests more commitment than the despatch of a constitutional document, and goes beyond the level of interference other Italophile peers were pursuing in Naples; it could even be considered treason.[89] Second, the mention of correspondence with Prince Pignatelli-Strongoli, an aide-de-camp of Murat who fought at Toletino, provides further evidence that the constitution sent with Binda was delivered. In Pignatelli's record of the conflict, he discusses being part of a group organised by Murat to formulate a constitution.[90] Pignatelli also states that Lord Holland came to the court at Naples in February and advised Murat with 'much deference' particularly on a new constitution, and that later on 8 May, weeks before their surrender, the Neapolitans drew up a constitution which contained 'qualche idea dell' Inglese Lord Holland'.[91] Holland's constitution damaged Anglo–Austrian relations, and was eventually published for an English readership as *Letter to a Neapolitan from an Englishman* (1818). As is discussed in Chapter 5, Naples would erupt again in 1820 and members of the Holland House set would make speeches against Austrian intervention. The constitution written by Holland proposes a bicameral system for the Neapolitan state, and aims to counter 'the foreign dynasties so lately restored, and so studiously, though incorrectly, denominated legitimate'.[92] Holland claims that the allied nations saw Naples as a prize given to 'nations unconnected with her people, and strangers even to Italy' and ends the constitution by boldly stating 'not a week, – no, not a day, – should be lost in putting it into execution'.[93] The intervention of the Holland House set extended to Parliament; Horner aggravated the government in his request for papers relating to treaties giving Naples to Austrian control, and championed the new constitution of Holland and Binda.[94] His speech in the Commons, along with his critique of the Aliens Bill, was among those that Foscolo translated in his first British work: *Discorsi nel Parlamento in morte di Francesco Horner*. The constitution, in its dismissal of the post-Vienna settlement and urgent nationalism, shares themes that Foscolo broached in his political and literary work. Binda's actions, as someone with connections in Naples to act as a go-between for British intervention in Italy, ignoring official state channels, is typical of the exiles' role as facilitators.[95]

As his actions in Naples illustrate, Binda was not simply a member of household staff: he was an active participant in the Holland House set who from 1815 to 1825 attended more than 800 dinners at the house among cabinet ministers, foreign ambassadors, and the leading lights of liberal culture. In one of his many roles at Holland House, it was Binda who introduced Foscolo to the set, organising a meeting between the Italian poet and Lord Holland in September 1816.[96] Not only did this allow

Foscolo to gain influence over Whig figures, and ingratiate himself with the *Edinburgh*, but his connection to Binda also allowed him to use the house's extensive library.[97] Where Binda facilitated literary and political interaction between English and Italian writers, his friend and fellow Holland House resident Serafino Buonaiuti was directly involved in literary production.[98] Buonaiuti had been writing libretti in London since at least 1799, and acted in Da Ponte's role as the poet to the King's Opera from 1809–1811.[99] In 1813 he edited an anthology for English readers of the poetry of Lorenzo de' Medici's court, including the work of Pulci that would be a profound influence on Byron.[100] But his role in promoting Italian literature in the periodicals began in earnest in 1817, when he became a contributor to the newly formed *Literary Gazette*. The *Gazette* was a weekly sixteen-page journal with articles of less than a side in length, apart from the cover piece that was given three pages. From its inception it devoted many pages to foreign literature and Buonaiuti was its most prolific writer on Italy. Buonaiuti got two of his articles on the front page, and by July 1818 he had been given a trimonthly 'Italian Literature' bulletin that provided news from the Italian literary scene.[101] Both front page articles were reviews of recent travelogues by English tourists in which Buonaiuti shares Foscolo's critical stance by correcting errors of fact with native knowledge: he castigates John Milford for his *Observations, Moral, Literary, and Antiquarian* (1818) as those observations never go 'beneath the surface of things', and Henry Sass for his *Journey to Rome and Naples* (1818) because its claim to contain 'an account of the present state of Society' is 'completely falsified' as its author 'does not appear from his publication to have been once in the company of Italians'.[102] Buonaiuti also encourages Byron's recent move to an Italian style: he reviewed the Hobhouse and Foscolo collaboration on notes for *Childe Harold IV*, calling it 'replete with intelligence', and wrote a long review praising *Beppo*.[103] Buonaiuti called Byron's ottava rima 'at the top of a style of writing with which England is not the most familiar', and sees Byron as between 'English sense and foreign refinements', a literary judgement of radical poetics in sharp distinction to those of conservative critics discussed in the next chapter.[104]

In a State of Open War with Writers of the Day

The elucidation of Italian culture for English readers taken on by Foscolo and Buonaiuti was not solely for the sake of art; they sustained Bozzi's wish 'to bring a pleasurable effect, and make ourselves useful in an effort for general society'.[105] Alfieri was the literary hero of many displaced Italians in the period, and the chapter 'Cosa siano lettere' in *Del principe e delle lettere* (1786) was the basis for the exiles' belief in criticism that was *utile et dulce*.[106] The exiles' pedagogy was corrective, aiming to promote Italy, its literature and history, over what they and the later Romantics saw as a pervasive 'French' school. Like Hunt and Byron, Foscolo stood firmly in favour of the 'Italian' over the 'French': he claims Pope is not 'of the first rank' and was part of a period in British verse which 'began to form itself upon the models of the French school'.[107] Foscolo's objection to Pope is based on his lack of originality and variety: 'when poetry is made by system, it may display artificial beauties, – but those of nature disappear'.[108] Foscolo finds an Italian parallel to this artificiality in the verse of the Accademia degli Arcadi. The Arcadians were founded in 1690 and had colonies in many cities in which they promoted the production of pastoral poetry (Mathias reached the rank of 'Pastore' in 1819).[109] Foscolo dismisses the Arcadians for their lack of original genius, and claims that poetry cannot be produced by giving someone 'a pastoral name, and a grant of lands in some romantic district of antient arcadia'.[110] In the 'Present State' essay, this charge of inauthenticity was extended to the diction used by two of the most famous Italian poets of the day, Melchiorre Cesarotti and Monti. He comments that Cesarotti's poems 'were spoilt and rendered inefficient; in the first place, by the intemperate and systematic use of *gallicisms*', and that Monti's work was 'infected with *Gallicisms*'.[111] His complaint is grounded in the 'systematic' adherence to French diction, which Foscolo views as unnatural. Later in the 'Present State' essay Foscolo, writing anonymously, appraises his own work. He claims to be an 'excellent scholar' and places his literary works in opposition to 'the preponderance of French power' which had 'infected the Italian language'.[112] Foscolo sets his poetry against a dominant 'French power' and situates his critical work in the same opposition. Foscolo's first victim is Ginguené, and three pages of his essay on Dante are devoted to probing the faults of the *Histoire*. Foscolo starts with one specific incident: Ginguené claims that he and Giambattista Corniani were the first people to suggest the *Tesoretto* (1260–1266) of Brunetto Latini was a possible model for the *Commedia*. Foscolo calls this assertion 'lamentable', points out that it was a link 'as old as the year 1400', and remarks that the *Tesoretto* did not influence Dante at all.[113] From this 'minute exposition' of a fault, Foscolo moves to general disdain, calls Ginguené a follower of Voltaire, the man who had damned the roughness of the Italian canon, and claims 'such inaccuracies and inconsistencies are inevitable in treating of a foreign literature'.[114] Foscolo then criticises the work of the Abbé de Sade, who like Ginguené 'had never been in Italy' beyond Tuscany, and reminds critics that they should 'avoid quoting foreign as native authority'.[115] In 'Narrative Poems' he extends his critique to a whole nation:

> M. Ginguené has criticised Pulci in the usual style of his countrymen. He attributes modern manners to ancient times, and takes it for granted that the gentlemen of every nation think and act like modern Frenchmen.[116]

Foscolo progresses from a mistake in Ginguené, to the inability of French criticism to effectively assess Italian literature, to these lines against what he perceives to be an arrogant French cultural position. A similar dismissal of the French nation occurs in Buonaiuti's claim that Stendhal is a 'clever, conceited, volatile, self-sufficient, Frenchman', in which the four adjectives prove he shared Foscolo's and Alfieri's contempt for Gallic cultural dominance.[117]

Foscolo's choice of target seems odd: Ginguené saw Italy as the motherland of European literature, and even defended Tasso in a manner strikingly similar to Foscolo.[118] There are two interrelated reasons for Foscolo's attack. The first involves Ginguené's relations with Foscolo's hero Alfieri. In his flight from Paris in 1793, the French government confiscated Alfieri's library; anticipating this, Alfieri had deposited some 150 volumes with Ginguené. But in his posthumously published *Vita* (1806) Alfieri accuses the Frenchman of not returning some 1600 volumes of his library.[119] Foscolo knew the *Vita* well and was often spoiling for a literary fight: his admiration for Alfieri and his works make it plausible that he could harbour ill feeling towards Ginguené over this incident.[120] The second reason for the criticisms of Ginguené relates to the earlier discussion of national binaries: that an oppressed national literature, in this case 'Italian', positions itself in binary opposition to the oppressor, 'France', and that an Italian critic's attempts at definition can only come through the degradation of a French critic.[121] This is the same national pride articulated in the *Orazione*, when Foscolo questions the failure of Italians to respond culturally to French and Austrian occupation and asks, 'A che vi querelate se i germi dell'italiano sapere sono coltivati dagli stranieri che ve gli usurpano?'.[122] Although it may appear a simplistic reading, these international relations can be nuanced if they are seen in the context of the British market for literary history and their use by the periodical press. Ginguené's work, along with that of the other great Francophone scholar Sismondi, was the authoritative account of Italian literature for British journals. In his earliest years of exile, Foscolo would have registered this esteem; one reviewer talked of the 'extreme utility' of the *Histoire,* and the *Quarterly* called Ginguené 'a masterly hand'.[123] Foscolo, a new arrival in English criticism, wanted to be the voice of Italian history in the periodical press, but found this role occupied by two French speakers. Furthermore, as Foscolo would have been aware, Ginguené was a member of the *Institut de France,* the learned society setup by the republican government in 1795, and was also a contributor to a number of volumes of the *Histoire littéraire de la France* (1814, 1817, 1820); he could be viewed not solely as an academic historian, but as a representative of French cultural power. To topple these two dominant voices, Foscolo recruited another binary nationalism: the English *versus* French opposition that produced the attacks on foreigners discussed in Chapter 1. He exploited the shared hostility to the 'French' to ingratiate himself with British readers. Just as he showed his congeniality by quoting Milton, Shakespeare, and Gray, here Foscolo appeals to antagonisms shared by Italians and the readers in his new home.

The two oppositions are quite different: British *versus* French opposes two competing European powers, where Italian *versus* French has Foscolo shed light upon the precarious situation of his national literature and language. Foscolo had lived in the Venetian republic before 'the treachery' of its cessation by Napoleon, had supported and lived in the Cisalpine Republic before the Congress of Vienna, and had developed in a cultural environment dominated by French criticism of Italian literature.[124] His work constantly reiterates the need for Italian natives to 'think and act like' modern Italians, and for English readers to prefer his native authority to the French. Foscolo's active resistance is more than a disagreement over critical practice; the encroachment of French culture into Italian life was a regular complaint of Italian nationalists who went to England. When Jacopo Ortis arrives in Milan and tries to buy some literature in Italian, the bookseller responds,

> [Q]uasi dispettoso mi disse, ch'ei non vendeva libri Italiani. La gente civile parla elegantemente il francese, e appena intende lo schietto toscano. I pubblici atti e le leggi sono scritti in una cotal lingua bastarda che le ignude frasi sugellano la ignoranza e la servitù di chi le detta.[125]

Foscolo shows his anger at a situation which goes further than thinking and acting like a modern Frenchman; language, one of the few potential unifying forces in the riven Italian Peninsula, becomes a sign of national servitude and subservience to the French. Foscolo mediates a widely felt concern through the fictional complaints of Jacopo, and this is the same tone he strikes in the *Orazione* when in his own voice he implores his countrymen to 'defend the language from usurpation and from calumny'.[126] Writing in the second issue of *L'Italico,* an anonymous exile recently arrived in Britain notes that the linguistic domination was complete in Lombardy and Piedmont, where the administrative language was now French.[127] Fighting against this French, and subsequently Austrian, cultural domination is one the earliest expressions of Italian nationalism. It is a dissenting voice that is rooted in Alfieri's critique of tyranny, a discussion of which ends this chapter. In his fiction, the young Foscolo vehemently opposed occupation and advocated Italian liberty; this opposition becomes more controlled in his British critical output. He still rages against the foreigner's 'claims to all the productions of the fruitful soil', and warns that 'the tythe of the poetry is claimed by the conquerors', but, as Marilyn Butler suggests, in a post-Waterloo climate this rage must take subtler forms – the periodical article over the novel, and the ear of powerful men over the rhetoric of an oration.[128]

Foscolo's oppositional stance should be seen in the context of similar opinions held by his closest British friends, Holland and Hobhouse. In spite of his multi-faceted criticism of the French, Foscolo had once written an ode 'A Bonaparte liberatore' (1797), and even his later disappointment in Napoleon did not stop him from calling himself 'a pupil of the revolution' in 1818.[129] To understand this statement we need to think beyond being simply 'for' or 'against' the French Revolution, as to do so, as Gregory Dart argues, is to accept the counter-revolutionary depiction of the Revolution as a 'monolithic phenomenon'.[130] These labels ignore the inherent difficulties in grouping together a man such as Foscolo, who was at best ambivalent about Napoleon, but who by 1816 was strongly in favour of the 'poor and weak' usurping a ruling class, with Holland or Hobhouse, who idolised Napoleon but were not avid republicans.[131] However, Foscolo, Hobhouse, and Holland shared opinions on national independence and personal liberty. Their reciprocity is based on opposition; Holland and Hobhouse were perennially in political opposition until the 1830s, and Holland House was a meeting place for the champions of liberal causes in Parliament. Foscolo too, as he claims in the Hobhouse collaboration, was in a 'state of open war' with established literature and politics of his day.[132] The remark is an act of self-fashioning to give a deliberate impression of his iconoclastic relationship with authority and tradition, and the congeniality of this opposition with Holland and Hobhouse gave Foscolo the opportunity, often denied to exiles, to disseminate ideas directly to the British public.[133]

Foscolo was deemed a large enough threat in 1814 to warrant an Austrian Secret Police report, which called him a 'manifold Proteus, infamous tongue at every time, another ringleader of the faction that in the last days of April agitated this region for independence'.[134] The Hollands shared Foscolo's hatred of Austria; Lady Holland called it 'that detested country' and Lord Holland spent much of his political career opposing it.[135] Indeed, the vehemence of Holland's attacks on Austrian occupation of Naples led to his being proscribed on a state list of European radicals who were not allowed to enter Hapsburg territory.[136] In keeping with this radical strain, Holland employed Italian political exiles such as Binda and gave them roles in his circle. These actions do not mean we should label Holland a 'radical': his lukewarm support for electoral reform and his distaste for popular uprisings would challenge that. In domestic politics Holland was what Gramsci would term a passive revolutionary 'satisfied by small doses, in a legal and reformist manner – in a way in which it was impossible to destroy the political and economic position of the old feudal classes'.[137] But, just as nuance is needed to classify a journal like the *Edinburgh*, so Holland's actions and opinions on European issues, and his hosting of exiles, are signs of more radical engagement with the Italian (and Spanish) cause.[138] These sympathies were also literary; during Holland's travels in Spain in the 1790s, his uncle Charles James Fox had persuaded him to go to Italy with a warning: 'if you do not go to Italy you never will learn thoroughly the Italian Language and for want of it be deprived of some of the greatest pleasure that you who love poetry can enjoy'.[139] Holland took his uncle's advice: he travelled in Italy, learnt the language, and read deeply in its poetry.[140] After Holland returned from his second trip in 1814 to 1815, he encouraged Rose to translate the works of Tasso and Francesco Berni; the latter translation was dedicated to Holland in 1823 as the peer who had 'wooed and won the Southern Muse'.[141] Hobhouse was also a guest at Holland House, dining there ten times between 1816 and 1825. He had spent time in Italy with Byron in 1816 and 1817; whilst in Milan he met many of the most important Italian writers, read widely in Italian literature, and returned home with a Sienese member of household staff.[142] In Italy, Hobhouse began to consider a political career; his opinions were taken seriously by the Italian liberals he met, and he notes that he had a 'willing audience' because he was 'a hater of the Congress Castlereagh system'.[143] After being in Italy, Hobhouse's opinions became decidedly more radical: he joined the Rota Club, stood as the Member of Parliament for Westminster with the support of Sir Francis

Burdett, and was jailed over a 'breach of privilege' in his pamphlet *A Trifling Mistake* (1819). His career was defined by opposition: he was welcomed in Italy because of his hatred of Castlereagh, happily recorded that he was extolled in the *Morning Chronicle* as 'a most important acquisition to the cause of liberty', and derived much fame, like Hunt, from his incarceration.[144]

On foreign politics, Holland, Hobhouse, and Foscolo shared a common sense of the futility of European war, and of the failure of the revolution in France to awaken liberty at home or on the continent. This feeling of futility would transform into the protests discussed in Chapter 5 and the realisation of failure in the poetry examined in Chapter 6. For Foscolo, the ceding of the previously protected Parga shows how 'we are to be rewarded for thirty years of suffering and bloodshed', just as for Holland the Austrians at Naples are 'incorrectly, denominated legitimate'.[145] Hobhouse believed that the distribution of power after 1815 was 'a restoration of all the old habits of the Empire' and made Northern Italy the 'most enslaved part of Europe'.[146] The shared opposition to British foreign policy and its post-Vienna alliances found an outlet in the attacks on policy makers, particularly Castlereagh. A second expression of opposition takes the form of attacks on figures who were once 'pupils of the revolution', but have since come to support the state. Echoing Hazlitt's remarks in 'On Court-Influence', Foscolo is highly critical of those writers who were once in favour of their national cause but now 'flatter governments and powerful individuals' and 'can never display independence of mind'.[147] Foscolo is not afraid to name names: in the 'Present State' essay he calls Cesarotti 'a poet who wrote by commission' and claims that 'his political conduct was not distinguished for its constancy'.[148] He reserves his longest attack for Monti, remarking that he

> has sustained the preponderating opinions, and he has invariably advocated the interests of the succeeding reigning powers. With such advantages it is not strange that he should have found many willing and eager readers; nor is it more strange that all the various governments, one after the other, should have continued to rank him amongst their partisans.[149]

Foscolo's diction – 'preponderating', 'invariably', 'succeeding', 'various' – exposes the inconsistency of Monti's partisanship. By August 1820 Byron was well read in the current literature of Italy and reached the same conclusion, calling Monti 'quel Giuda di Parnaso', and a month later claimed that Foscolo was 'a man of genius'.[150] Foscolo and the later Romantics shared a belief in the need to attack what they saw as the inconsistency of those poets, such as Monti, Wordsworth, and Southey, supporting and supported by the state.[151]

Foscolo's critique of inconsistency is based in the work of Alfieri. As discussed in the previous chapter, it was Alfieri's reinterpretation of Dante that had shown the innovativeness of the *Commedia*, for which Byron called Alfieri one of the writers 'changing the purposes of poetry'.[152] Foscolo devoted seventeen pages to Alfieri in the 'Present State' essay, praising his political vigour against the Popes of his day and his deep reading in Dante and Petrarch.[153] Later in the same essay, in the section appraising his own work, Foscolo calls himself a follower of Alfieri; as Mario Fubini has remarked, the revolutionary thought of Alfieri was always a presence in Foscolo's writing.[154] Regency readers could note the similarities between the two as Alfieri's life was translated in 1810 and his tragedies in 1815, making him the only writer discussed in the 'Essay', aside from Foscolo, available in English.[155] Foscolo's first works were tragedies in the manner of Alfieri, and in *Jacopo Ortis* his protagonist uses Alfieri's works for near-bibliomancy at moments of crisis.[156] When Jacopo pronounces 'the only mortal whom I wanted to meet was Vittorio Alfieri' it seems reasonable to see this as Foscolo's authorial expression of admiration for the hero he never met.[157] Foscolo learnt from Alfieri, but both shared a common teacher in Machiavelli, indeed what Lindon has called 'the nationalist millenarianism inaugurated by Alfieri and Foscolo' was the product of a Machiavellian moment in late eighteenth-century Italy.[158] Machiavelli, whose writings had been consistently attacked in Italy by religious conservatives, and who had become a byword for low cunning on the English stage, was becoming appreciated by Alfieri and others as an exposer of tyranny who offered hope in the darkest moments of the 1790s.[159] This reappraisal, which is strikingly similar to the change in Dante's critical reception in the same period, is the background to Foscolo's lines on Machiavelli in *Dei Sepolcri*:

Io quando il monumento
Vidi ove posa il corpo di quel grande
Che temprando lo scettro a' regnatori
Gli allòr ne sfronda, ed alle genti svela
Di che lagrime grondi e di che sangue.[160]

Machiavelli is first of the tombs considered, before even Dante and Alfieri. Foscolo controls his emotions, blending reverence with reality in the visceral but neatly balance last line. Machiavelli flattered rulers only to deceive, and is cast as a thinker who can unveil tyrannies which end not in tears but in blood. A few years after this poem, in the months following the *Orazione*, Foscolo wrote a long unfinished essay on the 'great one', and, as the next chapter shows, the idea of resurgence articulated in this Italian treatment of Machiavelli was integral to visionary strain of Byron and Shelley.[161]

Foscolo's critical works in England, although not filled with the direct quotation of *Jacopo Ortis*, evince an Alfierian root in their anti-Gallicism, their promotion of Dante, and their appeals to liberty. Foscolo's skill is his adaptation of Alfieri's prose, which largely rages against the slavery of patronage and the misrule of petty princes, to the post-revolutionary situation of foreign powers controlling Italy and its letters. The influence of Alfieri is seen in Foscolo's diction, as in this extract from the 'Present State':

> The foreigners who have by turns usurped the Italian provinces, have extended their claims to all the productions of that fruitful soil: not only the corn, and the wine, and the oil are put in requisition, but the tythe of the poetry is claimed by the conquerors.[162]

Foscolo's choice of 'usurped' echoes the use of the term in Alfieri's prose, and his agrarian imagery can be related to the image in *Del Principe* of Italians under foreign rule as plants who, have become warped under the stresses put upon them by 'il malvagio cultore'.[163] Over and above these similarities of diction and imagery is a shared belief in the power of words, in seeing literature as a central part of the life of a nation. Both writers educate the public about the structural enslavement that requires literature to pay its 'tythe': whether this is to patrons (as was the case with Metastasio in Alfieri's generation) or to foreign rulers (in the case of Monti in Foscolo's).[164]

Foscolo is attempting to explain the power a conqueror or nation-state has over its inhabitants; the 'tythe' is a symbol of the hegemonic control through which the state or invader controls not just agricultural output but also literary habits and trends.[165] Holland and Hobhouse were two friends who would have recognised the Alfierian tone of Foscolo's rhetoric. Hobhouse's Italian diary regularly discusses Alfieri, his work, and its proscription by the Austrian authorities. In addition, the diary constantly recounts stories of Alfieri's life; Hobhouse's fascination is shown by the amount of time he devotes to gossip concerning the Italian's hair, his tomb, and his habits in speech.[166] Hobhouse would have admired the decoration of Holland House; the topographer Thomas Faulkner commented on the portraits which covered the walls as of 'remarkable men, chiefly Italians'.[167] The Italians adorning the walls of Holland House were a roll-call of Renaissance Italy – Dante, Ca' della Scala, Petrarch, Ariosto, Tasso, Pulci, Benvenuto Cellini, Brunelleschi, and da Vinci – with one exception, a portrait of Alfieri. The dramatist's place amongst these giants of the Renaissance shows the esteem in which the Holland House set held him. Two invoices show that these portraits were commissioned at Florence in 1796 (along with a portrait of Holland himself) from Francois-Xavier Fabre, the man who had painted the famous Uffizi portrait of Alfieri three years earlier.[168] Holland not only admired the Italian's literature and politics but also wished to be portrayed as a radical in the Alfierian mould.

As Holland House was a nexus for exiled Italians and English promoters of liberty, such as Foscolo and Hobhouse, so the Veneto was an omphalos for English exiles attempting to connect with the Italian literary tradition. The literary heritage of the city and the hills to its west includes Petrarch, Alfieri, and Foscolo, and they became a locus for the Italian poetry of Byron and Shelley, poetry that follows the historical approach of Foscolo's criticism. Fleeing Milan, Jacopo goes to the Euganean Hills, where he makes a pilgrimage to Petrarch's house at Arquà; Luzzi has viewed this scene as Foscolo forging 'the cultural link between him[self] and a literary father'.[169] Jacopo constantly quotes lines from the *canzoniere* when he reaches Arquà, and again when he returns to the hills a few months later he quotes from canzone 320, 'Sento l'aura mia antica, e i dolci colli / veggio apparire'.[170] Jacopo is also reminded of Alfieri, who had made his own Petrarchan pilgrimage to Arquà; while among the Hills Alfieri records that he 'un giorno intero vi consecrai al pianto e alle rime', an action which produced the sonnet 'O cameretta, che già in te chiudesti'.[171] But there is more than a literary link being forged by Jacopo's memories of Petrarch and Alfieri. Jacopo cries 'Italia Mia', the opening line of Petrarch's nationalist canzone 128, for his nation overrun with 'barbarians', making a clear historical parallel, as he does in his English criticism, between Italy's current strife and the wars of Petrarch's age. Canzone 128 had long been a touchstone for the liberation of Italy, and it was with lines from this poem that Machiavelli chose to close his 'Esortazione a liberare la Italia da' barbari' at the end of *Il Principe* (1532).

After learning Italian with Cornelia Turner in 1814, Shelley had read widely in its literature, including Alfieri, and translated works by Dante and Cavalcanti.[172] Two items from the Marlow summer of 1817 show that Shelley had become increasingly interested in modern Italy. First, among fragments in a notebook used at Marlow, Shelley drafts what appears to be an advert in which he states that he is looking to exchange the lease on his house for a villa at Naples.[173] Second, in a recently discovered ledger that lists the books that Shelley left at Marlow before coming to Italy, are written the two words 'Jacopo Ortis'.[174] This entry proves what had only been suspected previously: that Shelley owned, and had likely read, Foscolo's epistolary novel. This discovery creates a new perspective on the opening of 'Lines written among the Euganean Hills' in which Shelley's narrator

> stood listening to the paean
> With which the legioned rooks did hail
> The sun's uprise majestical.[175]

Like Foscolo's Jacopo feeling the ancient breeze, the narrator devotes himself to the natural environment; Shelley is not just opening his ears to the rooks, but also to the Italian poets who found revelation and refuge here for half a millennium. As Alan Weinberg has shown, Shelley's phraseology shows his appreciation of place is indebted to his Italian forbears.[176] This is the beginning of Shelley's Italian poetry, infused more than Byron's in the traditional canon – with Dante and Petrarch as its two crowns – about which Foscolo had challenged prevailing attitudes in the pages of the *Edinburgh Review*. Byron, too, visited the Euganean Hills, even signing a guestbook at Arquà, but his real muse was Venice, the setting and the subject of *Beppo*, which was about to cause a 'great noise'.[177] The ottava rima of *Beppo* was discussed at length in Foscolo's essay on 'Narrative Poems', which provided the Regency readers with a history of the form in Pulci, Berni, and Casti. Four years after its publication the essay was still being referred to as 'an ingenious critique on the Italian Romantic poets'.[178] These articles, and their knowledgeable discussion of the history of the Italian Burlesque, were an integral part of Foscolo's 'open warfare' with entrenched critical perceptions of Italy and its verse. Foscolo was the figure – as poet, patriot, but more importantly as critic – who changed the British idea of Italy and its poetry. His work was part of the transformation in British engagement with Italian literature, which moved from a dilettante interest before 1815 to being one of the foremost literary topics of the quarterly and now monthly periodicals, and subsequently to the dominant formal and stylistic mode of second generation Romanticism.

CHAPTER 4

Veneto 1817–1819
Venice Redefined

Farewell, Monsieur Traveller: look you lisp and wear strange suits, disable all the benefits of your own country, be out of love with your nativity and almost chide God for making you that countenance you are, or I will scarce think you have swam in a gondola.

William Shakespeare, *As You Like It* (1599)

Venice is a pure signifier: 'a form in which men unceasingly put *meaning* (which they extract at will from their knowledge, their dreams, their history), without this meaning thereby ever being finite or fixed'.[1] The tendency of succeeding generations to define and redefine the city has left poetry written in Venice immediately after the European Peace caught in a critical penumbra. Romantic poetry set in Venice has been regarded as 'remote from contemporary life', often mistaken for the Grand Tour accounts which preceded it or the 'wistful Venetophilia' of the Victorians.[2] But the cultural pull of Venice from 1817 to 1819 produced a literature distinct from the aesthetic fascination of Ruskin or Proust; Byron and Shelley entered a state occupied for the second time in a decade, which provided on one hand an encounter with the strictures of post-Metternich Europe, and on the other the freedom of a demi-monde with traditional links to the carnivalesque. This chapter shows the importance of Venice for the Italian redefinition of Romantic poetry through a reading of the early works of Byron's and Shelley's exile. The analysis begins in the Euganean Hills, a viewing point for the 'Column, tower, and dome, and spire' of Venice, and the site of Shelley's first long poem composed in Italy, 'Lines written among the Euganean Hills'.[3] As Wasserman has argued, the poem is of a different cast to the transcendent poems of the Geneva summer, 'Hymn to Intellectual Beauty' and 'Mont Blanc'.[4] In the Veneto, Shelley was becoming absorbed in an Italian intellectual and poetic tradition, and this tradition underpins 'Euganean Hills'. The Shelleyan narrator's journey from a bitter north, across 'a deep wide sea of misery', to a nutritive exile in the warmth of Italy has clear parallels with the poet's personal journey, but the view over Venice is also epiphanic: it allows Shelley to redefine his poetic and political outlook through an interaction with republican and visionary Italian ideas.

The chapter then moves down from the hills, across the *laguna*, and into Venice itself, a place where foreigners had been seeking redefinition for centuries. Indeed, as Pocock has shown, the idea of the perfectly serene republic was as much a creation from without as it was an aspect of Venetian governance.[5] For Britons, Venice was an *exemplum* of both how to go right and how to go wrong, and these were lessons to be learnt in *La Serenissima* during their Grand Tour. Eighteenth-century treatments of Venice are caught between two poles: a predominantly Whig interpretation of a model civic polity and a conservative vision of vice and laxity.[6] The juxtaposition of edification and corruption was still active in 1818: Byron and Shelley had the opportunity to 'lisp and wear strange suits' when writing in and about a place bound to so many myths. After a discussion of the unique cultural moment that engulfed Venice in this period, I turn to *Beppo*, a poem Byron composed aware of the historical significance of a place he called both 'the greenest island of my imagination' and 'the Sea-sodom'.[7] *Beppo* is Byron's first ottava rima work of significant length and is often considered as an apprentice piece to *Don Juan*, a poem that he had not conceived of before Venice. *Beppo* is a revolution against what Byron refers to as his 'old style' of poetry and of thought.[8] He was now working in the same form as contemporary Venetians such as Pietro Buratti, and in the manner of Casti, and learning the potential for punning and ribaldry that this tradition offered. Byron's outlook was changing too: *Beppo* is a work in praise of variety, and even the poet's much-discussed debauchery was an attempt to experience life noble, middling, and low. The cosmopolitanism ingrained in Venice facilitated comparisons between England and Italy from the position of exile; a discussion of these comparisons concludes the chapter. Using an idea of Italy to question English values, Byron and Shelley flaunted their disinterest in domestic affairs, and yet as Gibbon's famous image of corrupt power reminds us, Britain was often seen in parallel with 'the Venetian history'.[9] The poets' persistent claims to pay little attention to British politics, and to have met no British travellers, belie their use of their exile status to attack and satirise the Regency.

To Our Healing Paradise

'Euganean Hills' was written at Este in October 1818.[10] Despite Shelley's own claim in the 'Advertisement' to *Rosalind and Helen* (1819) that the opening lines 'image forth the sudden relief of a state of deep despondency', the poem has long been viewed as melancholy.[11] This tradition was begun by Mary Shelley in her 1839 editorial commentary, which categorised 'Euganean Hills' among Shelley's poems of 'grief and despondency' and claimed that he had 'poured forth morbid but too natural bursts of discontent and sadness'.[12] Donald Reiman extended this depression to claim that Shelley's view of Venice reflected his sadness, so that 'there is, in fact, little except dross left within the city'.[13] John Pemble views this projection of an emotional state on to Venice as a common manoeuvre in the period:

> For most of the nineteenth century the Venice of literature was remote from contemporary life. It was a city of poetry and historical romance [. . .] for solitary sufferers who communed with themselves about the vicissitudes of human destiny [. . .] in the 1870s the Venice of literature changed. It became crowded with characters who wore modern dress and used modern language.[14]

But some poetry before 1870 was 'crowded' with modern dress and modern language, in particular later Romantic poetry about Venice interacted with and challenged contemporary language, custom, and morality. Venice is not a theatrical set in this literature but 'a peopled Labyrinth' (l. 13), to be seen in comparison with Regency London. The poetry I discuss is alert to the social aspects of current Venetian life and the political facts of its history. Pemble identifies pre-1870 writing about Venice as written by sufferers communing as near-solipsists, with literature about Venice itself in the same fallen state as the Serene Republic, and this feeling certainly existed: in the dirgeful 'Nessun maggior dolore' of the *gondoliere* in Rossini's *Otello* (1816), and in poems by Wordsworth and Byron.[15] But 'Euganean Hills' is not a poem of despondency, nor is the Venice it presents a relic of the past. It is a poem of the present, of the personal and geopolitical now, of a reckoning with exile that offers a new life grounded in a new landscape, and the potential for a new poetry drawn from the Italian tradition. This was the tradition that the Shelleys had read in with Leigh Hunt during the previous summer at Marlow, which would become central to both Mary's and Percy's later works.[16]

Hope is expressed in the first 150 lines of the 'Euganean Hills', which interpret the differences between England and Italy through a description of the landscape. The poem begins,

> Many a green isle needs must be
> In the deep wide sea of misery,
> Or the mariner, worn and wan,
> Never thus could voyage on.
>
> (ll. 1–4)

The unbalanced first couplet is weighted towards its depressed end as the forceful 'deep wide' and the doleful 'misery' break the hopefulness of the iambic opening. Shelley continues to stumble on the awkward similarity of 'mariner' and 'wan', and does not offer a regular rhythm until the fourth line. The next verse describes the 'beach of a northern sea', with a wind 'Howling, like a slaughtered town, / When a king in glory rides / Through the pomp of fratricides' (ll. 57–59). Shelley presents a bleak, presumably British, coast where the climate can be likened to the macabre processions of Ezzelin, Napoleon, and Alexander the Great, which will return in 'The Mask of Anarchy' and 'The Triumph of Life'. The lines above do little to counter Mary Shelley's reading of 'Euganean Hills', but this changes when the reader is taken to Italy.

> Aye, many flowering islands lie
> In the waters of wide Agony:
> To such a one this morn was led
> My bark by soft winds piloted:
> 'Mid the mountains Euganean.
>
> (ll. 66–70)

Shelley reworks the opening couplet, emphasising a move from despair on the northern shore to a healing south. The change to a trochee for the refrain 'Aye' carries an affirmative end to the narrator's grief; what previously was just a 'green isle' is replaced by 'many flowering islands', where the gerund gives a flourishing alternative to 'Agony'. A shift in mood causes a reciprocal shift in sound, as the uncomfortable rhythms of home give way to a more confident narrative voice. With 'such a one' the narrator moves to a specific place of relief and Shelley sustains the nautical imagery guided by 'soft winds'. The narrator then looks to the sky where

> th' eastern heaven
> Bursts, and then, as clouds of even,
> Flecked with fire and azure, lie
> In the unfathomable sky.
>
> (ll. 76–79)

The response becomes effusive in this discussion of the skyscape.[17] The change in climate from howling tempests to clear heaven 'Bursts' over the line-break in an image which returns at the close of 'England in 1819' ('from which a glorious Phantom may / Burst to illumine our tempestuous day').[18] Something in the environment overcomes the metrical constraint, breaking through to provide a hope that had previously been, in the dominant word of the paragraph, 'unfathomable'. Shelley's fervour is heightened as he looks over the plain of Lombardy, where 'Ocean's nursling, Venice lies, / A peopled labyrinth' (ll. 95–96). He then gives the reader a broader panorama.

> Lo! the sun upsprings behind,
> Broad, red, radiant, half-reclined
> On the level quivering line
> Of the waters crystalline;
> And before that chasm of light,
> As within a furnace bright,
> Column, tower, and dome, and spire,
> Shine like obelisks of fire.
>
> (ll. 100–107)

The material difference in the Italian landscape is underlined by the novelty of the many domed churches. Although he echoes the 'Ships, towers, domes' of Wordsworth's 'Composed upon Westminster Bridge', Shelley compresses his fascination with the domed skyscape into these lines, a fascination about which he had written to Mary Shelley, enraptured by 'Domes & steeples [. . .] on all sides', and told Peacock on his first sight of Venice 'the laguna with its domes & turrets glittering in a long line [. . .] is one of the finest architectural delusions in the world'.[19] 'Islanded' again recalls the first line, and the solace that the narrator sought is found in the Venetian archipelago, but Shelley's energy is voyeuristic as he looks in solitude on the 'peopled labyrinth' and buildings of urban Venice.[20] The perspective becomes total as his gaze moves up to the sun, down through the city, to the 'waters crystalline' below. The usually slow rise of the sun transcends time and 'upsprings', while the narrator's reactions are characterised by transition and change as the rising sun is 'half-reclined' and the apparently level waters quiver. This expressive visual landscape is then scattered with monuments in another list at the penultimate line – a profusion of radiant 'obelisks' far from 'sunless vapour, dim' of the northern shore.

By responding to this scene, Shelley is placing himself in a long tradition; Venetian landscapes were some of the most famous images in eighteenth-century visual culture. These views had their most famous appreciators in Canaletto and the *vedutisti* whose paintings of the Serene Republic hung in aristocratic homes and were available to a wider audience thanks to the burgeoning print industry.[21] Their subject was often the 'peopled' Venice of the *carnivale* and the *Spoziato del Mare* – the republic in its full pomp as described by Shelley. These views were also available in the panorama on the Strand, which Mary Shelley visited, and in descriptions in the literature of the Grand Tour and the Italianate Gothic.[22] So what separates Shelley's treatment of Venice from Ann Radcliffe's long descriptions in *The Mysteries of Udolpho* (1794)?[23] It differs because Shelley was not looking at the Republic of Venice, as Emily St. Aubert and the painters were, but at a newly acquired Austrian territory. Shelley is showing the islands in a 'darker day', which John Baker claim makes this Venice 'in fact a sepulcher that houses corruption'.[24] Baker's reading of Shelley's Venice fits with the view espoused in John Chetwode Eustace's *Classical Tour*, which laments the fall of the city 'to plunder, to slavery, and to indelible disgrace', and later by the narrator of Robert Browning's 'A Toccata of Galuppi's' in his wistful reminiscence that 'they lived once thus at Venice, where the merchants were the kings, / Where Saint Mark's is, where the Doges used to wed the sea with rings'.[25]

But for the previous fifty lines, Shelley portrays the city, as he views it specifically in October 1818, as an illuminating location: his Venice is a 'Sun-girt City' (l. 115). It has been thought that 'Sun-girt' is a misprint of Milton's and Thomson's 'Sea-girt', but Swinburne is right to appreciate that Shelley is not viewing a sinking Venice from Mestre, but redefining the city as illuminated from above.[26] Barthes wrote that the view over a city, 'permits us to transcend sensation and to see things *in their structure*', and this is precisely what Shelley does, he sees what Venice was, is, and could be.[27] To continue the analogy with landscape art, Shelley is using a view not in the manner of the *vedutisti*, but as a late eighteenth-century *capricci* painter.[28] A *capriccio* was a fictional landscape, which could include a mix of Classical, Gothic, and Renaissance buildings to, as Schoina argues, reinforce and complicate the 'imaginative connection between time and place'.[29] Like a *capriccio*, Shelley's poem can sustain in a single view Venice's glorious past, current problems, and, as I discuss, future regeneration. The next six verse paragraphs of 'Euganean Hills' are a discussion of the occupied Venetian territories, lines which Weinberg has argued show that for Shelley 'the sacrifice required of the city is nothing less than its physical existence: Venice is doomed, it must perish'.[30] The type of poetry that fits these claims produced some of the most enduring literature of the period: Wordsworth's 'On the Extinction of the Venetian Republic', which grieves 'when even the Shade / Of that which once was great is passed away', and Byron's talk of 'dying Glory' and 'palaces [. . .] crumbling to the shore'.[31] A similar funerary diction appears in Shelley's lines; Venice's towers have become

> Sepulchres, where human forms,
> Like pollution-nourished worms
> To the corpse of greatness cling,
> Murdered, and now mouldering.
> (ll. 146–149)

Shelley then extends this enslavement to Padua (ll 236–268). Mark Sandy has argued that Shelley shared Wordsworth's view of Venice, one concerned with 'ruins and the ruinous, decline and fall, death and decay', but although Shelley acknowledges that tyranny has come to the Veneto, this is not terminal as it was for Wordsworth.[32] The novelty of Shelley's idea of the Veneto, when compared to the English reactions of the previous twenty years, is caused by his interaction with an Italian intellectual tradition, from Petrarch to Machiavelli, and on to Vico and Alfieri. This engagement begins with the talk of 'Sepulchres', in the first line. Shelley knew that the Euganean Hills were important to the Italian tradition, reminding readers in the advertisement that he was 'where now is, the sepulchre of Petrarch' and opening a letter to Peacock, 'I'm writing to you from among sepulchres'.[33] In canzone 128, Petrarch asks his nation,

> che fan qui tante pellegrine spade?
> perché 'l verde terreno
> del barbarico sangue si depinga?[34]

Petrarch's hopeless questions address the role of Germanic mercenaries working in Italy for the lords of the various principalities. He sees their presence as part of a historical revenge in which Germanic mercenaries attack the gentle flocks of Italy in revenge for the actions of the Roman Marius, even though Nature has provided Italy with an alpine shield against 'la tedesca rabbia'.[35] Shelley transposes Petrarch's diction of Italy's maligned *campagna* to show the 'brutal Celt' now in control of Italy where 'many a lord / Like a weed whose shade is poison, / Overgrows this region's foison' (ll. 226–228).

Despite Shelley's adoption of this diction, 'Euganean Hills' is more hopeful than its Petrarchan analogue. The potential for change shown in the tense shift from 'Murdered' to 'mouldering' is confirmed in the line following those on sepulchres, beginning 'But if Freedom should awake' (ll. 150–165), which tentatively offers the possibility of resurgence for Venice. There follows a discussion of people Shelley associates with specific places, first Homer on the Scamander, Shakespeare on the Avon, then 'As the love from Petrarch's urn, / Yet amid yon hills doth burn' (ll. 200–201). The poet's grave is an active inspiration, and sepulchres, as they were to Foscolo, are a symbol of potential. The ability to hope for the resurgence of fallen Venice is a refutation of Petrarch's view of a suffering life redeemed in the Christian *eternitas*, and in this preference for a cyclical view of history Shelley shows debts to contemporary Italian thought.[36] In the first chapter of *Della tirannide,* Alfieri discusses his cyclical view of history, and states 'ogni uomo buono dee credere, e sperare, che non sia oramai molto lontana quella necessaria vicenda, per cui sottentrare al fin debba all'universale servaggio una quasi universal libertà'.[37] Alfieri boldest statement on the possibility of resurgence, and the poet's role in this process, is the concluding sonnet of the *Misogallo* (1798), 'Giorno verrà, tornerà il giorno'.[38] The poem is predominantly in the future tense, predicting a time when Italians will rise up against French incursions, but this changes after the volta:

> Gli odo già dirmi: O Vate nostro, in pravi
> Secoli nato, eppur create hai queste
> Sublimi età, che profetando andavi.[39]

There is a shift in time and tone to the present in which a grateful populace praise the vatic poet for his relentless prophesying of a better future. Shelley is never quite this rhetorically bold or ideologically secure, but he seems to share this view at the close of the 'Ode to the West Wind', in the claim that the 'incantation of this verse' could 'Be through my lips to unawakened Earth / The trumpet of a prophecy'.[40] The idea of a cyclical history, of the potential of earth to awaken from tyranny, finds its foundations in Vico's idea of 'corso' and 'ricorso'.[41] In this tradition, the overthrow of the historical bloc and the creation of an alternative cultural centre occurs when the control of the 'public mind' appears to be at its strongest. The engagement of Vico, Alfieri, and Foscolo with historical cycles was part of the radical reclamation of Machiavelli discussed in the previous chapter, and a slight reference in 'A Defence of Poetry' suggests that Shelley was aware of this intellectual lineage.[42] But Shelley's interaction with this Italian theory of cyclical renewal is of an earlier birth. It is present at the centre of 'Euganean Hills':

> Twining memories of old time
> With new virtues more sublime;
> If not, perish thou and they, –
> Clouds which stain truth's rising day
> By her sun consumed away,
> Earth can spare ye: while like flowers,
> In the waste of years and hours,
> From your dust new nations spring
> With more kindly blossoming.
> (ll. 158–166)

The panorama allows Shelley to twin past glory with a potential for a return to future liberty. The lines contain the national despair of Petrarch in the perishing inhabitants and the stained sky, but it ends in a hopeful vein. The line opening on 'Earth' is an expansive image going beyond the Veneto, and the national parameters discussed in the canzone, to a higher power. Ralph Pite has seen this broadening of perspective as part of the 'apocalyptic radicalism' that Shelley articulates in the poem, that the domination of Padua and Venice will be only a distraction from the 'Europe-wide conflagration of popular uprising that has been set in train by the original spark of Enlightenment learning'.[43] Within this larger historical process new nations can spring from dust just as the green isle is 'flowering' and Petrarch's ashes 'still burn'.[44] Shelley's depiction of Venice shows his ability to redefine notions of history and nation, and the power of exile to heal political and personal situations seemingly at their nadir.

After admiring the Venetian sunrise, 'Noon descends around' (l. 265) Shelley's narrator. He then experiences what O'Neill has called a 'visionary epiphany'; he looks south down the spine of Italy, 'the olive-sandall'd Apennine', and north to the Alps, before realising that all living things including his own spirit,

> Interpenetrated lie
> By the glory of the sky:
> Be it love, light, harmony,
> Odour, or the soul of all
> Which from Heaven like dew doth fall,
> Or the mind which feeds this verse
> Peopling the lone universe.
>
> (ll. 313–319)[45]

Like Satan 'pondering his voyage', Shelley feels himself alone in a singular universe, a position that lets him appreciate the scene, and thus life, in its entirety.[46] The interpenetration of the sensory, the imaginative, and the ideal presents a new reality in which poetry has a role to play in 'peopling', and producing change within, this world. Wasserman has seen things differently: 'the death of tyranny and the persistence of another Atlantis-like personal "isle" are prophecy and vision; the reality is a sea of Life and Agony, at best sprinkled with transient "flowering isles"'.[47] But surely in these lines we see the fruits of Shelley's reading in an Italian tradition in which 'reality' and 'prophecy' refuse to be separated so starkly. In a landscape which many contemporary Britons were casting as moribund, Shelley's spirit, 'so long / Darkened' (l. 312), found new life. This depiction of Venice and its environs remained with Shelley as he wrote the more assured rhythms of 'Julian and Maddalo: A Conversation'. In the talk

'Of all that earth has been or yet may be', the poem anticipates the visionary themes of 'The Witch of Atlas' and 'The Triumph of Life', but also reinforces the vivifying idea of the Veneto that is central to 'Euganean Hills'.[48] The 'rich emblazonry' of clouds at sunset, the alternative to the sunrise of 'Euganean Hills', is the subject of Julian's thirty-line description which contains the same excited listing of 'mountains, seas and vineyards and the towers / Of cities they encircle' (ll. 71, 58–9). Julian gazes to the north, to the 'aery Alps', before ending his description in the west to describe 'a wondrous hue / Brighter than burning gold' (ll. 68, 73–4). This final sensuous description is of 'Those famous Euganean hills, which bear [. . .] The likeness of a clump of peakèd isles' (ll. 77–79). Shelley's viewpoint has changed, from seeing Venice from the hills to looking from the Lido to the hills, but the ethereal brilliance and the solace provided by the 'flowering islands' remains. The lines are a fit tribute: it was among these hills that Shelley found solace in Italy – its climate, its history, its literature – and formed a belief in poetic and political resurgence that underpins his mature poetry.

Oh, Inverted World

For centuries, Britons and Europeans had come to the Venetian Carnival to spend a few weeks not being themselves. In some sense, Byron followed this tradition: his personal and poetic outlook underwent fundamental changes at Venice, a redefinition that came from engagement with the city and its cosmopolitan carnival. Shelley's major poems of the Veneto look on Venice from without; the view over the city encompasses its history and its ideas, and allows the exile to redefine himself in a visionary landscape. But Shelley does occasionally move into the urban landscape, and even briefly makes the traditional association of the Veneto and the carnival; his mention of 'a rapid masque of death' precedes the gaming of

> Those mute guests at festivals,
> Son and Mother, Death and Sin,
> Played at dice for Ezzelin,
> Till Death cried, 'I win, I win!'
> (ll. 237–240)

Tourists become Milton's Sin and Death accompanied by Ezzelino, a thirteenth-century Italian tyrant whose cruelty was discussed by Sismondi and Hallam.[49] The macabre cast are not playing dice for fun, or for the money to be won at the *Casinò*; at stake are the disputed Italian territories. As Dorothy George has shown, British caricaturists made much of the festivities and frivolities that took place at the Congress of Vienna, with one example showing the dancing monarchs dividing Europe while Castlereagh pays pipers to play.[50] Shelley takes this popular image and couches it in the language and pursuits of the carnival, a part of Venetian life that endured after 1815. Byron showed an interest in these typically Venetian themes in a letter to Augusta a week before his first Carnival. 'I am going out this evening – in my *cloak* & *Gondola* – there are two nice Mrs. Radcliffe words for you'.[51] Byron relishes the opportunity to use the diction of Venice. The phrases are almost gifts to Augusta, with which he conjures Radcliffe's *Udolpho,* a text that demarcates the Italian language by italicising foreign terms such as *lagune* and *zendaletto*.[52] Byron knows the conjuring power of these Venetian images, of which he now has first-hand experience. It is a power he uses to great effect in the carefully structured opening of *Childe Harold IV*, 'I stood in Venice, on the Bridge of Sighs; / A palace and a prison on each hand', in which the oft discussed ambiguity of the second line is contingent on the specificity of the first.[53] In *Beppo,* the tone is more jovial, but the point the same: 'Didst ever see a gondola? For fear / You should not, I'll describe it you exactly'.[54] Byron jests at the commonplace of gondolas in Shakespeare, Ben Jonson, and Thomas Otway, but what follows is a description from a writer who has seen one, to a readership that most likely has not. This discrepancy between knowing and not knowing is revealed in that seamless double shift of tense, in which Byron says 'have you seen a gondola in the past? Well you may not see one in the future, so I'll tell you about them right away'.

Byron's choice of *Udolpho* is important. Radcliffe's narrative of a foreigner's first visit to Venice, at the time of Carnival, with its outfits that 'defy all description', and St Mark's Square 'crowded with company' as the sun rises, was part of a literary tradition.[55] Venice had not been reinterpreted in the period during or immediately after the Napoleonic Wars. From 1790 to 1818, longer works written about Venice had not diverged from common eighteenth-century readings. In their depictions of Venice, Shelley and Byron exaggerate and play with these traditions by comparing Venice with the Britain they had left behind. This reinterpretation finds its most concentrated expression in *Beppo*, but before I turn to the poem I will consider three contexts that underpin it: the pre-existing images of Venice's carnival in British cultural life, the new geopolitical situation of Venice, and Byron's reaction to his new home in his correspondence. Venice was an open signifier: a city of the imagination, like classical Athens or Rome, but also a largely intact functioning polity. It had enjoyed strong diplomatic links with Britain until the 1790s, and British reformers had been interested in Venice since James Harrington's explicit comparisons between the brief English Republic and Venetian Republic.[56] These links were maintained in this period by the actions of Lord William Bentinck and William Macfarlane who, contrary to Foreign Office wishes, attempted to hold plebiscites on Italian independence at the fall of Napoleon. The rapturous reception for the two Englishmen angered the Austrians – who would blame the 'English Party' for stirring up discontent amongst Venetians – and led to their recall to London by Castlereagh.[57] Contrasting with this definition of Venice as a model republic was the association of the city with carnival, both the specific ritual and the carnivalesque as a wider social mode, which Rose claimed 'may surely be reckoned amongst the secondary causes which contribute to the indolence of the Italian'.[58] Writing on the Venetian Carnival is voluminous, and most of this literature shares the belief that the festival allowed for the effacement of normal distinctions. This could be expressed through a heightened sexual freedom, a mixing between plebeian and aristocratic participants, the blurring of the usual class signifiers through disguise, or an inversion of social conventions related to the Lord of Misrule. Elizabeth Crouzet-Pavan has shown medieval roots for some of these associations, for instance the early organisation of workshops led to 'the juxtaposition of ordinary and costly merchandise that seemed extraordinary'.[59] But this mixing also had a political dimension within the myth of Venice, especially the myth as viewed from abroad: the commonwealth was immortally serene because it represented a perfect balance of monarchy, aristocracy, and democracy.[60] This mixing extended to the visual arts, famously in Canaletto's *The Stone Mason's Yard* (c. 1725) with its scene of labouring life crossed with the *campanile* of Santa Maria della Carità, or inversely in *Venice: The Doge's Palace and the Riva degli Schiavoni* (c. 1738) where a knife-grinder's stall sits in front of St Marco's famous residence. The mix of plebeian and patrician was promoted by the masked socialising of the Venetian Carnival, a feature which did not occur in the equivalent celebrations at Rome.[61]

The dominant English representations of Venice were theatrical: *Othello* (1604), *The Merchant of Venice* (1605), *Volpone* (1606), and *Venice Preserv'd* (1682), all of which Byron and Hobhouse quote from in their Venetian correspondence.[62] But another play provides the epigraph to *Beppo*: *As You Like It*.[63] In Shakespeare's play the exiled Duke Senior finds himself sent 'to liberty and not to banishment', away like Shelley's narrator, from the 'churlish chiding of the winter's wind' to a 'life exempt from public haunt'.[64] The Duke's escape to an inverted land, along with the jests of Touchstone and the disguises of Rosalind and Celia, make the epigraph well suited. But rather than quote from one of the many speeches extolling the wonders of exile, its liberty, and freedom for invention, Byron chooses a retort of Rosalind to Jacques:

> Farewell, Monsieur Traveller: look you lisp and wear strange suits, disable all the benefits of your own country, be out of love with your nativity and almost chide God for making you that countenance you are, or I will scarce think you have swam in a gondola.[65]

The languid assonance of 'lisp and wear strange suits' hints at the debauchery of life abroad. Rosalind castigates the young man for his itinerant life, as Jacques's libertinism, and his choice to leave home, are judged to be debilitating. The symbol to carry these associations is the final foreign word, 'gondola', which is as potent a symbol for Shakespeare as it is for Radcliffe. The corrupt Venice that Byron presents in his epigram was a common reading of the city in the British cultural imagination. This reading would become more prominent after the Republic's fall but had earlier foundations. When Pope added a fourth book to *The Dunciad* in 1742, he included a satiric Grand Tour 'o'er seas and lands' which journeys to Italy, 'To happy Convents, bosom'd deep in vines, / Where slumber Abbots, purple as their wines'.[66] Language is slippery and images jar: the unusually happy convents are turned sordid by the sexual 'bosom'd', and beyond the medial caesura it is revealed that the monastery's peace is due to the abbots' inebriation. The climax of Pope's portrait of a world-upside-down is Venice: the shrine of 'Naked Venus', once a maritime power, now home to 'the smooth Eunuch and enamour'd swain'.[67] The reversal of Venice's position – and the actions of travellers there – echoes Eustace's later judgement that the islands 'instead of resounding to the stroke of the anvil, re-echoed to the dance and the concert'.[68] As John Eglin has argued, in a society undergoing such fundamental change there is also flux in language, and the perceptions and meanings it contains. He uses the example of the phrase 'Sono a Venezia', literally 'I am in Venice', which had an English meaning as 'We are in a place of Liberty'.[69] But what are the meanings of liberty for an English traveller? In the 1670s it presumably meant political liberty, but by 1770 it could be a justification for behaviour, particularly during *carnivale,* which was unacceptable in Britain. The ability of language to change and contradict itself is a central element of the carnivalesque, where a capacity for wordplay is linked to the mixing and reversals of its social gatherings.[70] The fact that Venice's name was homophonous with the goddess of love gave rise to ribald puns, as in the irregular ode of 1750 by a 'Captain Manly' entitled *A summer voyage to the Gulph of Venice.*[71]

This punning texture is apparent in Byron's letters: 'Yesterday being the feast of St. Stephen – every mouth was put in motion – there was nothing but fiddling and playing on the virginals – and all kinds of conceits and divertissements on every canal of this aquatic city'.[72] These puns make their way into the opening of *Beppo*:

> With fiddling, feasting, dancing, drinking, masquing,
> And other things which may be had for asking.[73]

Byron's only use of the archaic 'virginals' (a clavichord) plays on the young women he pursued at the opening of Carnival. But the heavy-handed pun is only part of what is going on here. Side by side with the *Beppo* extract the letter shows Venice's abundance. The dashed breathless sentence, the use of 'all' and twice repeated 'every', and the din of the voices and music which are their subject, characterise the linguistic carnivalesque of Byron's new style. Byron's readers also remembered the success of the British carnival, indeed in *Beppo* there is a reference to the masked balls which still occurred in early-nineteenth-century London. (Byron attended at least two at which dominoes were worn.)[74] Terry Castle has examined the London Haymarket masquerades run by the Venetian Madame Cornelys, who was also a supporter of the growing Italian opera at the venue. These festivities came about because 'the Nation has been honour'd with the Residence of a Number of Foreigners', which meant a mixture of the vitriol that greeted libidinous Grand Tourists and the diction of anti-immigrant attacks was used to castigate these masquerades.[75] A short pamphlet-poem by Richard Sheridan on a Ridotto at Bath shows the transfer of Venetian associations to these English events:[76]

> The VARIETY 'tis which so reign'd in the crew,
> That turn where one would the classes were new; [. . .]
> But like a chess table, part black and part white,
> 'Twas a delicate checquer of *low* and *polite*;
> The motley assemblage so blended together,
> 'Twas Mob, or Ridotto – 'twas both, or 'twas neither.[77]

What is improper about the event is its variety: of people mixing who are as different as the black and white of a chessboard (a game with strict rules on who can move where). These groups become assembled, and 'so blended together' due to the various ticket prices, that they cause a shift from top to bottom, bottom to top, so that, in the symmetry of the final line, opposites become one and the same. Byron's constant play on the mixed perceptions of Venice is to a knowing readership, that remembered a time when the levelling and inversion of the Carnival was regularly produced in miniature at London and Bath.

The trends discussed above bring the position of the Venetian Carnival up to the upheavals of the 1790s; a set of varied perceptions formed from fictional works, travel writing, and the masked balls of the eighteenth century. Bahktin and Castle would call time on the party here; by 1790 'the metaphor had lost its concrete grounding', 'laughter was cut down to cold humour', and there was an extinction of the carnival fires of Europe.[78] The abrupt end to discussion of the carnival is unfounded and has become entrenched by the limited research into the Hapsburg Veneto. The exclusion of occupied Venice is a consequence of falling into what David Laven has called the 'teleological trap' – believing too readily the myths of Austrian oppression that have dominated post-*Risorgimento* history.[79] There was an obvious agenda for liberals such as Holland and Hobhouse, and Italian historians writing in a unified Italy, to mythologise Venice in chains, oppressed by tyrannical foreigners, but modern historians have questioned whether this was the case.[80] Work by Rath and Laven has shown that, although the Austrians perpetuated some of the unpopular policies of the Napoleonic administration (notably conscription), the new regime was largely viewed by Venetians as an improvement on French administration: some even welcomed the Hapsburgs as liberators.[81] As the earlier discussion of 'Euganean Hills' has shown, critics have been keen to imbibe these narratives of oppression and use them in readings of literature. One popular historian has rendered Venice as if it was Rosselini's *città aperta* – complete with lion statues defaced by imperial decree and triumphs of foreign rulers.[82]

The basis for this sensationalism is the fact that Venice was under new rulers; taxes were levied on a population suffering from a Europe-wide economic recession, its men were conscripted, and many Austrian officials took important governmental roles.[83] The administration was keen to enforce a level of cultural control, putting in place a system of prepublication censorship on books and periodicals, outlawing any attempts to criticise the emperor, and introducing a number of laws to maintain public order. These regulations would result in a complete ban on Byron's work in Italian translation and lead to the imprisonment of Venetian poets. Despite this, the Hapsburgs (unlike the French) did not stop the Carnival, though they did increase regulations on it.[84] The new government newspaper, the *Gazzetta Privilegiata di Venezia*, carried mostly court bulletins, highly generalised foreign news, and notices on commercial regulations. For the first carnival under Austrian control, the paper featured a 'Foglio D'Avviso', signed by chief of police Anton von Raab. Masks were deemed lawful for the period on five conditions: they were not worn on Sundays or around sacred places; no wearing of costumes or insignia which insulted religion or authority; no carrying of weapons; no starting of fracas or quarrels; and no public discussions with offensive allusions to religion or custom whilst masked.[85] For the Austrians the show could go on, but only on their terms.

The new Carnival was not the Carnival at its peak where patrician and peasant could dress in a monk's cassock, and violent skirmishes and debauchery were common on the day of the *grassa*. But this epoch offered its own intrigues. Just as Shelley had used a landscape view to see regeneration, so the Carnival was an opportunity to see the endurance of a spirit in a place seemingly at its nadir. Byron relishes this decadent Venice in a letter to Murray:

> I do not even dislike the evident decay of the city – though I regret the singularity of its vanished costume – however there is much left still; – the Carnival too is coming.[86]

The first two clauses offer the 'fallen Venice' which British periodicals and travel writing had written about since the end of the republic, but Byron inverts this in the same sentence. The magic of Venice's costume and disguise has not vanished without trace, and as if to justify this the prospect of the carnival looms. For Wordsworth, St Bartholomew's Fair was a 'spectacle' that set 'The whole creative powers of man asleep!', but for Byron it was a spur to creativity.[87] In the same letter, he tells his publisher, 'Venice pleases me as much as I expected – and I expected much – it is one of those places which I know before I see them'. Byron's acknowledgement reveals the self-awareness that underpins *Beppo*: he knows Venice has its own set of preconceptions and conventions, and promotes many of these characteristics of the carnivalesque in his correspondence. Nowhere is this more apparent than in response to scandal being spread about his love life:

> Which 'piece' does he mean? – since last year I have run the Gauntlet; – is it the Tarruscelli – the Da Mosti – the Spineda – the Lotti – the Rizzato – the Eleanora – the Carlotta – the Giulietta – the Alvisi – the Zambieri – The Eleanora da Bezzi – (who was the King of Naples' Gioaschino's mistress – at least one of them) the Theresina of Mazzurati – the Glettenheimer – & her Sister – the Luigia & her mother – the Fornaretta – the Santa – the

> Caligari – the Portiera Vedova – the Bolognese figurante – the Tentora and her sister – cum multis aliis? – some of them are Countesses – & some of them Cobblers wives – some noble – some middling – some low – & all whores.[88]

Now on his third Carnival, Byron revels in playing the game – running the gauntlet of keeping multiple women happy and retaining his own sexual health. The odd use of 'the' before the family names makes the women appear like bridges or *palazzi*, as if they are his markers around the Venetian labyrinth. The list recalls Bernard Beatty's comparison of Goethe's and Byron's first reactions to Venice: the German bought a map to try and know his way around the city but for Byron, Venice's labyrinthine quality acted as 'a beloved replacement of our habitually dull life'.[89] Venice's ability to break the rhythms of everyday life is clear, as the list goes on as if it was a catalogue aria: a parenthetical aside seems to give information, but then undercuts itself; the excess of sleeping with two sisters is intensified by the next claim to have slept with 'Lugia & her mother'; and the second rhetorical question hints at more partners not mentioned. The mixing of the Carnival is captured in the last clause that shows the range Venice facilitates. Garbriel Matzneff has viewed this flaunting of sexual activity as a symptom of Byron's decline:

> Devenu, à Venise, un personnage de carnaval, il traîne, il drague: des filles auxquelles il néglige de demander leur prénom, corps anonymes, masques sans visages, des amours de carton qui sont à l'amour ce que le placebo est au médicament. Rien ne lui importe plus.[90]

But from Byron's long list, it appears he asked and remembered the names of his lovers, and that he attached some importance to his skill in doing so. Byron describes his sexual exploits not to cast himself as a casual loiterer as Matzneff claims, but as someone seeking out and revelling in variety.

The Style Is Not English – It Is Italian

It was during his time at Venice that Byron found a poetic form to accommodate his cosmopolitan passions, and his new passion for the cosmopolitan. At the end of his first carnival, Byron sent Murray the dramatic poem *Manfred* (1817), calling it a work 'too much in my old style'.[91] *Manfred* represents the apotheosis of the poetry that produced the brooding sinners Selim and Conrad, gave Byron his European fame, and lined the pockets of his publisher. Some did not warmly receive any change to the introspective verse that Byron had written at Geneva; Hobhouse wrote to Murray in 1819 worried about the 'combustibles' in this new Venetian poetry and advised the removal of a number of stanzas in drafts that he viewed as beneath 'the author of Childe Harold'.[92] Hobhouse's concern reveals the schism *Beppo* represents, and the hold that the 'old' Byron had over the reading public. Byron redefined his poetic style during his time in the Veneto. He sent a letter to Murray in September 1817, less than a month before *Beppo* was written, in which he states that the poets of the day are 'upon a wrong revolutionary poetical system'.[93] Byron claims that he, and the poets he mentions (a list which interestingly does not include Hunt), were far behind Pope in 'sense – harmony – effect – and even *Imagination* Passion – & *Invention*'.[94] This change in Venice may have been inspired by rereading Pope, but he did not find its formal foundations in the 'Queen Anne's Man'.[95] The roots of Byron's redefinition lie in his Italian form, the ottava rima, and his cosmopolitan life in Venice. That Byron was beginning to think in this form is confirmed in a later letter to Hobhouse. He reports that he has decided not to visit Florence, but to take a trip south and gather information on the characters from Canto V of the *Inferno* – as Byron puts it, to 'give Leigh Hunt some Nimini pimini for his "Rimini"'.[96] Triple rhymes were also necessary in the Spenserian stanza, in which Byron had written thousands of lines in *Childe Harold,* but the comic incongruity of the word and sound is characteristic of his Italian model. The triple rhyme of the ottava comes to Byron effortlessly and signals the ease with which the form tallied with his thinking.

The new style can be seen in any excerpt from *Beppo*; the stanza quoted below follows a discussion of Italian Lenten food with some advice to English travellers.

> And therefore humbly I would recommend
> 'The curious in fishsauce,' before they cross
> The sea, to bid their cook, or wife, or friend,
> Walk or ride to the Strand, and buy in gross
> (Or if set out beforehand these may send
> By any means least liable to loss),
> Ketchup, Soy, Chili-vinegar, and Harvey,
> Or, by the Lord! a Lent will well nigh starve ye.
> (st. 8)

The stanza begins 'And therefore', tethering itself to the preceding stanza to create a narrative thrust which is much harder to achieve after the terminal alexandrine of a Spenserian. *Beppo* contains twice as many stanzas opening with conjunctions as *Childe Harold IV*, a fluency taken further in the enjambed stanzas of *Don Juan*.[97] These openings give the effect of improvisation, an Italian tradition enjoyed by the Count in *Beppo*, as if each new stanza were a reaction to the previous one, unplanned until that moment.[98] Conjunctions play a role in the rest of the stanza with five uses of 'or' showing a new dynamism, and the abundance of subjects and locations available. Drummond Bone has written beautifully about the 'register-shifting' produced by the alternatives in the middle of this stanza, praising the 'purely formal pleasure' of satire without any object.[99] The shifty cadence of the narrative voice is added to by the parenthetical aside and finally the list of condiments, which in its words of Chinese, Japanese, Spanish, and French origin seems to contain the whole world. The stanza concludes with a pun on Harvey, the name of a popular fish sauce and close to the clergyman James Hervey previously lampooned by Byron, which in the context of Lent makes the two-word rhyme on 'starve ye' all the more scurrilous.[100] But this stanza has another trick up its sleeve. It has been assumed that the 'The curious in fish-sauce' is a quotation from an advertisement, and Byron's habit of bringing in other voices will later allow for dialogue and quotation in foreign languages to be accommodated into one polyphonic stanza. But the advertising slogan, which Byron mentions again in a letter of 1821, has not been identified.[101] The quotation is from an advert for John Burgess's 'Italian Warehouse' on the Strand that appeared from 1790 to 1820 in London daily newspapers, including the *Argus*, *London World*, *London Age*, *Morning Post*, and *True Briton* (an 'Italian Warehouse' was a term for grocers selling continental goods). The advert is split into sections beginning 'To the CURIOUS in' followed by a list of various types of a given product. The first section of the advert was always 'To the CURIOUS in FISH SAUCE', and began by stating 'J. Burgess begs leave to acquaint the Nobility and Gentry [. . .]', before listing sauces such as 'HARVEY'S', 'JAPAN SOY', and 'CHILLY VINEGAR'.[102] Knowing the source of the quotation, as contemporary readers would, makes the whole stanza a pastiche of an advertisement for Burgess – with 'therefore humbly I would recommend', the quotation of the slogan, and the list of condiments, all mirroring the structure of the original. By enabling a conversational quality that Spenserians precluded (but still retaining that stanza's musicality) the playful patterning of ottava rima gave Byron a new way of comically exalting the quotidian.

The haphazard and digressive quality of the fish sauce stanza is typical of the whole: only forty of ninety-nine stanzas in *Beppo* refer to the plot, which does not begin until the twenty-first stanza. A poem variously subtitled 'A Venetian Tale' and 'A Story', *Beppo* is as much concerned with quizzing digressions on the differences between England and Italy as it is with its narrative. Even during the story all is at play, as when the heroine is introduced, 'Her real name I know not, nor can guess, / And so we'll call her Laura, if you please, / Because it slips into my verse with ease' (st. 21). The indeterminacy in asking cook, wife, or friend, for fish-sauce, is again the case in naming our heroine, who we do not know, and cannot guess the name of, so decide on Laura. The prolix routine calls attention to a digressive style and cracks a literary joke, as Petrarch's famous muse is relegated to a metrical convenience. At a stroke, Byron rejects the spiritual canon of Dante and Petrarch, for a future largely preoccupied with the more demotic ottava rima works of Casti, Buratti, and later Pulci.[103] But while Bone is right to claim that this satire has no direct target, and is quite unlike the ad hominem attacks of *English Bards*, there is a common purpose to both these digressions from the narrative and the narrative itself. What the digressions at the level of the line and the stanza share with the plot of *Beppo* is a love of variety; the multiple voices, conjunctions, and interruptions are a partner to the narrator's cosmopolitan eye. Laura enters the Ridotto and 'To some she whispers, others speaks aloud; / To some she curtsies, and to some she dips' (st. 65), before 'She then surveys' seven different hairstyles in some detail. The appreciation of difference is a prelude to Laura's questions at the tale's dénouement. The smutty suggestion of Laura asking Beppo '"And are you, *really*, *truly*, now a Turk?"' (st. 92) has beneath it the poem's love of cosmopolitan freedom.

John Hookham Frere's 1817 poem *Whistlecraft* has been viewed as the inspiration for Byron's Venetian transformation.[104] Byron's comment to Murray that his tale was written 'in or after the excellent manner of Mr. Whistlecraft', has meant Frere's work is viewed as the key precursor to *Beppo*.[105] Andrew Rutherford has claimed that *Whistlecraft* 'transformed [Byron's] satirical technique', and in a recent essay Catherine Addison argued that Frere's work had an 'electrifying effect on Byron's creativity'.[106] Before examining the differences between the two poems, it is important to qualify Byron's statement to Murray about the 'manner of Mr. Whistlecraft'. Byron is writing to his publisher about *Beppo*, a poem that is the near-antithesis of his earlier style and that contained a politically incendiary commentary on Britain. By binding *Beppo* to Frere, a respectable Tory scholar and Murray's close friend, Byron conceals his upbraiding of British culture. There are similarities between *Beppo* and *Whistlecraft*. The capacity of English, with its lack of feminine rhymes, for incongruous and double-word rhymes is first used by Frere, whose couplets rhyme 'Mount Parnassus, / surpass us' and 'encumber'd / outnumber'd'. Frere also displays the same abundant listing as Byron, particularly in the culinary banquet at the opening of the first canto. But there are two qualifications to this apparent influence. First, as Albert Eichler has shown, Byron took these effects much further than did Frere.[107] Secondly, the origin of these traits in *Whistlecraft* is Italian: in a letter to Foscolo, whom Frere regularly asked for advice, he explains that *Whistlecraft* originated in reading extracts of Pulci in Ginguené's *Histoire*.[108]

The limitations of Frere's reading in the Italian tradition, and its second-hand nature, reveal why *Beppo* is a more comprehensively Italian poem. Frere learnt his ottava rima from reading Ginguené and from conversations with Foscolo, whereas Byron was living in a culture where this poetry was read and performed, and as Phillip Martin has argued, 'the impressions he received of Italian literature almost certainly filtered primarily through these living, oral contexts where poetry was offered as an entertainment'.[109] In addition to these oral contexts, *Whistlecraft* was not Byron's introduction to the 'manner' of the ottava rima on the page: he had written to Murray a month before reading *Whistlecraft*, discussing the octave 'measure'; he knew Casti's *Le novelle galanti* (1804) almost 'by heart'; and, if Stendhal is to be believed, had read the works of the Venetian satirist Buratti in October 1816.[110] Quite unlike Casti or Buratti, who were respectively exiled and imprisoned for their poetry, Frere was a member of the establishment who had been an admiral in the Peninsula Wars, and was involved in the foundation of the *Anti-Jacobin*. He was a friend of Scott, a friendship that left its mark on *Whistlecraft* as Frere justifies his Arthurian subject by the popularity of '*Madoc* and *Marmion*, and many more'.[111] Furthermore, the themes of the poem (its comparison of Launcelot to Wellington, for example), see Frere keeping up Scott's habit of making parallels between the individual hero of the romance tradition and the men of recent British victories.[112] The Scottian comparison illustrates the most obvious difference between the poems: *Beppo* is not a romance but a tale based on an anecdote from Venetian life. Byron discusses the current manners of a foreign society as his work eschews the British national past of Scott and Frere. The difference in mode affects the satire of the poems: Frere's pioneering form frames a mild lampoon on Arthurian legend where Byron uses the ottava rima for a tale of his new home and acid comments about British society. The immediacy of Byron's digressive jest is aided by the dynamism of the ottava rima, but Frere's style contains little speech or quotation, and often uses conventional romance techniques.[113] Even in digressions, something both poems share, we see a difference:

We must take care in our poetic cruise,
  And never hold a single tack too long;
Therefore my versatile ingenious Muse
  Takes leave of this illiterate, low-bred throng,
Intending to present superior views,
  Which to genteeler company belong,
And show the higher orders of society
Behaving with politeness and propriety.[114]

Although Frere shares Byron's apologetic tone, he does return to his narrative after his apology, where in *Beppo* these are mock-apologies and attempts to return to the narrative only lead to further digression.[115] Frere's tone is casual, a 'poetic cruise' of regular rhymes, but there is a certain formality in the largely end-stopped lines without the multiple caesurae of *Beppo*. The diction has none of Byron's range, from the rag fair to the last Pleiades, nor does the steady narration of Mr. Whistlecraft feature the polyphonous effects of *Beppo*. The differences between the two poems were reflected in their differing popularity: Murray wrote to Byron 'of *Beppo* I have sold Six times that [*Whistlecraft's*] quantity in a Sixth part of the time & before indeed it is generally known to be yours'.[116] For Southey, the difference between them was discernible beyond profits: *Whistlecraft* was 'too inoffensive to become popular; for it attacked nothing and nobody', whereas Byron's satires constituted 'an act of high treason on English poetry'.[117]

To form the style that the poet laureate judged as treasonable Byron looked to contemporary Italian satire – particularly the work of Casti. As discussed in Chapter 1, Da Ponte published *Gli animali parlanti* in London, and Casti also wrote two ottava rima poems: *Il poema tartaro* and *Le novelle galanti*. Byron had read the latter thoroughly before writing *Beppo*, and Casti's mocking tone is a clear influence on *Beppo*. The polite reaction to Casti has been harsh: Parini called him a 'dishonest and provocative satyr' and his *novelle* a 'polluted and lewd poem', and one modern critic has claimed '[Casti's] satire is not tempered by any moral purpose or by a zest to stir the imagination of men to nobler ideals'.[118] There has been critical acknowledgement that Casti's *novelle* influenced *Beppo* and *Don Juan* I–II, with Vassallo perceptively arguing they were a greater influence than Frere. But these arguments have been preoccupied with seeking out similarities in the stories themselves, with Vassallo going as far as to argue for 'plagiarism of plot' by Byron.[119] That there are similarities between the love triangles of Beppo, the Count, and Laura, and Don Juan, Don Alfonso, and Donna Julia is unsurprising: Casti's tales (themselves heavily reliant on Boccaccio) have the exploration of female chastity as one of their unifying themes. But over and above any narrative parallels it was the style and digressive tone of the *novelle* that influenced Byron. It is this style that Casti identifies in a prefatory stanza:

> Io so ben che lo stil delle novelle,
> Esser libero dee, gaio ed ameno,
> Ma trattar certe cose in pelle in pelle
> Conviensi, e porre alla licenza un freno,
> Nè offendervi le orecchie, o donne belle,
> Con termin grossolani, o tuono osceno,
> Tutto si può spiegar, tutto dir lice:
> Ma bisogna veder come si dice.[120]

It is this easy satirical tone that inspired Byron, created by the alliterative progression from 'libero' and 'licenza' on rhyming lines, the use of irregular punctuation, and the colloquial phrase 'in pelle in pelle'. As Byron chides himself for digression only to carry on digressing, Casti proclaims knowledge of his chosen style, observing the dangers of the demotic and invoking the beautiful women he won't offend, as the introduction to ribald and lewd tales. Byron announces in *Beppo* that he 'hates an author that's *all author*', and in Casti he found someone who knew how to puncture what is expected of a poet.[121]

Buratti was producing ottava rima poetry in Venice during Byron's residence and is possibly a further influence on *Beppo*. The claim for influence is speculative as we do not know whether Byron read Buratti, although Stendhal claims Byron did, and his friend Richard Belgrave Hoppner mentions the poet in a letter to him.[122] Nonetheless, an examination of Buratti's work is of interest: these satires show that in the Venetian culture of 1817–1819, a culture of which Byron was a part, ottava rima poetry was a favoured form in which to question contemporary social mores. Indeed, this type of poetry was also performed live: as Peter Cochran has shown, Buratti's satire was read aloud in the Venetian café society that Byron frequented.[123] Buratti grew up during the fall of the Republic and was a vocal member of the Venetian literati: he wrote an acerbic satire of French occupation under the title *Lamentazione al Prefetto di Venezia* (1812) and was imprisoned by the Austrian censor for his satire *L'Elefanteide* (1819). In this 1819 work numerous similarities in style between the two poets are evident. Quite unlike the chivalric rhymes of Frere, Buratti's satire is a tale of an escaped Elephant terrorising contemporary Venice, a city he mentions that is controlled by a censor and a mouthpiece, the *Gazzetta.* The resemblance is not perfect: Buratti's tale of a defecating and masturbating Elephant chased by feeble Imperial guards is far cruder than the worst of *Beppo* or *Don Juan*. Cochran has claimed that Byron only read contemporary Italian ottava poetry 'with a view to estimating what extremes to avoid', and as far as plot goes he is probably right.[124] But Buratti, like Casti, was a stylistic influence; the *Elefanteide* features jokes on the epic, digressive refrains, and reported dialogue, all of which are integral to Byron's Italianate poetry.[125] A parallel between the style of the contemporary Venetian and Byron can be seen in one particular technique shown here:

Cussi el puto nei ziri ingambarà
(E pur tanta superbia ghe xè in nù)
De quel nervo proposide chiamà
S' à visto molte volte andar zo e sù
Da L'Elefante in aria sbalotà,
Che dopo averse divertio de lù
(Per sie soldie comprar se pol la stampa)
El se l' à calumà soto una zampa.[126]

Buratti uses parentheses twice in the stanza: the first is a relatively typical narrative refrain pitying the child, but the second seems very Byronic. Almost like the slogan for fish-sauce, the narrator seems to be advertising, even giving the price, for the tragic tableau presented to the reader. With this intervention, the fate of the young boy is delayed and trivialised, and the focus shifted from his death to the forms art uses to represent it. The tone is now comic, as the only hope of tragedy is swiftly deflated in the strong couplet rhyme of 'la stampa' and 'una zampa'. The freedom to manipulate tone within the Italian stanza, particularly to make tragic events bathetic would become a hallmark of *Don Juan*, as pathetic episodes during the shipwreck or the Siege of Ismail are undercut in a witty line, or when we are given no time to grieve the dead highwayman due to the brilliance of 'But Tom's no more – and so no more of Tom'.[127]

When Casti, Buratti, and Frere are compared, it seems beyond doubt that the style of *Beppo* has its strongest origins in Italian verse. It could be that Byron does not mention these poets because of their perceived vulgarity, or because he lacked the confidence at this juncture to tie himself completely to relatively unknown Italian poets. But it was this tradition into which Byron was being placed by Foscolo, who in his 'Narrative Poems' essay discusses *Beppo* as a fit example of Italian ottava poetry.[128] When he was thinking about *Don Juan* at Venice in the second half of 1818, Byron was prepared to claim that 'the style is not English – it is Italian' and to call his new poem one 'in the style and manner of

"Beppo", encouraged by the good success of the same'.[129] By 1820, with *Don Juan* well under way, Byron would tell Murray, 'As to puffing *Whistlecraft – it won't do*', hinting that Frere's stanzas were laboured when judged against the ottava rima tradition. Perhaps Byron's later grounding in the more respectable Renaissance poetry of Berni and Pulci steeled him to announce the Italian formal source of his 'Human Epic'.

Byron's Italian formal preference is matched by the content of *Beppo*, which extols Venetian life over that of Regency London. The third and fourth stanzas go into great detail about the 'dresses, splendid but fantastical, / Masks of all times and nations' present at the Carnival, and these merits, freedoms, and novelties of Venetian culture are satirically compared to British life. Byron chooses the centre of the poem for this sustained comparison, which begins in the discussion of climate in stanzas 41 and 42. The fairer weather in Venice is linked to greater freedom: in nature with 'vines (not nail'd to walls)', but also for Byron himself to 'ride out' without being worried by rain. Stanza 42 uses the structure of the ottava rima to compare his old and new homes. Byron makes the terminal couplet a volta in which to turn the last six lines of praise on Italy into a comparison with rejected Britain. This structured juxtaposition continues into the next two stanzas with Byron's long list of likes. The effect of the list is to suggest that Byron could go on and on, not just improvising on Italy but, as became clear in *Don Juan*, that the poem itself is open to continual expansion. Each stanza begins in praise of Italy (its food, climate, language, and women) and turns in its couplet to Britain. Byron opens his list in stanza 43, 'I also like to dine on becaficas / To see the Sun set, sure he'll rise tomorrow'. As well as showing his ability to compare great things with small, Bryon's pleasure in eating songbirds shows the importance of food as a marker of cultural difference, a point made by William Rose, one of the friends Byron made in Venice. In his *Letters from the North of Italy* (1819), Rose notes that 'the customs of the kitchen are amongst the most permanent of national habits', and goes on to discuss the Italian preference for small birds which are 'rejected' in Britain.[130] Indeed, one English traveller in 1825 was disgusted to see beccafichi on a Livornese dinner table.[131] Byron's pleasure in these un-English tastes is partnered by the sibilance of the 'Sun set, sure' and its subsequent rise in a 'cloudless' sky, to convey his preference for the sensations of Italy. The section shares with 'Euganean Hills' the ability to see in everyday differences a better future for the exile, away from 'reeking London's smoky Cauldron'. It also shares Shelley's view that modern Venice, and more broadly Italy, is still a current cultural inspiration: in *Beppo* the 'the land which still is Paradise', a creative place quite apart from the 'dogeless city's vanish'd sway' of *Childe Harold IV*.[132] In the next two stanzas, Byron's gaze moves to Britain. Here he goes further than 'Euganean Hills' into a fluent comic mode that influenced 'Peter Bell the Third'.[133] The extended anaphora on British life begins with a quotation from Cowper, '"England! with all thy faults I love thee still!" / I said at Calais, and have not forgot it'. He may not have forgotten this line from *The Task*, but the lines that follow reject its sentiment.[134] The rejection comes through negation: he can present an apparent benefit of his homeland, to contradict it in an aside in the same line, as in 'I like the government (but that is not it)' and its corresponding line on habeas corpus. Byron's mock-praise is built up with the nine repetitions of 'I like' to the final exclamation of 'God save the Regent, Church, and King!' – the chant of crowds at the Gordon Riots and a call of the anti-Jacobin press.[135] At the centre of his first ottava rima poem, Byron begins his praise of the Italian everyday in sharp contrast to the British status quo that is undercuts by comic exposition. These ten stanzas mark the beginning of a new type of satire; a satire that aimed to confront British hegemony in a manner many reviewers saw as dangerous.

We Dread an Amalgamation with the Continent

The reception of *Beppo* is a useful starting point for a discussion of what made Byron's satire so different, and why it was deemed a threat to the public mind. The chapter will then conclude by examining why Byron's and Shelley's self-fashioning as exiles aided their attacks on English cant. The *Edinburgh* called *Beppo* a work 'which our English literature has hitherto afforded very few examples' and enjoyed it as a 'piece of lively and loquacious prattling'.[136] For the *Edinburgh,* the cosmopolitan novelty and abundance of *Beppo* were the reasons for its success, but these traits made it a work of 'immorality' for conservative periodicals.[137] The *British Review* responded to Byron's satire by reproducing their criticism of *Rimini,* in which they had castigated 'Mr Hunt's levelling doctrines in poetic composition'. *Beppo* was a 'new entertainment [...] rising fast in fashion and favour in the country', which in style was 'not much unlike that which in the political world, is called the levelling principal'.[138] The 'restless pursuit' of Byron's quizzing style brings out the same defence of the public mind that was seen in the reaction against *Rimini* and *Parisina*; it was a trend to be watched by 'those who exercise any guardianship over the morals of the community'.[139] As the article progresses, the reviewer moves from censure of *Beppo* to rebuke 'Lord Byron, an English nobleman, an English husband, and an English father' for sending a work 'reeking from the stews of Venice'.[140] Byron, not only an Englishman but also an aristocrat, is accused of spreading a corrupt alien form into British culture. The reviewer goes on to rehash earlier rhetoric against foreigners:

> We dread an amalgamation with the Continent; we feel quite persuaded that our nationality and our morality have so long mutually upheld each other that they cannot be separated without mutual injury.[141]

An argument based on national manners is used to define ideas geographically, and sees continental influences as a threat to 'our nationality'. The language in this 1819 review harkens back to the 1790s, to the pages of the *Anti-Jacobin* or the *British Critic*. During the revolutionary decade, the conservative press was not concerned per se with the violence in France but feared the possibility of the revolutionary contagion being exported to Britain. To counter the possible spread of these foreign ideas, the Pitt government increased anti-radical legislation and its supporters in the periodical press attacked Jacobinism.

When considering *Beppo*, and the reaction against, it must be remembered that satire was the predominant form used to attack cultural Jacobinism. In the company of Pitt the Younger at 169 Piccadilly, Frere, Gifford, and Mathias would draft editions of the *Anti-Jacobin* that strenuously maintained Church-and-King values in literary reviews and satirical verse. Gifford made his name savaging the Della Cruscans as poets who 'cherish Arno and his flux of song' rather than British forms and traditions, and inspired Mathias to write *The Pursuits of Literature,* which ran to fourteen editions by 1808.[142] The satire was Popean, its politics orthodox, and its targets individuals whose actions went against the status quo. Mathias explains in an 'Introductory Letter' to *The Pursuits* what he saw as the purpose of this poetry. 'Satire is an instrument, and a powerful instrument, to maintain and enforce public order, morality religion, literature, and good manners'.[143] Satire was a vehicle used to defend the state and preserve the 'public mind', it was a prop used to pursue what Mathias called 'lawful war' against the enemies of the state.[144] This satiric mode is not the Romantic satire studied today, not the world of William Hone's caricatures and *Don Juan*: as Gary Dyer has argued, it requires a great leap of the historical imagination to understand that the satire we now read is untypical in both form and approach for the dominant strain of the age.[145] Satiric reactions to *Beppo* penned between 1818 and 1819 support Dyer's argument, and show that the mode of Mathias and Gifford was still the tradition. The most pointed verse attack on *Beppo* takes the form of a satire in regular couplets written from Cambridge, which condemns Byron's as a 'Degenerate Son', and castigates his new style that prefers 'The pause – the gap – the interrupted line, / Which fancy cannot fill, nor reason join'.[146] The form tallies with 1790s satire, as do the explanatory notes at the foot of each page that cite Scott, Mathias, and Gifford. The anonymous author directly addresses Byron's dissent:

For to write satire is a bold pretence
To learning, judgment, wit, refinement, sense;
Not venom'd spite, and vulgar insolence;
Good satire is of a politer school.[147]

As he discusses at the centre of *Beppo*, Byron is writing in an era that featured the same suspension of habeas corpus and press controls as the revolutionary epoch policed by Mathias and Gifford.[148] From Venice, a place where he had redefined his own poetic style, Byron choose to redefine the purpose of satire from 'lawful' to – as Southey suggests – treasonable war. Byron's challenge to a conservative genre, which had asserted some control over the public mind, is part of a wider articulation of Italian ideas that aimed to overturn existing conventions in *Rimini*, 'Euganean Hills', and *Beppo*. For their radical critique of English society and culture to be effective, and to grow into the later productions of the Pisan circle, the group needed the freedom of Italy. To gain this freedom, the exiles do something quite odd. Byron and Shelley regularly claim in correspondence and verse to be no longer interested in England and its politics. Shelley's claim at the opening of 'The Mask of Anarchy' to be 'asleep in Italy' is an example of a trait that finds its clearest expression in the claim in 'A Defence of Poetry' that 'a Poet is a nightingale who sits in darkness, and sings to cheer its own solitude with sweet sounds'.[149] In Byron's correspondence, this develops into a hermitic pose, which has him claim that, 'There are no English here [Venice] at present', 'There are no English here', 'of England I know nothing – hear nothing (never looking into a paper foreign or Italian) and desire to hear nothing', '"English gentlemen" are very rare – at least in Venice – I doubt whether there are at present any'.[150] It was an attitude noticed by one traveller, an English Divinity tutor, who passed Byron's villa on Lake Geneva when the Shelleys and Claire Clairmont were nearby, and who concluded, 'Lord Byron lives, in a sullen and disgraceful seclusion. Besides his servants, his only companions are two wicked women. He sees no company'.[151]

From these public statements critics have argued, as they have in readings of 'Euganean Hills', that verse about post-Waterloo Italy, and specifically

Venice, is meditative and introverted. Joseph Luzzi claims Shelley and Byron saw 'an Italy without Italians' which they used 'as a backdrop for solitary meditation'.[152] Tony Tanner views Byron in Venice as

> a man without a home, a party, a country; he had given up on politics as he had given up on family and England (he specifically asks not to have any political news from England, adding that he reads neither English nor Italian newspapers).[153]

But Tanner and Luzzi have been duped by the exiles' claims to 'know nothing – hear nothing', which are truly only a mask.[154] Byron is protesting too much in his articulations about ignoring England and the English: he certainly had not 'given up' on home. Byron wrote to Douglas Kinnaird, praising his 'popular eloquence & speech', which he read in 'the Italian Gazettes'; he complained to Murray about Caroline Lamb's *Glenarvon* (1816), which he had read about in 'the Venice papers'; and wrote to Murray about rumours spread by Henry Brougham concerning his separation.[155] In a letter to Hobhouse, Byron claims, 'I saw your late Speech in Galignani's newspaper', which shows he was reading *Galignani's Messenger*, a tri-weekly and later daily summary of English-language newspapers and international news distributed on the Continent, which avoided expensive English stamp duties.[156] Jane Stabler has shown that a number of the most famous incidents in *Don Juan* seemed to have been sparked by news reported in *Galignani*, and Byron's and Shelley's later comments and poetry about the trial of Queen Caroline were only possible through information garnered from sources of English news available in Italy.[157] Shelley's attachment to his homeland can be traced in Mary Shelley's journal, which regularly mentions the *Edinburgh*; his correspondence also shows an arrangement with Thomas Love Peacock to receive clipped editions of the *Examiner*, and he shared copies of the *Quarterly* with Byron.[158] Furthermore, the poets' own claims to have encountered no English are untrue. There were many English visitors in Venice during this period: a random month-long sample of the *Arrivi in Venezia* column of the *Gazzetta* in 1817 shows a dozen English men arriving, including a member of Parliament and a peer.[159] For the period as a whole, the English, apart from Italians and Austrians, are the most frequent visitors. As Rose noted of Venice, 'Here, all foreigners are well received; but, to be an Englishman, is to bring with you a sure letter of recommendation'.[160] Byron and Shelley did not avoid this prominent community; on the contrary they made friends within it, with the Venetian consul Richard Belgrave Hoppner, with John and Maria Gisborne, and with Rose himself.

What was the purpose of these masks? They gave the poets the appearance of exclusivity: to be in Italy without the English, and writing English poetry from a foreign window. Their freedom allowed for a different 'revolutionary poetical system', built around an Anglo-Italian grouping with a deep interest in Italian literature. As Cox has discussed, readings of poetry in this period need to be recalibrated to appreciate the power of groups 'as a means of cultural production and also as a site of opposition'.[161] Groups need not be based around a communal living space as in Pisa, or a meeting place like Holland House. They can be larger networks of shared interests, in this case exiles in both London and Italy who shared a realisation of the radical potential of Italy and its literature. Shelley was beginning to think of a sympathetic set of readers not defined by geographical location, like earlier communal circles at Marlow or the Villa Diodati. He wrote to his publisher Charles Ollier and asked for a copy of all his published work to be sent to 'Mr Hunt Godwin Hogg Peacock Keats Thos. Moore Hor. Smith Lord Byron'.[162] Hunt starts this list and there were plans for the editor of the *Examiner* to visit Venice, with Shelley telling him that Byron 'wished you would come to Italy & bade me tell you that he would lend you money for the journey'.[163] What the three would do in Venice is unclear, but in a 1818 letter Byron had presciently hinted at their future collaboration on the *Liberal*: 'an English newspaper here would be a prodigy, and an opposition one a monster'.[164] Byron's redefinition was born in Venice, and it cut already frayed ties between him and the conservative defenders of British culture. Shelley's political verse would likewise mature into a sustained attack on the stifling morality he saw in Britain. Yet this verse was not entirely alienated from or alienating to Regency readers; it aligned itself with a growing taste for Italian literature critically appreciated by Foscolo and Buonaiuti, and with wider Italian cultural forms reviewed by Hazlitt and Hunt. The poets' links to this wider cultural phenomenon allowed for the formation of network bound by Italian forms and an increasing disaffection with the Lake Poets. The Veneto is a refuge for Shelley in 'Euganean Hills', but it also gave him space to mock the political shift of the 'beastly and pitiful wretch that Wordsworth', and in 'Peter Bell the Third' he could parody the deeper egotistical turn in his verse.[165] What little notice Shelley's poetry had garnered in the British press before 1818 was predominantly scornful, and in 'Peter Bell the Third' he took aim at the periodicals for their attacks on Wordsworth, which he thought were partly to blame for the elder poet's decline. In a curious repurposing of the *Frankenstein* problematic, the satiric question at the centre of 'Peter

Bell the Third' is whether Wordsworth was attacked by the press because he was egotistically monstrous, or whether he became so because of these attacks. Likewise, Byron's satirical gaze became increasingly focused on the Lake School and its apostasy, reserving his greatest scorn for Southey. The growing fissure between the two schools of so-called Romantic poetry is comparable to the division during the 1790s between Radicals and Anti-Jacobins, and it is no coincidence that from 1819 to 1821, when this split intensified, Britain came closest to its own revolution.[166] Venice, thanks to its peculiar historical situation, nurtured this rejection of British cultural politics, with Italy becoming a paradisal simulacrum and literary resource. Here there was the freedom of a signifier written into cliché over the previous hundred years, ripe for redefinition by poets aware of its visual and festive traditions. At home, Italy and Italians were about to be discussed on the front pages of every major newspaper: Queen Caroline was set to return from her long exile in Italy and turn London into a radical carnival for the summer of 1820.

CHAPTER 5

London and Naples, 1819–1821
An Almost Revolutionary Queen

> Do you recollect the eye of that hoary pander from Trieste? Did he not look, as the great poet of Italy describes the hoary letcher in the infernal regions to have looked, when he says that he regarded him with the eye, the gloating eye of an ancient tailor peeping through the eye of his needle?
>
> **Henry Brougham to the House of Lords, 1820**

So far, this study has highlighted the growing interest radical and liberal writers showed in Italian literature in the aftermath of Waterloo. The work of exiled Italians in London and British writers in Italy played a significant role in intensifying the Regency's fascination with Italy and Italian culture. These writers' interest in Italian ideas flourished beside other interactions taking place in London, such as the promotion of Italian literature in the lectures of Hazlitt and Coleridge. In the first of his lectures on the English poets, Hazlitt claimed that Boccaccio, alongside Bunyan and Defoe, was the closest that prose had to the 'essence and the power of poetry', and that Dante was 'the father of modern poetry'.[1] Coleridge gave thorough consideration to Ariosto, Tasso, and Boccaccio in the third of his 1818 lectures on European literature and devoted the tenth lecture of this series to Dante. Coleridge gave another lecture on Dante in a series at the Crown and Anchor in 1819, calling him 'picturesque beyond all, modern or ancient'.[2] The lecture promoted Henry Cary's 1814 translation *The Vision of Dante Alighieri*, which, with the help of a positive appraisal by Foscolo, was given a second edition in 1819.[3] The *Commedia* was now available to thousands of English readers. Listening audiences were also offered new experiences: at the King's Theatre, the Italian opera came under the control of Leigh Hunt's friend William Ayrton, who reformed its baroque and Metastasian repertoire to belatedly bring Mozart's and Da Ponte's *Don Giovanni* (1787) and the works of Rossini to London. In urban architecture the Italophile John Nash was growing in prominence thanks to the patronage of the Prince Regent. Nash took the Palladian style he had developed at Sandridge Park and created, from Piccadilly to Regent's Park, the Italianate London we know today.

The importance of Italian culture to the metropolitan radicalism that flourished between Waterloo and Peterloo can be seen in Leigh Hunt's 1819 publication *The Literary Pocket Book*. The book is a diary and London directory for 'the Lover of Nature and Art' and features poetry by Keats and Shelley.[4] It opens with the claim that:

> The intellectual power of society indeed has so much increased of late, and has become so prominent, as one of the ruling or controuling [*sic*] authorities, that it seems proper and necessary it should have a sort of Court Calendar of its own.[5]

The new 'intellectual power' of society described by Hunt is an equal to the official calendar that governs the operation of state. Hunt sees a reformist metropolitan public as an alternative hegemony to rival established forms of state power. The public Hunt describes was central to the radical actions of the period 1819–1821 and found its voice through print and protest: as one pamphlet would put it in 1820, '*Vox Populi* now is *Vox Dei* we know, / As the progress of intellect serveth show'.[6] Alongside its claim for an increased public role in society, the *Pocket Book* is also notable for its promotion of Italian culture. The diary includes twenty-two famous birthdays, eight of which are foreign; seven of these (Ariosto, Michelangelo, Petrarch, Poliziano, Pulci, Raphael, and Tasso) are Italian. In the same manner as the decorative choices at Holland House, Hunt is attempting to make a clear connection between his work and the politically involved authors of the Italian Renaissance. But the scope of the *Pocket Book* is not confined to canonical figures: modern Italians appear regularly in the lists of eminent authors, artists, and musicians 'native and foreign'; furthermore, they feature heavily in the London directory of musical performers, teachers, and language instructors, including the publisher, translator, and former secretary of Alfieri, Gaetano Polidori. Any group aspiring to supplant the existing hegemony must do more than simply protest on the streets, oppose the status quo in print, or engage with controversial literature. Hunt realises this: to be effective, a counter-hegemony must offer alternative praxes (the methods of bringing ideas to a practical application in life). The *Pocket Book* may seem only an organizer and diary, but it offers a new practical method of living life through radical ideas of history, literature, and cosmopolitanism, and attempts to instil a consciousness in its readers of being part of a new culture.

In a movement related to the increasing power of 'society' claimed by Hunt, the previously dilettantish interest in Italian language and culture was now expanding its influence among a burgeoning middle class. Thanks in part to an active migrant community, manifold cultural forms were becoming Italianate, and Italian became a widely available form of expression: a leader in Hunt's *Examiner* called it a language 'so much cultivated now-a-days'.[7] By examining the growth of a metropolitan culture that goes beyond patrician boundaries I am opposing E. P. Thompson's dichotomy of the 'Theatre of state' and the 'counter-theatre' of radicalism that has been used to describe post-Waterloo England.[8] This chapter in particular, and the study in general, takes the view outlined in the *Pocket Book*: this period witnessed far greater challenges to hegemony than Thompson's split between a patrician society and a plebeian culture supposes. It was a period in which landscapes of Italy in the manner of J. M. W. Turner and Joseph Wright of Derby could be found in the Panorama on the Strand for pennies; when the radical weekly *Examiner* carried a column on Italian opera; and when broadside satires and caricatures played on the multiple meanings of Italian phrases. I instead see a split between two antagonistic cultural blocs: the hegemony of the state and a developing counter-hegemony. From 1819 to 1821 this alternative bloc was formed of politicians, intellectuals, poets, and publishers, and had almost the requisite mixture of class identities to succeed.[9]

If two blocs did exist, then at the time of Caroline of Brunswick's return to England from Italy a counter-hegemony was as close to overthrowing an established culture as it had ever been. It was an arrival that brought people to the streets, drew special attention to international issues in a way that Peterloo and the Cato Street Conspiracy could not, and put Italians and their culture under scrutiny. The role of all things Italian in London life was substantially altered by Queen Caroline's landing at Dover, and her subsequent trial in the House of Lords.[10] The ascendancy of Italian literature and culture was challenged by these two events. Some Britons reverted to seeing Italians as pernicious and unreliable, as they were believed to be during the 1790s, while others saw them as a people struggling for freedom at Naples. That both of these strands had revolutionary implications is significant; as Thompson has observed, opposition groups did not 'look forward complacently to 1832 and all that; it was more natural in 1819, when two incompatible social forces confronted each other, to remember 1789'.[11] With the Queen dead and the Neapolitan Revolution quelled in 1821, the dominant feeling within these groups changed to failure. The artistic engagement with the disappointment of liberals and radicals across Europe to form a new hegemony is explored in the next chapter.

This chapter is divided between an analysis of the very different reactions to Italians in London and in Naples. The geopolitical scale of the Queen's trial and the Neapolitan revolution allows for an analysis across the spectrum of opposition politics, from radicals such as Alderman Wood and William Cobbett, to the Holland House Whigs Earl Grey and Sir James Mackintosh. The two men that link these disparate groups are Henry Brougham and Leigh Hunt. Brougham was a founder of the *Edinburgh Review* and the head of Queen Caroline's defence. Hunt's politics were too democratic for Holland House, and Brougham was not radical enough for Cobbett or Wood, but the two men were sufficiently close to link the groups. They knew one another: Brougham was Hunt's lawyer when he was prosecuted for libelling the Regent in 1812 and visited him in his Italianate prison cell; Hunt wrote to Brougham before leaving for Italy at the end of 1821, and after Brougham was made Lord Chancellor in 1830, John Hunt wrote to his brother claiming 'you have certainly contributed to his fame'.[12] The chapter begins by looking at responses to Queen Caroline's arrival, including Shelley's satirical tragedy *Oedipus Tyrannus; or, Swellfoot the Tyrant* (1820). It then moves to a close reading of certain moments in the House of Lords proceedings, and finally considers the manifold responses to the case and the effect these had on public attitudes to the Neapolitan Revolution. The chapter analyses the pervasive effect that the Queen's return had on the idea of Italians in visual culture, parliamentary debate, opera, verse satire, and periodical literature.

In the People's Bosom

Caroline Elizabeth Amelia of Brunswick-Wolfenbüttel married the Prince of Wales, later George IV, in April 1795. Their marriage was in trouble from the outset. The pair lived apart from 1797 and rumours of affairs were the constant talk of society. The public was more sympathetic to the Princess than to the Prince, who was seen as a pleasure-seeking glutton; he regularly went to the opera at the King's Theatre with Mrs. Maria Fitzherbert or the Countess of Jersey (Frances Villiers), both known to be his mistresses. Caroline also regularly attended the Italian opera, and on one occasion, during a particular period of bitterness in the marriage, she was greeted with applause and huzzahs by the pit – a premonition of the support she would enjoy during her trial.[13] The increasingly difficult relationship between Prince and Princess led to a secret government attempt in 1806 to prove Caroline's infidelities and grant George a separation. The so-called 'Delicate Investigation' employed spies to monitor Caroline and she was advised to 'sacrifice all society and give up going to the opera'.[14] The perceived injustices against the Princess, inflicted by an increasingly unpopular Prince and his ministers, caused a swell of support from liberal and radical journalists who depicted Caroline as a damsel in distress. With an allowance secured, Caroline left England for Europe, returning to Brunswick and then embarking on a tour before settling in northern Italy; the diaries of travellers who rushed to see Italy after the peace of 1815 show that attempting to spot the Princess at her villa was a popular pursuit.[15]

After a tour which included north Africa, Greece, Palestine, and the court of Naples, Caroline settled in Pesaro with a mostly Italian household. Caroline's actions and choice of company at this time were monitored by the Prince's spies within her staff and Austrian informants in contact with the ministry. Together these two groups compiled evidence for another separation attempt based around Caroline's supposed infidelity with her courtier Bartolomeo Bergami.[16] The death of George III in 1820 precipitated Caroline's return to Britain in June of the same year. Caroline came to defend her position as the rightful Queen, following the Regent's offer of a greater annuity to stay in Italy and the omission of her name from the liturgy of the Church of England. Once the Regent was informed of Caroline's planned return, he instructed his ministers to prepare a Bill of Pains and Penalties, so she could be tried in the House of Lords. From the middle of May 1820, radical and anti-ministerial newspapers recommenced their support of the Queen. By 26 May the excitement was palpable: a report from Calais by the *Morning Chronicle* reassured its readers, 'The instant The Queen of ENGLAND arrives here, you shall have the earliest communication'.[17] Before her departure, Caroline had been depicted as the wronged Princess, often cast, as Iain McCalman claims, as 'the heroine of a gothic-romance fantasy', but the manner of and reaction to her arrival in June of 1820 shows that she was now seen in a different light.[18]

Caroline's journey from Calais to London contributed to her transformation from a victim of an unfortunate royal marriage to an independent woman seeking justice. The Royal Yacht was denied to Caroline. She refused to wait for alternative arrangements, boarded a packet ferry, and on arrival she took refreshment at the Ship Hotel in Dover: both decisions endeared her to the public. For *The Times* Caroline's landing could be interpreted in revolutionary terms: its article begins, 'there have been disembarkations on the British Coast bringing war and revolutions in the state, ere now'.[19] It then compares her to the Prince of Orange and

William the Conqueror but not even at these events 'were the people's bosom of this metropolis so much agitated as they were tonight'. Caroline entered Britain as a threat: she was a member of the ruling elite, from a prestigious European royal line, and the rightful queen, yet she was hated by her husband and his ministers, and represented the same destabilising potential as her Dutch and French antecedents. She found her welcome in 'the people's bosom', and radical journalists were quick to link the ministry's persecution of the Queen with the attempts of the 'Yeomanry sabres at Manchester' to suppress democratic rights.[20] As one anonymous pamphlet put it, 'what Manchester left undone, the persecution of the Queen has nearly accomplished'.[21] The journey taken by the Queen from Dover to London was rich with radical symbolism that became significant in Shelley's late poetry. Caroline's carriage entered Canterbury late at night to be greeted by hundreds of flaming torches and a population insistent on drawing her through the town; the public manner of her welcome and this outdoor politics was thoroughly reported in newspapers such as *The Times*, the *Morning Chronicle*, and the *Traveller*.[22] Her landing was also making international news. The *Gazzetta Privilegiata di Venezia* devoted six columns to the journey, calling it 'un continuo trionfo' and discussing the people's shouts of '*viva la Regina Carolina*'.[23] Caroline's progress towards London over Shooter's Hill increased the number of her 'attendant cavalcade' and it was claimed that not 'since the days of Queen Elizabeth' had 'its neighbourhood ever produced a more lively scene'.[24] The triumphal procession became a tumult once it arrived in London; the activity of her supporters was typical of the period immediately after Peterloo, a time when, as Mary Fairclough has argued, radicals began to believe that 'physical gatherings of the populace constitute[d] a material representation of the political will of the nation at large'.[25] The mass mobilisation of supporters changed the metropolis into a kind of radical carnival. Hobhouse walked home on the night of Caroline's return to see 'a dozen link boys calling out "Lights!" Heard that windows were broken', and the *Traveller* claimed later 'the town was yesterday illuminated in many parts, on account of the Queen'.[26] Caroline's ability to mix between classes was crucial to her popularity. She chose to stay with the radical Member of Parliament Alderman Wood, rather than amongst nobility, and when she arrived at his house on South Audley Street she finished her journey with a piece of radical theatre. Caroline addressed the crowds from the balcony, in a gesture that allowed spectators to draw comparisons with Henry 'Orator' Hunt's famous harangue from the first floor of Merlin's Cave tavern in the winter of 1816.[27]

The People of England Will Not Listen to Italian Witnesses

Marx's clarification of Hegel that opens the *Eighteenth Brumaire* – that events occur first as tragedy, and then are repeated as farce – is illustrated by the arrival of the Italian witnesses against the Queen.[28] They arrived at Dover a month after Caroline had passed through, and were greeted by 'the men, women, and children, of this humane, loyal, and public-spirited Town'.[29] The mob had been waiting at the quay for the 'bugs and frogs' who would testify against the Queen and set about them with sticks, leaving one witness partially deaf and another badly beaten in what the press jeeringly called the Dover Massacre. The event was a gift to caricaturists, as seen in *John Bull Peppering the Italian Rascals – or a Kick from Harwich to Holland* (1820) in which John Bull boots terrified Italians into the sea shouting, 'This is *Freedom's* own Land, 'tis the *land of the Queen*, / Where no *hired traducers* shall ever be seen'.[30] The witnesses fled through streets lined with the same crowds that had welcomed the Queen and sought refuge in The Ship, the very hotel in which Caroline stayed. Their journey to London was as chaotic as their arrival at Dover: they were jeered and pelted by missiles in every town by the people who had carried Caroline in triumph, before being kept under state protection in the Cotton Yard, a building on the west side of Parliament.

The same pamphleteers and caricaturists who defended the Queen began characterising the Italian arrivals. Some chose to see them as the effeminate 'persons who are occasionally imported from Italy to sing Tenor notes in some of our theatres'.[31] Others revived 1790s conceptions of Italians as a beggarly people. Just like earlier immigrants, the witnesses were characterised by their poverty of dress: one anonymous pamphlet entitled *Arrival of the Italian Wretches* claimed 'such a set of ragged Rascals never were seen before'.[32] The caricaturist claims to have never seen such people as those who arrived at Dover, but in the next sentence a simile finds a point of comparison with the Italian organ-grinders and entertainers on the streets of London: 'Such Wretches as go about with dancing dogs and monkies, white mice, tame snakes, and land-turtles'. Although the tactics used by radicals mimicked those used by anti-Jacobin satire twenty years earlier, a fundamental reversal has occurred in these later formulations. In the 1790s John Bull was resolutely on the side of the King and Pitt's government, persecuting French and Italian migrants for the revolutionary contagion they carried to English shores. But here the recruitment of John Bull to kick foreigners from 'Harwich to Holland' was part of a counter-hegemonic movement against the witnesses of the

Crown and Government. The change from state attacks on Italianism for its revolutionary and reformist ideas to state support of Italian witnesses inspired a new xenophobia in radical attacks. This xenophobia within reform movements presented a problem for those writers who both espoused a radical idea of Italy, and supported the Queen's cause against the King. The pamphleteer's link between the witnesses and earlier immigrants became established, and was made a unified stereotype in William Hone's famous image of:

> Two hundred RAGG'D ITALIANS,
> With dancing-dogs and mice,
> Prepar'd for any dirty job,
> And for all sorts of vice,
> Thus, for a crust of bread and cheese,
> Delightfully did sing
> "O what a pleasant dainty dish
> We'll set before the King!"[33]

Here the Italians are not just 'RAGG'D' entertainers on the London streets, but also the easily bought witnesses who would do 'all sorts of vice' and sing their royal employer's tune with typical musicality. Hone's portrayal of the witnesses as 'Two Hundred RAGG'D ITALIANS' went into eight editions, and affected the lives of Italian immigrants living in London. *The Times* carried an article less than a year after the witnesses' arrival that detailed the rounding up of Italians, 'miserable boys who have so long infested the streets of the metropolis', they were convicted at Bow Street, it was decided that 'the government is to provide a vessel to take them back to Italy'.[34] The deportation of these Italians could be a coincidence, but with Hone's caricature of Italians as parasitic street dwellers, and the slurs in broadside satire discussed below, this seems unlikely.

The most innovative of the satirical attacks on the Italian witnesses can be found in a bound collection of printed ephemera kept at the British Library, entitled 'Satirical Songs and Miscellaneous Papers Connected with the Trial of Queen Caroline'.[35] One of these handbills deserves particular scrutiny.[36] It purports to be a public notice informing 'SCAVENGERS, NIGHTMEN, AND OTHERS' of 'vast quantities of Filth and Nastiness lately imported from various parts of the Continent' which have now become 'highly noxious to the Public'. It then goes on to tender the removal of this filth on 'Vessels in the Bone Trade (or Dung Barges)' to willing contractors, who must 'give a bond against re-landing it in this Country'. Along with its textual mimicry of official language and formatting the handbill carries two signifiers at its head which confer state authority: the royal crest and motto 'Dieu et Mon Droit', which is flanked by Admiral Nelson's famous signal on the eve of Trafalgar, 'England expects That every Man Will do His Duty'. At first glance this handbill could be mistaken for an authentic notice, but a Regency reader would know that the description of the 'SCAVENGERS GENERAL' as 'Messrs. L——H and Company' is a reference to Sir John Leach, often called Leech in radical works such as *Oedipus Tyrannus*, and drawn as a parasitic leech in caricatures.[37] Leach was the vice-chancellor who organised the Crown's witnesses in Milan, which explains the otherwise confusing reference to the transportation of waste 'at an enormous Expense, by a R——l Commission House in the Milanese'. Two notes at the bottom of the bill gloss the text to confirm its satirical intent. We are told that 'Specimens [of the waste] may be obtained either at Liverpool, Wellington, or other large Towns', playing on Lord Liverpool (Richard Jenkinson) and the Duke of Wellington being influential members of the ministry, and a further note warns that the vessels must be quarantined on their return, '*Cotton* Goods being apt to retain the Plague', which is a riff on the witnesses' London address at Cotton Yard. The satirist's conventional attack on the immorality and infectiousness of Italians is made innovative by being masked as an official document complete with the seal of King George himself.

The radical press published much pre-trial material that ridiculed Italians and attempted to outline the Queen's innocence in some detail. When seen as a whole this literature represents a public defence of the Queen before the state prosecution had made their case. The tract *The Queen's Case Stated* (1820) by the celebrated barrister Charles Phillips ran to twenty-two editions, and in it Phillips claims, 'the people of England will not listen to Italian witnesses, nor ought they'.[38] The next four pages are an assault on the Italian national character as a people of 'habitual invention', who are 'infected freight' shipped from Italy to Westminster and on 'which [we] should have performed quarantine before it vomited its *moral pestilence* amongst us'.[39] Only months after the renewal of the draconian Aliens Bill, the tract implores the court:

> Send back, then, to Italy, those alien adventurers; the land of their birth, and the habits of their lives, alike unfit them for an English court of justice.[40]

The tract is a radical document published by Hone and yet it invokes in convoluted prose the statist power of the 'English court of justice' to eject aliens and later 'the purity of [England's] moral atmosphere'.[41] As in the handbill on the export of waste, here the vox populi speaks in the manner of the state before the state has tried the Queen. One member of Parliament who was about to hear the Queen's case mimics the negative depiction of Italians promulgated by radical writers. In a letter attempting to stop the trial before it had begun, Lord John Russell asserts that the witnesses represent 'the *jetsam* and *flotsam* of a licentious people – from the eaves-droppers of the whole Continent', and carries in higher diction the radicals' sense of Italians as waste washed ashore.[42]

At the Baths of San Giuliano, Shelley's interest was piqued by Caroline's arrival in England and the potential for reform and revolution it presented. Shelley craved information about the royal intrigue, asking friends in London about 'this vulgar cook-maid they call a Queen'.[43] What he saw as 'mummery' in his letter to the Gisbornes, provoked deeper thought twelve days later when Shelley mentions the Queen to Peacock:

> [The King], no less than his ministers, are so odious that everything, however disgusting, which is opposed to them, is admirable. The Paris paper, which I take in, copied some excellent remarks from the *Examiner* about it.[44]

Shelley remained perturbed by the sordid nature of proceedings but, like radical writers in London, saw the unifying potential of Caroline. The 'Paris paper' is *Galignani's Messenger*, which allowed Shelley to receive news about Caroline with a lag of only two or three days. Mary Shelley's journal shows that this reading led to a satire on the Queen Caroline affair, begun in late August 1820 as her trial was about to begin.[45] Shelley's *Oedipus Tyrannus; or, Swellfoot the Tyrant* is a two-act play that presents itself as a Sophoclean tragedy, but is undercut by a *dramatis personae* made up of livestock, which Mary claims was 'suggested by the pigs at the fair of St. Giuliano'.[46] The Italian *festa* may have been the cue for *Swellfoot*, and the generic code that it subverts may be classical, but the remarkable feature of the play is its interaction with radical metropolitan satire. With only the articles excerpted in *Galignani*, the correspondence from his London friends, and the 'conversation among the English' in Italy, Shelley was prepared to write a poem on the 'circumstances of the day'.[47] The material allowed for what Shelley later called a 'display of newspaper erudition', a phrase that captures both his interest in and separation from events.[48] *Swellfoot* could be mistaken for a radical London satire: as in early caricatures, Sir John Leach is cast as a Leech, who sucks the blood of the state; the chorus of swine chant in unison supporting the Iona Taurina (the Queen), as the papers reported the crowds did from Dover to London; and the long speech (II. i. 157–182) of Iona Taurina at the

'Public Sty', in which she throws 'herself, her cause, her life, her all' (II. i. 162) to the bosom of the people, seems an obvious reference to Caroline's speech from a city balcony.[49] Two of the most cutting satirical images in the play – the oinking of the choral 'swinish multitude' and the depiction of the Queen as Iona Taurina (i.e. Joan Bull) – rely on the reclamation of conservative terms by radicals in the 1790s and after Waterloo. Shelley's satiric play furthers the linguistic campaign of the London pamphleteers who had earlier claimed the formulation 'the public mind' and the figure of John Bull for their cause.

In material terms, *Swellfoot* was recognisably part of the pro-Caroline pamphlet movement. As an anonymous, short (39-page) octavo pamphlet, published in Cheapside by J. Johnston, who had published other pro-Caroline material, Shelley's work paraded its radicalism within its bibliographic features.[50] The epigraph, at the centre of the first page, is a prophecy that is repeated twice more in the play. The epigraph version contains an important omission:

> ————Choose Reform or civil war,
> When through thy streets, instead of hare with dogs,
> A CONSORT-QUEEN shall hunt a KING with hogs,
> Riding on the IONIAN MINOTAUR.

In its next appearance 'Boeotia' is inserted at the opening (I. i. 113–16) and in its final use 'Thebes' is inserted (II. i. 153–6), but here the subject is uncertain. It could have been this prophecy on the front page, with its call to revolution and its inversion of the King to a fox hunted by hogs, which led to the pamphlet's suppression.[51] Michael Rossington and Laura Barlow have plausibly suggested 'England' is the word implied to fill this gap, but it could also be left blank, as the capitalised 'C' suggests, providing a stark imperative to readers.[52] In spite of these similarities, *Swellfoot* has one stark difference from the satires discussed above: its attitude towards Italy and Italians. Shelley does not situate the Italian other as the enemy of the people. The character Purganax mentions that the rumour about the Queen was that she was involved with 'milk-white bulls that feed / Beside Clitumnus' (II. i. 60–1), but this play on Virgil's description of Umbria is a far cry from the xenophobic description and diction of disease analysed above. As discussed in the previous chapter, Shelley had spent time and emotion on an idea of Italy that radically read its literary tradition and saw a landscape of liberty in its vistas and panoramas. The conspicuous absence of the popular language of xenophobia allows the farmyard satire to work on a larger European level: 'Choose Reform or civil war' could apply equally to King Ferdinand at Naples or Swellfoot George in London. In a similar way to the view over Venice in 'Euganean Hills', Shelley's rejection of the xenophobic attacks in other pamphlets shows that a radical engagement with Italy and its literature allows for the conception of revolution and reform on a continental scale. Like Hunt in his *Pocket Book*, Shelley is attempting to re-organise how we translate ideas into action. *Swellfoot* contains political protest in its opposition to the King's actions, but Shelley also realised that the publications around the Queen's trial that he imitated were not simply protest: radicals were attempting to change praxis, to challenge which structures and which forms of literature spoke for the political will. Shelley uses these new methods of practically realising a challenge to hegemony, with a literary distance from straightforward political action or physical resistance, to push for the transcontinental resurgence of liberty that he had been advocating since 1818.

Non Mi Ricordo

The Queen's trial began on the morning of 17 August; the army blocked the roads around Parliament to reserve space for carriages taking Lords to the House. Inside, Sir John Soane had erected temporary galleries to cope with peers and their guests.[53] The Queen's choice of legal counsel reflected two notable characteristics of her case: the importance of popular support for Caroline, and the centrality of Italian people, language, and culture, to proceedings. As her solicitor-general she chose Thomas Denman, a man who made his name as the defender of the Luddites in 1817. Denman was an ideal choice; he was both a recognisable name to Caroline's thousands of radical supporters and a Parliamentarian who contributed to the *Edinburgh Review*. Denman's establishment connections extended to Holland House where, in preparing the Queen's defence, he 'luxuriated in an admirable library, and the best company in the world': presumably the Italian residents at the House provided insights into much of the testimony.[54] Over the period of the trial (June 1820 to November 1820) Denman dined and stayed the night at Holland House eleven times. On all but two of these occasions the Queen's attorney general Henry Brougham was present (he dined at Holland House more than thirty times during the trial). Brougham was a founder of the *Edinburgh Review* and a long-standing defender of the Queen's cause. His perceived radicalism, and the threat he posed to the state, was felt keenly by Wordsworth who had vociferously opposed his election to a seat in Westmoreland in 1818, claiming his election would 'produce infinite mischief not to

Westmoreland only, but to the whole kingdom'.[55] His abilities as a speechmaker and fluent Italian speaker were central to the failure of the case against Caroline. Brougham was knowledgeable and passionate about Italy and Italian culture: his family home, High-Head Castle, had been rebuilt and decorated by Italian workmen after his great-grandfather had become 'so imbued with Italian taste' during a tour in the early eighteenth century; and in 1804, before he was called to the bar, Brougham had travelled to Italy under American papers.[56] He spent time at Florian's in Venice, visited the galleries and churches of Rome, and admired the English men-of-war in the bay at Naples.[57] In 1819 he wrote a long review of Stendhal's *Histoire de la peinture en Italie* (1817) for the *Edinburgh* in which he confidently charted the progress of Italian painting from Cimabue to the present day and discussed the 'traits of Neapolitan courage' during the attempted revolution of 1815.[58] The sum of his learning would be essential to the defence of the Queen.

As the defence in the trial proper began discrediting the Crown's Italian witnesses, it was clear that radical depictions had stuck in their minds. In his opening remarks, Brougham recalled earlier testimony by an Italian witness. He opened by claiming there is a 'general sameness in the conduct of these witnesses', and continued with the specific example of the inn keeper Pietro Cuchi, who claimed to have observed Bergami leave Caroline's room by looking through a key hole:

> Do your lordships recollect Pietro Cuchi, the waiter from Trieste? Can any man who saw him have forgotten him? Does he not rise before your faces the instant I mention his name – unless many of your lordships should recollect the face, the never-to-be-forgotten expression of face, although the name may have escaped you? Do your lordships recollect that expression of physiognomy – those eyes – that nose – that lecherous mouth with which the wretch stood here to detail impurities which he has invented [. . .] Do you recollect the eye of that hoary pander from Trieste? Did he not look, as the great poet of Italy describes the hoary letcher in the infernal regions to have looked, when he says that he regarded him with the eye, the gloating eye of an ancient tailor peeping through the eye of his needle?[59]

Brougham could be describing a character in the radical prints discussed earlier, an Italian whose moral and sexual baseness is written on his 'physiognomy', even reminding the Lords that if they cannot recall the witness they can remember his 'never-to-be-forgotten expression'. It is a base caricature that he clearly wishes to extend to all; Brougham concludes his speech on Cuchi by remarking, 'I dismiss the other witnesses of the same description. I take this filthy cargo by sample purposely'.[60] The extract is remarkable for Brougham's final question, which goes beyond radical caricature to invoke the Regency interest in Italian literature. Brougham knows his Dante and is confident that without naming him directly the Lords would know 'the great poet of Italy' and specifically the moment in *Inferno* XV from which he makes his comparison.[61] These lines were discussed by Warton in his *History of English Poetry*, and Pite has shown that this passage was popular with English readers.[62] The reference to Dante serves two purposes. First, Brougham links 'lecherous' Cuchi with the man who looks at Dante with 'the gloating eye'. To make this link he condenses the two and a half tercets that precede the pilgrim's encounter with Brunetto Latini, when Dante meets those who have sinned against the flesh:

> quando incontrammo d'anime una schiera
> che venian lungo l'argine, e ciascuna
> ci riguardava come suol da sera
> guardare uno altro sotto nuova luna;
> e sì ver' noi aguzzavan le ciglia
> come 'l vecchio sartor fa ne la cruna.
>
> Così adocchiato da cotal famiglia,
> fui conscuito da un.[63]

Brougham's speech only mentions the simile of the tailor's eye. He uses the reference to castigate Cuchi, yet Dante's simile refers to a 'cotal famiglia', a group of people, not a single 'hoary lecher'. Furthermore, these two lines do not imply the 'gloating' or the sexual perversion that Brougham tries to place on Cuchi. In the same vein as Mathias in the *Componimenti* and Hunt in *Rimini,* Brougham adapts the *Commedia* to his purpose: it is the lines before in which the souls look the pilgrim up and down as some men do in the darkest nights (often interpreted as signalling homosexual intent) and it is in the next lines that Dante switches from a collective to being recognized 'da un' (by one individual sinner). Brougham condenses these lines to allow the reference to the tailor to carry all the perversity of the carnal sinners, and with this casts Cuchi's physiognomy, and that of the Italian witnesses in general, as a product of moral failure. The defence is encouraging the Italians to be viewed as suffering the same *contrapasso* in their wretched appearance as that which deforms the inhabitants of the *Inferno.*[64]

The allusion is part of Brougham's technique of using the growing British interest in and knowledge of Italy to aid his argument. The defence's erudite knowledge of Italian culture was used repeatedly during the trial to discredit witnesses and exonerate the Queen. The defence embellishes established radical stereotypes with its wider knowledge of Italy and the Italian language, a process which came full circle as pamphleteers based further satires on the trial.[65] Brougham uses Italian culture, in this instance Dante, for the opposite purpose to that analysed in previous chapters, despite using the same techniques of literary appreciation and adaptation. In *Beppo,* 'Euganean Hills', and Foscolo's essays in the *Edinburgh*, Italy is viewed through an exposition of its art, literature, and climate, as an equal, if not superior, culture to Britain. The defence uses the improved knowledge of Italy in British culture as a means to persuade the Lords, and Britons who assiduously followed the trial, to believe their demeaning stereotypes of the Italian witnesses. Brougham was not someone whose views of Italy and its culture before or after the trial could conceivably tally with the stereotypes he was propagating in the Lords. Yet he saw short-term gain in siding with a radical xenophobia to benefit his case, contradicting his long-standing commitment to cosmopolitanism. Brougham's self-contradiction was reversed later in the trial as promoted the need to appropriate foreign habits and customs when abroad, which in turn helped recruit radical voices to the cause of Neapolitan independence.

After lengthy opening statements by the Crown and the Defence, Theodore Majocchi (or Majoochi) was called from the Cotton Yard to the stand on 21 August. Majocchi was to become the most infamous man in Britain for his recollection of the Queen's behaviour in Italy. Before evidence could be given, two interpreters were called to translate from Italian to English. The defence chose Mr Binetto Cohen, a man about whom little is known aside from the fact that he was Jewish.[66] Cohen's role was limited to giving occasional alternative translations to those of the Crown's interpreter, Nicholas Dorier, the Marchese di Spineto. Spineto was a Cambridge tutor in Italian from (at least) 1808 to 1832 and a member of the Cambridge Garrick Club in the 1830s.[67] After Spineto's first day at the trial, and before the cross-examination of Majocchi by Brougham, Countess Granville (Harriet Leveson-Gower) described him in a letter:

> The interpreter is the man that delights them all. His name is Spinetto [*sic*]; he is an Italian teacher at one of the Universities, as quick as lightning, all gesticulation, and so eager he often answers instead of the witness. Between them they act all the evidence, and at times they say this is so irresistibly comic that the noble lords forget all decorum and are in a roar of laughter.[68]

The serious activity of gathering evidence becomes, thanks to the interpreter, a farcical and inexact exchange. Granville's claim that the interpreter and witness 'act all the evidence' and rely on 'gesticulation' was prescient: the absurdity of exact verbal translation would become the central problem for the Crown once Majocchi was questioned by the defence. The gesticulating, acting, and translating commented on by the Countess Granville took place during the Crown's examination of Majocchi. The Italian answered precisely, revealing table plans for dinners on the Queen's yacht, complex room layouts on board, and the duration of private conferences between Caroline and her supposed lover Bergami; Majocchi even imitated a waltz they had danced.[69] Brougham had relatively few objections to these lines of questioning, aside from a point of order to clarify if the witness spoke any English: he did not. Majocchi was cross-examined by Brougham on the following day and, despite his certainty earlier certainty, uttered the phrase 'non mi ricordo' over eighty times.[70] The literal and figurative meanings of this phrase were to occupy the Lords during Majocchi's testimony, and its terse power was a boon to Caroline's supporters. Brougham questioned many of the Italian phrases for their lack of precision during cross-examination: he queried the difference between 'sempre' (always) and 'sempre le piu parti' (for the most part), asked whether 'lontano' (far off) could also mean 'separated', and sought clarification over which members of service were included in the phrase 'Le Corte' (entourage).[71] Brougham apparently used his knowledge of Italian to clarify testimony, but it had the opposite effect. It created a further separation between the original Italian and the English heard by the peers. The tactic applied to the Italian language by the defence served both to muddle the previously certain evidence of Majocchi and twist it to fit Brougham's interpretation.

The slipperiness of Italian phraseology, and by extension the duplicity of the Crown's witnesses, was established in a disagreement over the proper meaning of the phrase 'non mi ricordo'. What makes the 'non mi ricordo' controversy of central importance lies in a debate about what the phrase actually meant. This debate was reported widely during and after the trial:

> The interpreter explained, that these words meant "I don't remember, or I don't know;" and that they answered to the French phrase "Je ne sais pas." Mr. Brougham considered the correct translation of the words to be of much consequence; and he dissented from that which had been put upon them by the Marchese: upon which the Marchese Spineto begged that their Lordships would apply to the interpreter for her Majesty, who was behind him, and would correct him if he was wrong. Their Lordships desired Mr. Cohen, accordingly, to be asked, which was done by Mr. Brougham.

> How do you translate the words 'Non mi ricordo?' – 'I do not recollect.' How do you render 'I don't know' – 'No so.'[72]

Not content with making Majocchi appear to lack the knowledge that he had claimed a day earlier, the defence pursued the slippery nature of his oft-repeated phrase. Brougham managed to render the phrase toxic by the convolutions he added to its meaning: first, the argument itself is a pause in testimony, then the interpreter explains the phrase means 'I don't remember, or I don't know', two very different things, one which implies having known and now forgotten and the other that Majocchi never knew. The translator then offered an equivalent in another foreign language, with which again Brougham seemed to be unsatisfied, which causes Cohen's disagreement with Spineto, as he implies that 'Non mi ricordo' only means 'I don't recollect', as opposed to 'I don't know'. The linguistic exposition lingers over a phrase that is already absurd from Majocchi's repetition of it, and allows Brougham to separate the witness from his ability to control his testimony in his native language. The tactic of taking linguistic power from the Italian witnesses is made clear as the 'non mi ricordo' debate continues:

> Mr. Brougham then appealed to their lordships. It would be the most childish thing in the world in him were he to talk of his knowledge of the Italian language; because their lordships had appointed an interpreter, and they were to take the witness's answer through him. But if it appeared that they always translated 'Non mi ricordo' 'I don't recollect', it seemed to him that it might be allowable for a person – even, who was only a Tramontane, like himself – to doubt whether the same words could sometimes mean 'I don't recollect' and at others 'I don't know'.[73]

Brougham is playing to the gallery. He coyly suggests that it would be childish for him to use his Italian as 'their lordships had appointed an interpreter', and yet this lengthy interruption relies on undermining Spineto and showing this knowledge. 'Tramontane' allows Brougham to admit that he was not Italian, as he is 'one from beyond the mountains', yet he uses an Italian term to make this claim. The faux-appeal for clarity had its desired effect: once proceedings had resumed, two Lords interrupted again to doubt the meaning of 'non mi ricordo'.[74] Brougham shares the wish of much pre-trial literature to see the Queen acquitted, but he had also learned from the radicals' techniques. The legal process operates within the strict rules of the state, within it language is forced to perform inside controlled boundaries, and rhetoric is confined to the logic of question and answer. But the polyvalence of 'non mi ricordo' interrupts the form of these proceedings, and creates a symbol that not only identifies a flawed case but also suggests the corruption endemic in the state's process.

News of the controversy spread quickly in the press and the phrase became a locus for further radical satire; some weeks later Brougham reflected on 'the extraordinary fact of that answer being dropped by the other witnesses, as soon as the impression which the repetition had made on the public mind was fully understood'.[75] 'Non mi ricordo' is concise and tangibly foreign, allowing it to become a slogan for the perceived absurdity of the case against the Queen. A contemporary print attests to the use of the phrase on banners at rallies in support of Caroline, but its roots in dialogue and its easy feminine rhyme meant 'non mi ricordo' was more suitable for literary and musical satire.[76] A broadside called 'The Italian Witness: A New Song', is typical of this use, and it begins,

> My name it is Majocchi;
> I bow to all my Lords-O,
> And have you any Christian name?
> *Signor, non mi ricordo*:
> I've quite forgot the word-O.[77]

The writer creates a mock-Italian argot for Majocchi's speeches which causes a jaunty rhythm through odd word order, the insertion of 'O' in the rhyme words, and the repetition of 'my' and 'mi'. The italics on '*non mi ricordo*' not only follow the convention of italicising foreign terms, but can also be seen as emphasising Majocchi's stock answer to mark a chorus for sung performance. The techniques used in the song also appear in two works by Leigh Hunt written less than a week after the cross-examination.[78] The differences between this satire and those by other radicals show Hunt's loyalty to an Italian-inflected cosmopolitanism. Hunt wrote his pro-Caroline verse under the pseudonym 'Harry Brown', who had a more considered approach than 'John Bull', and who saw larger forces at work in the Queen's mistreatment. 'Memory and Want of Memory or Rather No than Yes' appropriates the form of the trial by splitting its fifteen stanzas between 'Counsel for the Plaintiff' and 'Counsel for Defence', both of whom perform a mock-examination of Majocchi. The first line of each quatrain begins with a question or statement by counsel and this line always ends with the witnesses' fawning agreement 'Signor, si', which is followed, in the 'Plaintiff' stanzas, with another question to which the answer is again 'Si, Signor'. The constant flow of affirmatives creates an obsequious tone that is reversed in the second half of the poem by the 'Defence'. The 'Counsel for Defence' begins:

Now look at me – 'Oh signor, si' –
Pray who gives you your board O,
And when did you last take your tea?
'O Sair – Non mi ricordo'.
(ll. 25–8)

Hunt's fictional Brougham begins with an imperative that changes the relationship between witness and council into an interrogatory mode: it is this that brings the following stanzas to end 'Non mi ricordo'. Thematically, Hunt's defence questions the corrupt nature of the Crown for paying the witnesses 'tea' and 'board', rather than mocking the unreliability of Italians; the Majocchi character is portrayed as having been coached, once responding 'Yes. No; No, – Yes; more I than me' (l. 47), and admitting in his garbled English 'upon my vord O, / you [Brougham] put soach cònfuse into me' (ll. 42–43). Hunt's song was something of a hit: it was anthologised among more caustically anti-Italian numbers in *The Non Mi Ricordo Song Book* (1820?), a sixteen-page collection of songs riffing on the famous phrase.[79]

The second pro-Caroline poem in the August 27 edition of the *Examiner,* 'Non Mi Ricordo', continues this attack on the government and King. Hunt begins by claiming that most people have 'a favourite phrase [. . .] To swear by or to save their wits' (ll. 1–3), before offering some suggested oaths, 'Some say by George and some by Gosh, / Some put their trust in Goles' (ll. 5–6). That some people swear by God (the derivative of 'Goles' and Gosh') and George (Patron Saint of England) seems an innocuous point, yet with the future George IV as the plaintiff the poem opens by mocking those who swear by 'Church and King'. It is in this class of oaths that Hunt places 'that pregnant phrase / Divine, *Non mi ricordo'.* Majocchi's phrase is 'pregnant' due to the satirical reaction it brought forth from radicals, but also, at the level of the poem, for the anaphora it initiates to find its meaning. Hunt spends the next thirty lines offering entirely different things which the phrase can mean: a 'waistcoat' and 'trousers', 'dinner' and 'breakfast', 'day' and 'night', and 'no' and 'yes'. At the end of the increasingly ridiculous list Hunt asserts,

That being well interpreted
It means it has no meaning.

It means a thief, it means some beef,
It means a shabby villain;
It means 'mine host o' the Garter' here
Who longs to bring his Bill in.
(ll. 51–56)

That something can be 'well interpreted' to have 'no meaning' alludes to Brougham's dismantling of translated testimony in the Lords and concludes the list of possible definitions of 'non mi ricordo'. The next stanza signals a change in subject and begins with 'beef' and 'thief', a pair without an apparent link beyond rhyme. But 'beef', 'thief', and 'shabby villain' can be connected in a reading that turns the poem towards a more complex satirical message. There can be no doubt that the 'host o' the Garter' is the Regent, who awarded the Order of the Garter, and 'Who longs to bring his Bill' of Pain and Penalties against Caroline. The Regent can also be the subject of the two preceding lines. Radicals often called George a 'thief' because of his constant demands on the public purse, and he was partial to 'some beef' (observing his corpulence was what landed Hunt in Surrey Gaol in 1812). If we take 'shabby' to mean contemptibly mean, ungenerous, or dishonourable, then that fits with the widely held view of the King's behaviour in attempting to separate from the Queen.[80] The reading of the subject as George is strengthened by the direct quotation of the phrase 'mine host o' the Garter' from *The Merry Wives of Windsor* (1602).[81] The line is Falstaff's greeting on entering the Garter Inn; Hunt's allusion to a play that revolves around its rotund protagonist's shabby behaviour towards women buttresses a reading that sees the poem attempt to change focus from pointing out the absurdity of an Italian witness to mocking the King himself.

Just as Shelley had done a few months earlier in *Swellfoot,* Hunt aims to expose the ridiculousness of the situation rather than inciting violent reaction, and directs his satire towards the monarch rather than Italians. Hunt's motive for diverting the satirical current becomes clear when his activity during the period is considered. Hunt's work in the previous decade had two linked concerns: the championing of Italian culture in his poetry, essays, and opera reviews, and the creation of an active middle-class radicalism that encouraged reform and challenged the Prince and his ministers. To be a user of Hunt's Italianate materials in the *Pocket Book* or a reader of the *Examiner,* and to enjoy *The Story of Rimini* or to champion Mozart, suggested opposition to a hegemonic culture. Hunt's poetic output in the months preceding the trial of the Queen make clear his absorption in Italian culture, and at the start of 1820 he began his translation of Tasso's *Aminta.* In his recently founded literary periodical the *Indicator,* Hunt had championed the Italian subjects chosen by his friends. He praised Shelley's *The Cenci* (1819) and showed his own interest in Roman history, and when in a review of *Lamia, Isabella, The Eve of St. Agnes, and Other Poems* (1820) he misquotes the address to Boccaccio asking pardon for the work as an 'Echo of him in the worth-wind sung', we see Hunt share Keats's awe for the Italian tradition.[82] As the reading of the two satires shows, Hunt, unlike Brougham, is unwilling to engage in attacks on a people and a culture to which he had been devoted for more than a decade. Instead, he views English radicals in a wider continental frame; in an article about the Queen, he describes 'an English multitude, which like all civilized multitudes, becomes more and more every day a representative of disappointed Europe at large'.[83] Hunt attempts to turn the discourse towards a cosmopolitan discussion of the failure of liberty in peacetime Europe, with events like the Queen's trial and Peterloo as national examples of a continental malaise. The effectiveness of his vision was bolstered by events occurring more than a thousand miles away at Naples.

Revolution at Naples!!!

A few weeks before the trial began, Mary Shelley wrote to Maria Gisborne, who was visiting London. Mary Shelley did not view the Queen as a flawless heroine, but she nevertheless writes, 'I wish with all my heart downfall to her enemies'.[84] She then changes the subject to inform Gisborne of the uprising at Naples that occurred on 1 July:

> Are you not, or will you not be delighted to hear of the revolution at Naples [. . .] [W]hat a glorious thing it will be if Lombardy regains its freedom – and Tuscany – all is so mild there that it will be the last, and yet in the end I hope the people here will raise their fallen souls and bodies, and become something better than they are.[85]

Mary Shelley sees the revolution in Naples as the catalyst for a return to republican city states across 'fallen' Italy. It was a view shared by Hunt who devoted a front page of the *Examiner* to the revolution, claiming like Mary Shelley, that thanks to Naples '[t]he fire is kindled; it warms the nations'.[86] Hunt's idea that Italy was seeing a new dawn of liberty is inspired by a poem discussed in the previous chapter: Shelley's 'Lines written among the Euganean Hills'. Hunt quotes twenty-seven lines of the poem in the *Examiner*, and ends his extract on an apostrophe.

> O tyranny, beholdest now
> Light around thee, and thou hearest
> The loud flames ascend, and fearest.[87]

The quotation supports the earlier reading: although Shelley portrays Italy as 'Trampled out by tyranny' he predicts that soon the agents of her suppression will be put on the pyre.[88] Hunt's choice to end the extract on these lines not only provides the fire metaphor for his description of the Neapolitan Revolution, but also reminds the reader of the radicals who illuminated houses and shouted in protest to produce the 'Light around thee' and 'loud flames' at London and Naples in July 1820.[89] Anticipating the events of 1848, Hunt uses Shelley – who in *Swellfoot* made the same connection – to encourage his readers to realise that a transcontinental conflagration of liberty was possible. The day after Mary Shelley's letter, Hobhouse records '*Revolution at Naples*!!!' in his diary: this was the moment that the British public became aware of events on the continent.[90] General Guglielmo Pepe and his revolutionary troops had taken Naples with little resistance, and a constitutional monarchy was declared under the Bourbon King Ferdinand. Two days later, Hobhouse dined with 'Captain Clive of the Guards', who told him that 'the citizens are in a great fright' about troops garrisoned in London to prevent disturbances at the Queen's arrival; Hobhouse then wrote, 'the military revolution at Naples will add to this fright'.[91] The link made here between the Queen's return and the Neapolitan situation, which appears coincidental in Mary Shelley's letter, became increasingly common as the trial progressed, so much so that an emergency debate on the revolution, called by Lord Holland and Earl Grey, interrupted the Queen's trial in the Lords. A number of intellectual currents swelled around these two events; the final part of this chapter will look at the role that Naples played in shaping the international dimension of the trial.

Naples, with its surrounding coastline, was established in the British imagination before the revolutions of 1815 and 1820. That Naples was better known than the coast of Puglia or the Maremma was largely due to its popularity in topographical watercolours and landscapes by artists like Thomas Jones, John Robert Cozens, and William Marlow. Views of Naples appeared in panoramas on London streets, and views of the city were a common subject for landscape painters in training.[92] British perceptions of Naples changed from a known and admired landscape to a place of political importance during the continental war. There was a brief pro-French republic at Naples in 1799 after a successful revolution against King Ferdinand, but with the assistance of the British Navy under the command of Nelson, the king was restored and there was a violent repression of revolutionary sympathisers.[93] Italian revolutionaries such as Vincenzo Cuoco and Foscolo raged against the British actions of 1799, as did Charles James Fox in the House of Commons, but by the end of the Napoleonic Wars liberal Neapolitans saw an intervention by the British government as their best hope of reform.[94] Ferdinand had remained ruler of Sicily thanks to the assistance of Lord Bentinck and the British, while Murat ruled Naples for Napoleon before he was dethroned during the Hundred Days. Ferdinand was then restored as King of Naples. The prospect of a British-supported Bourbon king was an enticing one for Neapolitan liberals: the British had forced the Bourbon Spanish king to agree to constitutional reform in 1812, and Bentinck had put significant and effective pressure on Ferdinand to implement constitutional reform in Sicily in the same year.[95] Many British Whigs who wished for reform in Naples and across Europe, such as Lord and Lady Holland, and Lord John Russell, wintered in the city at this time. A list of 'English at Naples in the Winter of 1814–1815' written by the antiquarian William Gell, who accompanied Queen Caroline to Naples, shows that they formed a substantial expatriate community of more than fifty families.[96] There was a brief hope – from the beginning of 1814 to early 1816 – among English and Italian reformers that the same change to constitutional monarchy that occurred in Spain could occur at Naples.[97] This hope led Holland to write his constitution, and it also produced a vogue for British culture in the city, with Bentinck claiming in a letter to William Hamilton of January 1816, 'there is no part of the world where the British name is equally respected. It is love and admiration without alloy. They look upon us as the natural friends of independence'.[98]

An important expression of Neapolitan Anglophilia was Rossini's opera *Elisabetta regina D'Inghilterra,* which premiered at Naples's San Carlo in October 1815.[99] Musically the opera borrowed a number of parts from earlier works, but its variety of choruses and the casting of Isabella Colbran as Elisabetta made it an impressive premiere. The opera concerns the machinations of the Elizabethan court, as Elizabeth confronts the lies of the Duke of Norfolk and placates her populace. The Queen as head of state acts for the common good and the action closes with a chorus singing 'Viva Elisabetta! L'eroina, / lo splendor di nostra età'.[100] As Richard Osborne has observed, the subject of English freedom was a shrewd choice for Naples in 1815.[101] *Elisabetta* was a flop in London, and played only four times in 1818; although it is impossible to know, one would imagine that its portrayal of a deceived but ultimately victorious English queen may have fared better with the King's Theatre audience in 1821. In 1815 supporters of reform in Britain and Naples were entertaining false hope. A 'Treaty of Friendship' was made between the Bourbon king and the Hapsburgs that allowed Ferdinand to mobilise the Austrian army of the central Po.[102] Additionally, although British foreign policy was theoretically in support of constitutional reform, the government was not prepared to sacrifice its alliance with Austria for the sake of the Italian states. Lord Holland had angered the government with his constitution and Lord Liverpool thought Bentinck 'mad'.[103] These two problems would re-emerge in the attempt for Neapolitan liberty five years later. In the period immediately preceding the Bourbon Restoration, Caroline had been on her travels and spent four months in the last days of Napoleonic Naples. The Queen was highly influenced by the court culture at Naples: when she left the city, Murat gave her a coach that the Comtesse de Boigne (Adèle d'Osmond) reported was a 'phaeton, constructed like a sea-shell, covered with gilding and mother-of-pearl' led by English servants dressed in Neapolitan livery.[104] The same witness claims that having left Naples, Caroline attempted to persuade the now politically incapacitated Bentinck to 'unite the English with the Neapolitan arms'.[105]

The connection made between the Queen and European liberty became more clearly outlined in the Queen's trial, especially when the defence began to state their case. The prosecution saw the opportunity to portray the Queen as profligate in her travels, mimicking anti-Grand Tour discourse by depicting Italy as an environment conducive to her alleged adultery with Bergami. To a large extent the viability of this portrayal rested on Caroline's behaviour during three evenings at Naples: Brougham cast the prosecution's tales of the city in a mock-Shakespearean light, 'where the scene is laid which is first so sedulously brought before your lordships'.[106] The Government's tactic was myopic: just as radical British interest in Naples had been aroused by political events, so the participants in the most important trial of the Regency were beginning to discuss the recent Anglo-Italian history of the city. On the Queen's first or second night at Naples (reports vary) she had gone to watch the opera. Her maid Louise Demont claimed under examination that Caroline had left the San Carlo early, with Bergami, and returned to her bedroom, from which she did not rise again until eleven in the morning.[107] Crucially, Demont claimed to have seen Bergami leaving Caroline's room in only a shirt and slippers. The entertainments on the second and third evenings were masquerades. The first was also at the San Carlo; Caroline attended with Demont and Bergami, and the Prosecution claimed two serious indiscretions occurred. The party arrived in a small coach by a private road without the regalia of the British state, which the Crown argued was so that Caroline could go with Bergami unnoticed, and Caroline's dress was deemed inappropriate, in an outfit described by Demont as 'very ugly, monstrous'.[108] The third night was a ball given by Caroline in honour of

Murat. Again costume was an issue as Caroline wore three outfits – a Neapolitan peasant, a Genius of History with 'arms and breast bare', and a Turkish slave – all deemed to be inappropriate. Furthermore, according to Demont, Bergami had aided the Queen in changing between them in an antechamber.[109] Like Byron at Venice, Caroline used the opportunity of being in a foreign land to wear strange suits.

The Defence dealt with these charges by diverting the argument from the Queen to the Neapolitan cultural norms she was observing: the debate was now over the customs of the cosmopolitan traveller. Lord Llandaff (Henry Matthews), who had been at Naples, was called and claimed that visiting a lady in her bedroom was 'very common practice in Italy' (a custom that had been discussed in earlier travel literature).[110] Caroline's servant John Jacob Sicard was questioned as to why Bergami did not breakfast with other servants, and preferred to wait on the Queen in chamber; he answered, 'they do not take breakfasts in Italy [. . .] not one out of a thousand'.[111] When it came to her behaviour in public, the cosmopolitan Brougham remarked that the attorney general had shown he did not know anything of the 'Royal Recreations of Murat's court' as 'strange as it may appear to my learned friend, a person at a masquerade endeavours to be disguised'.[112] He then called Gell and asked him to describe the Genius of History costume. Gell answered that Caroline's body was 'very much draped' and that the outfit was 'best exemplified by the Townley Cariatides [*sic*] in the British Museum', before listing the large number of English and Italian aristocratic families who visited the Queen at Naples.[113] Caroline was not only following the Neapolitan social norms but also the best classical examples, which the Lords could see for themselves a mile away on Great Russell Street. The line of argument pursued by the Defence rests on authentic experience, and is noticeably similar to Foscolo's attacks against English critics of Italian literature; as Brougham observed of the attorney general, his argument was not informed, as 'he had never been in Italy' and was not sufficiently cosmopolitan to appreciate cultural difference.[114] And yet, only weeks earlier the Defence had appropriated the xenophobic rhetoric of the 1790s to depict Italians as a singularly mendacious, filthy, and immoral people: was this the same culture whose conventions Brougham praised the Queen for observing? The Queen's actions in Italy, and the current revolutionary activity in Naples reported across Britain, allowed Brougham to adopt a liberal and cosmopolitan idea of Italy of which he was a more comfortable proponent. The daily papers, which had mounted the harshest attacks on Italians, mimicked Brougham's praise of the Queen's travel to further this paradox. The *British Press* asked, 'Is it extraordinary that persons going to a masquerade should study concealment?' and, 'What there was indecent and licentious in the character which [Caroline] assumed?'.[115] A pamphlet published by the radical John Fairburn went further by containing the testimony of an 'Eye-Witness' who wished to 'state a few *facts* which fell under his observation' in two years spent in Italy 'from which country he has just returned', one of which was that 'the *costume* of a Neapolitan peasant, completely excludes every thing indecent'.[116] A broadsheet published by Gowland Summers in Sunderland vindicated all the Queen's actions whilst in Italy as taking in sights 'by which the classical, the ingenious, and the inquisitive traveller is attracted and delighted'.[117]

Why was travel to Naples, and the Queen's actions whilst there, now acceptable to a radical press that had appropriated the xenophobia of John Bull weeks before, and whose readers would have been highly unlikely to visit Italy? To an extent their attitude was led by Brougham's speeches in the Lords, in that they supported and reproduced any argument that helped the Queen's cause, but it was also aided by the revolutionary events of 1820. This was an association raised by the constant discussion of Naples in Parliament, the Queen's links to the revolution, and, most importantly, the similarity of the demands of English and Neapolitan reformers. The first parliamentary discussion of the situation at Naples was an interruption of Caroline's trial by Lord Holland and Earl Grey, which began a series of interjections during Lords debates about the Queen by members of the Holland House set.[118] The association between the injustice of not intervening at Naples and the unfairness of Caroline's trial was strengthened by the Queen's links to the revolution. In 1814 and 1815 she had become close friends with the leader of the insurrection, General Pepe. When Caroline returned to London, she offered him residence in Britain, which he accepted after defeat by the Austrians. He arrived to find the Queen dead, he did though dine at Holland House in 1821, and used London as a base to write in favour of reform and plot a revolution in Dalmatia.[119] Furthermore, the first British account of the revolution was written by a former chamberlain of the Queen, Richard Keppel Craven, who lived at Naples, from whence he was forced to return for her trial. Keppel Craven derived his authority from writing the account 'in the carriage during his rapid journey homeward from the immediate scene of the action' and in it rebukes 'some English newspapers' for their misrepresentation of the revolution as atheistic.[120] As radicals had supported Caroline, so too did they support a revolution which has been described as 'adopted in the spirit of originating an earthly paradise', and wished for some of the Neapolitan reforms, such as a wider franchise and constitutionally guaranteed free speech, to be implemented in Britain.[121] Not only did radicals support Caroline and the Neapolitans, but they also, like the Lords, associated the two. A radical broadside attacking the mayor of Rochester for claiming impartiality as the reason for refusing a meeting in support of the Queen, asked in a threatening postscript, 'Have you heard what the SOLDIERS have done in Naples? You will say, I suppose, they have *prejudged the question*!'[122] The *Weekly Intelligencer and British Luminary* devoted an October front page to the 'Present State of Public Affairs'; the page was evenly split between events in Naples and the Queen.[123] The article opens with a sentence that puts the magnitude of events in no doubt, 'The History of Nations has been marked from time to time by certain memorable epochs, the transactions of which influenced or fixed the condition of mankind for many succeeding centuries'. The Queen and Naples were not national or independent issues to be discussed, as Peterloo was, in the context of English affairs, but of 'nations' with effects that would shape Europe for centuries. Some radicals pressed the need for this panoramic view of events further, criticising the government for the insularity of its 'odious transactions' against Caroline 'whilst the People of Naples and Portugal were asserting their rights as freemen, and overthrowing the corruption of ages'.[124]

Members of the Holland House circle now approached the issue of Naples in Parliament, knowing that they were 'supported by the universal voice of the people of this country'.[125] In content these speeches were a continuation of Fox's speech against Nelson in 1800, but in rhetoric and form they were something else entirely. Debates over Naples were nothing like the technical cut and thrust of the trial; the speeches were long, replete with abstract concepts and metaphorical language, designed to be printed and read in newspapers or Hansard volumes. These speeches fit with Matthew Bevis's argument that over the course of the nineteenth century Parliament grew to be 'seen as a form of literary entertainment', where orators began to consider 'how printed words and private scenes of reading might form reflective yet engaged counterpoints to fast-paced vocal utterances and immediate crowd responses'.[126] The speeches of Holland House Whigs are indebted to the expansive rhetoric of their friend Foscolo and to the prose of Alfieri, whose portrait hung in the house's library. Earl Grey saw the threat of Austrian occupation in Naples as part of 'the monarchical principle' which if 'successfully maintained the triumph of tyranny would be complete, and the chains of mankind would be rivetted for ever'.[127] The Foxite Marquis of Lansdowne (Henry Petty-Fitzmaurice) asked 'are the subjects of an independent state to be for ever debarred from political regeneration?', and James Mackintosh shared Shelley's grand historical reflection that, 'the whole of the Neapolitan territories should once more be overrun by the barbarous hordes of the North, by modern tyrants of regions, which were in former ages the cradle of those rude warriors who desolated Italy'.[128] In 1820, the public mind appears to, albeit briefly, have changed how it thought: the idea that liberty could be conceived of beyond the statutory limits of nations, free of xenophobic prejudices, was now a practical belief held in common by Hunt and Shelley; radical English pamphleteers, journalists, and newspapers; and Whig parliamentarians. In this brief moment, these usually distinct groups seem not only to have shared something at the level of ideas, but to have been convinced that they had the requisite praxes to make this a new social reality.[129]

The rhetoric, protest, and publications of this nascent counter-hegemony were in vain: the meeting of the allied powers at the Congress of Troppau in October 1820, and the Congress of Laibach in January 1821, reinstated the absolute monarchy of Ferdinand with the support of Austrian troops. The British Ministry expressed its disappointment at the failure of constitutionalism but, as in 1815, was unprepared to intervene to guarantee this.[130] The 'intellectual power of society', that Hunt saw on the rise in 1819, which had produced hundreds of publications and taken up weeks of Parliamentary debate, had ultimately failed to have a meaningful impact on the Neapolitan question. The Queen's situation was no better; although Caroline's defence had won the day, and the King's minister did not put the bill through the Commons, her victory, like General Pepe's at Naples, was essentially pyrrhic. Caroline's support quickly waned. The trial ended in early November and Parliament was not recalled until January, which meant Caroline and her supporters had to wait before any changes to the liturgy or her annuity could be demanded. In the meantime, government supporters rallied, particularly through articles in Theodore Hook's newly founded *John Bull*, and began a concerted campaign to show that Caroline was still unfit to be queen.[131] In the King's Speech of 23 January 1821 the government took the momentum by granting the Queen the larger annuity she desired.

After two failed attempts to have her name restored to the liturgy, Caroline angered her radical supporters by accepting a larger annuity. Caroline was now seen in the same vein as her husband, and not as a principled champion of the people. Her greatest ignominy came on the morning of 19 July 1821. Having tried to force her way into Westminster Abbey for the coronation of her husband, Caroline was rejected and jeered by the crowds who had been her bulwark months before. She died suddenly of a heart attack a month later. These two seemingly epoch-defining events with which Italy and British Italianism were bound ended not with a bang but a whimper. They were the last showing of the 1790s spirit; Mary Shelley claimed in 1820 that 'thirty years ago was the era for Republics, and they all fell – This is the era for *constitutions*', but the next two decades were the era of state supremacy, punctuated with only the mild respite of the 1832 Reform Act.[132] In some cases the reaction to failure maintained post-Waterloo idealism; Lord Ellenborough (Edward Law) claimed 'the blood of the Neapolitans, would be the seed of the liberties of Italy'.[133] The response was more subtle at the King's Theatre where Hunt's friend, and *Examiner* contributor, William Ayrton was musical director. Aware of the cosmopolitan investment in the Queen and Naples, Ayrton chose May 1821 to give London premieres to two works by Rossini: *Il Turco in Italia* (1814) and *La Gazza Ladra* (1817). The Neapolitan setting of *Il Turco* kept the landscape of the failed revolution in the public mind, with one review commenting, 'the view of Naples first by day-light, and afterwards by moon-light, is among the finest instances of art'.[134] The power of *La Gazza* was more immediately obvious: its tale of the draconian power of the state to publicly try a wrongly accused woman had clear parallels with Caroline's fate. The xenophobia that came to the surface during the Queen's trial and the snub to independence bound up in the Troppau protocol were felt keenly at Pisa and Ravenna, and caused Shelley and his circle to reflect on the failure of cosmopolitanism and liberty. In what was the last great articulation of radical Anglo-Italian literary culture, these exiles created poetry that used its deep commitment to Italian forms and ideas to come to terms with the failure of opposition.

CHAPTER 6

Pisa 1820–1822
Sailing in the Wind's Eye

Italy is the place for you – the very place – The Paradise of exiles – the retreat of Pariahs.

Percy Shelley to Thomas Medwin, 1820

Three poets who had been engaged with Italy and its literature since 1815 attempted to form a literary coterie at Pisa in 1822; over seven years they had developed a radical idea of Italy, while their hopes for European revolution were frequently disappointed. Byron and Shelley were settled in a land that in climate, landscape, and culture could be their paradise, but were also aware that their poetry, convictions, and morality had made them pariahs in England. The belated arrival of Hunt at Livorno, only a week before Shelley's death, makes him a fit subject for the coda, as his disaffection with Italy when he experienced it at first hand anticipates the changes to Anglo-Italian culture after 1823. The chapter begins by briefly considering Byron's development in the ottava rima while at Ravenna in 1820 and most of 1821: his deeper engagement mirrors Shelley's accretive study of Italian forms at Pisa. In the aftermath of the failed Carbonari uprising and with expulsion from the Romagna looming, Shelley implored Byron to 'undertake a great Poem' and persuaded him to join the exiles at Pisa.[1] The chapter looks at the formation of this doomed coterie. There was a pre-existent community of exiles and misfits at Pisa, many of whom shared Shelley's literary and political inclinations, but it was the willingness of Shelley, although the least renowned of the trio, to conduct the 'two thunderbolts', Byron and Hunt, that forged this group.[2] A discussion of Shelley's self-fashioning as the Lucifer of this Pisan community forms the contextual background to a reading of 'The Triumph of Life'. Most of this chapter is given over to a consideration of Shelley's last long poem, which I read as a product both of his immersion in the Italian canon and his relentlessly hopeful approach to a bleak European present.

Pisa was a suitable place for the formation of a coterie: it was close enough to Livorno for an easy supply of books and periodicals, and the area also had an established exile community, whose beliefs tallied with those of Shelley's circle. The community did not consist of the English tourists who were again visiting Italy; Margaret Mason wrote to Shelley to reassure him of this before his arrival, 'Here there are very few [English] as yet, and I do not hear of any that are expected'.[3] Mason's claim is corroborated by travellers' diaries of the period; Pisa was not on the standard route of the shorter post-war Italian tour, and those who did visit would typically only spend a day seeing the Piazza del Duomo and the Torre della Muda.[4] In the *Liberal*, the journal intended to be the literary expression of this circle, Hunt welcomes this peace and claims, 'What renders Pisa interesting now, and will continue to render it so long as it exists, is its being left to a comparative solitude'.[5] This solitude provided a few years of calm following personal and political turmoil, a calm in which Shelley wrote 'The Triumph of Life', a poem ingrained with the failure of European radicalism.

While Shelley was settling in to life in Pisa, Byron was at Ravenna, where he undertook further reading in and translation of the Italian tradition that had inspired *Beppo*. From the composition of *Don Juan* IV onwards, Byron's reading went beyond the contemporary poetry of Casti: he read and studied Francesco Berni's *Orlando Innamorato* (1524–1531) and began to be strongly influenced by the *Morgante* of Luigi Pulci. Byron began a translation of the first canto of Pulci's mock epic in 1819, aiming to 'present [the *Morgante*] in an English dress', which was eventually published in the fourth number of the *Liberal*.[6] Pulci's poem is a sprawling burlesque in ottava rima, which loosely follows Orlando and his companion the giant Morgante on their adventures around Europe. Its ribaldry and criticism of religious zealots earned it a place on Savonarola's *falò delle vanità*.[7] The influence of the *Morgante* on *Don Juan* has long been established in criticism, but Byron's interaction can be further appreciated by considering it in the context of the Italian literary revival in London, and particularly Romantic critics' estimation of Pulci.[8] In the 1790s, Roscoe had included verse by Pulci in the appendix to his *Life of Lorenzo,* and in the 1810s the Holland House resident Serafino Buonaiuti edited *Risorgimento della Poesia Italiana*, a two-part anthology of Pulci and his contemporaries.[9] In the preface Buonaiuti praises this group as reformers who had revived Italian verse after it had 'ricadde nell'antica rozzezza'.[10] Ginguené gave a long analysis of the *Morgante* in the fourth volume of his *Histoire* and likewise saw his style as reformist: it was an antidote to the proliferation of Petrarchan lyrics and a return to 'les dictons familiers dont la langue toscane abonde'.[11] As Byron claims in the preface to his translation of Pulci, and shows in the increasingly digressive and self-descriptive *Don Juan*, he wanted his work to be viewed in the same reformist vein, as part of a 'new style of poetry lately sprung up in England'.[12]

However, as with many of Byron's interactions with Italian ideas, he both observes and diverges from the recent English interest in the *Morgante*. Byron engages more deeply with the *Morgante* and embraces its serio-comic coarseness that had been criticized by a number of Romantic critics.[13] Pulci featured in one of Coleridge's lectures, and in his notes he wrote, 'the heartless spirit of Jest and Buffoonery its [the *Morgante's*] chief demerit – sovereigns and their courtiers were flattered by the degradation of nature'.[14] It was precisely this spirit that Byron looked for, calling Pulci 'the parent [. . .] of all jocose Italian poetry'.[15] Pulci also provided a defence against the outcry of the 'public mind' against *Don Juan*: as Byron claimed to Murray, when reading the *Morgante,* 'you will see what was permitted in a Catholic country and a bigotted age to a Churchman on the score of religion'.[16] What Byron gained from Pulci's ottava rima is not easily identifiable by similarities of plot; rather the *Morgante* gave *Don Juan* a new dynamism. It allowed Byron to 'perch upon a humbler promontory / Amidst life's infinite variety' to accommodate different languages, registers, and people, to tell a tale of maids, pirates, and highwaymen.[17] Byron's Italian freedom in the resumed *Don Juan* was not praised in *Blackwood's*: 'Lord B.'s residence in Italy has been much too long protracted. He has positively lost his ear, not only for the harmony of English verse, but the very jingle of English rhymes'.[18] Life in Italy not only lead to the disintegration of Byron's moral fabric but also corrupted the form of his verse. The perceived threat to tradition is based on national values, as it has been throughout this study; Byron's easy style is unpatriotic as it fails to pay respect to the 'harmony' and 'jingle' of his native tongue. Shelley was well versed in *Beppo*, and Byron had read the first canto of *Don Juan* aloud to him in 1818; Shelley was now considering the 'jingle' of this Italian form.[19] In July 1820 Shelley loosely translated the Homeric hymn to Hermes in ottava rima as the 'Hymn to Mercury', and a month later composed 'The Witch of Atlas'. Byron's ottava rima was an obvious spur to these experiments – Shelley seems to acknowledge as much in a recently discovered letter to Ollier – but he was also indebted to his reading of Niccolò Forteguerri's *Il Riccardetto* (1738).[20] The interest in Forteguerri was timely: Murray was about to publish Merivale's translation, *The Two*

First Cantos of Richardetto (1820). The claim in Merivale's preface that 'the genius of English literature more nearly assimilates with that of the Italian than of any other European nation', shows the high-water mark of Italian influence on English culture, an esteem that would be inconceivable a decade before or after.[21] But Shelley seems to have had no serious thought of returning home to ride this wave: his time in Italy was, like Byron's, changing from a long tour to a 'residence'.

After leaving Venice, the Shelleys led an itinerant life, moving from Naples, to Rome, and Florence. They had faced the trauma of losing two children, the problem of dealing with Claire Clairmont and her daughter Allegra, and the scandal surrounding the pregnancy of their maid Elise Foggi.[22] In the context of this final 'calumny', Shelley visited Byron at Ravenna, and wrote to Mary Shelley of his wish,

> to form for ourselves a society of our own class, as much as possible, in intellect or in feelings: & to connect ourselves with the interests of that society. – Our roots were never struck so deeply as at Pisa & the transplanted tree flourishes not.[23]

Shelley believed that to flourish, he and Mary must reject passivity. He wanted to 'connect' within a group, and grow roots to take greater nourishment from the Italian soil. Shelley's time in Italy, whether in Venice, Bagni di Lucca, or Pisa, is a search for an imaginative home, and Michael O'Neill has appreciated this quest for home as a paradox inherent in the Shelleyan view of Italy as both a paradise and a retreat.[24] This need for home or sanctuary has an earlier basis in his interaction with Italian verse. Among the poems appended to *Alastor* (1816) is a translation of Dante's sonnet to Guido Cavalcanti, in which he wishes to 'ascend / A magic ship' (ll. 2–3) and sail with fellow-poets to a place where 'even satiety should still enhance / Between our hearts their strict community'.[25] It was during his residence at Pisa five years later that Shelley wrote his most Dantescan poetry, and this earlier desire to travel among like minds resonated with him as he organised a circle which was 'strict' in the now obsolete sense of close and intimate.[26]

Newfound stability brought a change in culture for the Shelleys. They were now residents, not travellers, and their leisure time shifted from touring galleries and monuments to socialising with an established community. When the Shelleys arrived in Pisa they found an intellectually animated group of expatriates and Italians with whom they could discuss literature and politics.[27] After a month or so, the Shelleys made the acquaintance of Francesco Pacchiani, a sometime-professor at the

University of Pisa, whom Mary Shelley initially described in a letter to Hunt as 'il solo Italiano che ha cuore ed anima'.[28] Although their friendship cooled rapidly, it was Pacchiani who introduced the Shelleys to Alexander Mavrocordato on 2 December 1820. Mavrocordato was a Byzantine Greek in exile: as calls for Greek independence swelled towards the end of the 1810s, Mavrocordato left Wallachia for Italy to plan for Greek freedom among the exile community at the University of Pisa.[29] For a time, Mavrocordato was Mary Shelley's tutor in Greek, and was the dedicatee of Shelley's verse drama *Hellas* (1821).[30] Another Pisa resident whom the Shelleys met via Pacchiani was the Irish belletrist John Taaffe. While at university in Edinburgh, Taaffe became involved with a married woman and the repercussions of the affair led to a life in exile. This began with travels around Portugal, Spain, and north Africa, during which he wrote his Byronic tale, *Padilla* (1815). Taaffe arrived at Pisa in 1815, and his name is remembered today primarily because of his involvement in the so-called 'Pisan affray' at the end of March 1822, the event that heralded the end of Shelley's literary circle.[31] But at Pisa Taaffe was also involved in a decade-long study of Dante that produced a translation of the *Inferno* and a long commentary (the first volume of which was published as *Comment on the Divine Comedy of Dante Aligheri* (1822)).

Scholars have generally dismissed the *Comment*, with Timothy Webb claiming, 'Although Shelley was too kind to say so openly he obviously considered that the literary merits of Taaffe's work were negligible'.[32] It is clear from Shelley's parodic fragment 'A capering, squalid, squalling one' that he thought little of Taaffe's translation of Dante, and Mary Shelley found Taaffe personally overbearing.[33] But there is no evidence that this was Shelley's opinion of the *Comment*; on the contrary, he, Byron, and Hunt praised the work and attempted to get it published.[34] Byron, having written that Taaffe's translation 'is *not* good; but the Comment is really valuable', did persuade Murray to publish the first volume in 1822.[35] Moreover, when the *Comment* is assessed in the context of the Dante resurgence in London, its literary worth is not negligible. As Ralph Pite has suggested, the *Comment* is 'one of the fruits of Dante's suddenly increased popularity in England after Waterloo'.[36] The *Comment* distils aspects of the new Dante scholarship flourishing in Italy, and its later recapitulation in England. Like Mathias, Foscolo, and Buonaiuti before him, Taaffe's work begins with his credentials:

> A long residence in Italy (I have lived in it for several years and am likely to continue) and many consequent facilities might render me fitter for my undertaking than my competitors.[37]

The use of his immigrant position mimics the Italian exiles' recourse to native status, and suggests his work is of greater authority than English scholarship. The *Comment* follows the work of Italians in London by dismissing 'French' critics of Dante: Taaffe calls Sismondi 'incorrect' for questioning Dante's political importance, stating that his view seems 'much more suggested by a desire of novelty, than a judicious survey of events'.[38] The climax of this argument for a politically engaged poet comes in Taaffe's statement on Dante's Italy: 'the Italian republics were in full possession of their boasted, though insecure, feverish independence [. . .] ere the modern literature was begotten, or the ancient had emerged from the hiding-places of the monasteries'.[39] Taaffe's judgement blends Foscolo's argument for the civic role of the poet in the Tuscan republic with Shelley's claim in 'A Defence of Poetry', written at Pisa, that Dante's poetry 'may be considered as the bridge thrown over the stream of time, which unites the modern and antient world'.[40] The concurrence here is more than a coincidence; at Pisa, Shelley was now in an environment where Dante's poetry was discussed at an expert level.

The Shelleys' closest friend in Pisa was Margaret Mason, born Margaret King and for a time Lady Mount Cashell. She had been tutored as a child by Mary Wollstonecraft, and was a passionate anti-Unionist who identified as a United Irishwoman.[41] Her radical position was reflected in the unusual company she kept as the wife of a Tory peer: in the 1790s, she met Godwin and Thomas Hardy in London, and toured Europe from 1801 to 1803, seeking out audiences with Thomas Holcroft and Thomas Paine in Paris, and with Alfieri at Florence.[42] After her separation from Lord Mount Cashell, she visited London and regularly called on the Godwins, dined at their house in Skinner Street, and had a book published in their *Juvenile Library* series.[43] Mason was now settled in Pisa: her radical life and history with her mother made her a point of contact for Mary Shelley. They corresponded on the political state of England, with Mason claiming 'the Box of Pandora is opening a little more and a little more every day,' and she encouraged the couple's move to Pisa.[44] Once they had arrived in late October 1820, Mason was a guest and host of the Shelleys, and the dairies of Mary Shelley and Claire Clairmont reveal that her experience of failed revolution in Ireland was still on her mind.[45] Mason's society was predominantly Italian; her political beliefs and estrangement from her husband made interaction with the English difficult. One of her closest friends was the surgeon Andrea Vaccà, doctor to Byron, Shelley, and Marianne Hunt. Vaccà had a radical past. While studying at Paris he participated in the Storming of the Bastille, leading Mary Shelley to call him 'a great republican & no Xtian'.[46] The Europe of the Vienna settlement was a political failure for Mason, Mavrocordato, and Vaccà. Their sense of unfulfilled promise in France, Ireland, and most recently in Britain and Naples chimed with Shelley's growing disillusionment. In a letter trying to bring Thomas Medwin to Pisa, this feeling is expressed in a clarification of a well-known line: 'Italy is the place for you – the very place – The Paradise of exiles – the retreat of Pariahs'.[47] Shelley's original line has the Englishman Julian apostrophise 'Thou Paradise of exiles, Italy!' and go on to praise his new Italian home.[48] At Pisa, after the failure of radicalism in 1819 and 1820, Shelley keeps the idea of 'Paradise' as a resting place for the just, but also accepts the role of Italy as a safe haven for outcasts. Shelley's correspondence carries a defeatist sense that '[e]very thing seems to conspire against Reform', and Byron too in 1821, just before asking if the two could 'contrive to meet this summer', writes that the 'late failure of the Italians has latterly disappointed me'.[49]

The Lucifer of That Starry Flock

The balance of hope and failure that operates between 'paradise' and 'retreat' permeates Shelley's later poetry. The Italian situation of Shelley's poetry allows him to discuss the past, present, and future of Europe within a landscape that was already impressed upon the Regency imagination. In Shelley's last years the ability of this location to function as a political–visionary space is heightened by using established British conceptions of the Italian landscape and climate, playing on the fact that, as Rose claimed, 'Italy's skies and suns have passed into a proverb'.[50] The symbolic function of natural phenomena can be seen in the 'Ode to Liberty':

> England yet sleeps: was she not called of old?
> Spain calls her now, as with its thrilling thunder
> Vesuvius wakens Aetna, and the cold
> Snow-crags by its reply are cloven in sunder.[51]

The similar metrical structure of the first three lines demands a comparison between sleeping England, calling Spain, and bright Naples. England is dormant and the modifying 'yet' implies it has been so for some time: its lethargy is set against the interconnected geology of the continent. G. M. Matthews has discussed the prevalence of this image cluster in Shelley's Italian poetry and correspondence, arguing that volcanoes are an image of 'revolutionary activity in the external world and in the human mind – of irrepressible collective energy contained by repressive power'.[52] The function of these images in the external world is also one of interconnectedness;

the geological chain means Vesuvius ignites Etna, and reveals a process by which more dormant landscapes could be awakened. As Hunt had claimed of the Neapolitan revolution, 'The fire is kindled; it warms the nations'.[53]

Shelley's reading of this landscape is radical, but his habit of viewing the Italian landscape in the round, as a panorama, is conventional: of the sixty-three plates in Elizabeth Batty's popular *Italian Scenery* (1820), thirty-eight are panoramic views, and in his travelogue of 1820 H. W. Williams claimed of Florence that '[t]o give you any idea of this beautiful classical city [. . .] I must describe it from one of its lofty towers'.[54] Shelley's image in the 'Ode to Liberty' was particularly conventional: the view of Vesuvius's eruption was 'the timeless stock-in-trade of topographers and panorama painters' in Britain.[55] In works from Wright of Derby to Turner and later John Martin, Vesuvius is represented as a bursting flare in a sky of darkness.[56] Pite has argued that Shelley's Italian poetry appropriates traits from British paintings of Italian landscapes and then 'alters the pictorial conventions he invokes'.[57] So here Shelley takes a famous scene and changes its fire to function as an image of European struggle. Just as reformers after Waterloo redefined hegemonic terms such as the 'public mind', and Shelley himself reclaimed the diction of monarchy and religion against the institutions they represent, so here popular views of Italian scenery are repurposed for radical ends. Even after Britain's failure to intervene in the suppression of the Neapolitans, these natural images of catching fire remained integral to Shelley's poetry: in the 'Triumph' Rousseau maintains his intellectual power because 'there rise / A thousand beacons from the spark I bore' and Francis Bacon is praised as he 'leapt / Like lightning out of darkness'.[58]

In a letter to Hunt of 1821, Shelley suggests that the Pisa circle was a similar point of light in the gloom of Metternich's Europe. 'I wish you could bring [T. J. Hogg] with you – he will say that I am like Lucifer who has seduced the third part of the starry flock'.[59] Frederick Jones's footnote to these lines directs the reader to the following lines from *Paradise Lost*:

> His countenance, as the morning star that guides
> The starry flock, allured them, and with lies
> Drew after him the third part of heaven's host.[60]

Shelley's use of 'Lucifer', if read as meaning the morning star Venus, follows the pattern observed above: Shelley identifies himself and his project as a light in the night sky. But in the letter Shelley changes Milton's 'morning star' to 'Lucifer'. The terms are synonymous – Lucifer literally means 'Light-Bearer' – but the claim is quite different if 'Lucifer' replaces 'morning star'. Milton's lines do not read 'His countenance as the morning star'; the comma makes a metaphor, and creates one of what Alastair Fowler has called the 'radical ambiguities' in the syntax of *Paradise Lost*.[61] Satan was a guide to the rebel angels as the star Lucifer is to sheep at night. It is not the 'star' that 'allured' the rebel angels but Satan himself. Shelley elides the two meanings: he can be the morning star, which, in its associations with liberty, was for W. B. Yeats 'the most important, the most precise of all Shelley's symbols, the one he uses with the fullest knowledge of its meaning', but also harness Satan's power among the rebel angels to lure his friends to join him at Pisa.[62]

Six months before this letter, Shelley wrote 'A Defence of Poetry' in which Milton's Satan is an image of power in failure: 'one who perseveres in some purpose which he has conceived to be excellent in spite of adversity and torture'.[63] In the 'Defence', Milton is a figure who 'stood alone illuminating an age unworthy of him' (520) and Dante was 'the Lucifer of that starry flock which in the thirteenth century shone forth from republican Italy, as from a heaven, into the darkness of the benighted world' (528). Shelley's allusion to *Paradise Lost* in a reference to Dante reaffirms the connection between Milton and the Italian tradition shown throughout this study. Again, the deliberate misquotation of 'Lucifer' for 'morning star' occurs. Dante can be seen as the morning star, the 'first awakener of an entranced Europe', but with this change he is also, like Shelley, the exile and rebel, cast out but retaining his ability to enlighten 'the benighted world'. Dante is the poet Shelley refers to most in the 'Defence', and it was during the residence at Pisa that he made his pilgrimage, as he had to Arquà for Petrarch, to Dante's tomb, where he 'worshipped the sacred spot'.[64] Percy and Mary Shelley were also reading and re-reading Dante and Petrarch whilst at Pisa, particularly the *Purgatorio* and *Trionfi* (1351).[65] The result of this study was 'The Triumph of Life', which uses these two Italian analogues as a means of reckoning between the paradise of isolation and the fact that Shelley's hopes for liberty were all but extinguished. Shelley's manipulation of these sources within the political current of his own time is complicated by the unfinished state of the 'Triumph'. The poem is fragmentary; as Orrin Wang has suggested, it 'invites its reader to approach it as a series of historical and textual fragments' through its interaction with multiple genres and sources.[66] Shelley's use of the Italian tradition resembles what scholars of Terence and Plautus have called *contaminatio*: using an additional source (the *Commedia*) to alter the relationship with a primary analogue (the *Trionfi*). In *De la Littérature du Midi de l'Europe*, Sismondi chooses not to discuss the *Trionfi*, as he deemed it too similar to the *Commedia*, but Shelley's careful reading shows the important differences between Dante and Petrarch, particularly in their contrasting modes of narration.[67] The *contaminatio* of the 'Triumph' is subtle – Petrarch and Dante share a genre (visionary epic), and a form (terza rima) – and Shelley's ability to distinguish between these poems demonstrates his engagement with the Italian tradition at Pisa.

Shelley's absorption in these two poems also produced a very different terza rima from that of the 'Ode to the West Wind'.[68] This development from 1819 to 1822 occurs in part because of deeper reading and writing in the form: the Dantescan fragment 'The Tower of Famine', written in December 1820, shows Shelley moving away from the logical and punctuated tercets of the ode, and towards the concentrated but syntactically open style of the 'Triumph'.[69] But it was also a change fostered by a community within which Shelley could discuss the mechanics of the form: with Byron, who wrote *The Prophecy of Dante* (1819) in tercets; with his cousin Thomas Medwin, who was translating the Ugolino episode for his *Sketches in Hindoostan* (1821); and particularly with Taaffe, who devotes twenty pages of the *Comment* to a discussion of the terza rima. In the preface to the *Comment,* the 'wondrous flexibility' of terza rima is praised, but for Taaffe the element that made the form integral to any reading of the *Commedia* is its concision; this was 'the chief peculiarity of Dante's style'.[70] For Foscolo too, the way Dante 'compresses his narration' was central to the laconic style of the *Commedia*, and Hallam claimed 'No poet ever excelled him in conciseness, and in the rare talent of finishing his pictures by a few bold touches'.[71] The concision and fluency of Shelley's terza rima in the 'Triumph' is a practical expression of the renewed critical interest in Dante's form.[72] One example of this new terza rima, notable for how self-consciously Shelley alludes to Dante, is in Rousseau's digression before his vision:

> [']Behold a wonder worthy of the rhyme
>
> 'Of him who from the lowest depths of Hell
> Through every Paradise and through all glory
> Love led serene, and who returned to tell
>
> 'In words of hate and awe the wondrous story
> How all things are transfigured, except Love;
> For deaf as is a sea which wrath makes hoary
>
> 'The world can hear not the sweet notes that move
> The sphere whose light is melody to lovers—
> A wonder worthy of his rhyme[']
>
> (ll. 471–480)

The first clause is quickened by repetition and alliteration, only to be slowed by the spondaic 'Love led' to end on the contemplative 'serene'. The next two clauses also end on love, so that the central theme of Shelley's Platonic reading of Dante becomes a sustained feature of his poetic construction. The concentrated description of Dante's language as 'words of hate and awe' gives, in the manner of the *Commedia*, complex sense in simple phrases and illustrates the concision that Taaffe and Foscolo admired. These lines also display Shelley's ability to mould Dante's craft into English diction, and act as a tribute to his predecessor. The reference to the 'sweet notes that move / The sphere whose light is melody to lovers' is a verbal echo of the final line of the *Commedia*, 'l'amor che move il sole e l'altre stelle', and more obliquely to the pilgrim's reaction to Casella's song, '*Amor che ne la mente mi ragiona*'.[73] There is a further tribute in not directly naming 'him': Dante is named by his deeds, in homage to a technique that Dante uses to describe Aristotle in Limbo (a scene Shelley had in mind when writing the 'Triumph').[74]

Despite the importance of Dante to Shelley's poem, the later poet is not overly dutiful; the 'Triumph' does not suffer from what Thomas Greene has called 'the characteristic risk' of imitative verse by not making 'a vital emergence from the tradition'.[75] Shelley pursues strategies that mark the originality of his work. Although enjambment within tercets occurs in the *Commedia*, it never occurs on the scale used in the 'Triumph', and the enjambment between tercets in the extract above is infrequent in Dante.[76] The change creates a greater narrative drive, with the terza metrically forcing the progress and wild dance of the triumphal procession. The second point of novelty is in the effrontery of Rousseau's claim, made twice, to tell 'a wonder worthy of the rhyme' of Dante. As William Keach has remarked, it is no accident that Shelley rhymes on 'rhyme' when alluding to Dante, and then reinforces this comparison by repeating the worthiness of his subject at the end of the digression.[77] The manuscript of the 'Triumph' supports this claim for Shelley's purposeful rhyme. Line 471 originally had 'a wonder worthy of the rime', which was then altered to 'rhyme'; although the use of Italian term would clearly signal a Dantescan tribute, Shelley may have seen it as a bit overblown.[78] The stylistic homage of these lines should be read in the voice of the poet, as a statement in which, after a sustained study of Italian forms, Shelley ranks his English tercets as an equal to Dante's.

Of All That Is, Has Been, or Will Be Done

The first forty lines of the 'Triumph' present the narrator in an Italian setting, 'athwart the steep / Of a green Apennine' (ll. 25–6), from which he will experience the 'strange trance' of Life's procession. It is sunrise, the birds are singing their 'matin lay', the ocean its orison, and between the two of them there is 'Sweet talk in music through the enamoured air' (l. 39). As it was at the opening of 'Euganean Hills', the rise of the sun is an enriching dawn:

> Swift as a spirit hastening to his task
> Of glory and of good, the Sun sprang forth
> Rejoicing in his splendour, and the mask
>
> Of darkness fell from the awakened Earth.
> The smokeless altars of the mountain snows
> Flamed above crimson clouds, and at the birth
>
> Of light, the Ocean's orison arose
> To which the birds tempered their matin lay.
> (ll. 1–8)

The dactylic opening to a first line that breaks the pentameter signals the pace that will be the defining characteristic of the poem. The scene is one of harmony; all the subjects – the Sun, Earth, snow, clouds, Ocean, and birds – are free from human interference. The lines are filled with images of production and novelty, in the Sun which 'sprang forth', the revelation of a new day in unmasking the old, and in the 'birth / Of light' enjambed across tercets. Again the imagery concerns the play of light, but what was just a bright star or a flare of volcanic eruption becomes over the eight lines a fully illuminated landscape. Behind this is Uriel's description of creation in *Paradise Lost* III, in which 'darkness fled, / Light shone', and 'Swift to their several quarters hasted then / The cumbrous elements'.[79] But, in a manner typical of Shelley's elision of Milton and Dante in the 'Defence', there is also a nod to Shelley's deeper source: *Purgatorio* I. Dante's pilgrim climbs onto *terra firma,* after thirty-three cantos of darkness, to be greeted by the dawn star Lucifer. In this natural world Dante is approached by Cato, who announces that the sun is rising and that it will be his guide up the Purgatorial mountain. After their conversation Dante notices his new environment:

> L'alba vinceva l'ora mattutina
> che fuggia innanzi, sì che di lontano
> conobbi il tremolar de la marina.[80]

As in the 'Triumph', Dante's sunrise is characterised by its speed in the vanquishing of the dawn over the matin hour. There is also an unveiling: the light cast by the sun reveals the sea to the pilgrim, a new clarity of vision that hints at the possibility of cleansing in this new canticle. Misreading of this opening can occur if Shelley's Dantean source is ignored. In an influential reading, Paul de Man has claimed the Sun's rise 'occurs by *imposition*' in a violent image associated with Life's later tyranny.[81] But this reading does not appreciate Shelley's established technique of reclaiming the diction of power ('glory', 'Rejoicing', 'altar', 'orison') for radical ends, nor does it recognise the importance of his source: for Dante's pilgrim morning has broken like the first morning, and the sunrise signals a process of change.[82]

Pite has claimed that the 'Triumph' 'makes use of the world created by *Purgatorio*'; more precisely it makes use of its first two books, the stage after Hell and before Purgatory, the *Antepurgatorio*, which Mary Shelley reports contained Shelley's 'most favourite passage'.[83] Shelley chooses this source for two connected reasons: the figure of Cato appears at this point in Dante and is below the surface of Shelley's poem, and these cantos represent 'the birth of light' for the pilgrim as they do in the opening of the 'Triumph'. On the first point, Mary Shelley records that she and Percy had taken up reading the *Purgatorio* in August 1819 along with a study of Lucan's *Pharsalia*, both works in which Cato plays an important role.[84] Cato is an anomalous figure in the *Purgatorio*; as a pagan and a suicide he should be in *Inferno*, but is held by Dante 'degno di tanta reverenza in vista, / che più non dee a padre alcun figliuolo'.[85] Dante opens the Christian process of Purgatory with a Roman Man of Law who was prepared to die for liberty. Shelley's decision to open his poem in a landscape associated with Cato, as opposed to a nonspecific *locus amoenus*, means an icon of liberty, and an enduring icon despite his failure, precedes an exposition of what Shelley calls 'Caesar's crime' in establishing an empire. The crime of the Roman Empire was also of symbolic resonance for Euthanasia, the republican heroine of Mary Shelley's *Valperga* (1823), who weeps 'why did not Cato live?', when entering Rome.[86]

The second reason for Shelley's use of this Dantescan landscape is that the sun functions within *Purgatorio* as a cleanser; as the reader later learns, the pilgrims may only climb the purgatorial mountain during the hours of sunlight. Cato uses the imagery of light to compare the possibility of a cleansed future in *Purgatorio* with the infinite suffering of those in *Inferno:*

> 'Chi v'ha guidati, o che vi fu lucerna,
>   uscendo fuor de la profonde notte
>   che sempre nere fa la valle inferna?[87]

The answer, not given due to the pilgrim's awe, is Virgil, who is a 'lucerna' just as Rousseau, Shelley's guide, bears a spark. The clash is between the light of Purgatory and the 'profonde' and 'sempre nere'; in the *Inferno* there is no light, and thus no prospect of forgiveness. Shelley inverts the scheme of the *Commedia*, which moves from the *Inferno* to the light of *Purgatorio*, by opening with the 'birth of light' and the possibility of a changed future, before reflecting on the historical failure of liberty. In a manoeuvre typical of Shelley's confidence in altering his sources, Dante's aubade is turned on its head when the narrator makes his orientation clear: 'before me fled / The night; behind me rose the day' (ll. 26–27). These lines appear in an earlier manuscript as, 'Before me fled the ~~day~~ night; behind me ~~sunk~~ rose the ~~night~~ day'.[88] Unlike Dante, Shelley's narrator turns his back on the sun. The correction in the manuscript inverts the typical dawn-gazing pose of the aubade, and provides a transition to the central vision of Shelley's poem. The narrative itself now turns away from the light of Cato, and from the possibility of a new dawn, towards the procession of Life's tyrannical power.

Once the narrator falls into his vision Shelley begins his engagement with the Italian triumphal tradition, and specifically with Petrarch's *Trionfi*. A triumph was the highest honour given to a general upon his return to Rome, with monuments such as the Arch of Titus built to celebrate such events.[89] Shelley saw this arch, which commemorates the sacking of Jerusalem, in 1819. His reaction is recorded in a prose fragment: Shelley begins by looking at the conquered, 'the desolation of our City' and the degradation of 'matrons & virgins & children & old men', before moving on to 'a procession of the victors'.[90] His account appreciates the central duality of the triumph as an event both to garner praise and to revel in the subjugation of the conquered. Shelley had read Gibbon's two essays on this subject, 'On the Triumphs of the Romans' and 'On the Triumphal Shows and Ceremonies', which saw the triumph as the ultimate display of imperial power, with Gibbon claiming that because of it 'military virtue was forever associated with religion in the imagination of the Romans'.[91] Although the Roman triumph was largely obsolete by the Byzantine period, Shelley was inspired by the revival of triumphs in the statecraft and art of modern Europe. The public triumph was brought into the political theatre of the early nineteenth century by Napoleon, who entered Paris in 1810 and passed under an early version of the Arc de Triomphe.[92] Shelley casts Napoleon in the 'Triumph' as the 'Child of a fierce hour' (l. 217): an agent of Life, and one who obscured the dawn brought by the French Revolution. The journey of Queen Caroline to London from

Dover was also regularly viewed as a triumphal procession. In one print of 1820, Caroline is portrayed as Boadicea on a chariot, armed with a spear and trampling her bewigged enemies as her supporters follow behind, and another print from 1821 has Caroline pulled by Lions, like Mark Antony, in a chariot covered in Union Jacks.[93]

The Roman triumph had a related afterlife as a cultural image in the art and literature of the Italian Middle Ages and Renaissance, where the triumphal procession of an allegorical figure was a common subject.[94] Unlike the northern European triumph, which was characterised by its *tableaux vivants* and static poses, the Italian triumph gains its creative energy from its moving procession.[95] The Italian allegorical triumph is the basis of Petrarch's *Trionfi*, the work that is 'the legitimate progenitor' of Shelley's 'Triumph'.[96] Shelley's triumph is Italian in character; it is a vision that occurs on 'a green Apennine' (l. 26), and features an extended simile on the song of a Brescian shepherd (ll. 421–22). The 'Triumph' is rhetorically, formally, and thematically engaged with its analogue but it is not an imitation or extension of Petrarch's poem.[97] Shelley syncretises the work of Petrarch and Dante through his emotional state at Pisa, as he is forced to confront the pre-emptive triumphs of Napoleon and Queen Caroline. To analyse the role of the *Trionfi* in Shelley's 'Triumph' requires an outline of Petrarch's poem.[98] The *Trionfi* is in six chapters each containing a triumph of an allegorical figure, beginning with Love (*Cupidinus*) and ending in Eternity (*Eternitatis*) with the fulfilment of the God's 'promessa a chi si fida in lui'.[99] Petrarch describes the form and character of each allegorical figure. Death is introduced in the following manner:

> et una donna involta in vesta negra,
> con un furor qual io non so se mai
> al tempo de' giganti fusse a Flegra[100]

Although a conventional depiction, the figure of Death has entire control over the tercet, with the frailty of her concealment negated by her gigantic superiority. Each allegorical figure in triumph also comes with an associated train. The procession of *Fame*, which is like those 'in Campidoglio al tempo antico / talora o per Via Sacra o per Via Lata / venian tutti', is the most strictly organised of the triumphs.[101] Before the 400-line description of the pageant, Petrarch states that the retinue of Fame approached him in the specific order that his narrative follows (*Fame* I 31). This hierarchical *enumeratio* begins with the men of civic Rome, followed by the heroes of Persia and Greece, then the biblical tradition, and ends in the next book with women of Antiquity. The final book begins with the narrator's head turned 'a l'altro lato', and gives a humanist progress of philosophy.[102] Unlike Dante's encounters, Petrarch's *enumeratio* do not discuss these characters in any detail, nor does the narrator converse with them; the list exists to vivify the famous through their synecdochal power. The figures are paragons of a great age available to the poet only through imagination. The absence of contemporary figures, and the invective against the Crusaders' failure to recapture Jerusalem, creates Petrarch's visionary world in which present is inferior to past.[103]

A number of rhetorical devices are used to break the regularity and heighten the register of these *enumeratio*. When a new group is to be considered, a transitional tercet is often supplied, in which Petrarch reflects on his visionary task, the quantity of people still to be discussed, and his current viewpoint.[104] Petrarch also groups the cast into twos and threes, so we encounter, 'Duo altri Fabii, e duo Caton con esso, / e duo Pauli, duo Bruti e duo Marcelli', as the heroes proceed by a rhetorical technique that allows for the compression of ten characters into two lines.[105] A more complex form of number-based rhetoric in the *Trionfi*, drawing on the significance of the sixteen virtues and the Pythagorean thirty-two in *Pudicitie,* has been analysed by Alistair Fowler, who claims that more than being a mere catalogue the triumph represents 'an ordered array and conveys meaning by its spatial arrangement'.[106] These rhetorical tropes, along with the division, on the basis of gender, geography, and profession, are part of a stylistic formality, which mimetically enforces the stateliness, and in the case of *Fame* the imperialism, of the triumphs described. Petrarch's descriptions of the allegorical triumph and its attendants is the template for Shelley's triumph of Life (ll. 41–181). The starkest difference between the two interpretations is that where Petrarch has a secure foundation in Christian and pagan traditions, Shelley chooses to represent Life. His Life is a visionary allegory of the hegemonic forces active throughout society, which function outside the temporal logic of Death, Fame, and Eternity. Through the exposition of this allegorical figure Shelley can mount a critique of nineteenth-century tyranny, while also making a larger claim about hegemonic restrictions on freedom throughout history. In a reversal of Petrarch's scheme the reader is shown the procession first. They are a multitude,

> All hastening onward, yet none seemed to know
>   Whither he went, or whence he came, or why
> He made one of the multitude, yet so
>
> (ll. 47–49)

The pauses and relative adverbs reveal a purposeless group far from the orderly devotion in *Fame* and *Cupidinus,* and an atmosphere of uncertainty is transmitted through the disorientating syntax and repetitions. When Life arrives it appears

> Beneath a dusky hood and double cape
> Crouching within the shadow of a tomb;
> And o'er what seemed the head a cloud-like crape
>
> Was bent, a dun and faint etherial gloom
> (ll. 89–92)

Although the entrance of Life in hood and cape suggests Petrarch's Death, it has none of her fury. Again, Shelley's Italian relationship is mediated through Milton, with his description sharing the equivocal nature of Death's introduction in *Paradise Lost.*[107] The figure is obscured by the colour and size of its clothing, its stature, and its positioning within the shadow of the tomb. Where Petrarch's Death was greater than giants here the narrator can only indeterminately make out Life's head. It is not that Life is any less powerful than Petrarch's Death, but rather that Life's power is so great that it need not boast and revel in its entire tyranny. Life's power is total but it is without the symbolism and grandeur of Death; Shelley's almost postmodern conception is of the barely perceptible ('dun and faint etherial') everyday suppression of liberty by those who have controlled the 'public mind' from the time of Cato to Castlereagh.

Shelley's style is also distinct from Petrarch's. He can appropriate the stately tempo of the Italian tradition as his procession moves 'with solemn speed majestically on' (l. 106), as when Shelley goes to great lengths in the manuscript to pull off the rhetorical trick of withholding Napoleon's name until the final clause (ll. 215–224), a technique used by Petrarch in his introduction of Claudian in *Fame.*[108] But for every nod towards a higher register there is a corresponding distortion. Shelley's chariot moves like the 'conqueror's advance' (l. 112) through Rome, but the crowd surrounding it negate any sense of order with 'fierce song and maniac dance' (l. 110). Shelley may be recalling the *feste* that took place at Lerici, which Mary Shelley describes in a letter as containing local people who 'pass the whole night in dancing on the sands close to our door running into the sea then back again & screaming in one perpetuel [*sic*] air'.[109] The mania of the triumphal dance is enacted in the syntax: lines are rarely end-stopped, tercets regularly run on, and the proliferation of conjunctions and interrogative terms denies the reader a grand style. Shelley does not change his triumph only for the sake of poetic difference. Life is the triumphant victor in a procession that has nothing like the Roman separation of the subjugated foe and a proud citizenry; Shelley's multitude is mixed into one subservient mass. Gibbon realised that the Roman Triumph 'converted the spectators into actors', as the watching populace becomes proud of, but also implicated in, the state's militarism, a point referred to when Rousseau tell the narrator 'follow thou, and from spectator turn / Actor or victim in this wretchedness' (ll. 305–306).[110] Gibbon's theoretical conversion of innocent spectators to culpable actors is practically realised in the 'Triumph': Shelleys 'living sea' takes its members from 'senate-house and prison and theatre' (ll. 113–114), or in an earlier draft from 'senators & gladiators and slaves', lists which in their profusion recall the 'matrons & virgins & children & old men' of the prose fragment on the Arch of Titus.[111] Shelley's alteration of Petrarch's scheme conveys the larger dominance of Life's tyranny, not just in individual governments or in certain periods, but in so many forms that there can be no split between conquerors and conquered. The crowds that Gibbon had described at Rome, in awe of the state and its victorious power, were not unlike those at the London victory rallies in 1815, and when Shelley wrote the 'Triumph' crowds had a new radical significance at St Peter's Field in 1819 and at Caroline's entrance into London in 1820. But Shelley's crowd has neither the subservience of 1815, nor the organised protest against the 'public mind' of the later period: it a single, transhistorical, and uninvolved mass.

The crowd that surrounds the triumph is disorganised. None of the elaborate enumeration of the *Trionfi* remains, as the narrator cannot distinguish between members of the train by any of Petrarch's criteria. The reader is presented with figures from all ages: Aristotle, Alexander the Great, Catherine the Great, Frederick the Great, Kant, Leopold II, Napoleon, Plato, the Roman emperors from Caesar to Constantine, and Rousseau. The narrator's inability to differentiate is addressed as the triumph approaches, 'Old age and youth, manhood and infancy, / [?Whirled] in one mighty torrent did appear' (ll. 52–53). The effect is not only to condense the quantity of characters described, but also to imagine them as a single tableau of European history. Life as the *Janus Quadrifrons* has the power to rule as an all-seeing transhistorical deity, but six lines later any benefits to this scope are punctured by the revelation that all four faces 'Had their eyes banded' (l. 100). Shelley's triumph contains those who were positive enlighteners of their time, and those who abused their power, but in the scheme of the triumph this is of secondary importance. There is no hierarchy in this train; all are acolytes and slaves to the 'Janus-visaged Shadow' (l. 94).

The devotion or slavery to Life that Shelley's train displays is central to the recasting of Petrarch's framework. Where Petrarch develops a historical process from Death to Fame, which in Time fades but is redeemed in Eternity, Shelley's Life has the ability to see all history, but fails to guide in any direction. And this transhistorical failure makes the 'Triumph' not – or not just – an exposition of the tyranny of today but a wider critique of the process of tyranny. The futility of Life can be accommodated in Petrarch's worldview through Eternity, as a Christian salvation when 'le tre parti sue vidi ristrette / ad un sola'.[112] The Christian redemption of Eternity is unavailable, and after many defeats in the fight for liberty, Shelley questions his earlier belief in the possibility of resurgence proposed by Machiavelli, Vico, and Alfieri. Shelley meditation on this political failure is inflected with elements of Petrarch's *Triumphus Mortis*, a triumph that crucially occurs before the redemption of Eternity. In Death's speech, which proudly opens 'Io ho condutto al fin la gente greca / e la troiana, a l'ultimo i romani', Petrarch's narrator reflects on the figures before him:[113]

> Ivi eran quei che fur detti felici,
> pontefici, regnanti, imperadori;
> or sono ignude, miseri e mendici.
> U' sono or le richezze? u' son gli onori?
> e le gemme e gli scettri e le corone,
> e le mitre e i purpurei colori?[114]

The movement from power to irrelevance signalled by the imperfect 'eran' is the fate of the men who occupy the second line. The run of nouns inspires the lists that follow: first of suffering, then a succession of the material symbols of power. There is emptiness when the abundance of symbols is put against the narrator's rhetorical questions and Petrarch faith in eternity. Shelley changes this reflective pose into a dialogic relationship when his narrator asks Rousseau:

> 'And who are those chained to the car?' 'The Wise,
>
> 'The great, the unforgotten: they who wore
> Mitres and helms and crowns, or wreaths of light,
> Signs of thought's empire over thought;
> (ll. 208–11)

Later, Rousseau points out the emperors, from Caesar to Constantine, who,

> Had founded many a sceptre-bearing line
> And spread the plague of blood and gold abroad,
> And mitre-cinctured phantoms, men divine
>
> Who rose like shadows between man and god
> (ll. 286–289)

Shelley commemorates those in power who wielded symbols of control, but where Petrarch's heroes are 'naked, poor, of all bereft', Shelley's 'great' retain a hold over thought; what was an exposition of the futility of worldly achievement has become a revelation of the perpetual power of tyranny. Two expansive images, one geographical (of the empire), the other chronological (of a blood line), convey the power of the 'plague' Shelley sees gripping man. It is this tyranny that obscures the relationship between man and God and usurps 'thought', to not only control ideas, but also the praxis to bring them into reality. The epithet 'great' prepares the reader for the approach of Alexander, Frederick, and Catherine, and the choice of 'unforgotten' hints in its structure at the absent many. Petrarch's triumph can commemorate a superior past in the context of a barbarous present, where Shelley's vision shows an emphatically continuous process, enacted by hyphenated compound images, that sees Life's tyranny in 'all that is, has been, or will be done' (l. 104).

The perpetual tyranny of Life is at the centre of the 'Triumph', but, as the Pisa circle itself tried to balance failure with hope, so there is a possibility of a brighter future in the poem. The act of accepting and assessing Life's perpetual tyranny is in itself a positive act: Shelley's ability to discern the 'etherial gloom' (l. 92) that constitutes the ultimate sign of 'thought's empire over thought' (l. 211) displays the consciousness necessary to effectively propose an alternative hegemony. Furthermore, the 'birth of light' at the opening of the 'Triumph' gives symbolic value, in the very diction of Church power it opposes, to a new dawn that could enlighten the world. The possibility of change creeps back into the poem during the dialogue between the narrator and the spark-bearer Rousseau (ll. 180–308). The dialogue between Shelley and Rousseau, based on the relationship between Virgil and Dante, is characterised by constant questioning, probing Life's purpose and power in search of explication. De Man calls these questions acts 'within the pathos of [the poem's] own indetermination' and 'tangles of meaning and of figuration', but with the revelatory dialogues of Dante and Virgil as precursor, and Shelley's praise of the great inquirers Bacon, Rousseau, Christ, and Socrates, questioning must be a positive act.[115] These questions and answers precede Rousseau's narrative, which begins on line 308 and takes the form of a dream vision. In keeping with its generic status, the dialogue before the dream is the subject and the prompt for the vision. During the dialogue, Rousseau discusses figures associated with the French Revolution, the event Shelley called 'the master theme of the epoch in which we live'.[116] Rousseau first describes Napoleon, who 'sought to win / The world, and lost all it did contain of greatness', and is ultimately left fallen (ll. 216–217), then Voltaire, who tried to break tyranny by preparing the intellectual foundations of the Revolution, but 'in the battle Life and they did wage / She remained conqueror' (ll. 239–240). The dialogue is the background to Rousseau's vision, which begins with obvious echoes of the poem's opening. He is 'asleep / Under a mountain' (ll. 311–312) and experiences a vision which begins, as in *Purgatorio* I, under the light of the morning star. From here Rousseau,

> [']arose and for a space
> The scene of woods and waters seemed to keep,
>
> 'Though it was now broad day, a gentle trace
> Of light diviner than the common Sun
> Sheds on the common Earth[']
>
> (ll. 335–339)

Again this is more than a 'common' sunrise; Rousseau, after the cleansing of the 'oblivious spell', now walks in a light unlike the 'harsh world' where he had met Shelley's narrator. In an allegorical reading, it is a dream vision after all, he now wakes in post-revolutionary Europe after the success of the battle waged by the Enlightenment on Life.

On to this scene arrives 'A shape all light', who could be thought of as Napoleon himself, that apparently represents a complete embodiment of the new revolutionary dawn. By calling Napoleon the 'Child of a fierce hour' (l. 217), Shelley sees him as the very embodiment of the Revolution, as Pitt the Younger did in a speech recorded by Coleridge in February 1800. On the rise of Napoleon, Pitt claims: 'to this Jacobinism we are now to reconcile ourselves, because all its arts and all its energies are united under one person, the child and the champion of Jacobinism, who has been reared in its principles, who has fought its battles; who has systematised its ambition'.[117] And yet, what was a revolution represented by a pastoral idyll with a 'gentle trace of light' and 'soft grass' now features 'silver music' and 'golden dew', and the shape carries a 'crystal glass / Mantling with bright Nepenthe' (ll. 358–359). The ideal of the Revolution has been perverted through 'light's severe excess' (l. 424), and the vision moves to the imperial rule of Napoleon. Into this changed world, Life reappears. She enters 'from some dread war / Triumphantly returning' (ll. 436–437) with a 'moving arch of victory' built in celebration (l. 439). The cycle from the end of tyranny as a result of the Revolution to the return of Life under Napoleon, anticipates Marx's claim that France in these years 'draped itself alternately as the Roman Republic and as the Roman Empire'.[118] Life returns triumphantly from the war waged against her by the Enlightenment, just as Napoleon entered Paris in 1810. Napoleon is seen as 'fall'n' in an echo of Shelley's earlier sonnet in which the Emperor is chided for choosing a 'frail and bloody pomp'.[119] Napoleon 'mightst have built' a paradise from the materials of the Enlightenment, but he became too attracted by Life's triumph.[120]

In the 'Triumph', Shelley looks back from Pisa with the liberal cause at its lowest ebb, to see the last thirty years as a false dawn. But to even consider the prospect of a change to the tyranny of Life is a small victory in the face of failure. Two months before moving to Pisa, Shelley wrote a letter to John Gisborne in which he asked a series of rhetorical questions extolling the Greeks. He then wonders, what if 'Rome might have been all that its intellectual condition entitled it to be [. . .] What then should we have been?'[121] The conditional question, and the 'mightst' of 'Feelings of a Republican on the Fall of Bonaparte', is the basis of the reflection on the failure of Cato, Rousseau, Napoleon, and ultimately of Shelley himself. As life in Pisa was a compromise between the freedom of living without censure and separation from the cultural centre in London, so the poem balances the consistent disappointments of the republican cause, at Utica, Vienna, and Troppau, with the possibility of a future dawn achieved through questioning Life's tyranny. It reflects the pariah status of Shelley and his work in the periodical press, but also the perseverance, and possibility of resurgence captured in Lucan's reflection on defeat: 'Victrix causa deis placuit, sed victa Catoni'.[122] The victory of those who had opposed the radicalism that Shelley, Hunt, and Byron had pursued in Italian forms was beginning to seem certain. Southey wrote to the *Courier* early in 1822, calling Hunt, Byron, and Shelley, 'the personalities which disgrace our current literature', 'enemies to the religion, the institutions, & the domestic morals of their country', and claimed that Byron was 'their founder and leader'.[123] The demise of this literary circle was confirmed with Shelley's drowning on 8 July 1822: the repercussions of this loss for

Byron and Hunt are considered in the Coda. There is a pathetic circularity in a death by shipwreck when we remember Shelley's wish to ascend a 'magic ship' in the Dante sonnet of 1816, his exchange of lakes for ocean in 1818, and the more than a dozen boat drawings that litter the margin of the 'Triumph' manuscript.[124]

Shelley's death was the subject of another notice in the *Courier*: 'SHELLEY, the writer of some infidel poetry, for the republication of which a man of the name of CLARKE either has been, or is about to be, prosecuted, is dead'.[125] The defenders of the 'public mind', with the judicial powers of state behind them, tried to have the last laugh on Shelley's radicalism. John Hay wrote to Byron in September 1822 about the *Courier* notice, claiming it 'shocked him in a manner impossible to describe' and that 'the paragraph is too infamous to transcribe'.[126] Byron was emboldened by the cruelty of the report: he told Murray, 'You are all brutally mistaken about Shelley', and his defiance was expressed poetically at the opening of *Don Juan* X, written in the immediate aftermath of Shelley's death.[127] The withering satire of the London cantos is the final stage of a long development, as Byron became increasingly concerned with a radical idea of Italy and antagonistic towards the cant of British culture, moving beyond the questioning of the state in *Parisina* to the comparisons of Italy and England in *Beppo* and finally to Don Juan's satirical *nostos*. This oppositional stance has a particularly Shelleyan ring in the fourth stanza of Canto X:

> In the Wind's Eye I've sailed, and sail; but for
>   The stars, I own my telescope is dim;
> But at the least I've Shunned the common shore,
>   And leaving land far out of sight, would skim
> The Ocean of Eternity; the roar
>   Of breakers has not daunted my slight, trim,
> But *still* sea-worthy skiff, and she may float
> Where ships have foundered, as doth many a boat.
>
> (*DJ* X iv)

The nautical metaphor for a poetic journey is a nod to Pulci: canto openings in the *Morgante* often used this imagery to describe poetic peregrinations, and Pulci begins his mock epic by launching his 'barchetta', and invokes God at the opening of canto III as 'colui che 'l mio legno movesti / e 'nsino al porto aiutar mi dicesti'.[128] Byron acknowledges his debt to this sprawling work, and pokes fun at those British poets without their sea legs. Wordsworth is mocked in a recollection of Byron's earlier play on the Lake Poet's wish for '"a boat" to sail the deeps—/ Of Ocean?—No, of air', and even the admission of inadequacy, 'I own my telescope is dim', hints at the lofty themes of Coleridge and Wordsworth that Byron had derided.[129] The clarifications 'and sail' and the italicised '*still*' bookend the stanza, and show Byron's renewed defiance and commitment to a foreign poetic tradition. The new *Don Juan* is a reinvigorated attack, inspired by Byron's time at Pisa among a group of exiles, which vindicates poetic and personal choices against 'the roar / Of breakers'. Shelley's recent death could be the cause of the unnerving stumble in the final line, but it also burnishes the central image. The stressed 'Shunned' and 'shore' create the defiant cadence that precedes 'The Ocean of Eternity', an allusion to Shelley's own reference to Byron as the 'Pilgrim of Eternity' in *Adonais* (1821).[130] There is a poignant sense of community in the placement of an inter-elegiac image at the heart of the stanza: Byron allows melancholy to creep into the proem of the otherwise humorous tale of Juan's voyage, to remember Shelley and to show himself as a keeper of the flame for 'infidel poetry'. The poetic outcomes of Byron and Shelley's reading at Pisa are as different in tone and scope as the Italian predecessors they favoured, but they share a willingness, born out of Italian ideas, to maintain a challenge to the established views of the nation which had made them pariahs.

Coda

Leigh Hunt – the poet and journalist who had spent a decade promoting Italian literature for radical ends – set sail for Italy on 13 May 1822. His arrival at Pisa should have heralded a fruitful engagement with Byron and Shelley, the other central English expounders of a radical idea of Italy. This coda begins by examining the diary of Hunt's Mediterranean crossing and first months abroad, to show the diminishment of Hunt's radicalism when engaged with Italy at first hand. I then discuss the aftermath of Shelley's death, the disbandment of the Pisan circle, and why its journal, *The Liberal: Verse and Prose from the South,* ran for only four issues. It was this series of events that led Hunt to reflect on his Italian experience a number of years later: 'we have the best part of Italy in books; and this we can enjoy in England'.[1] During this time, conservative journalists in London attacked the radical promotion of the South with increased venom, and Italian exiles in London were unable to defend their culture from sustained criticism: Foscolo was near-bankrupt and no longer in favour with the major journals, and immigrants such as Bozzi and Panizzi had taken public roles that limited their ability to criticise hegemonic power. In literary culture travel works eclipsed radical writing, and these had little interest in Italy's political or poetical potential. By the middle of the 1820s writers looking for foreign forms and ideas with which to reform English culture looked more often to Germany than over the Simplon Pass.

Nicholas Roe has drawn attention to the diary of Hunt's journey to Italy in the summer of 1822.[2] Unlike the well-travelled Byron, Shelley, and Foscolo, this was Hunt's first journey abroad; he was migrating to Italy, where he had located much of his poetry and prose, and whose culture he had promoted for a decade. Hunt's detached thoughts during this journey bear out Washington Irving's observation that, 'to one given to day-dreaming, and fond of losing himself in reveries, a sea voyage is full of subjects for meditation'.[3] As Hunt passed through the Straits of Gibraltar on 25 May, he noted 'Dante's Ulysses', a reference that shows his habit of embedding new experiences in a literary frame.[4] These associations continue as Hunt 'passed into the Mediterranean' and remarked, 'I kept repeating the word Mediterranean, not the word in phrase, but the word in verse, as if stood at the beginning of one of my lines'.[5] The 'word in verse' could be the 'summer dreams' of the Mediterranean in the 'Ode to the West Wind', but beyond any specific allusion, the incantation shows Hunt projecting his wonder on to his literary preoccupation with Italy.[6] Hunt had argued for an authentic engagement with Italian politics and literary culture, but on arrival seems to succumb to the same effusive praise as the travellers now pouring in to Italy. Hunt's idea of Italy came from the *Parnaso Italiano*, a work he was proud to return 'to its native land'.[7] Hunt's idealising tendency remained with him once he had settled in Italy, and is shown in a letter to his sister-in-law Elizabeth Kent trying to persuade her join them in Genoa: 'say to yourself this instant, and as many future instants as you please. "With the early spring I certainly go to Italy" – "certainly" and to "Italy" – "to Italy, the land of perpetual sunshine, and fruits, and flowers, and mountain walks, and Petrarch, and Ariosto, and Buccaccio [*sic*]".[8] "Italy" is more than a place; it is an ideal that, like 'Mediterranean', can signify paradise. Although these effusive words share in their abundance something of Byron's first reactions to Venice, they have none of Byron's satirical thrust or grounding in the present.

By January 1823 Hunt was complaining of a 'surprising winter' that had none of the 'perpetual sunshine' which he had imagined, but even while his ideal was being challenged he kept up the facade of his Italian idyll.[9] Just as the Mediterranean was tied 'to vignettes in the *Parnaso Italiano*',[10] and "Italy" was the land of 'Petrarch, and Ariosto, and Buccaccio', so when Hunt speculates on where he should live in Italy, he considers, 'Florence, or Lucca, or the Baths of Pisa, or what other world of beauty and aboraceousness. I thought of 'Vallombrosa', but they tell me there are no inhabitants there but the monks'.[11] Despite mourning the death of Shelley and a cooling of his friendship with Byron, Hunt maintained an idea of Italy as a catalogue of beauty and 'aboraceousness'. Unlike the reasonable places he begins by considering, his suggestion of 'Vallombrosa' is odd. Hunt considers Vallombrosa, and it is written in inverted commas, because he is quoting Milton's description of Satan's legion 'Thick as the autumnal leaves that strew the brooks / In Vallombrosa'.[12] Vallombrosa had only ever been an abbey, rather than a town or village, and by its inclusion Hunt reveals his idea of Italy. He wishes to live at Vallombrosa, where William Parsons had sought the muse in *The Florence Miscellany*, a shrine visited by many English literary tourists but never mentioned by

Shelley or Byron.[13] When Hunt experienced Italy first hand it did not offer a new perspective with which to challenge native literary and political orthodoxies; his reaction was instead a more typically English adoration of its landscape and cultural past. Italy for Hunt was, like Vallombrosa, a place in inverted commas.

In the diary of his voyage Hunt tempered his idealising through an allusion that suggests he foresaw the doomed nature of his migration. The reminder of Ulysses's final journey may have put Hunt in a sombre mood. A page after the discussion of the 'Mediterranean' Hunt notes 'Ovid – Tristia – Lib. 1 Eleg. 2', which suggests he was reading, or at least remembering, Ovid's most melancholy reflection on exile. Quiet seas and kind winds cannot stem Ovid's melancholy, based on the future pain of never again seeing the Ausonian shores and having no further part in Roman culture. These emotions would have been poignant for Hunt, who felt forced to leave his homeland for reasons both practical (his increasing financial debts) and ideological (the failure of radical actions he had been at the centre of promoting in 1819 and 1820). Although Italy was Hunt's paradise, he was also a pariah. This status had allowed Shelley and Byron to explore their disappointments and criticise the homeland they had left behind, but they did so as poets settled socially and intellectually in Italy. Before Shelley's death, and Byron's departure for Greece, Hunt did not have the time or the predilection to grow roots and become engaged as a resident in Italy's current literary and political culture. The diary of his journey contains a premonition of this failure through its idealised depiction of Italy and classical allusion to the misery of exile. His worst fears were realised when Shelley, the man who saw himself as the link between 'the two thunderbolts' Hunt and Byron, died in a squall off the coast of Viareggio.[14]

I Longed to Bathe Myself in the Grassy Balm of My Native Fields

Shelley's death caused grief to become the dominant emotion of the Pisan circle. The lasting effect of this was the distinctly melancholy and escapist cast of the *Liberal*. In the same notebook as his Mediterranean diary, Hunt reacts to the loss of Shelley:

> One has been taken, & the other left.
>
> Instead of the health which I looked for in his society to restore the springs of life, I waste them with the perpetual pall of sorrow.[15]

Jeffrey Cox has suggested that the enigmatic first line could refer to Shelley being taken while Hunt remains, or 'refer to Shelley who has been taken and Keats who left Hunt in England'.[16] I am reluctant to accept a reading that suggests Hunt is reflecting on the departure of Keats for Italy years earlier. The note, and the notebook as a whole, is Hunt's record of his time in Italy and in it he is concerned with Shelley's 'society', both his friend's companionship and the 'strict community' Shelley had formed at Pisa. Cox's first reading, that Hunt is reflecting on his own loneliness in the wake of Shelley's death, is supported if we appreciate the allusion: Hunt is remembering his Wordsworth and behind that Matthew's Gospel, 'one is dead and gone; / The other, left behind', in a gesture of kinship to mourn the loss of a poetic brother.[17]

The rear pastedown of Hunt's diary contains what appears to be a statement of intent after Shelley's death: 'To show ~~& vindicate~~ his real possession of religion – of the purest and devoutest kind'.[18] The vehicle of this exposition was the *Liberal*: Hunt remembers Shelley in the preface to the first issue as 'one of the noblest of human beings' and attacks the *Courier* for its notice of his death.[19] Hunt's attempts to enhance Shelley's posthumous reputation were shared by Byron, who hoped that the world 'will, perhaps, do him justice *now*, when he can be no better for it'.[20] Byron used the preface to 'The Vision of Judgment', his major contribution to the first issue of the *Liberal*, to counter accusations of Satanism in the Pisan circle. He expanded upon Hunt's earlier remarks and claimed that the group 'have done more good in the charities of life to their fellow-creatures in any one year' than Southey had done in his entire life.[21] The preface is an extended attack on Southey, calling his insults to English exiles those of 'apostate jacobins' and mocking 'his *public* career' in the diction of the republican discourse against courtiers. Byron's vitriol against the Laureate is maintained throughout his poem, which also contains a tribute to Shelley's radical verse in its portrait of the late George III as an 'old, blind, mad, helpless, weak, poor worm'.[22] Byron's attack on the King and Laureate guaranteed that the *Liberal* would be noticed in London, but the journal was a commercial disappointment and ran for only four issues. In his comprehensive study, William H. Marshall takes his lead from Thomas Medwin's 1824 *Conversations with Lord Byron*, and argues that the reason for the failure of the *Liberal* was the breakdown in the personal relationship between Hunt and Byron.[23] In Marshall's view, the *Liberal* failed because Byron and Teresa Guiccioli disliked the company of Hunt, his wife, and their children. Murray making public misgivings about Hunt that Byron had sent him in private correspondence worsened this enmity.

Marshall's argument is persuasive, particularly when applied to Hunt's and Byron's move to Genoa after the first issue, but, as he himself admits, it pays limited attention to the literary content of their journal.[24]

If the *Liberal*, rather than Byron and Hunt, is placed at the centre of analysis, two factors can be shown to have created a journal that ineffectively engaged with radical Italian ideas. The most obvious reason for the failure of the *Liberal* is a practical one: without Shelley, they had lost a substantial proportion of the material for the journal. Hunt writes to Byron in January 1822 imagining the *Liberal* as a publication 'of entirely Pisan origin [. . .] essays, stories, poetry, poetical translation, especially from the Italian', but without Shelley this was an impossible task.[25] Byron's extensive contributions to the first two volumes, 'The Vision of Judgment' and 'The Blues' (1821), took up some space but still left the majority of pages to be filled. To solve this problem, Hunt had to write a great deal of the journal himself and seek contributions from England.[26] With articles by Hazlitt and Horace Smith, the *Liberal* struggled to maintain a coherent Anglo-Italian voice and could not live up to its subtitle of *Verse and Prose from the South*.

The second reason for the failure of the *Liberal* rests on the emotional state of its editor and main contributor. After the death of Shelley, Hunt's idea of Italy changed from his earlier interactions in *Rimini* or in the *Examiner* during Caroline's trial. Hunt's 'Letters from Abroad', his most substantial contribution to the *Liberal*, show this idea in flux. Each issue of the journal contained a travelogue in the form of a letter written by Hunt. In the first of these, devoted to Pisa, Hunt begins by describing the Leaning Tower, which causes him to reflect on a visit to the Piazza del Duomo with Shelley days before his death: 'Good God! what a day that was, compared with all that have followed it! I had my friend with me, arm-in-arm, after a separation of years: he was looking better than I had ever seen him – we talked of a thousand things – we anticipated a thousand pleasures – – – I must plunge again into my writing, that I may try to forget it'.[27] In 'we anticipated' there is an intimation of future pleasures never to be realised, and in the imperative 'must' is a present obligation to forget, but this is the only glimpse in the article into Hunt's troubled state of mind. In his notebook Hunt more openly expresses his emotions on the same scenes when he writes, 'The Cathedral of Pisa, when we heard the music together . . . ~~beg~~ beg that it may not be so', but the dominant tone of the 'Letter' on Pisa is warm and complimentary.[28] To avoid the 'perpetual pall of sorrow', Hunt found solace in the Italian past.[29] Hunt claims in the 'Letter' that the very first thing a foreigner does in Italy is recover 'from the surprise' caused by the clash between 'your dreams and matter-of-fact', but the difference between an ideal 'Italy' and the Pisa he was describing is one he fails to reconcile.[30] In the 'Letter' Pisa is cast as another 'Vallombrosa'; it was the home of Ugolino where 'the commonest door-way, or the ceiling of a room' was the product of 'Michael Angelo', where the university was the home to Galileo, and the Arno was the 'river of Dante, Petrarch, and Boccaccio'.[31]

The description of the Arno shows Hunt's need to tether his appreciation of Pisa to his life in England, what Schoina has called the idiosyncrasy of his 'mental cartography'.[32] To describe the size of the river, Hunt tell his reader that it is 'as wide as the Isis'; for the Leaning Tower he writes, 'Let the reader imagine the Monument of London'; in the Piazza del Duomo he asks the reader to 'suppose the new square at Westminster Abbey'; and the Campo Santo is described as 'about the size of Stratford Place'.[33] This manner of seeing Pisa through the sites of London is part of a wider trope in travel writing that prizes the familiar and sees Italy through unashamedly British eyes. H. W. Williams was pleased to give particular praise in his published travels of 1820 to the *campagna* around Parma for being 'not unlike the counties of Huntingdon and Cambridge'.[34] This is a formative change: travel no longer had what Chloe Chard has called 'a demand for some form of dramatic departure from the familiar and the mundane'.[35] A change from prizing the originality of a scene to seeking familiarity not only controls the activities of the tourist but also how they view a landscape. The cause of Hunt's touristic style was his homesickness, as he wrote in his *Autobiography*, 'I longed to bathe myself in the grassy balm of my native fields'.[36] The effect was a travelogue that does not seek to show the alterity of foreign climes, and one that does not see Italy as a modern culture that could enable a challenge to Regency hegemony. In fact, Hunt's writing on Pisa parades two traits commonly found in British writing – the reduction of Italy to a ruin of its past glory and a limited engagement with contemporary Italy – which he had previously deplored.

Strong English Prejudices Delivered in the Strong Clear Language of England

In the 'Letters from Abroad', Hunt does not follow Foscolo, Byron, and Bozzi by using the Italian past to comment upon the current political situation of Italy or Britain. But the *Liberal* was still a politically antagonistic journal, which in its first issue attacked Wellington and Southey, and ended with an epigram cruelly mocking Castlereagh's recent suicide. The angry reaction to the *Liberal* from those who defended the hegemonic bloc of the Regency took a familiar form. Wordsworth predicted the bent of the *Liberal* before it was published, claiming it was 'reported' that the Pisan circle were preparing a journal, which was to be 'directed against everything in religion, in morals, and probably in government and literature, which our Forefathers have been accustomed to reverence'.[37] For Wordsworth, an alliance of Hunt, Byron, and Shelley would perforce constitute an attack on established values. In the mention of 'Forefathers', Wordsworth signals his belief that custom is the centre of a native cultural tradition, a tradition which sees literature, government, religion, and morals as a product of a national family, under threat from 'some Town in Italy'.[38] The *John Bull*, the journal that was fundamental in turning the public mood against Queen Caroline, was more forceful in its censure of the *Liberal*. It used 2,500 words to attack what it called the 'non-sensical blasphemy' of the *Liberal* in the hope that they could 'effectually *prevent* the spreading of a *contagion*'.[39] As has been the case throughout this study, the language of disease is used to describe Italian ideas that needed to be eradicated from the British 'public mind'.

Byron was the main target of the attacks on the *Liberal*, on the grounds that the kind of radicalism it expressed was expected of Hunt, but not of a Peer of the Realm. Hazlitt saw the reaction against the *Liberal's* alliance 'between the Patrician and "the Newspaper man"' as an example of cultural intransigence. The class barriers that had been briefly lowered in the grand coalition that successful defended Queen Caroline were now raised again by the failure of the literary establishment, and Byron's friends, to see Hunt's and Byron's shared belief in 'the Muse, the public favour, and the public good'.[40] Timothy Tickler's letters in *Blackwood's* expressed their disgust that Byron was among 'the deluded drivellers of Cockaigne', and contrasted the *Liberal* with the work of Southey and Gifford which gave 'strong English prejudices delivered in the strong clear language of England!'[41] Attacks that saw exiles writing in foreign traditions as effeminate and weak were not a novelty: they were part of the same construction of national manners and morals that had seen Italian immigrants and Italian witnesses as wretches and beggars. But the existence of the *Liberal* allowed these comments to apply uniformly to a group of writers rather than appreciating the different strands of Anglo-Italian radicalism expressed by Hunt, Byron, and Shelley. The writers that the establishment had long suspected were a 'Satanic', 'Italian', and 'Cockney' school were now presenting themselves as such, and could be denounced en masse.

The Illiberal! is the best example of how the formal association of the Pisan circle caused by the *Liberal* was used by satirists.[42] Thomas Wise attributed the twenty-page pamphlet to Gifford, although he gives no proof for this attribution.[43] Wise also claims, and Marshall agrees, that this work was unpublished. They claim this because they knew of only one copy of the pamphlet, now kept at the British Library. In fact there is at least one more extant copy of *The Illiberal!*, which suggests that the pamphlet could have been circulated more widely than has been previously thought.[44] The work is subtitled 'Verse and Prose from the North!!' and takes the form of a play set in Byron's Pisan home. It begins with Byron repenting for his 'immoral work, *Don Juan*' before Hunt and his children interrupt him with poetry for the second issue of the *Liberal*.[45] The Hunt character recites a work entitled 'From Hampstead I have Looked upon St Paul', mocking Hunt's sonnet 'On Hampstead' in *Foliage*, and uses odd Italian words and cockneyisms, such as 'Sol shone bright' and 'everything was mum', to send up Hunt's style.[46] The satirist uses the shared domestic setting as a way into the shared authorship of Byron and Hunt, which creates a complete caricature of the cultural and political opinions of the Pisan circle. The play ends when Byron receives a letter from Hell in which Shelley begs him to repent for his immorality. Shelley tells Byron how he came to be damned:

> Suffice it that our boat perchance was wreck'd,
> And I with all my sins to Hades pack'd.[47]

An end-stopped couplet conveys a simple moral in simple diction: Hell beckons for those who lead a life of sin. The fifty-line letter is in Popean couplets; the same balanced and regular form that Gifford and Mathias had used for their anti-Jacobin satires of the 1790s was now being used against the foreign contagion of the *Liberal*. With the earlier role of conservative satirists in mind, the author's choice of epigraph for *The Illiberal* is apt:

> Let such forego the Poet's sacred name,
> Who rack their brains for lucre, not for fame:
> Still for stern Mammon may they toil in vain!
> And sadly gaze on gold they cannot gain!
> Such be their meed, such still the just reward
> Of prostituted muse and hireling bard![48]

These lines from *English Bards and Scotch Reviewers* show Hunt and Byron how far they have 'prostituted' themselves by falling for a foreign Muse and straying from the culture and politics of the North. In his early verse

Byron was proud to take 'The path which Pope and Gifford trod before', and in the epigraph tries to expose the degree of Byron's corruption abroad.[49]

The six chapters of this study have argued that from 1815 to 1823 there was a significant Anglo-Italian interaction between Italy and London, and shown how groups in these two places communicated with and supported one another. The attacks on the *Liberal* were not countered by the exiled Italians who had promoted Italian culture and supported radical Italianate English poetry since 1815. These writers were unable to defend their homeland from the slurs of conservative periodicals for a number of reasons. It was the combination of the smaller role that Italians had in London cultural life after 1823, and the disbandment of the exile circle in northern Italy, due to Shelley's death and Byron's migration, that caused the importance of radical ideas of Italy to dwindle. Foscolo was the exile who was best equipped to defend the Pisan circle and maintain the public interest in Italy. He had educated the British public about Italian literature, its cultural background, and the need to support the current Italian opposition to Austrian domination. Foscolo had also specifically promoted Hunt's *Rimini* in 1818 and explicated the Italian formal tradition behind *Beppo* and *Don Juan* in 1819.[50] But by 1822, the cooling of Foscolo's friendship with Hobhouse and Holland, along with his many debts, caused the beginning of the Italian's tremendous decline. Foscolo did not stop producing critical works after 1822 – his seminal *Essays on Petrarch* were published by Murray in 1823, and in 1825 Pickering published his *Discorso sul testo della 'Commedia' di Dante* – but he was no longer given space in journals with the esteem or the circulation of the *Edinburgh*, and he no longer dined at Holland House.[51] Foscolo's work after 1821 was scholarly, and often tied to larger editorial or translation projects, but contained fewer of the attacks on tyranny and repression that had angered the conservative press.[52] The academic tenor of his later work did not mean the defenders of the 'public mind' treated Foscolo more kindly. Lockhart, in the guise of Timothy Tickler, claimed in *Blackwood's* that allowing Foscolo to write in 'the periodical literature of this great and civilised empire, this, I maintain is indefensible and atrocious quackery'.[53] Foscolo's status as a foreigner was set to cause him far bigger problems than these slurs: he had paid for a house in Regent's Park that under the Aliens Act he could not legally own, and then borrowed against this property from several lenders. By 1823 there were a number of warrants out for his arrest and he ended up in debtors' prison in November 1824. Foscolo was forced to leave his home and move farther and farther away from the literary soirées he had once been the toast of: first to Hendon in 1824, and then Totteridge in 1825, before dying in poverty at Turnham Green in September 1827.[54]

Giuseppe Binda, Foscolo's Holland House friend, chose to follow Da Ponte and leave England for America: he met and married Fanny Sumter in 1824, settling in New York in 1827.[55] Other Italians stopped thinking of themselves as exiles and began to assimilate into English culture. Augustus Bozzi did not maintain the radicalism he had shown in *L'Italico*: he became a West End physician in 1818 and by 1829 he was the president of the Westminster Medical Society. Bozzi's willingness and ability to criticise the historical bloc was restricted when he took up a prominent professional role within it. Antonio Panizzi faced the same predicament in 1828 when he became Professor in Italian at the University of London, and again in 1837 when he became Keeper of Printed Books at the British Museum. Panizzi came to England in May 1823, having left Italy to avoid a trial for treason.[56] He found little work in London and moved to Liverpool, where he became part of Roscoe's circle. Although Panizzi gave a well-received series of lectures on Ariosto and Tasso in 1825, he wrote only a handful of essays for the periodical press in his first five years in England. His output was limited, and often published in smaller journals, such as the *Foreign Review and Continental Miscellany*.[57] In these works Panizzi did not promote Italian literature as part of a republican poetic tradition or publish long works correcting British attitudes towards Italy, in the manner of Buonaiuti and Foscolo. He was born in 1797 and was part of a different generation from the Italian and British writers who had written during the French Revolution and the Napoleonic Wars: Panizzi's politics were formed in the age of congresses and constitutions. Foscolo's description of himself in a letter to Panizzi a year before the older man's death shows this difference. He chooses a slightly altered line from the *Orlando Furioso* to describe his condition:

> Non son, non son io quel che paio in viso,
> Quel ch'era Orlando un tempo or è sotterra.[58]

Foscolo, the knight-errant who had been in 'a state of open war' with Austrian tyranny and English conservatism, is now defeated and devoid of purpose. Foscolo's radicalism needed the bold action of the *Orazione* or the 'Essay on the Present State', but Panizzi was a gradualist who hoped that by professional progress, and by maintaining friendships with men like Brougham and William Gladstone, he could change Italy's political and cultural destiny.

Italy Was at a Discount

The *Foreign Quarterly Review* was founded in 1827 and the composition of its early issues provides an example of the decreasing significance of Italy and Italian literature in English culture. Of the fifty-seven articles in the first five numbers of the *Foreign Quarterly* there were only seven on Italian subjects, with fourteen on German and eighteen on French topics.[59] The demise of Foscolo, the departure of other first-wave exiles, and the death of Byron and Shelley were not the only causes of diminished coverage of Italian culture in the periodical press. There were wider social factors that meant Italy was no longer a major influence on cosmopolitan Londoners. What had made Italy interesting to radicals and liberals from 1815 to 1823 was literature that was associated with an opposition to established forms and rules, and a political situation in which a number of Italian states were hotbeds for reform and revolution. After the suppression of independence movements at Troppau and Laibach, Italian independence had lost its position among liberals and radicals as a cause with a genuine chance of success. In 1828, after three years in Italy, Henry Beste reflected on the prospect of Italian independence: 'Nothing, however, that may happen in the future history of the world, appears now more improbable, than this independence and union'.[60] For more than two decades, Lord Holland had been involved in the promotion of Italian literature, and of Italian freedom at Naples, but by 1823 he wrote to Foscolo in a postscript to a letter, 'Will Greece succeed better than Italy? God grant she may'.[61] For Holland the fight for Liberty in Italy had been lost and Greece was the new cause, as it was for Byron who left Genoa for Missolonghi in July 1823. Furthermore, the virulent opposition of men such as Brougham and Holland to the ministry's prosecution of Caroline and its foreign policy over Naples had left them marginalised in a British political scene dominated by Tory administrations until 1830.[62]

As the Italian peninsula was becoming a less relevant theatre of revolution and reform, so tourists visited in greater numbers. Peace in Europe meant a resumption of continental travel, but the surge in tourism after 1821 inaugurated a different type of traveller. Various advances in infrastructure had reduced the cost of living and transport, making travel available to a wider class of people on shorter itineraries.[63] From 1821 there was a steam-operated ferry between Dover and Calais. One traveller in 1826, a Becky Calvert, noted in her diary that she left London at 10 a.m. and arrived at Calais on the 'Atwood Steam Packet' at 10:30 p.m. that evening; no longer were travellers subject to lengthy and expensive delays waiting on the wind.[64] On arrival in major French and Italian cities, there were hotels specially marketed at English tourists, such as the Hotel de Londres (Florence), the Hotel des Etrangers (Paris and Nice), and the Hotel D'Europa (Milan and Naples). Calvert felt at home during her stay at Rome in January 1827: she visited the English church every Sunday, went to see 'a race of English Horses about 5 miles from Rome', and took part in a fox-hunt.[65] The Italian cities were now safe, at least for twenty years, from the danger of uprisings, and an infrastructure for English tourists was being built. In 1818, Byron had recommended that those 'curious in fish sauce' should bring condiments with them to Italy, but a decade later Henry Beste notes that in Italy one can now find 'English shops' selling 'tea and fish sauces, and almanacks, and books of common prayer'.[66] Mary Shelley, who contributed three articles to the *Liberal* after Shelley's death, returned to England in August 1823.[67] She observed in a *Westminster Review* article in 1826 that the new generation of tourists could enjoy 'the elegant steam-packet, and the improved state of the continental hotels', and goes on to comment on the attitude of these new English visitors: 'We fly to Italy; we eat the lotus; we cannot tear ourselves away'.[68] Those who did tear themselves away often fantasised about the Italian idyll they left behind. Arthur Hallam, whose father had written *View of the State of Europe during the Middle Ages*, visited Italy for eight months in 1827 and this youthful interaction informed his verse.[69] His sonnet 'Lady I Bid Thee to a Sunny Dome' invites his female lover to 'magic halls', which ring with the 'echoes of Italian song', where 'Old Dante's voice encircles all the air' and one can hear 'the keen sweetness of Petrarca's moan'.[70] Dante and Petrarch are here for local colour rather than as part of an interaction with Italy and its literary tradition. In this paradise, Hallam and his lover could 'feast on the music' and gorge themselves on lotus flowers: Italy functions as a sensual alternative not just to English life but to any real existence. The sonnet was published a decade after 'The Triumph of Life', and its lack of political conviction or deep-reading in the Italian tradition is characteristic of an interaction which saw an Italy like that in Hunt's Pisan travelogue rather than in the manner of Byron and Shelley.

The Parmanese author and patriot Antonio Gallenga arrived in England from America in 1839 and became a successful author, journalist, and Italian teacher. He was a member of Giuseppe Mazzini's unificatory and republican group *Giovine Italia* and campaigned for Italian independence while in Boston and London. In his 1884 autobiography he lamented the standing of Italian culture in England in the early Victorian period: 'These were no longer the days of Byron and Shelley, of Roscoe, Leigh Hunt, Rogers, Landor, and those other stars of the Regency, who had caused all their educated countrymen to rave about Italy [. . .] Italy was at a discount after Queen Victoria's marriage, and German had come into fashion'.[71] Gallegna's nostalgia for the Anglo-Italian interaction of the immediate post-war years is surprising. Mazzini had arrived in London only two years before him, and was soon writing for the periodical press, and befriending the likes of the Carlyles and Dickens. Gallegna is writing at a peak of Italian activity in London and yet he still pines for a two-way interaction, for not just Italian writers to be printed in the London press but for the British engagement with Italian ideas that had been so important to Byron, Shelley, and Hunt. The role of German ideas in filling the vacuum for radical writing among 'educated countrymen' had occurred some years before Queen Victoria's marriage. In 1819 *Blackwood's*, the journal that had been most antagonistic to radical Italian ideas, began its *Horae Germanicae* that ran for twenty-five articles until August 1828. The first article ended by claiming 'a fine field lies open' for the man who possessed 'the two richest languages in Europe – the German and the English'.[72] The work of Robert Gillies and Lockhart in *Blackwood's* was central to the growing belief that Germany was the 'land of ideas', and that it offered a philosophical tradition with which to influence and reform British culture.[73]

As Rosemary Ashton has argued, the fact that Coleridge, Carlyle, G. H. Lewes, and George Eliot were simultaneously Germanists and the most important British thinkers of the first half the nineteenth century is no coincidence.[74] By the same token, it is not a coincidence that from 1815 to 1823 the most important radical politicians, poets, and journalists were deeply read in the history and current state of Italy. The literature and wider culture of Italy provided approaches to opposition: it offered forms of poetry, political history, and, in the case of the carnival, sociability, that could be used to counter the conservative control of the 'public mind' at home. Hunt captures the importance of Italianism to these expressions of opposition in the preface to the first number of the *Liberal*:

> The object of our work is not political, except inasmuch as all writing now-a-days must involve something to that effect, the connexion between politics and all other subjects of interest to mankind having been discovered, never again to be done away.[75]

The *Liberal* did not live up to this idea of an inherently political literature, but the statement reflects the importance of the radical Italian ideas that

Hunt and others had disseminated. In the "hot chronology" of 1815 to 1823, a number of groups and cultural trends intersected with Italy as their central point. Early in this period, Foscolo's critical works for the *Edinburgh* increased the British appreciation of the radical potential of Italian literature and history. In the period 1820 to 1823, the market was flooded with commentary on Italian morals, in the caricatures of the Italian witnesses at the Queen's trial, and the Italian travelogues that were filling up booksellers' stalls. But there was, concurrently, an authentic engagement with Italian culture and history. The established presence of Italy in British visual culture was reconfigured into visionary poetic landscapes, while Italian politics at Venice and Naples gave British reformers and radicals the opportunity to participate in revolutionary struggles. This involvement created an awareness of a trans-European opposition to hegemony, and the idea that political liberty was important beyond national boundaries had much in common with the cosmopolitan approach of radical English poets engaging with Italian literature. Italian poetry past and present, and the philosophy of Alfieri and Machiavelli, was used to break customs surrounding poetic forms, question the 'French' school's notions of refinement, and create radical new kinds of English satire. The coincidence of these interactions over such a brief period created a unique literary moment in Italy and in London, a moment that many of the greatest works of Byron, Foscolo, Hunt, and Shelley are a product of.

Notes

Preface

1 John Keats, 'Happy is England! I could be content' [1816], *Poems of John Keats*, ed. Jack Stillinger (Cambridge, MA: Harvard University Press, 1978), 55, ll. 5–6.

2 Jane Austen, *Northanger Abbey and Persuasion*, 4 vols. (London, 1818), IV 155–156; Thomas Love Peacock, *Nightmare Abbey* (London, 1818), 52–54; Henry Cary, *The Vision, or, Hell, Purgatory, and Paradise, of Dante Alighieri* (London, 1814, 2nd ed., 1819); Leigh Hunt, *Amyntas: A Tale of the Woods* (London, 1820).

3 Rosemary Ashton, *The German Idea* (Cambridge: Cambridge University Press, 1980), 2.

4 *OED,* definition 7 c) for 'radical'.

5 The literature on what Italy is, or whether it exists at all, is voluminous. The classic work on the question for English readers of the Romantic period was Giuseppe Baretti, *An Account of the Manners and Customs of Italy* (London, 1768). Two notable works on this subject are Giacomo Leopardi, *Discorso sopra lo stato presente dei costumi degl'italiani* [composed 1824, first pub. 1906], ed. Marco Dondero (Milan: Biblioteca universale Rizzioli, 1998); and Giulio Bollati, *L'italiano* (Turin: Einaudi, 1996).

6 Bollati, *L'italiano*, 50, 'laying claim to a tradition both of the greatness and of the primacy of Italy, and teaching the blind and careless visitors how it is possible to at least detect a living continuity among the glorious contests in literature and the arts'.

7 Claude Lévi-Strauss, *La Pensée sauvage* [1962] (London: Weidenfeld and Nicholson, 1966), 258–259. See the discussion of Lévi-Strauss in James Chandler, *England in 1819* (Chicago, IL: Chicago University Press, 1998), 3–46.

8 Byron, *Don Juan* XI 82. All references to *Don Juan* I–XV [1819–1824] are from *LBCPW* V 1–663 and are given as *DJ* with canto and stanza number.

9 Christopher Ricks, 'Literary Principles against Theory', *Essays in Appreciation* (Oxford: Oxford University Press, 1996), 314.

10 See 'Childe Harold IV' [1818], *LBCPW* II 120–186, st. 56. All further references will be to *CHIV* followed by stanza number. Boccaccio was also

popular in the visual arts. See Thomas Stothard's 'The Scene of Boccaccio's Tales'; and Henry Fuseli's 'Theodore and Honoria' (1818).

11 The classic study of Boccaccio's reputation in England is Herbert G. Wright, *Boccaccio in England* (London: Athlone Press, 1957); for the Romantic period, see pp. 331–478. Jane Stabler includes a chapter on the role of Boccaccio in romantic appreciation of the Italian *campagna* in *The Artistry of Exile* (Oxford: Oxford University Press, 2013), 118–156; and Cox has an excellent discussion of 'Cockney Boccaccio' in *Romanticism in the Shadow of War* (Cambridge: Cambridge University Press, 2014), 194–207.

12 See Nanora Sweet, '"Lorenzo's" Liverpool and "Corinne's" Coppet: The Italianate Salon and Romantic Education' in *Lessons of Romanticism,* ed. Thomas Pfau and Robert Gleckner (Durham, NC: Duke University Press, 1998), 244–260. The best discussions of translation occur in: C. P. Brand, *Italy and the English Romantics* (Cambridge: Cambridge University Press, 1957); Ralph Pite, *The Circle of Our Vision* (Oxford: Oxford University Press, 1994); Ralph Pite's chapter 'Italian' in, *The Oxford History of Literary Translation in English*, vol. 4, ed. Peter France and Kenneth Haynes (Oxford: Oxford University Press, 2006), 246–260; Nicholas Havely, *Dante's British Public* (Oxford: Oxford University Press, 2014), 128–153; and Diego Saglia, *European Literatures in Britain, 1815–1832* (Cambridge: Cambridge University Press, 2018), 110–147.

13 Brand, *Italy and the English Romantics*, ix.

14 Joseph Luzzi, *Romantic Europe and the Ghost of Italy* (New Haven, CT: Yale University Press, 2008), 54.

15 Felicia Hemans, *The Restoration of the Works of Art to Italy* (Oxford, 1816), 7.

16 Ibid., 7–8.

17 Ibid., 8.

18 'living continuity', see 6n. Hemans's poem is similar to her next work, *Modern Greece* (London, 1817). Byron, having left for Italy the year before, dismissed it as, 'Good for nothing – written by someone who has never been there' (*BLJ* V. 262). The reaction reveals a crucial difference between the sentimental current of *Childe Harold* and the poetry of Byron's exile, which gives primacy to interaction with foreign cultures.

19 'Ink and Inkcapability', *Blackadder the Third*, written by Richard Curtis and Ben Elton. First aired 24 September 1987.

Introduction

1 A first-hand account of late July and August 1814 is given in Joseph Farington, *The Farington Diary*, ed. James Greig, 8 vols. (London: Hutchinson, 1922–1928), VII 261–275.

2 See Robert Southey to Henry Southey, August 23 1815, *The Correspondence of Robert Southey*, ed. Charles Cuthbert Southey, 6 vols. (London, 1850), IV 121–123.

3 Robert Southey, 'An Inquiry into the Causes of the General Poverty and Dependence of Mankind', *Quarterly Review* (October 1816): 226.

4 See J. Ann Hone, *For the Cause of Truth* (Oxford: Oxford University Press, 1982), 271–273.

5 For further discussion of this shift, see Will Bowers, 'The Dilemma of a "Romantic" Anthology', *Publishing History* 67 (2010): 65–89.

6 Nicholas Roe, 'Leigh Hunt and Romantic Biography', *Romanticism, History, Historicism,* ed. Damian Walford Davies (London: Routledge, 2009), 203.

7 Gregory Dart, *Rousseau, Robespierre and English Romanticism* (Cambridge: Cambridge University Press, 1999); Nicholas Halmi, *The Genealogy of the Romantic Symbol* (Oxford: Oxford University Press, 2007); Ashton, *The German Idea*; Paul Hamilton, *Realpoetik* (Oxford: Oxford University Press, 2013), Saglia, *European Literatures in Britain, 1815–1832.*

8 This revitalising aspect is discussed in Walter Jackson Bate, *The Burden of the Past and the English Poet* (London: Chatto and Windus, 1971), 22.

9 See Friedrich Nietzsche, *Der Fall Wagner* (Leipzig, 1888), 'Il faut méditerraniser la musique' (music must be mediterraneanised), 3.

10 Arturo Graf, *L'anglomania e l'influsso inglese in Italia nel secolo xviii* (Turin: Ermanno Loescher, 1911). A new edition is forthcoming: Arturo Graf, *L'anglomania e l'influsso inglese in Italia nel secolo xviii*, ed. Francesco Rognoni and Pierangelo Gofffi (Naples: La scuola di Pitagora editrice, 2020).

11 Maura O'Connor, *The Romance of Italy and the English Political Imagination* (London: Macmillan, 1998); Roderick Cavaliero, *Italia Romantica* (London: Macmillan, 2005); *Immaginando l'Italia*, ed. Lilla Maria Crisafulli (Bologna: Clueb, 2002). For a study of British literary responses to Italian art, see Maureen McCue, *British Romanticism and the Reception of Italian Old Master Art* (Aldershot: Ashgate, 2014).

12 Stabler, *The Artistry of Exile*; Maria Schoina, *Romantic 'Anglo-Italians'* (Aldershot: Ashgate, 2009).

13 Peter Vassallo, *Byron, The Italian Literary Influence* (London: Macmillan, 1984); Alan Weinberg, *Shelley's Italian Experience* (London: Macmillan, 1991).

14 Pite, *The Circle of Our Vision*; *Dante and Italy in British Romanticism,* ed. Fredrick Burwick and Paul Douglass (Basingstoke: Palgrave Macmillan, 2011); Antonella Braida, *Dante and the Romantics* (Basingstoke: Palgrave Macmillan, 2004); Steve Ellis, *Dante and English Poetry* (Cambridge: Cambridge University Press, 1983).

15 Crisafulli, 'Introduzione', *Immaginando l'Italia,* 14. 'Freedom, and liberation from rigid social and behavioural codes'.

16 The exclamation 'Thou Paradise of exiles, Italy!' in 'Julian and Maddalo: A Conversation' [1819], *LongmanPS* II 666, l. 57.

17 This is discussed throughout Stabler's *The Artistry of Exile,* esp. 4–6; see the discussion of James Joyce in Edward W. Said, 'Reflections on Exile' in *Reflections on Exile* (Cambridge, MA: Harvard University Press, 2000), 182–183.

18 'The Liberal', *John Bull* (28 July 1822), 780.

19 *PL* II 255–256.

20 'the new flower of foreign speech'.
21 *LPBS* II 170.
22 For a discussion of the failure of nomenclature, see Chandler, *England in 1819*, 174–194.
23 Said, 'Reflections on Exile', 186.
24 Jeffrey N. Cox, 'Keats in the Cockney School', *Romanticism* 2 (1996), 28.
25 Jerome McGann, *A Critique of Modern Textual Criticism* (Chicago, IL: Chicago University Press, 1983), 48; Francis Mulhern, *Culture/Metaculture* (London: Routledge, 2000), xvii; Alan Liu, 'The Power of Formalism: The New Historicism', *English Literary History*, 56 (1989), 723.
26 Terry Eagleton, *Heathcliff and the Great Hunger: Studies in Irish Culture* (London: Verso, 1995), 27.
27 Antonio Gramsci, *Quaderni del carcere,* ed. Valentino Gerratana (Turin: Einaudi, 1975), 869. He is paraphrasing a statement in Marx's *A Contribution to the Critique from Hegel's Philosophy of Right* (London, 1844).
28 'Public opinion is the undeniable mistress of the world. Public opinion is always the offspring of persuasion in some form, and never of force'. *Principe,* III x 213.
29 My inspiration in mapping the usage and changes of the term comes from chapter 3 of James Epstein, *Radical Expression* (Oxford: Oxford University Press, 1994), 70–99; and J. G. A. Pocock's discussion of how 'conceptual vocabularies' change over time in *The Machiavellian Moment* (Princeton, NJ: Princeton University Press, 1975), 57.
30 J. G. A. Pocock, *Virtue, Commerce, and History* (Cambridge: Cambridge University Press, 1976), 48.
31 Oliver Goldsmith, 'The Traveller, or, a Prospect of Society' [1764], *The Poems of Gray, Collins, and Goldsmith,* ed. Roger Lonsdale (London: Longman, 1969), 622–57, ll. 73–74.
32 Ibid., ll. 124, 405.
33 Pocock, *The Machiavellian Moment,* 334.
34 See for example, Mark Akenside, 'To the Right Reverend Benjamin Lord Bishop of Winchester' [1754], *Poetical Works,* ed. Robin Dix (Madison, NJ: Farleigh Dickinson University Press, 1996), 326; Henry Boyd, 'To the Right Honorable the Earl of Charlemont', *Poems, Chiefly Dramatic and Lyric* (Dublin, 1793), 642.
35 Raymond Williams, *Marxism and Literature* (Oxford: Oxford University Press, 1977), 112.
36 William Cobbett, ed., *Cobbett's Parliamentary History* XXXIV (London, 1806–1819), 988.
37 Arthur Young, *An Enquiry into the State of the Public Mind* (Dublin, 1798), 14; 'The St. Alban's Street Plot,' *Monthly Meteor* (June 1810): 559, 562; Samuel Taylor Coleridge, *Biographia Literaria*, 2 vols. (London, 1817), II 285.
38 *LPBS* II 166.
39 J. G. A. Pocock, 'The Machiavellian Moment Revisited: A Study in History and Ideology', *Journal of Modern History* 53 (1981): 50.

40 James J. Sack, *From Jacobite to Conservative* (Cambridge: Cambridge University Press, 1993), 21–22.
41 Kevin Gilmartin, *Writing Against Revolution* (Cambridge: Cambridge University Press, 2007), 96. Nonetheless, pamphlets were still relevant: broadside songs, caricatures, and poems are at the centre of the discussion of Queen Caroline's Trial in Chapter 5.
42 William St. Clair estimates the combined sales of the *Quarterly* and *Edinburgh* was 27,000 copies in 1816. These editions would then pass through, in the average family, four hands. See *The Reading Nation in the Romantic Period* (Cambridge: Cambridge University Press, 2004), 573–574.
43 Epstein, *Radical Expression*, 77.
44 William Cobbett, 'Nottingham', *Cobbett's Political Register* (London, 20 May 1815): 621.
45 'March of the Public Mind', *Black Dwarf* (2 June 1819), 343. 'England in 1819' [1819?], ll. 2–3, *LongmanPS* III 190.
46 Jon P. Klancher, *The Making of English Reading Audiences, 1790–1832* (Madison, WI: University of Wisconsin Press, 1987), 100.
47 Pocock, *Virtue, Commerce, and History*, 283–285.
48 William Hazlitt, 'Character of Cobbett' [1821], *The Selected Writings of William Hazlitt*, ed. Duncan Wu et al., 9 vols. (London: Pickering, 1998), VI 43. All further references are to this edition.
49 Hazlitt, 'Letter to William Gifford' [1819], *Selected Writings,* V 362.
50 William Shakespeare, *Othello* [1603], ed. E. A. J. Honigmann (Walton: Arden, 1997), IV ii 60–61.
51 For a discussion of this definition of revolution, see Christopher Hill, *A Nation of Change and Novelty* (London: Routledge, 1990), 83.
52 Pocock, *Machiavelian Moment*, 407.
53 Ibid., 387.
54 William Hazlitt, 'Christabel: Kubla Khan, a Vision', *Edinburgh Review* (September 1816): 67.
55 Gramsci, *Quaderni del carcere*, 1250.
56 Stuart Curran, *Poetic Form and British Romanticism* (New York: Oxford University Press, 1986), 5.
57 Cox, *Romanticism in the Shadow of War*, 164.
58 Kelvin Everest, 'Shelley's Doubles: An Approach to "Julian and Maddalo"', *Shelley Revalued*, ed. Kelvin Everest (Leicester: Leicester University Press, 1983), 74. See 'Euganean Hills', ll. 72–3, *LongmanPS* II 433 and 'Ode to Liberty', l. 193, *LongmanPS* III 408.

1 Italians and the 'Public Mind' before 1815

1 'It was a matter of great shame to Italian nationals and of great wonder even to educated foreigners to see circulating in London so many periodicals in the German, French, Spanish, and Portuguese languages, alongside an immense

quantity in English of differing opinions and various forms; yet amongst so many Journals, Newspapers, Periodicals, and Magazines not one single pamphlet was to be found in the glorious Italian language'. Augustus Bozzi, 'Introduzione', *L'Italico*, no.1 (May 1813): I 3–4.

2 William Roscoe, *The Life of Lorenzo de' Medici* [1795], 2nd ed. (London, 1796), I xix.

3 Ibid., I ii.

4 Pierre-Louis Ginguené, *Histoire Littèraire d'Italie*, 14 vols. (Paris, 1811–1835). Hereafter, *Histoire Littèraire d'Italie.*

5 Ginguené, *Histoire Littèraire d'Italie*, II 2, 'created a new poetic system, a new poetry'.

6 Jean Charles Léonard de Sismondi, *De la littérature du Midi de l'Europe*, 4 vols. (Paris, 1813), I 5. Hereafter, *De la littérature du Midi de l'Europe.* 'three intellectual pursuits that are generally thought to be so dissimilar, politics, religion, poetry'.

7 *De la littérature du Midi de l'Europe*, I 350. 'the most important of the Italians', 'the crude materials'.

8 Note to 'Hellas' [1821], *SPP*, 462.

9 Henry Hallam, *View of the State of Europe during the Middle Ages*, 2 vols. (London, 1818), I 233; II 563.

10 The religious bent to Smollett's attack is shown when his tour of the churches finds them littered with 'implements of popish superstition', and the works on display are 'indecent' and 'indelicate'. Outside the church, Italian women are full of 'atrocious vice' and we are told often of the 'filth' of the streets. See Tobias Smollett, *Travels through France and Italy*, 2 vols. (London, 1766), II 120, 56, 94–97.

11 The best of the many discussions of Smollett's treatment of homosexuality in this passage is Cameron McFarlane, *The Sodomite in Fiction and Satire, 1660–1750* (New York: Columbia University Press, 1997), ch. 3.

12 Tobias Smollett, *The Adventures of Peregrine Pickle*, 4 vols. (London, 1751), II 89–90. The lines from *Il pastor fido* are in English: 'As one infirm, who longs to taste the forbidden medicine – so have I longed, consumed with amorous thirst'.

13 Smollett, *The Adventures of Peregrine Pickle*, II 90–91.

14 George Eliot, *The Mill on the Floss*, 3 vols. (Edinburgh, 1860), I 51.

15 For the sense of this as 'the classic age of English caricature', see Dorothy George, *English Political Caricature*, 2 vols. (Oxford: Clarendon Press, 1959), II 150–177.

16 I am indebted here to Peter McNeil's, *Pretty Gentlemen* (New Haven, CT: Yale University Press, 2018).

17 Ibid., 90–92.

18 Ibid., 93–100, 52–56.

19 Sympathetic representations of Italians occur in Laurence Sterne, *A Sentimental Journey through France and Italy* (London, 1768); Horace Walpole, *The Castle of Otranto* (London, 1764); Giuseppe Baretti, *Remarks*

on the Italian Language and Writers (London, 1753); Giuseppe Baretti, *An Appendix to the Account of Italy* (London, 1768).

20 George F. E. Rudé, 'The Gordon Riots: A Study of the Rioters and Their Victims', *Transactions of the Royal Historical Society* 6 (1956): 93–114.

21 Robert Merry, Hester Thrale Piozzi, Bertie Greatheed, William Parsons et al., *The Florence Miscellany* (Florence, 1785), 196. Further references will be given in page numbers after the text.

22 William Gifford, *The Baviad* [1791] (London, 1793), 35, 45. Hereafter *Baviad.*

23 Ibid., 17.

24 A *tenzone* is a poetic exchange, usually in sonnets, often with participants repeating each other's rhyme words. Jerome McGann, *The Poetics of Sensibility* (Oxford: Oxford University Press, 1996), 80–81.

25 *Baviad,* 33.

26 Michael Gamer, *Romanticism, Self-Canonization, and the Business of Poetry* (Cambridge: Cambridge University Press, 2017), 98.

27 W. N. Hargreaves-Mawdsley, *The English Della Cruscans and Their Time, 1783–1828* (The Hague: Martin Nijhoff, 1967), 1.

28 See Michael Duffy, *The Englishman and the Foreigner* (London: Chadwyck-Healey, 1986), 13.

29 Ibid., 13–19.

30 *Cobbett's Parliamentary History* XXX (London, 1817), 176.

31 Ibid. 175–177. See also Vaughan Bevan, *The Development of British Immigration Law* (London: Croom Helm, 1986), 58–64; and T. W. Haycroft, 'Alien Legislation and the Prerogative of the Crown', *Law Quarterly Review* 50 (1897): 180–183.

32 Giuseppe Naldi, *The Alien; or an Answer to Mr. Greville's Statement with Respect to Mr. Naldi's Action for Arrears of Salary* (London, 1811), 55, 81.

33 *Cobbett's Parliamentary History* XXX, 157.

34 Ibid., 197, 176.

35 The count makes five appearances in *The Diary of William Godwin*, ed. Victoria Myers, David O'Shaughnessy, and Mark Philp (Oxford: Oxford Digital Library, 2010), http://godwindiary.bodleian.ox.ac.uk/people/ZEN01.html, and produced work such as *An Address to the People of England* (London, 1792).

36 Warwick Lister, *Amico: The Life of Giovanni Battista Viotti* (Oxford: Oxford University Press, 2009), 218.

37 Quoted in J. R. Dinwiddy, 'The Use of the Crown's Power of Deportation under the Aliens Act, 1793–1826', *Historical Research* 41, no. 104 (1968): 193–211.

38 Charles Dibdin, *The Songs of Charles Dibdin*, 2 vols. (London, 1848). See 'The Jew in Grain', 353; 'The Jew Money Lender', 422; and 'The Jew Pedlar', 344.

39 See particularly, 'Jack at the Opera', Dibdin, *Songs,* 269, in which a demobbed soldier mistakes the Haymarket Opera for Drury Lane and is disgusted by the singing ('With their squeaking, so mollyish, tender, and soft, / One should

scarcely know ma'am from mounseer') and escapes to watch 'old Billy Shakespeare'.

40 Charles Dibdin, *The Professional Life of Mr. Dibdin*, 4 vols. (London, 1803), IV 158.

41 Charles Dibdin, 'Ballad. In England against Italy', *Collection of Songs*, 2 vols. (London, 1814), II 96–97.

42 See Nicolas Boileau, 'Satire IX' [1666], *Œuvres poétiques*, 2 vols. (Paris, 1872), I 139: 'A Malherbe, à Racan, préférer Théophile / Et le clinquant du Tasse à tout l'or de Virgile'.

43 Pope's sketch was first printed in Owen Ruffhead, *The Life of Alexander Pope* (London, 1769), 425. For the letter, see Thomas Warton, *The Poetical Works of the Late Thomas Warton*, 2 vols. (Oxford: Oxford University Press, 1802), I lviii–lxi. The letter is dated 15 April 1770. David Fairer has shown how both the Pope and Gray models were available to Romantic readers in his essay 'Southey's Literary History', in *Robert Southey and the Contexts of English Romanticism*, ed. Lynda Pratt (Aldershot: Ashgate, 2006), 5–7.

44 This is Voltaire's address on his entrance to the Académie française; see François-Marie Arouet de Voltaire, *Oeuvres completes de Voltaire*, 52 vols. (Paris, 1877–1885), XXIII 205–217. For more on these climate theories and their effect on poetics, see Will Bowers, 'Byron's Rhyming Clime', *Essays in Criticism* 69 (2019): 157–177.

45 This phrase is also rendered as 'Inglese Italianato è un diavolo incarnato'. See George B. Parks, 'The First Italianate Englishman', *Studies in the Renaissance* VIII (1961), 199–200. 'Satanic' in the preface to Robert Southey, *A Vision of Judgment* (London, 1821), 17–22; and 'Italian' in a letter to Walter Savage Landor, 20 February 1820, *Correspondence*, V 21.

46 *DJ*, 'Dedication' V.

47 The standard view of the political arc of the First Generation, as young radicals and old conservatives, has been debated. The extent of Coleridge's revolutionary sympathies in the 1790s has been examined by a number of writers who make convincing arguments that Coleridge was radical and that his work was seditious. See, E. P. Thompson, '"Bliss was it in that dawn", The Matter of Coleridge's Revolutionary Youth' [1971] in *The Romantics* (Rendelsham: Merlin Press, 1997), 108–132. A thorough examination of the radical circles that Wordsworth and Coleridge developed within is given in Nicholas Roe, *Wordsworth and Coleridge: The Radical Years* (Oxford: Oxford University Press, 1988). For a view of Coleridge as a Burkean conservative in his early years, see Alan P. Gregory, *Coleridge and the Conservative Imagination* (Macon, GA: Mercer University Press, 2002), 1–27.

48 William Christie, 'Francis Jeffrey in Recent Whig Interpretations of Romantic Literary History', *English Literary History* 76 (2009): 593.

49 'Composed in a Valley Near Dover', [1802] *WWMW*, 284, ll. 12–13, 9; William Wordsworth, *The Excursion* [1814], ed. Sally Bushell, James Butler, and Michael Jaye (Ithaca, NY: Cornell University Press, 2007), 196–197, bk VI ll. 1–75; see also Samuel Taylor Coleridge, *The Friend* (London, 1812),

355, for his claim that 'in short, his COUNTRY should have a place by every Englishman's fireside'.

50 Hazlitt, 'On Court-Influence' [1819], *Selected Writings,* IV 217.
51 'Michael', [1800], *WWMW,* 224 ll. 37–39.
52 Ugo Foscolo, Gaetano Polidori, Antonio Panizzi, and Giuseppe Pecchio all taught Italian in England for a time.
53 See Brand, *Italy and the English Romantics*, 36–45.
54 Timothy Webb has shown that even experienced Italian speakers, such as the Shelleys and Byron, encountered difficulties with these regional languages. See Webb, 'Syllables of the Sweet South: Figuring the Sound of Italian in the Romantic Period', in *Dante and Italy in British Romanticism,* 210–211.
55 Cesare Bruno, *Studio italiano* (London, 1815, 2nd ed., 1818).
56 Antonio Montucci, *Italian Extracts* (Edinburgh, 1806; 2nd ed., London, 1818); Vittorio Alfieri, *Quindici tragedie di Vittorio Alfieri da Asti in tre volume*, ed. A. Montucci (Edinburgh, 1806).
57 Benedict Anderson, *Imagined Communities*, 2nd ed. (London: Verso, 2004), 40–46.
58 For the importance of English political culture to the promotion of the Italian language by exiles in London, see Isabella Maurizio, *Risorgimento in Exile* (Oxford: Oxford University Press, 2009), 111–146.
59 Schoina, *Romantic Anglo-Italians*, 57; see also 57–63.
60 Luisa Calè, *Fuseli's Milton Gallery* (Oxford: Oxford University Press, 2006), 55.
61 Polidori, Gaetano, trans., John Milton, *Il Licida, L'Allegro, ed Il Penseroso* (London, 1814), v.
62 Thomas Mathias, *Componimenti lirici de' piu illustri poeti d' Italia*, 3 vols. (London, 1802), I xix. 'tante cicalate, pazzìe, e ciance di certi Francesi e Tedeschi moderni, che germogliano in copia smisurata, come piante mal sane in un terreno salvatico e guasto'.
63 William Spaggiari, 'The Canon of the Classics: Italian Writers and Romantic-Period Anthologies of Italian Literature in Britain' in *British Romanticism and Italian Literature*, ed. Laura Bandiera and Diego Saglia (Amsterdam: Rodopi, 2005), 27. Saglia, *European Literatures in Britain*, 74.
64 Lorenzo Da Ponte, *Memoirs*, trans. Elizabeth Abbott (New York: New York Review of Books, 2000), 297. This is based on the Laterza edition of the *Memorie,* ed. G. Gambarin and F. Nicolini (Bari, 1918).
65 Mathias, *Componimenti* (1802), I ix, I xxiv.
66 'Componimenti lirici de' piu illustri poeti d'Italia'. *Edinburgh Review* (October 1804): 64.
67 The best English account of this period is Sheila Hodges, *Lorenzo Da Ponte* (London: Granada, 1985), 10–23.
68 Da Ponte, *Memoirs*, 300.
69 Ibid.
70 This is the second lower endpaper of his edition of Casti's *Gli animali parlanti,* discussed later. See 73n.

71 The 1804 catalogue is available at the British Library (S.C. 834. 12). Its title is 'CATALOGUE Of the valuable splendid and fine Collection of BOOKS, Consisting of almost every Author in the Italian Language many of which are the greatest rarity . . . THE GENUINE PROPERTY OF MR. L. DAPONTE, BOOKSELLER'. The sale began on the 16 April 1804. Dante, Petrarch, Ariosto, Tasso, and Metastasio are available in dozens of editions.

72 Two examples of sales of Italian book sales from the period show this. In the sale catalogue for Mr. King (*BL* C.194, b. 223 1–12), No. 8 is the catalogue of 'M De Mauregard, Gone abroad;' a sale which took place on 25 February 1801. Although it lists many of the classics of Italian poetry, it features only a few poets after Metastasio. The catalogue for a sale at Mr. Stanley's (*BL* RB.23.a.21540) on 9 July 1816, entitled 'A catalogue of a valuable collection of rare and curious books, consigned from Italy [. . .] the property of an Italian gentleman dec.', features the canon and a selection of manuscripts (including a fourteenth-century *Sonetti e Triumphi di Petrarca*) but includes no poetical work in Italian published after the seventeenth century.

73 Torquato Tasso, *Aminta* (London, 1800).

74 Giovanni Battista Casti, *Gli animali parlanti,* 2 vols. (London, 1803).

75 'to set out an entire political history, revealing the vices and defects of political systems'. Casti, *Gli animali parlanti,* ed. Gabrielle Muresu (Ravenna: A. Longo, 1978), 61.

76 Da Ponte, 'Al Lettore', *Gli animali parlanti*, I iii, 'We may, without fear of being accused of exaggerating, assure the public that this work adds new splendour to our times and new glory to the Italian Parnassus'.

77 Ugo Foscolo, 'Narrative and Romantic Poems of the Italians'. *Quarterly Review* (April 1819): 486–556.

78 Gabrielle Muresu, 'Introduzione', *Gli animali parlanti*, 12.

79 *Gli animali parlanti*, I 9: 'Thus those most prudent animals, legislators, philosophers, politicans all, to remedy many ills, made synthetic and analytic examination of all governments, the good or harmful, republican, monarchial or mixed'. See also I 29.

80 Mathias, *Componimenti lirici de' piu illustri poeti d'Italia*; *Aggiunta ai componimenti lirici de'più illustri poeti d'Italia,* 3 vols. (London, 1808); *Componimenti lirici de'più illustri poeti d'Italia,* 4 vols. (Naples, 1819).

81 Saglia, *European Literatures in Britain*, 75.

82 *Componimenti* (1802) I xxi–xxii. 'because ignorance of so many poets, or their being forgot, is the sole or chief reason for the obscurity in which they [the works of Italy] lie neglected *amongst us*; I too am desirous, as much as my force allows me, to work with this Resurgence of Italian Poetry and Literature *in England* to their ancient and accustomed power [. . .]as in the century, poetical above all others, of our august and royal Virgin queen, ELIZABETH, sovereign protector of arms, arts, learning, and OF POETS.'

83 Ibid., vi–vii. 'Thus I may hear again the highest melody from the lips of future bards with sufficient breath to fill their sounding trumpets'.

84 *Purgatorio*, I 4–8. 'I will sing of that second realm where the human spirit is purged and becomes fit to ascend to Heaven. But here let dead poetry rise again, O holy Muses'.
85 *British Critic* (January 1803): 32; see also *Critical Review* (May 1803): 72–78; *Monthly Review* (September 1805): 13–24. William Stewart Rose also praises Mathias's understanding of Italian in *Letters from the North of Italy*, 2 vols. (London, 1819), II 24–25.
86 For Mathias's translations and original poetry in Italian, see Kathleen Speight, 'An English Writer of Italian Verse', *Studies in Philology* 43 (1946): 70–88.
87 *Componimenti* (1819), 36. 'in unrestrained triumph are halied again in our respected country'.
88 *L'Italico,* 3 vols. References are given by number, date, volume, and page number. It contains reviews of a number of editions of Italian literature published in London. For example Zotti's six-volume poetical works of Metastasio, in *L' Italico* no. 2 (June 1813): I 262–267; his *Orlando Furioso, Italico* no. 2 (June 1813): I 268–270; and a review of Dulau's two-volume *Vita di Vittorio Alfieri, L'Italico* no. 2 (June 1813): I 270–273.
89 Augustus Bozzi, *Appeal to Alexander, Emperor and Autocrat of All the Russians* (London, 1814), 6.
90 'the convulsions and tremors that agitate the continent'. *L'Italico*, no. 1 (May 1813): I 3.
91 In June 1814, Bozzi met Foscolo at Milan and discussed a project for an Italian kingdom under Sardinian rule. See Augustus Bozzi Granville, *Autobiography,* 2 vols. (London, 1874), I 358–360.
92 Reuben John Rath, *The Provisional Austrian Regime in the Lombardy-Venetia, 1814–1815* (Austin, TX: University of Texas Press, 1969), 171–177.
93 For more on the foundation of *L'Italico,* see Renato Sóriga, 'Augustus Bozzi Granville e la Rivista "L'Italico"', *Bollettino della Società pavese di storia patria* 14 (1914): 265–301.
94 Periodical writing on Italian culture before 1816 appeared occasionally in *The New Annual Register* (1780–1825); *The English Review* (1783–1795); and *The Literary Magazine* (1797–1806).
95 John Herman Merivale, 'Account of the Morgante of Luigi Fulci' [*sic*], *Monthly Magazine* (May 1806): 304–308; then under the title, 'Remarks on the Morgante Maggiore of Luigi Pulci', *Monthly Magazine* (June 1806): 510–513; *Monthly Magazine* (August 1806): 34–36; *Monthly Magazine* (October 1806): 238–240; *Monthly Magazine* (January 1807): 532–535; *Monthly Magazine* (February 1807): 16–19; *Monthly Magazine* (June 1807): 439–442; *Monthly Magazine* (July 1807): 699–702.
96 Merivale, 'Account of the Morgante of Luigi Fulci', 304.
97 *L'Italico,* no. 2 (May 1813): I 122–144; no. 3 (August 1813): I 326–348.
98 *L'Italico,* no. 1 (May 1813): I 3.
99 *L'Italico*, no. 2 (June 1813): I 212.
100 *L'Italico* no. 1 (May 1813): I 5. 'we cannot rest under the shaded laurel of the Ancient Fathers'.

101 Ibid., I 4 'le aure di vera libertà respirano, si fossero addormentati come le loro speranze per il risorgimento dell'antica nazionale lor gloria'.
102 *L'Italico*, no. 2 (June 1813): I 198–199.
103 Ibid., I 201–202. 'Their object was to condemn and proscribe our Tragedian Alfieri: his free and proud sentiments, his character and his language, that of a great soul, were a source of displeasure, and were incompatible with the base and corrupt men of this shameful age'.
104 *L'Italico*, no. 1 (May 1813): I 13. 'un effetto delli sforzi che facciamo per riportar loro le consolanti notizie in Italia ignorante'.
105 Ibid., I 5. 'cercar di sollevare piacevolmente, e rendersi utili in una parola alla società generale'.
106 Fabio Camilletti, *Classicism and Romanticism in Italian Literature* (London: Pickering and Chatto, 2013), 2–3.
107 *Memoirs*, 307.
108 Thomas Mathias, *The Shade of Alexander Pope* (London, 1799), 50.
109 See Fiona MacCarthy, *Byron: Life and Legend* (London: John Murray, 2002), 263–282; Ralph Pite, 'Shelley and Italy' in *The Oxford Handbook of Percy Bysshe Shelley*, ed. Michael O'Neill and Anthony Howe, with the assistance of Madeleine Callaghan (Oxford: Oxford University Press, 2013), 34–35; Roe, *Fiery Heart*, 332–335.
110 Pite, 'Shelley and Italy', 33.

2 London 1816

1 'My little garden, from you, that are my city, palace, and lodge, to me thou 'rt vineyard, field, and meadow, and wood'.
2 Dante's Paolo is called Paulo by Hunt.
3 Webb, 'Stories of Rimini: Leigh Hunt, Lord Byron, and the Fate of Francesca', *Dante in the Nineteenth Century*, ed. Nick Havely (Oxford: Peter Lang, 2011), 31.
4 *BLJ* III 228.
5 A rare reading of *Parisina* by a major critic is Robert F. Gleckner, *Byron and the Ruins of Paradise* (Baltimore, MD: Johns Hopkins Press, 1967), 177–190.
6 '*The Siege of Corinth*, *Parisina* and *The Story of Rimini*', *British Review* (May 1816): 452.
7 Leigh Hunt to Marianne Kent, 30 May 1809, University of Iowa, Brewer-Leigh Hunt Collection, MSL H94hum2 leaf 96, 2.
8 'The Political Examiner', *Examiner* (17 January 1813): 34.
9 Leigh Hunt, *Correspondence*, ed. Thornton Hunt, 2 vols. (London: 1862), I 79; Hunt, *Autobiography*, ed. J. E. Morpurgo (London: Cresset Press, 1949), 243.
10 Hunt created a tall tale concerning Mozart's childhood trips to Italy in which he 'caught the fine spark from southern sunshine', 'Theatrical Examiner', *Examiner* (23 March 1817): 189; and later called him 'German by nation, and Italian by nature', 'Theatrical Examiner', *Examiner* (22 March 1818): 188.

11 Hunt, *Autobiography*, 414.
12 *Parnaso Italiano,* ed. Andrea Rubbi, 56 vols. (Venice, 1784–1791).
13 'The present state of literature in Italy', *Monthly Magazine* (January 1805): 482.
14 'The source of all our poetic wisdom', *Parnaso Italiano,* III 8.
15 Other works include *Elogi Italiani,* 12 vols. (Venice, 1782–1783), and *Il giornale poetico* (Venice, 1789). Rubbi mocks Voltaire's judgement of Dante in *Parnaso Italiano,* III 7. 'always with the intention to hold back French arrogance', Graf, *L'anglomania e l'influsso inglese in Italia*, 30.
16 Juvenal and Persius, *Satires*, V 187–188. 'Everything is in Greek: when it is more shameful for our Romans to be ignorant of Latin'.
17 Hunt, *Correspondence*, I 146.
18 See Greg Kucich, '"The Wit in the Dungeon": Leigh Hunt and the Insolent Politics of Cockney Coteries', *Romanticism on Net* 14 (1999). He lists the following as visitors to Hunt's cell: Bentham, Brougham, Byron, Edgeworth, Haydon, Hazlitt, the Lambs, and Moore.
19 Their trip into the garden is related in Leigh Hunt, *Lord Byron and Some of His Contemporaries*, 2nd ed., 2 vols. (London: 1828), I 292–293.
20 This is shown in a letter to Marianne Hunt, in *Leigh Hunt: A Life in Letters,* ed. Eleanor M. Gates (Essex, CT: Falls River Publications, 1998), 41; and in *Lord Byron and Some of His Contemporaries*, I 4.
21 See Webb, 'Stories of Rimini', 45.
22 For his reading, see *BLJ* II 27–31, 34–35; and for the Webster comment, see *BLJ* III 132–133.
23 Vassallo, *Byron: The Italian Literary Influence*, 7–23. See Byron's list of reading on Italy recommended to Annabella Milbanke at *BLJ* IV 161.
24 Byron translated *Inferno* V for Teresa Guiciolli in 1820 (*LBCPW* IV 280–285), and discusses it in a letter to Augusta at *BLJ* VI 129–130, to Hobhouse at *BLJ* VI 187–190, and considers writing a play on the subject at *BLJ* VIII 36–37.
25 Lord Byron, preface to *Parisina* [1816], *LBCPW* III 358–375. Hereafter, line number cited in parentheses after quotations.
26 The similarity was first realised, albeit only briefly, in Frederick L. Beatty, 'Byron and the Story of Francesca da Rimini', *PMLA* 75 (1960): 399.
27 Leigh Hunt, *The Story of Rimini* (London: 1816), II 62–3; see also III 21–29, III 55–66. Hereafter, line and canto number cited in parentheses after quotations.
28 See *Rimini* I 115–120, IV 213, IV 315, IV 373–375, IV 404, V 161–206, and *Parisina* ll. 56, 460, 404–429.
29 *The Siege of Corinth* [1816], ll. 31, 37, *LBCPW* III 322–355. For topographical description, see ll. 9–10, 46–48, and *The Giaour* [1813], ll. 7–10, 105–113, *LBCPW* III 39–82.
30 Compare *Parisina*, ll. 250–315 to *The Siege of Corinth*, ll. 261–262.
31 Gleckner, *Byron and the Ruins of Paradise*, 183.
32 Hunt, *Autobiography,* 258.

33 Edward Gibbon, 'Antiquities of the House of Brunswick', *Miscellaneous Works*, 3 vols. (Dublin: 1796), III 463.

34 McGann, in notes to *LBCPW* III 489.

35 *LBCPW* III 479–480; 489.

36 One McGann himself adopts, see Jerome McGann, *Fiery Dust* (Chicago, IL: Chicago University Press, 1968), 190–191.

37 This is lot 166 in the 1816 sale catalogue of Byron's library, listed as '*Gibbon's Miscellaneous Works*, 3 vol., 1796'. See Andrew Nicholson (ed.), *Lord Byron the Miscellaneous Prose* (Oxford: Clarendon Press, 1991), 237.

38 *LBCPW* III 297, VII 90.

39 *LBCPW* III 297.

40 *LBCPW*, *The Bride of Abydos* [1813], l. 16, III 108. Andrew Rutherford, *Byron: A Critical Study* (Palo Alto, CA: Stanford University Press, 1961), 37.

41 See *BLJ* IV 17. An interesting reading of the role of the name Francesca occurs in Susan Wolfson, *Formal Charges* (Princeton, NJ: Princeton University Press, 1997), 162.

42 Murray to Byron, 1 April 1816, *LJM*, 153.

43 The manuscript is *BL* Ashley Ms. 906, and is the only known example of Byron offering suggestions to a contemporary poet on his text. There is only a record of Byron's comments on Cantos II and III, with Hunt admitting that he had rubbed out comments on Canto I for fear of objections from his publisher. For more, see Webb, 'Stories of Rimini', 34–35.

44 *BL* Ashley Ms. 906, ff. 2^{v}, 3^{v}, 5^{r}, 7^{v}, 20^{v}. For more of Byron's praise of *Rimini*, see *BLJ* IV 324–326, *BLJ* IV 329–331, and Murray's description to Hunt of Byron's praise for the poem as a 'tempting encomium' in a letter from Hunt to Byron in *NLS* Ms. 43449.

45 Webb, 'Stories of Rimini', 33. See also Timothy Webb, 'Leigh Hunt's Letters to Byron from Horsemonger Lane Gaol: A Commentary', *The Byron Journal* 37 (2009): 21–32, 26; Webb, 'After Horsemonger Lane: Leigh Hunt's London Letters to Byron (1815–1816)', *Romanticism* 16 (2010): 233–266.

46 The manuscript shows that the phrases 'more robust the other finelier' (Ms. 906 f. 5^{r} / *Rimini* III 27), and Paolo's 'graceful nose' (Ms. 906 f. 6^{r} / *Rimini* III 46) were based on Byron's amendments. It appears that most of Byron's suggestions were contrary to Hunt's aims for a new style, as shown in a letter of 30 October 1815 (*NLS* Ms. 43449) in which Hunt justifies his rejection of the changes to Byron. Although Byron's editorial interventions had little impact, in his role as literary agent he encouraged Hunt to finish the poem, and put in a good word with John Murray. For Byron's encouragement see *BLJ* IV 295, and for Murray's involvement in the publication see *LJM* 145; *LJM* 148–149.

47 Roe, *Fiery Heart* (London: Pimlico, 2005), 244.

48 Hunt, *Autobiography*, 257.

49 *BLJ* V 32.

50 *British Review* (May 1816): 452; John Lockhart, 'On the Cockney School of Poetry II'; *Blackwood's* (November 1817): 196.

51 St. Clair, *The Reading Nation in the Romantic Period,* 215.

52 Scott's romances were a significant influence on the love of disguises and hero-villains in the 'Turkish' tales; see Susan Oliver, 'Crossing "Dark Barriers": Intertextuality and Dialogue between Lord Byron and Sir Walter Scott', *Studies in Romanticism* 47 (2008): 15–35.

53 Curran, *Poetic Form and British Romanticism,* 130.

54 Walter Scott, *Marmion* [1808] *Poetical Works,* ed. J. Logie Robertson (Oxford: Oxford University Press, 1913), 89–90.

55 Ibid., 90; Simon Bainbridge, *British Poetry and the Revolutionary and Napoleonic Wars* (Oxford: Oxford University Press, 2003), 136.

56 *Marmion,* 91.

57 Walter Scott, *Waverley,* 3 vols. (Edinburgh: 1814), I 9–10.

58 For a later discussion of this in Scott, see the invocation of the military concept of 'neutral ground' that exists between 'the large proportions of manners and sentiments which are common to us and our ancestors, which have been handed down unaltered from them to us, or which, arising out of principles of our common nature, must have existed alike in either state of society', in the 'Dedicatory Epistle' to *Ivanhoe,* 2nd ed., 3 vols. (Edinburgh: 1820), I xix.

59 Battle is another aspect which is absent from *Parisina,* but is integral to *The Corsair, Lara, The Bride of Abydos,* and *The Siege of Corinth.*

60 See *Parisina,* ll. 553–556: 'The deepest ice which ever froze / Can only o'er the surface close – / the living stream lies quick below, / And flows – and cannot cease to flow'.

61 *Parisina* l. 30; *DJ* II 111. This is not the only echo of *Parisina* in *Don Juan*: the famous lines on Milton, '*He* did not loathe the sire to laud the son' (*DJ* 'Dedication', 10) echo the shared infidelity of Azo and Hugo, 'As erred the sire, so erred the son' (l. 314).

62 *Marmion,* 91, 100, 112, 124, 136, 152.

63 'On the Cockney School of Poetry II', 194.

64 See Greg Kucich, 'Hunt, Keats, and the Aesthetic of Excess', in *Leigh Hunt: Life, Poetics, Politics,* ed. Nicholas Roe (London: Routledge, 2003), 125–127.

65 Edmund Burke, *Reflections on the Revolution in France,* ed. L. G. Mitchell (Oxford: Oxford University Press, 1999), 76. This is not the only allusion to Burke in *Parisina*: see also the detailed final image of the state as a tree 'with tainted branches' (ll. 579–586), which recalls Burke's image of the law-abiding thousands 'reposed beneath the shadow of the British oak' (*Reflections,* 85).

66 Davd Duff, *Romance and Revolution* (Cambridge: Cambridge University Press, 1994), 3. In a letter discussing the run-up to the 1831 Reform Bill, Scott remembers 'a similar crisis' in 'about 1792', and claims 'Burke appeared, and all the gibberish about the superior legislation of the French dissolved like an enchanted castle when the destined knight blows his horn before it', *The Letters of Sir Walter Scott,* ed. H. J. C. Grierson, 12 vols ((London: Constable, 1932–1937), XI 455.

67 'The Round Table', *Examiner* (1 January 1815): 13.
68 Duff, *Romance and Revolution*, 117.
69 Curran, *Poetic Form and British Romanticism*, 6.
70 *Rimini*, 'Preface', x–xiii.
71 Cox, 'Re-visioning Rimini: Dante in the Cockney School', 183.
72 Webb, 'Stories of Rimini', 41.
73 See Friedrich Schelling 'Über Dante in philosophischer Beziehung' [1803], in *Werke,* ed. M. Schroter, 6 vols. (München: Beck, 1927–1928), III 573. Giuseppe Mazzotta, 'Life of Dante' in *The Cambridge Companion to Dante* (Cambridge: Cambridge University Press, 1993), 1: 'the turning of himself into an archetypal literary character, such as Ulysses, Faust, or any of those medieval Knights Errant'.
74 For Voltaire on Dante, see Lettre XXII ('Sur M. Pope et Quelques autres poètes fameux'), *Lettres Philosophiques, Oeuvres completes* (1734), XXII 174; the entry in the *Dictionnaire philosophique* (1765), *Oeuvres completes,* XVIII 312–315; Lettre XII ('Sur le Dante, et sur un pauvre homme nommé Martinelli'), *Lettres Chinoises et Indiennes* (1776), *Oeuvres completes,* XXIX 495–498.
75 Thomas Warton, *The History of English Poetry,* 3 vols. (London, 1774–1781), III 236–255, 241, 249, 255.
76 *Parisina,* 'Preface'.
77 The discussion of Dante occurs in *Principe* II 3, 58–64: 'which suited his times', 60, 'contaminated themselves with so much vile adulation and falsehood', 60.
78 Francesco Torti, *Prospetto del Parnaso Italiano* (Milan: 1806), 37, 53: '*Dante* did not follow any model'; 'to consider nature from an entirely new perspective'.
79 Torti, *Prospetto,* 39–46.
80 These themes still exist to an extent in modern criticism, but the reading of Dante as a symbol of independence (especially republican nationalism) has been contradicted by study of Dante's output beyond the *Inferno,* e.g. *Purgatorio* XVI 106–108 and *De Monarchia* (1312–1313?).
81 Saglia, 'Translation and Cultural Appropriation', 102; Michael Caesar, *Dante: The Critical Heritage* (London: Routledge, 1989), 53; Pite, *Circle of Our Vision,* 1.
82 Hunt's interpretation is quite different to the allegorical reading of the castle given in Ginguené, *Histoire Littèraire d'Italie,* II 41.
83 'soli eravamo', *Inferno,* V 129.
84 *Inferno,* IV 65, 106–8, 'the wood'; 'to the foot of a noble castle, seven times encircled by lofty walls and defended round about by a fair stream'.
85 *Inferno,* IV 111, 'a meadow fresh of fresh verdure'; *Inferno* IV. 45.
86 *Inferno* IV 94, 'the fair school'; *Inferno* IV. 48 'the company of six'.
87 *Inferno,* IV 104–105, 'things it is well to pass in silence, even as it was well to speak of them there'.
88 *Inferno,* IV 101, 'they made me one of their company'.
89 *Inferno,* V 71, 'knights and ladies of ancient times'.

90 *Inferno*, V 100–108.
91 *Inferno*, V 137, 'A Gallehault was the book and he who wrote it'.
92 *Inferno*, V 39, 'who subject reason to desire'.
93 *Rimini*, 'Preface'.
94 *Inferno*, IV. 111. 'meadow of fresh verdure'.
95 Hunt, *Lord Byron and Some of His Contemporaries*, II 257; Hunt uses the full three-line quotation in a letter to Mary Shelley of 1819, *Correspondence*, I 146.
96 *Parnaso Italiano*, XXIII 304. 'From you, that are my city, palace, and lodge'.
97 Elizabeth Jones, 'Suburban Sinners: Sex and Disease in the Cockney School', in *Leigh Hunt Life, Poetics, Politics*, 88–89.
98 *BLJ* IV 49–50.
99 Hunt, *Autobiography*, 258.
100 Samuel Johnson, 'Life of Pope', *Lives of the Poets* [1779–1781], ed. Roger Lonsdale, 4 vols. (Oxford: Oxford University Press, 2006) IV 62; *Gentleman's Magazine* (June 1789): 510.
101 William Bowman Piper, *The Heroic Couplet* (Cleveland, OH: Case Western University Press, 1969), 151; Earl Wasserman, 'The Return of the Enjambed Couplet', *English Literary History* 7 (1940): 245.
102 Hunt mentions the work in a letter to Haydon of November 1812, see *Leigh Hunt: A Life in Letters*, 27. Joseph Warton, *An Essay on the Writings and Genius of Pope* (London: 1756), iv.
103 Bate, *The Burden of the Past and the English Poet*, 31–57, esp. 44.
104 Robert Griffin, *Wordsworth's Pope* (Cambridge: Cambridge University Press, 1995), 26.
105 To view Pope's prosody as 'mere mechanic art' misrepresents his immense variety; see for example the use of a plodding metre for the pagan gods and the regular pauses to enact ratiocination in early sections of 'An Essay on Man', *PoAP*, 501–548, I 61–68, I 123–130; and the imitative quality of his form in 'An Essay on Criticism', 143, 168, ll. 345–384.
106 Thomas Warton's edition of Milton's shorter poems in English, Italian, and Latin (*Poems upon Several Occasions* (1785)) is an important text in this reassessment. William Hazlitt, *Lectures on the English Poets* (London: 1818), 137.
107 See for example, Wordsworth's incredulity that Johnson began *The Lives of the Poets* with Cowley in 'Essay, Supplementary to the Preface', *Poems*, 2 vols. (London, 1815), I 366.
108 Hazlitt, *Lectures on the English Poets*, 148.
109 See Upali Amarasinghe, *Dryden and Pope in the Early Nineteenth Century* (Cambridge: Cambridge University Press, 1962), 95.
110 Francis Jeffrey, 'Thalaba, the Destroyer', *Edinburgh Review* (October 1802): 63; John Lockhart, 'On the Cockney School of Poetry IV' *Blackwood's* (August 1818): 520. For more defences of Pope see: 'Scott's Swift', *Edinburgh Review* (September 1816): 1–58; 'Spence's *Anecdotes of Pope*', *Edinburgh Review* (May 1820): 302–330; 'Spence's *Anecdotes of Pope*', *Quarterly Review* (July 1820): 400–434.

111 See J. J. Van Rennes, *Bowles, Byron, and the Pope Controversy* (Amsterdam: H. J. Paris, 1927); James Chandler, 'The Pope Controversy: Romantic Poetics and the English Canon', *Critical Inquiry* 10 (1984): 481–509.
112 Wordsworth, 'Essay, Supplementary to the Preface', I 356, 366–367.
113 *Rimini,* 'Preface'.
114 Ibid.
115 See Southey, *Specimens,* I xxiii, for the claim that the Elizabethans were not Italian, and that aside from there use of sonnets 'there is little other reason for this assertion'.
116 Pascale Casanova, 'Combative Literatures', *New Left Review* 72 (2011): 128.
117 Leigh Hunt, *The Feast of the Poets* (London: 1814), 52.
118 *BLJ* IV 49–50.
119 Letter of 10 February 1814 from Hunt to Byron in *NLS* Ms. 43449.
120 'Of Italian learning he does not appear to have ever made much use in his subsequent studies'; Johnson, 'Life of Pope', *Lives of the Poets,* IV. 3.
121 See for example *BLJ* V 265.
122 'English Bards and Scotch Reviewers', [1809] *LBCPW* I 227–264, ll. 799–805.
123 Chandler, 'The Pope Controversy', 505. Byron had the same conditional admiration for Scott of whom he later claims 'his poetry as good as any – if not better (only on an erroneous system)' (*BLJ* VIII 23).
124 'Beppo' [1818], *LBCPW* IV 129–160, ll. 404. This turn against the couplet was not forever, see Jane Stabler, *Byron, Poetics, and History* (Cambridge: Cambridge University Press, 2002), 173–180.
125 *BL* Ms. 906 f. 19^{v}.
126 Michael O'Neill, '"Even now while I write": Leigh Hunt and Romantic Spontaneity', *Leigh Hunt: Life, Poetics, Politics,* 135.
127 'The Divina Commedia of Dante Alighieri', *Edinburgh Review* (January 1803): 307.
128 William Hazlitt, 'De la Litterature du Midi de l'Europe', *Edinburgh Review* (June 1815): 31–32.
129 Ibid., 46–47.
130 William Hazlitt, *The Letters of William Hazlitt,* ed. Herschel M. Sikes (New York: New York University Press, 1978), 153; Francis Jeffrey, 'The Excursion', *Edinburgh Review* (November 1814): 1.
131 William Hazlitt, 'The Story of Rimini', *Edinburgh Review* (June 1816): 476.
132 Hunt, *Autobiography,* 258.
133 Shelley, 'Julian and Maddalo', ll. 1–3, *LongmanPS* II 663; 'Endymion: A Poetic Romance', *Quarterly Review* (April 1818), 204.
134 *British Review* (May 1816): 452.
135 Pocock, *Machiavellian Moment,* 17–18.
136 William Keach, 'Cockney Couplets: Keats and the Politics of Style' in *Romanticism,* ed. Michael O'Neill and Mark Sandy, 2 vols. (London: Routledge, 2006), II 165.
137 Roe, *Fiery Heart,* 166.

138 Roe, *Keats and the Culture of Dissent* (Oxford: Oxford University Press, 1997), 122.
139 Cox, *Romanticism in the Shadow of War*, 179.
140 Wolfson, *Formal Charges*, 1–30; Peter Manning, *Reading Romantics* (Oxford: Oxford University Press, 1990), 300–320.
141 *BLJ* IV 326; *BLJ* V 35.
142 T. C. W. Blanning, *The Culture of Power and the Power of Culture* (Oxford: Oxford University Press, 2002), 2.
143 Ibid., 11.
144 *Parisina*, 'Dedication'.
145 A theory of 'public opinion' which finds its origins in Gramsci, *Quaderni del carcere*, 1638.
146 Robert Hunt, 'Fine Arts', *Examiner* (18 June 1809): 77.
147 An exception to this is Cronin's chapter on Keats and Hunt in *The Politics of Romantic Poetry,* esp. pp. 181–183. For an example of this criticism see Cox, *Poetry and Politics in the Cockney School*, 30–31, 'poetry was judged on political grounds; put simply one's reception was dependent upon one's views of the government of Castlereagh, Sidmouth, and Eldon'.
148 A pamphlet that defended Hunt against this criticism also focused on the poetic novelty of *Rimini*: see Charles Cowden Clarke, *An Address to that Quarterly Reviewer who touched upon Mr. Leigh Hunt's 'Story of Rimini'* (London: 1816), 3–18.
149 'The Story of Rimini', *Quarterly Review,* 474, 477.
150 A convincing argument for the personal tenor of these attacks is given in Kim Wheatley, 'The Blackwood's Attacks on Leigh Hunt', *Nineteenth-Century Literature* 47 (1992): 1–31.
151 'On the Cockney School of Poetry', *Blackwood's* (October 1817): 38.
152 *British Review* (May 1816): 452.
153 Hunt, *Feast of the Poets,* xiv.
154 Rimini, 'Preface', xii.
155 *'The Siege of Corinth* [. . .] *Parisina* [. . .] *The Story of Rimini'*, *British Review* (May 1816): 454–456.
156 'On the Cockney School of Poetry II', 201.
157 Chapter II of *Poetry and Politics in the Cockney School* is entitled 'The Hunt era', 38–81.
158 Hunt, 'To Lord Byron, On His Departure to Italy' *Examiner* (28 April 1816): 266.

3 London 1817–1819

1 Ugo Foscolo, *Discorsi nel parlamento in morte di Francesco Horner* (London, 1817), iv. 'And whilst you, young man, follow in the footsteps of that citizen and boldly continue on life's ways, I, tired and without country, shall go looking back on my safe repose'.
2 Additionally, Foscolo kept editing *Le Grazie* in London until his death in 1827.

3 Mario Fubini, *Ugo Foscolo* (Florence: La Nuova Italia, 1962), 254. 'the last phase in the development of his personality as it had manifested itself in the preceding periods of his life'.

4 William Stewart Rose, *The Court of the Beasts* (London, 1816), 4. The final line reads, 'As an expert in both languages'. A reworking of *Horace, Odes* III 8 l. 5, which begins with the vocative, 'docte'.

5 Walter Scott, *The Journal of Sir Walter Scott*, 2 vols. (Edinburgh, 1890), entry of 24 November 1825, I 29.

6 See Foscolo's disastrous meeting with Wordsworth in E. R. Vincent, *Ugo Foscolo* (Cambridge: Cambridge University Press, 1953), 14–18, and the comparisons with Baretti, in Carlo Maria Franzero, *A Life in Exile* (London: W. H. Allen, 1977), 26. A more nuanced view of Foscolo's plight in London is provided in Carlo Dionisotti, *Appunti sui moderni* (Bologna: Mulino, 1988), 55–78.

7 For Foscolo as the announcer of '[l]a nuova letteratura', see Francesco De Sanctis, *Storia della Letteratura Italiana,* ed. by Morano (Naples, 1879), 420–428; see also Benedetto Croce, 'Ugo Foscolo' [1922], *Filosofia, Poesia, Storia* (Milan: Ricciardi, 1955), 825–835; Fubini, *Ugo Foscolo* (1962) is a minor classic on Foscolo and John Lindon, *Studi sul Foscolo 'inglese'* (Pisa: Giardini, 1987), is also excellent.

8 John Cam Hobhouse, *Diary*, 19 October 1816, 28 November 1816. I am indebted to the editorial labours of Peter Cochran on Hobhouse's dairy, available at http://petercochran.wordpress.com/hobhouses-diary/ (2009). All future references will be given as *Hobhouse*, followed by the date for the entry.

9 'The Letters of Ortis to Lorenzo, &c.' *Monthly Meteor* (March 1814): 283.

10 Roscoe to Holland, 28 February 1818, *BL* Add MS 51650 f. 110^{r}.

11 The best work in this mould is Vincent's *Ugo Foscolo,* which charts Foscolo's rise and fall in high society, particularly his solecisms at dinner parties and his amorous quests.

12 John Cam Hobhouse, *Historical Illustrations of the Fourth Canto of Childe Harold* (London, 1818), 347–491.

13 For a discussion of the 'Italian Romanticism' controversy see Camilletti, *Classicism and Romanticism in Italian Literature*, 1–58; and for the role of Hobhouse and Foscolo within it, see Grazia Avitabile, *The Controversy on Romanticism in Italy* (New York: Vanni, 1959). For an anthology of the primary texts relating to the controversy, see Egido Bellorini (ed.), *Discussioni e Polemiche sul Romanticismo* (Bari: Laterza, 1943).

14 E. R. Vincent, *Byron, Hobhouse and Foscolo* (Cambridge: Cambridge University Press, 1949) is the standard work on this collaboration and includes copious quotation from previously unpublished letters. Useful context for the reception of the essay appears in Nick Havely, '*This Infernal Essay:* English Contexts for Foscolo's Essay on the Present State of Italian Literature', *Immaginando L'Italia*, 233–250; and Lilla Maria Crisafulli 'An Infernal Triangle: Foscolo, Byron, Di Breme, and the Italian Context of "The Essay on the Present Literature of Italy"', *Immaginando L'Italia*, 251–295.

15 *Discorsi nel parlamento in morte di Francesco Horner tradotti dall' Inglese* (London, 1817); *Ultime Lettere di Jacopo Ortis* (London, 1817), further references as *Ortis (Murray)*; 'Dante', *Edinburgh Review* (February 1818): 453–474, further references as 'Dante 1'; 'Dante', *Edinburgh Review* (September 1818): 317–351, further references as 'Dante 2'; 'Essay on the Present State of Italian Literature', in *Historical Illustrations of the Fourth Canto of Childe Harold*, 347–491, further references as 'Present State'; 'Pius VI', *Edinburgh Review* (March 1819): 271–295; 'Narrative and Romantic Poems of the Italians' *Quarterly Review* (April 1819): 486–556, further references as 'Narrative Poems'; 'Parga', *Edinburgh Review* (October 1819): 264–293.

16 An excellent narrative of Foscolo's literary career from 1819–1822, especially his work on Petrarch and his relationship with Henry Brougham and Lady Dacre, is given in Saglia, *European Literatures in Britain*, 122–147.

17 Information on attendance from dinner is from The Holland House dinner books, a record of diners at Holland House from 1799–1840, kept under shelfmark *BL* Add MS 51950–51957. I am indebted to Christopher Wright, whose work has allowed me to ascertain the dining frequency of various Italian exiles.

18 'Pius VI' and 'Parga' both open their issues.

19 Isabella, *Risorgimento in Exile,* 24.

20 'Dante 2', 340. 'The passage that we select is from the episode of '*Francesca da Rimini*,' as being most familiar to the English reader, both from its own popularity, and from the beautiful amplification of it which Mr. Hunt has lately given to the public'.

21 For Milton see, 'Narrative Poems', 524–525, 546. For Gray, see the reinstatement of Foscolo's '*Naturae clamat ab ipso / vox tumulo*', a Latin translation from Gray's 'Elegy Written in a Country Churchyard', in *Ortis (Murray).*

22 'Proceedings in Parga', *Quarterly Review* (May 1820): 111–136, 111.

23 Ibid., 112, 116, 120.

24 Ibid., 125, 126.

25 Foscolo to Lady Dacre (29 March 1821), *ENUF* XXI 258. 'My cousin has brought dozens of letters here, which urge me strongly to intervene in Greek affairs, so that I shall end by being deported under the Aliens Act.'

26 Carlo Cattaneo, *Ugo Foscolo e L'Italia* (Milan, 1861), 34. 'E così Ugo Foscolo diede alla nuova Italia una nuova istituzione: *l'esilio*'.

27 Ugo Foscolo, *Ultime Lettere di Jacopo ,Ortis*, [1802], *ENUF* IV 137. 'My name is on the list of those proscribed'. See also the inset narrative 'Frammento della Storia di Lauretta' where the theme of exile is similarly omnipresent (IV 185–189). All further references to this edition will be as *Ortis.*

28 *BLJ* VIII 125, 'those Scoundrels appear to be organizing a system of abuse against me; – because I am in their "list" – you know – I suppose that they actually need a list of all individuals in Italy – who dislike them – It must be numerous'.

29 *Ortis*, 137. 'the first persecutions, and the most ferocious'.

30 *Ortis,* 138. 'Or at most, brief and sterile compassion, the only comfort which civilised nations offer an alien'.
31 Ugo Foscolo, 'A Zacinto', [1802–1803], ll. 1–2 *ENUF* I 95. 'No more shall I touch those sacred shores, / where as a boy my body lay'.
32 Nick Havely, '*Francesca Franciosa*: Exile, Language and History in Foscolo's Articles on Dante', in *Dante in the Nineteenth Century*, 56–58.
33 Plutarch, 'On Exile', *Moralia* VII, trans. Phillip H. De Lacy (London: Loeb, 1959), 525. 'Why, we look for a fire, a bath-house, a cloak, a roof: in a rainstorm we do not sit idle or lament'.
34 Ibid., 567.
35 John Lindon. 'Foscolo as Literary Critic', *Reflexivity – Critical Themes in the Italian Cultural Tradition,* ed. John Took and Prue Shaw (Ravenna: A. Longo, 2000), 148.
36 Foscolo to Monti, (5 December 1808), *ENUF* XV 535, 'to speak philosophically and eloquently the history of the literature of all ages and all people'.
37 'Dante 1', 454.
38 This comparison appears again in 'Narrative Poems', 487, 501.
39 Ugo Foscolo, 'Classic Tours', *European Review* (October 1824): 136. Other exiled Italian journalists in London also dismissed travel literature, see for example, Serafino Buonaiuti, 'A Journey to Rome and Naples', *Literary Gazette* (21 November 1818): 737.
40 See also the claim for 'Authenticity' in Serafino Buonaiuti and James Godby, *Italian Scenery; Representing the Manners, Customs, and Amusements of the Different States of Italy* (London, 1806).
41 Foscolo, *Orazione,* 111.
42 Ibid., 144, 141: 'The literature that illuminates truth'.
43 Ibid.,143. 'but where is a history of Italy? [. . .] How will you repay our fathers' vigil if you do not make use of the documents that they prepared for you?'
44 'Pius VI', 272.
45 Ibid., 272–275.
46 Ibid., 276, 281, 286.
47 'Parga', 274–284.
48 'Parga', 264.
49 In the *Edinburgh* articles by Foscolo on Dante, some four and a half pages are written by Samuel Rogers ('Dante 1' 469–474) owing to a mistake by Sir James Mackintosh (the translator) and Jeffrey (the editor). This mistake has been discussed in detail by Beatrice Corrigan in 'Foscolo's Articles on Dante in the *Edinburgh Review*: A Study in Collaboration', in *Collected Essays on Italian Language and Literature Presented to Kathleen Speight,* ed. Giovanni Aquilecchia (Manchester: Manchester University Press, 1971), 214–220.
50 For further examples, see 'Narrative poems', 487, 522.
51 'Dante 1', 454.
52 'Dante 2', 321.

53 Ibid., 331.
54 'Dante 2', 323. The historian in question is William Robertson in *The History of the Reign of the Emperor Charles V* (1769).
55 'Dante 2', 323.
56 'To the Editor', *Anti-Jacobin Review* (August 1804): 416, 418.
57 John Ring, *The Beauties of the Edinburgh Review* (London, 1807): 79.
58 Samuel Smiles, *Memoirs and Correspondence of John Murray*, 2 vols. (London, 1891), I 93.
59 'Whig' is a term that is nearly always preceded by an epithet, e.g. 'radical', 'Foxite', 'high', 'Vulgar'; for further discussion, see J. W. Burrow, *Whigs and Liberals* (Oxford: Clarendon Press, 1988), 40–60.
60 Jennifer Mori, *The Culture of Diplomacy* (Manchester: Manchester University Press, 2010), 30–31. She is quoting from a letter from Gilbert Eliot to James Harris of 18 May 1784.
61 *Edinburgh Review* (October 1808): 215–234.
62 For Southey's reaction, see his letter to Grosvenor Bedford, 6 January 1809, *The Correspondence of Robert Southey*, III 205. For Scott's departure from the *Edinburgh*, see *The Letters of Sir Walter Scott*, II 100–153.
63 Francis Jeffrey to Francis Horner (12 March 1815), in Henry Cockburn, *Life of Lord Jeffrey*, 2 vols. (Edinburgh, 1852), II 152.
64 Ibid., II 107.
65 For a detailed discussion of this opposition, see William Christie, *The Edinburgh Review in the Literary Culture of Romantic Britain* (London: Pickering and Chatto, 2009), 147–166.
66 Mark Schoenfield, *British Periodicals and Romantic Identity* (London: Palgrave, 2009), 100.
67 Schoenfield. *British Periodicals and Romantic Identity*, 101. The article appears in *Blackwood's* (February 1818): 558.
68 Mentioned in 'On the Cockney School of Poetry I' (October 1817): 40, and again as 'austere and simple' in 'On the Cockney School of Poetry II' (November 1817), 199.
69 'On Mr. Campbell's Specimens of English Poetry', *Blackwood's* (March 1819): 696.
70 'Dante 2', 321.
71 'Remarks on Schlegel's History of Literature', *Blackwood's* (August 1818): 500.
72 'Dante 2', 334–335. The relevant lines are *Inferno* XV 22–104.
73 'Dante 2', 336–345. The lines which Ariosto re-works are *Purgatorio* XIV 109–111; Dante meets Casella at *Purgatorio* II 76–114.
74 'Dante', 464.
75 'Present State', 364.
76 Ibid., 377–379.
77 *Hobhouse,* 28 March 1818. Foscolo provides the dates for Dante's birth, banishment, and death. It was this information that ignited the doomed collaboration between the two writers later that year.

78 For more on this, see Will Bowers, 'The Many Rooms of Holland House', *Re-evaluating the Literary Coterie*, ed. Will Bowers and H. L. Crumme (London: Palgrave, 2016), 159–180.
79 Whishaw's Diary quoted in *The "Pope" of Holland House,* ed. Lady Seymour (London, 1906), 119–21.
80 The fate of Naples at the end of the European wars was uncertain. It was presumed it would not remain under the control of Joachim Murat if Napoleon was defeated. The two most discussed possibilities were the restoration of Ferdinand IV (as part of the Kingdom of the Two Sicilies) or an independent republic. The eventual restoration of Ferdinand, with Austrian assistance, is discussed in Chapter 5.
81 *Italiani. L'ora è venuta* (Rimini, 1815), 1 sheet. 'Italians. The hour has come when you must accomplish your highest destiny'.
82 For this view, see John Rosselli, *Lord William Bentinck* (Delhi: Thomson, 1974), 167–179. Mitchell, *Holland House*, 205.
83 The source is a letter from Lord Burgesh to Bentinck, 20 April 1815, *Correspondence of Lord Burgesh* (London: John Murray, 1912), 152–153. The tale of Binda being intercepted is told in Mitchell, *Holland House*, 204–205, and repeated in Saglia, *European Literatures in Britain*, 118.
84 'Naples the Ministry of Foreign Affairs'. This is marked on *BL* Add MS 51643 f. 49^{v}.
85 'I am extremely content in my present situation, and shall remember with eternal gratitude him that I owe for it'. *BL* Add MS 51643 ff. 47^{r-v}.
86 *Correspondence of Lord Burgesh*, 152.
87 'My Lord, I had just given a letter to General Pignatelli on your behalf, when he received yours at this moment of the 23rd of this month', *BL* Add MS 51643, f. 49^{r}.
88 For Pignatelli's Jacobinism, see Harold Acton, *The Bourbons of Naples* [1957] (London: Prion 1998), 266–267, 284.
89 See for example, *Correspondence of Lord Burgesh,* 151–156. Bentinck and Burgesh were hoping for an independent Naples but were not prepared, as it seems Holland was, to keep the current regime in power for the sake of depriving the Austrians.
90 Francesco Pignatelli Strongoli, *Memorie intorno alla storia del Regno di Napoli dall' anno 1805 al 1815* (Naples, 1820), 185–189.
91 Franceso Pignatelli, *Memorie di Un Generale*, ed. Nino Cortese, 2 vols. (Bari: Laterza, 1927), II 230. 'added some ideas of the Englishman Lord Holland'.
92 Lord Holland, *Letter to a Neapolitan from an Englishman* (London, 1818), v,
93 Ibid., 3, 40.
94 See Francis Horner, *The Horner Papers*, ed. Bourne and Taylor (Edinburgh: Edinburgh University Press, 1994), 804, 861.
95 Another example of this is Franceco Mami's furnishing Foscolo with material for 'Pius VI' – Mami had previously held diplomatic posts in Rome. See Giorgio Lelli-Mami, *Francesco Mami, Cesenate amico di Ugo Foscolo* (Cesena: Sintini, 1984), 39–41.

96 Binda to Foscolo, 16 September 1816, *ENUF* XX 8.
97 Foscolo to Binda, December 1816, *ENUF* XX 263. Binda provided Foscolo with stanzas from Berni's *Orlando Innamorato* for 'Narrative Poems'.
98 Like Binda, Buonaiuti was a regular at the Hollands' dinner table, attending more than 250 dinners from 1799–1822.
99 For Buonaiuti's works, see *Music Entries at Stationer's Hall 1710–1818*, compiled by Michael Kassler (Aldershot: Ashgate, 2004), 617, 624, 629, 631.
100 Serafino Buonaiuti (ed.), *Risorgimento della Poesia Italiana dopo Il Petrarca* (London: 1813).
101 'Italian Literature' began in *Literary Gazette* (25 July 1818): 469, and carried on every three months thereafter.
102 'Observations, Moral, Literary and Antiquarian, Made during a Tour', *Literary Gazette* (24 January 1818): 53;. 'Journey to Rome and Naples', *Literary Gazette* (21 November 1818): 737.
103 'Historical Illustrations of the Fourth Canto of Childe Harold', *Literary Gazette* (9 May 1818): 292.
104 'Beppo: a Venetian Story', *Literary Gazette* (14 March 1818): 162, 164.
105 'Introduzione', *L'Italico,* no. 1 (May 1813): I 5.
106 *Principe,* I iii 18, 'What Is Literature?' – 'le lettere sono l'arte d'insegnar dilettando, e di commuovere, coltivare, e ben indizziare gli umani affetti'. 'Literature is the art of instructing delightfully, and of touching and cultivating, and directing well the human emotions'.
107 'Dante 1', 467.
108 Ibid., 467.
109 Mathias is named 'Pastore Arcade in Roma' in the *Componimenti* (1819) frontispiece.
110 'Pius VI', 279.
111 'Present State', 359, 455.
112 'Present State', 456.
113 'Dante 2', 332.
114 Ibid.
115 Ibid.
116 'Narrative Poems', 520.
117 'Book Review', *Literary Gazette* (27 December 1817): 402.
118 See Ginguené, *Histoire*, I 319, for a defence of Italian literature, especially the 'vengeance poetique' of Alfieri against France. See V 345–346 for the defence of Tasso which is similar to Foscolo's at 'Narrative Poems', 544.
119 Vittorio Alfieri, *Vita di Vittorio Alfieri,* 2 vols. (London [i.e. Firenze]: 1804 [i.e. 1806]), II 191–192. See also, Cristina Trinchero, *Pierre-Louis Ginguené e L'Identità Nazionale Italiana Nel Contesto Culutral Europeo* (Rome: Bulzoni, 2004), 28–29.
120 For Foscolo's reading of the *Vita,* see, T. O'Neill, 'The Figure of Alfieri in "Dei Sepolcri"', *Italica* 55 (1978): 321–337.
121 Casanova, 'Combative Literatures', 123.

122 'Whom do you think is to blame if the seeds of Italian knowledge are cultivated by the foreigners who have usurped you?', *Orazione*, 142.
123 'Literary Intelligence', *Literary Gazette* (31 July 1819): 493; 'Whistlecraft', *Quarterly Review* (April 1819): 486; see also, 'Book Review', *Monthly Review* (December 1818): 370.
124 'Present State', 454.
125 *Ortis,* 235. 'somewhat spitefully, that he did not sell Italian books. The civilian population speaks French elegantly, and pure Tuscan is hardly known. Public acts and laws are written in a bastard language, so that the naked phrases bear witness to the ignorance and servitude of those who dictate them'.
126 *Orazione,* 141; for the French influence on the Italian language in the late eighteenth century, see Graf, *l'anglomania e l'influsso inglese in Italia nel secolo xviii,* 4–7.
127 Bozzi, 'Lettera Scritta da un Italiano agli Estensori del Giornale *Italico*', *L'Italico* (June 1813): I 200–201.
128 'Present State', 365. See Butler, *Romantics, Rebels and Reactionaries* (Oxford: Oxford University Press, 1981), 189.
129 'Present State', 482. On Napoleon see 'Pius VI', 290.
130 Dart, *Rousseau, Robespierre and English Romanticism,* 14.
131 *Orazione*, 104.
132 'Present State', 477.
133 'Present State', 477.
134 This is translated in Glauco Cambon, *Ugo Foscolo* (Princeton, NJ: Princeton University Press, 1980), 310–311.
135 See *Elizabeth, Lady Holland to Her Son*, ed. Lord Ilchester (London: John Murray, 1946), 171.
136 See Mitchell, *Holland House,* 203–204.
137 *Quaderni del carcere*, 1127. ('furono soddisfatte a piccolo dosi, legalmente, riformisticamente, e si riuscì così a salvare la posizione politica ed economica delle vecchie classi feudali').
138 See also Holland's speech on the Aliens Bill at *Hansard* I lxxxi 17–23. For Holland and Spain, see Diego Saglia, *Poetic Castles in Spain* (Amsterdam: Rodopi, 2000), 26–32.
139 Letter from Fox to Holland 17 September 1793, *BL* Add MS 47571 f. 60^{r}.
140 The letters between Holland and Fox on the Italian language and literature between 1793 and 1795 are *BL* Add MS 47571 ff. 60–150.
141 This discussion is in a letter from Rose to Holland, 16 November 1819, *BL* Add MS 51650. f. 186^{r}. The dedication occurs in William Stewart Rose (trans.), *Orlando Innamorato* (Edinburgh: 1823), I 3.
142 For meetings with Di Breme and Monti see *Hobhouse,* 11 October 1816 to 3 November 1816. For the servant called Baptista / Battista, see *Hobhouse,* 8 January 1818, 6 October 1818, 13 March 1819, 25 March 1819, 3 May 1819.
143 *Hobhouse*, 17 October 1816.

144 *Hobhouse,* 14 July 1818.
145 'Parga', 263; Holland, *Letter to a Neapolitan from an Englishman,* 5.
146 *Hobhouse,* 14 November 1816.
147 'Dante 1', 455.
148 'Present State', 360–361.
149 Ibid., 424.
150 *BLJ* VII 151, 'that Judas of Parnassus'; *BLJ* VII 194.
151 i.e. in Wordsworth's employment as Distributor of Stamps for Westmorland, Southey's position as Poet Laureate, and Monti's attempts to ingratiate himself to the Austrian conqueror in *Il Mistico Omaggio* (1815) and *Il Ritorno di Astrea* (1816).
152 *Parisina,* 'Advertisement'. Byron saw Alfieri's *Mirra* in 1819 and claims it sent him into convulsions (*BLJ* VI 206). Alfieri's tragedies were also influential in the writing of *Marino Faliero* in 1820, see *BLJ* VII 181–182.
153 'Present State', 406–407.
154 'Present State', 450–451. 'Dietro il Foscolo sta, ed egli non se ne dimenticherà mai, l'opera così profundamente rivoluzionaria dell'Alfieri', Mario Fubini, *Ugo Foscolo: Saggi, studi, note* (Florence : La Nuova Italia, 1978), 270.
155 Vittorio Alfieri, *Memoirs of the Life and Writings of Victor Alfieri* (London: 1810); Vittorio Alfieri, *The Tragedies of Vittorio Alfieri,* trans. Charles Lloyd, 3 vols. (London: 1815).
156 *Ortis,* 270. 'Jacopo prese il primo libro così come fu lasciato aperta da Odoardo' – 'Jacopo took up the first book as it was left open by Odoardo'. The book is Alfieri's tragedies from which he quotes ten lines from *Saul* III 4, then opening the same volume again at random, he reads three lines from *Sofonisba* IV. 4.
157 Ibid., 228. 'L'unico mortale ch'io desiderava conoscere era Vittorio Alfieri'.
158 John Lindon, 'Italy 1799', *Romance Studies* 18 (2000): 19.
159 For Alfieri on Machiavelli, see *Principe* II ix 111–112. The classic study of this reception is Luigi Firpo 'Le origini dell'antimachiavellismo' *Il Pensiero Politico* 2 (1969): 337–367.
160 *Dei Sepolcri* (1807), ll. 154–158, *ENUF* I 129 ('When I saw the monument / in which lies the body of the great one / who tempering the sceptre to the rulers / trims their laurels, and to the nations reveals / what tears and what blood pour from them.')
161 See 'I Frammenti sul Machiavelli' [1809–1811], *ENUF* VIII 1–63.
162 'Present State', 365
163 The verb to usurp, and its derivatives, are common in Alfieri. For one small passage with three uses, see *Della tirannide* (Kehl: 1795), I xi 117; 'the evil cultivators', *Principe* III xi 218.
164 In *Vita* I 138, Alfieri calls Metastasio 'una Musa appigionata o venduta', 'a muse rented out or sold', for his loyalty to Joseph II in Vienna.
165 The role that literature could play in freeing a state, and the need for this in modern Italy, is discussed in *Principe,* III ix–xi.
166 See *Hobhouse* 13 October 1816, 14 October 1816, 22 December 1817, and 29 December 1817.

167 Thomas Faulkner, *History and Antiquities of Kensington* (London, 1820), 114.
168 The first invoice is *BL* Add MS 51637 ff. 51^{r-v} which details the order of portraits from Fabre is dated 17 April 1796. The next but one extant letter, *BL* Add MS 51637 ff. 53^{r-v}, informs Holland of the completion of the Alfieri portrait and is dated 10/05/1796.
169 Luzzi, *Romantic Europe and the Ghost of Italy*, 5.
170 *RIME*, 'Canzone 320', 'I feel the old breeze, and I see appearing the sweet hills'.
171 'consecrated there a whole day to tears and verse', *Vita* I 100. Alfieri, 'Sonneto LVIII', *Rime* (Kehl: 1789), 35.
172 For learning Italian, see *LPBS*, I 384; Alfieri appears in the Shelleys' reading list for 1814, see *MSJ* I 86. The two poems are 'Sonnet. From the Italian of Dante Alighieri to Guido Cavalcanti' [1815] and 'Guido Cavalcanti to Dante Alighieri', [1815], see *LongmanPS* I 451, 453.
173 *Bodleian* MS. Shelley adds. e. 10, p. 130.
174 *Pforzheimer* MS Shelleyana 1082 contains ten leaves which record more than 300 titles. An edition of the list, edited by Nora Crook, is forthcoming on *Romantic Circles* (www.rc.umd.edu).
175 'Lines written among the Euganean Hills' [1818], *LongmanPS II* 427–443, ll. 71–73.
176 Weinberg, *Shelley's Italian Experience*, 22–24.
177 For the visit to Arquà, see Countess of Blessington, *Conversations with Lord Byron*, ed. Ernest J. Lovell (Princeton, NJ: Princeton University Press, 1969), 75; *Hobhouse*, 13 March 1818.
178 Rose, *Orlando Inammorato*, xv.

4 Veneto 1817–1819

1 Roland Barthes, *The Eiffel Tower and Other Mythologies*, [1977], trans. Howard (Berkeley: University of California Press, 1997), 5.
2 John Eglin, *Venice Transfigured* (New York: Palgrave, 2001), 203; John Pemble, *Venice Rediscovered* (Oxford: Oxford University Press, 1995), 15.
3 'Lines written among the Euganean Hills' [1818], *LongmanPS* II 427–443, l. 106. All further references are given by line number in the body of the text.
4 Earl Wasserman, *Shelley: A Critical Reading* (Baltimore, MD: Johns Hopkins University Press, 1971), 197.
5 Pocock, *Machiavellian Moment*, 99–100.
6 See Linda Colley, *Britons: Forging the Nation 1707–1837* (New Haven, CT: Yale University Press, 2005), 67.
7 *BLJ* V 129, *BLJ* VI 262.
8 *BLJ* V 183.
9 See Edward Gibbon, *Memoirs of My Life*, ed. Georges L. Bonnard (London: Thomas Nelson, 1966), 15.
10 Aside from ll. 167–205, which were added in December 1818. See *LongmanPS* II 430.

11 Percy Shelley, *Rosalind and Helen* (London, 1819), 6.
12 Percy Bysshe Shelley, *Poetical Works of Percy Bysshe Shelley*, ed. Mary Shelley, 4 vols (London, 1839), I xi; Mary Shelley, 'Notes to the Poems of 1818', quoted in *MSJ* I 244. The dominance of this reading is perhaps because the writing of 'Euganean Hills' coincides with the death of the Shelleys' daughter Clara and the anniversary of the suicide of Mary Wollstonecraft's daughter, Fanny Imlay.
13 Donald H. Reiman, 'Structure, Symbol, and Theme in "Lines written among the Euganean Hills"', *PMLA* 77 (1962), 407.
14 Pemble, *Venice Rediscovered*, 15.
15 Byron saw *Otello* on 20 February 1818, *BLJ* VI 13.
16 See the Marlow inventory (*Pforzheimer* Shelleyana 1082) for a sample of the Italian literature read during this period, including Ariosto, Dante, Foscolo, Guarini, and Tasso.
17 See also *LPBS*, II 3 and Ibid., II 2.
18 'England in 1819' [1819?], *LongmanPS* III 189–192, ll. 13–14.
19 'Composed upon Westminster Bridge, September 2, 1802' [1802], *WWMW* 285, l. 6. *LPBS* II 33; *LPBS* II 42. See also 'View from the Pitti Palace', *Shelley's Prose Works*, ed. H. Buxton Forman, 4 vols. (London: 1880), III 50–51.
20 'Home at Grasmere' [1816], *WWMW* 174, ll. 5–6.
21 See J. G. Links, *Canaletto and His Patrons* (London: Paul Elek, 1977).
22 *MSJ* I 193.
23 See for example Ann Radcliffe, *The Mysteries of Udolpho*, 2nd ed., 4 vols. (London, 1794), II 35, 'its islets, palaces, and towers rising out of the sea, whose clear surface reflected the tremulous picture in all its colours. The sun, sinking in the west, tinted the waves and the lofty mountains of Friuli'. Hereafter, *Udolpho*.
24 John Jay Baker, 'Myth, Subjectivity and the Problem of Historical Time in Shelley's "Lines written among the Euganean Hills"', *English Literary History* 56 (1989): 152.
25 John Chetwode Eustace, *A Classical Tour Through Italy*, 3rd ed., 3 vols. (London, 1815), I 182. Robert Browning, 'A Toccata of Galuppi's' [1853], *Selected Poems*, ed. John Woolford et al. (London: Longman, 2010), 370, ll. 5–6.
26 See Algernon Charles Swinburne, 'Notes on the Text of Shelley', *Essays and Studies* (London, 1876), 199.
27 Barthes, *The Eiffel Tower and Other Mythologies*, 9.
28 See *Capricci veneziani del Settecento*, ed. Dario Succi (Turin: Allemandi, 1988).
29 Schoina, *Romantic 'Anglo-Italians'*, 36.
30 Weinberg, *Shelley's Italian Experience*, 32; see also Reiman, 'Structure, Symbol, and Theme', 407.
31 'On the Extinction of the Venetian Republic', *WWMW* 268, ll. 13–14; *CHIV* st. 3.
32 Mark Sandy, 'Reimagining Venice and the Visions of Decay in Wordsworth, the Shelleys and Thomas Mann', *Venice and the Cultural Imagination*, ed. Michael O'Neill, Mark Sandy, and Sarah Wooton (London: Pickering and Chatto, 2012), 29.

33 See the advertisement in *Rosalind and Helen,* 6; *LPBS* II 75.
34 *RIME*, 'Canzone 128', ll. 20–22. 'what are so many foreign swords doing here? Why is the green earth coloured with barbarian blood?'
35 'the Teutonic rage'.
36 For Shelley's reading of Alfieri during his stay in Este, see *MSJ* II 220–229.
37 *Della tirannide*, I i 18, 'every good man must believe, and hope, that not far from now there will be an inevitable change, in which a near universal liberty must supplant universal servitude'. For a further Alfierian reference, compare Shelley's lines on Padua to Alfieri's line at *Della tiranide*, I iii 32, 'ogni giorno nella tirannide il coltivatore, oppresso dalle arbitrarie gravezze, menare una vita stentata e infelice' ('every day under tyranny, the farmer, oppressed by arbitrary taxes, leads a harsh and unhappy life').
38 Vittorio Alfieri, *Il Misogallo* (London, 1799), 179. ('The day will come, the day will return').
39 Ibid. ('I already hear them tell me: Oh Bard of ours, in depraved / ages born, you have nonetheless created these / Sublime ages, which you went on prophesising').
40 'Ode to the West Wind' [1819], *LongmanPS* III 200–212, ll. 65, 68–69.
41 For an outline of this theory, see Giambattista Vico, *New Science* [1744], trans. David Marsh (London: Penguin, 2000), 395–458.
42 'But as Machiavelli says of political institutions, that life may be preserved and renewed, if men should arise capable of bringing back the drama to its principles', 'A Defence of Poetry' [1821], *SPP* 521. See also, *LPBS* II 277–278.
43 Pite, 'Shelley and Italy', 40.
44 The idea of an apocalyptic re-beginning, after successive clashes of 'the spirit of freedom and the spirit of tyranny,' dominates 'A Philosophical View of Reform'. See 'A Philosophical View of Reform' [1819–1820], *SC* VI 969.
45 Michael O'Neill, *Romanticism and the Self-Conscious Poem* (Oxford: Clarendon Press, 1997), 143.
46 *PL* II 919.
47 Wasserman, *Shelley*, 203.
48 'Julian and Maddalo', l. 43, see also the swift sun at l. 75 and the meeting on the public way ll. 369–71. Further references are given by line number in parentheses of the text.
49 Sismondi, *Histoire des Républiques*, III 33–34; Hallam, *View of the State of Europe*, 266–267.
50 George, *English Political Caricature*, II 159. The caricature in question is *Amusement at Vienna, Alias Harmony at Congress, i.e. Paying the Pipers* (London, 1815).
51 *BLJ* V 145.
52 For examples in *Udolpho,* see 61 ('*Bravissimo*', '*canzonettes*'); 93–95 ('*zendaletto*'); 158 ('*Excellenza*'); 162 ('*Lagune*'); 166 ('*Campagne*').
53 *CH IV*, st. 1.
54 *Beppo* [1818], *LBCPW* IV 129–161), st. 19. All further references are to this edition as *Beppo.* Stanza numbers are given in the text.

55 Radcliffe, *Udolpho,* 42, 66.
56 See James Harrington, *The Common-Wealth of Oceana* (London, 1656).
57 Police reports from Anton von Raab and Baron Franz von Hager quoted in Rath, *The Provisional Austrian Regime*, 178–179.
58 Rose, *Letters from the North of Italy*, II 172.
59 Elizabeth Crouzet-Pavan, *Venice Triumphant*, trans. Lydia Cochrane (Baltimore, MD: Johns Hopkins University Press, 2002), 157. See also the history of relaxed laws on prostitution, 159.
60 See Pocock, *Machiavellian Moment*, 102–103.
61 In Rome, the aristocracy and prelates would not mix with the peasants whose main celebration surrounded the horse race in the Piazza del Popolo.
62 See *BLJ* V 129–132 for a discussion of this theatrical history.
63 Mentioned at *BLJ* VI 19–20.
64 William Shakespeare, *As You Like It* [1599], II i 7, 15, ed. Juliet Dunisberre (Walton: Arden, 2006), 190.
65 *As You Like It,* IV i 30–35, 288.
66 'The Dunciad in Four Books' [1743], *PoAP*, 709–805, IV 301–303.
67 Ibid., IV 309–10.
68 Eustace, *Classical Tour,* I 180.
69 Eglin, *Venice Transfigured*, 80.
70 Mikhail Bahktin, *Rabelais and His World* [1965], trans. Helen Iswolsky (London: MIT Press, 1968), 5.
71 *A summer voyage to the Gulph of Venice, in the Southwell frigate, Captain Manley junr. commander; an irregular ode* (1750).
72 *BLJ* V 151.
73 *Beppo*, st. 1.
74 See *Beppo*, st. 56, and *BLJ* IV 135–136.
75 Quoted in Terry Castle, *Masquerade and Civilization* (London: Meuthen, 1986), 8.
76 A poet on Byron's mind in 1818, see *BLJ* VI 66.
77 Richard Sheridan, *The Ridotto of Bath* (Bath, 1771).
78 Castle, *Masquerade and Civilisation,* 332; Bahktin, *Rabelais and His World,* 37–43.
79 See David Laven, *Venice and the Venetia Under the Hapsburgs, 1815–1835* (Oxford: Oxford University Press, 2002), 8–10.
80 These comments appear regularly in *Hobhouse* 3 November 1816 to 5 December 1816. See also a contemporary British report that 'the bucentaur is rotten, and there is no longer any Doge to wed the Adriatic', 'Present State of the City in Venice', *Blackwood's* (April 1817), 16.
81 See Laven, *Venice and the Venetia under the Hapsburgs*, 54–55, and the testament of residents quoted in Rath, *The Provisional Austrian Regime,* 145.
82 See John Julius Norwich, *Venice: The Greatness and The Fall* (London: Penguin, 1981), 374; and Norwich, *Paradise of Cities* (London: Viking, 2003), 6–12.
83 For a survey of these changes, see Alvise Zorzi, *Venezia Austriaca 1798–1866* (Rome: Laterza, 1985), 157–238.

84 These restrictions had been increasing throughout the eighteenth century; see Stefania Bertelli, *Il Carnevale di Venezia nel Settecento* (Rome: Jouvence, 1992).

85 'Foglio D'Avviso', *Gazzetta Privilegiata di Venezia,* no. 6, Gennaio 1816. The entire print run of the *Gazzetta* is available at the *Biblioteca Marciana.*

86 *BLJ* V 132.

87 See 'The Prelude' [1805], *WWMW* 374–590, VII 652–679.

88 *BLJ* VI 92.

89 Bernard Beatty, A '"More Beloved Existence": From Shakespeare's "Venice" to Byron's Venice', *Venice and the Cultural Imagination,* 13–14.

90 Gabriel Matzneff, *La diététique de Lord Byron* (Paris: La Table Ronde, 1984), 187. ('Having become, in Venice, a carnival character, he loiters, on the pull: girls whose names he forgets to ask, anonymous bodies, masks without faces, cardboard love stores that are to love what the placebo is to medicine. Nothing is important to him anymore').

91 *BLJ* V 185.

92 John Cam Hobhouse to John Murray, early 1819. *NLS* Ms. 42288, ff. 43–44. See also *BL* Add MS 36457 f. 437.

93 *BLJ* V 265.

94 Ibid.

95 Ibid.

96 *BLJ* V 214. The ottava rima is an eight-line stanza, usually in pentameter, rhyming *abababcc.* The Spenserian stanza rhymes *ababbcbcc* and ends with an alexandrine. The ottava rima was used in the heroic Italian tradition (Tasso and Ariosto) but most often in comic and satirical verse.

97 *Beppo,* see stanzas 3, 5, 7, 8, 20, 21, 27, 29, 31, 35, 37, 38, 40, 50; *CHIV,* see stanzas 4, 20, 23, 24, 25, 32, 48.

98 *Beppo* st. 33, 'He patronised the Improvisatori,/ Nay, could himself extemporize some stanzas'.

99 Drummond Bone, '*Beppo*: The Liberation of Fiction', *Byron and the Limits of Ficiton,* ed. Bernard Beatty and Vincent Newey (Liverpool: Liverpool University Press, 1998), 99–100.

100 See 'The Composite Merits of Hervey's Fish Sauce and Hervey's Meditations' [1811], *LBCPW* II 348.

101 *BLJ* VIII 228. McGann does not identify the quotation in *LBCPW,* and Andrew Nicholson is not able to find its source in *The Manuscripts of the Younger Romantics: Lord Byron* XII, ed. Nicholson (New York: Garland, 1998), 298.

102 *The Argus,* 11 November 1790, 1.

103 An exception is *The Prophecy of Dante* (1821), but this work was written at the bequest of Teresa Guiccioli and is something of a one off. For more Byron's plays on the venerability of *tre corone,* see Saglia, 'Where shall I turn me?': Italy and irony in *Beppo* and *Don Juan', Byron and Italy,* ed. Alan Rawes and Diego Saglia (Manchester: Manchester University Press, 2017), 211–215.

104 *Prospectus and Specimen of an Intended National Work, by William and Robert Whistlecraft* (London, 1817). All further references as *Whistlecraft.*

105 *BLJ* V 267.
106 Rutherford, *Byron: A Critical Study*, 108; Catherine Addison 'Heritage and Innovation in Byron's Narrative Stanza', in *Byron: Heritage and Legacy*, ed. Cheryl Wilson (London: Palgrave, 2009), 127–138, 133.
107 Albert Eichler, *John Hookham Frere* (Wien: W. Braumüller, 1905), 170–184.
108 Frere to Foscolo (8 May 1818), *ENUF* XX 318–320.
109 Philip W. Martin, *Byron: A Poet before His Public* (Cambridge: Cambridge University Press, 1982), 177.
110 *BLJ* V 266; see *BLJ* V 80, thanking Pryce Gordon for giving him the *Novelle*; for Stendhal's claim that Byron read Buratti, see Stendhal, *Vie de Rossini,* 2 vols. (Paris: Le Divan, 1929), II 267.
111 *Whistlecraft*, Proem viii.
112 *Whistlecraft*, I xiii.
113 See *Whistlecraft,* I xv, xvi.
114 *Whistlecraft,* I ix.
115 See *Beppo,* sts. 50, 63.
116 *LJM,* 253.
117 Southey, *Life and Letters of Robert Southey*, V 21.
118 Giuseepe Parini, 'Sonneto XLVI', *Opere,* ed. Ettore Bonore (Milan: Ugo Mursia, 1969), 435; Vassallo, *Byron: The Italian Literary Influence*, 47.
119 See Roberto Sangiorgi, 'Giambattista Casti's *Novelle galanti* and Lord Byron's *Beppo*', *Italica* 28 (1951): 261–269; and Vassallo, *Byron: The Italian Literary Influence,* 46–63.
120 Giovanni Battista Casti, *Novelle galanti* (London: 1793), Protesta Dell'Autore st. viii. 'I know full well that the style of these tales, must be free cheerful and amusing, but treating certain things on the surface is a good idea, as is putting a curb on one's license and not offending your ears, o beautiful ladies, with uncouth terms or obscene shouting; everything can be explained, and everything said, but we have to watch how we say it'.
121 *Beppo*, st. 75.
122 Stendhal, *Vie de Rossini,* II 267; Hoppner's letter to Byron on 27 October 1819 at *NLS* Ms. 43448.
123 Peter Cochran, *Byron and Italy* (Newcastle: Cambridge Scholars Press, 2012), 189–190.
124 Ibid., 191.
125 Pietro Buratti, *Elefanteide,* ed. by Tiziano Rizzo (Venice: Fillipi, 1988). For the effects mentioned, see sts. 4, 54; 2, 9, 5, 13, 20; 14, 58; 30, 62, 61, 88–92. Hereafter, *Elefanteide.*
126 *Elefanteide,* st. 44. 'Just so the boy entangled in the coils/ (and yet what pride there is in us!)/ of that nerve known as a trunk/ was seen flying several times up and down/ thrown up into the air by the Elephant,/ which after having had his fun with him/ (you can buy the engraving of this for a few pence)/ crushed him under his foot'. Translation of the Venetian dialect kindly provided by Gregory Dowling.

127 *DJ* XI 20.
128 'Narrative Poems', 505.
129 *BLJ* VI 24; VI 67; VII 113.
130 Rose, *Letters from the North of Italy*, I 156–157.
131 Margaret Bewicke, 'Tour in France, Switzerland and Italy made in the years 1824 & 1825', *Beinecke* MS Osborn d534, 254.
132 *Beppo* st. 46, *CH IV*, st. 4.
133 'Peter Bell The Third', [1819] *Longman PS* III 70–153, particularly the lists in I iv and rhymes at I vi. Shelleys claims he wrote 'Peter Bell' in a week and that '[t]he verses and language, I have let come as they would', *LPBS* II 135.
134 William Cowper, *The Task*, ed. by James Sambrook (London, 1994), II 206–207.
135 A chant which returns at *DJ* VIII 50.
136 'Beppo', *Edinburgh Review* (February 1818): 302.
137 'Beppo', *British Critic* (March 1818): 301.
138 *British Review* (May 1818): 327.
139 Ibid., 328.
140 Ibid., 328–329.
141 Ibid., 329.
142 *Baviad*, 43.
143 Thomas Mathias, *The Pursuits of Literature*, 14th ed. (London, 1808), 7.
144 Ibid.
145 Gary Dyer, *British Satire and the Politics of Style 1789–1832* (Cambridge: Cambridge University Press, 1997), 23.
146 *A poetical epistle from Alma mater to Lord Byron* (Cambridge, 1819), 1, 11.
147 Ibid., 6. See also *More News from Venice, By Beppo* (Oxford, 1818).
148 *Beppo*, st. 47.
149 'The Mask of Anarchy', [1819] *Longman PS* III 27–64), l. 1; 'A Defence of Poetry', *SPP* 516.
150 *BLJ* V 132, V 146, V 168, V 192.
151 'Journal of a Tour on the Continent, Dr. John Pye-Smith Vol. II' (1816), *Bodleian* MS. Eng. Misc. e. 1376, f. 1[r].
152 Luzzi, *Romantic Europe and the Ghost of Italy*, 59.
153 Tony Tanner, *Venice Desired* (Cambridge, MA: Harvard University Press, 1992), 22.
154 Laven has argued that Marchand's depiction of Byron in Venice also suffers from this oversight. See 'Sex, Self-Fashioning and Spelling: (Auto)biographical Distortion, Prostitution, and Byron's Venetian Residence', *Literaria Pragensia*, 23:46 (2013): 38–52.
155 *BLJ* VI 59, V 204, VI 86–87.
156 *BLJ* VI 89.
157 Stabler, *Byron, Poetics, and History*, 139–148. For poems on Queen Caroline, see Shelley's *Swellfoot the Tyrant* (1820) and the opening of Byron's *The Irish Avatar* (1822).

158 *LPBS* II 18, II 119 , II 44.
159 This takes in *Gazzetta,* No. 5, Mercoledi, 8 gennaio, 1817 to No. 26, sabato, 1 febbraio, 1817. The MP mentioned is Sir John Lowther and the peer is Stephen Moore, 3rd Earl Mount Cashell. This does not tell the whole story of arrivals, as only the senior male of any party is announced and as not all British to visitors made it into the paper, e.g. the 2nd Baron Ashburton's visit to Venice from 1818 to 1819, recorded in the diary *Beinecke* Gen. Ms. vol. 132, is not announced in the *Gazzetta.*
160 Rose, *Letters from the North of Italy,* I 293.
161 Cox, *Poetry and Politics in the Cockney School,* 11.
162 *LPBS* II 118.
163 *LPBS* II 67.
164 *BLJ* VI 66.
165 He is discussing the pamphlet at the Westmoreland election, *LPBS* II 26.
166 See E. P. Thompson, *The Making of the English Working Class* (London: Penguin, 1968), 691–780.

5 London and Naples, 1819–1821

1 Hazlitt, *Lectures on the English Poets,* 27, 34.
2 Samuel Taylor Coleridge, 'Lectures on European Literature 1818', Lectures 3 and 10, *The Collected Works of Samuel Taylor Coleridge: Lectures 1808–1819: on Literature,* ed. Reginald A. Foakes, 2 vols. (Princeton, NJ: Princeton University Press, 1988), II 89–105, 184–186; Coleridge, '1819 Lectures on Shakespeare &c', Lecture 5, Ibid., II 397–403, 401.
3 *The Vision of Dante Alighieri,* trans. H. F. Cary (London, 1819). For Foscolo's comments on Cary, see Chapter 3.
4 Leigh Hunt, *The Literary Pocket Book* (London, 1818), 27, 32. Hunt also published work by Shelley in later versions of the *Pocket Book,* e.g. the sonnet 'Ye hasten to the grave!' published in *The Literary Pocket Book* (London, 1822), 112.
5 Ibid., 1.
6 Rosco (pseud.), *Horrida Bella, Pains and Penalties versus Truth and Justice* (London, 1820), 19.
7 'A Summary of the Proceedings against her Majesty', *Examiner* (3 September 1820): 563.
8 E. P. Thompson, 'Patrician Society, Plebeian Culture', *Journal of Social History* 7 (1974): 387. It is a dichotomy used in Iain McCalman, *Radical Underworld* (Cambridge: Cambridge University Press, 1988), 163–170.
9 For a discussion of the need for partnership across classes in the formation of a counter-hegemony, and the need to reform not just ideas but practice, see Gramsci, Note IV of the preliminary points for the 'Appunti per una introduzione e un avviamento all studio della filosofia e della storia della cultura', *Quaderni del Carcere,* 1377–1395.

10 Technically speaking, the method used by the Regent to separate from Caroline was a 'Pain and Penalties Bill'. Both contemporary and modern literature has called it a trial, a convention I have kept.
11 E. P. Thompson, 'Peterloo', [1969], collected in *Making History* (New York: The New Press, 1994), 189.
12 John Hunt letter to Leigh Hunt, 5 January 1831, University of Iowa Brewer-Leigh Hunt Collection, Ms LH932 no. 10, f. 1^{v}.
13 Flora Fraser, *The Unruly Queen* (Berkeley, CA: University of California Press, 1997), 85–86.
14 Lord Thurlow quoted in Ibid., 114. See also Ibid., 95.
15 See Anon, '1816 July–November', *Beinecke* MS Osborn d416 entry for 6 October 1816, 42; and 'Anon Diary' September / October 1816, *Beinecke* MS Osborn d190, f. 21^{v} .
16 This name is given as Bergami in contemporary British sources, but his actual title was Barone Pergami della Franchina.
17 *Morning Chronicle*, 26 March 1820.
18 McCalman, *Radical Underworld*, 163.
19 'The Queen', *The Times*, 6 June 1820, 3.
20 William Cobbett, 'A LETTER TO MR. CANNING, On the Cruel Treatment of the Queen', *Cobbett's Political Register*, 8 July 1820, 1179.
21 Anon., *A Letter to the People of England upon Passing Events* (London, 1820), 5.
22 For the arrival at Canterbury see, *The Times*, 7 June 1820.
23 *Gazzetta*, no. 141 'Inghilterra, Londra 7 Giugno', 26 June 1820, 1. 'a continuous triumph'; 'Long Live Queen Caroline'.
24 *The Times*, 7 June 1820.
25 Mary Fairclough, *The Romantic Crowd* (Cambridge: Cambridge University Press, 2013), 126.
26 *Hobhouse*, 6 June 1820; *Traveller*, 8 June 1820, 1.
27 For a contemporary print that gives some idea of Hunt's setting, see *The Spa Fields Orator Hunt-ing for Popularity to Do-good!!* (London, 1817).
28 Karl Marx, 'The Eighteenth Brumaire of Louis Bonaparte' [1852] in Karl Marx and Friedrich Engels, *Collected Works*, 50 vols., trans. Richard Dixon et al. (London: Lawrence and Wishart, 1975–2004), XI 103.
29 'Arrival of the Italian Wretches'. Anonymous broadsheet labelled: 'Dover, Friday, 7 July 1820'.
30 Anon., *John Bull Peppering the Italian Rascals – or a Kick from Harwich to Holland* (London, 1820).
31 'The English Man' not dated, but *circa* 8 July 1820. See also: 'GLORIOUS ARRIVAL OF THE FRIENDS OF THE QUEEN' (London, n.d.).
32 Anon, 'Arrival of the Italian Wretches', dated 7 July 1820.
33 William Hone and George Cruikshank, *The Green Bag: A Dainty Dish to Set before a King* (London, 1820), 8–9.
34 'Italian Begging Boys', *The Times*, 23 June 1821, 3.
35 *BL* 1852. b. 9 contains ninety-one items from before, during, and after the trial, including broadsheets, pamphlets, and prints.

36 *BL* 1852. b. 9 (34). The handbill which follows (35) is a tamer attempt at a similar satire. It is a notice of an upcoming auction by a 'Dealers in Cat's Meat [. . .] *by order of John Bull'* in which is sold the effects of 'Messrs. *Muddlepool, Derry-down* and Co.', which were common titles for Liverpool and Castlereagh. Lot. 1 is an attack on the witnesses as, 'A large quantity of Cat's meat, made from an amphibious animal lately found on the sea-coast at Brighton. Had arms and legs similar to a human being, except the toes and fingers were webbed like a goose's foot'.
37 e.g. 'The Great Milan Leech', *BL* 1852. b. 9. (32).
38 Charles Phillips, *The Queen's Case Stated* (London, 1820), 20.
39 Ibid., 21–22.
40 Ibid., 22.
41 Ibid., 23.
42 Lord John Russell, *A Letter to Mr. Wilberforce and a Petition to the King* (London, 1820), 25.
43 *LPBS* II 207.
44 *LPBS* II 213.
45 *MSJ* I 330.
46 Ibid.
47 Percy Shelley, 'A Note on Oedipus Tyrannus', *Poetical Works of Percy Bysshe Shelley*, ed. Mary Shelley (London, 1840 [1839]), 191.
48 'Preface to Hellas' [1821], *SPP*, 431.
49 *Oedipus Tyrannus; or Swellfoot the Tyrant*, [1820] *LongmanPS* III 649–710, I i 292; I i 324. Further references will be in given by act, scene, and line number in parentheses in the text.
50 Two examples of pro-Caroline work published by Johnston are: *The Kettle Abusing the Pot. A Satirical Poem* (London, 1820) and *Plenipo and the Devil! or, the Upshot of the Plot* (London, 1820).
51 See Donald H. Reiman, 'Shelley's *Swellfoot*: Critics' Stepchild', *SC* X 772–812.
52 *LongmanPS* III 654.
53 An idea of the crowd is given in George Hayter's painting *The Trial of Queen Caroline* (1820).
54 Denman's 1820 journal is quoted entire in Joseph Arnold, *Memoir of Thomas, First Lord Denman*, 2 vols. (London, 1873). See, I 171.
55 See Stephen Gill, *William Wordsworth: A Life* (Oxford: Clarendon Press, 1989), 328–330. William Wordsworth to Lord Lonsdale, 18 January 1818, *The Letters of William and Dorothy Wordsworth: the Middle Years, Part 2*, ed. Ernest de Selincourt, rev. Alan Hill (Oxford: Clarendon Press, 1970), 411.
56 Henry Brougham, *The Life and Times of Henry Lord Brougham*, 3 vols. (Edinburgh, 1871), I 303.
57 Ibid., I 292–293, 300, 307.
58 'Histoire de la Peinture en Italie', *Edinburgh Review* (October 1819): 320–339, 335.
59 *Hansard*, II ii 188.

60 *Hansard,* II ii 189.
61 See also a speech of 1825 in which Brougham praises Dante for his style and precision, calling him 'the great poet of modern Italy' in Henry Brougham, *Speeches of Henry Lord Brougham,* 4 vols. (London, 1838), III 90.
62 It occurs in Warton, *History of English Poetry,* III 238–239. Pite, *Circle of Our Vision,* 13, 27–29.
63 *Inferno* XV 16–21. 'we met a troop of souls that were coming alongside the bank, and each looked at us as men look at one another under a new moon at dusk; and they knit their brows at us as the tailor does at the eye of his needle. Eyed thus by that company, I was recognized by one'.
64 *Contrapasso* is a term used for the physical or mental punishment given to the sinners in *Inferno* which is supposed to be both proportional and relatable to their sins on Earth. See *Inferno* XXVIII 142.
65 Later, Brougham used his superior knowledge to clarify when the Queen left a garden at Naples. As Hunt reported in 'A Summary of the Proceedings against her Majesty', *Examiner* 663 (3 September 1820): 562, 'the hour at which the Queen was in a garden with Bergami, actually formed part of the Attorney General's instructions and would have been established upon the House, had not Mr. Brougham been acquainted with the Italian method of reckoning time, which turned the supposed midnight into evening'.
66 He took his oath on the Old Testament, *Hansard,* II ii 804.
67 *Hobhouse* 22 August 1822 claims that Spineto was one of his old Cambridge masters, and Hobhouse graduated BA in 1808; he is mentioned in 1832 as a Cambridge don in Joseph Romilly, *Romilly's Cambridge Diary, 1832–42* (Cambridge: Cambridge University Press, 1967), 11, 17, 38, 40. For the Garrick, see *The Album of the Cambridge Garrick Club* (Cambridge, 1836), 151, 220, 231.
68 Granville to Lady Morpeth, 22 August 1820, *Letters of Harriet, Countess Granville,* 2 vols. (London, 1894), I 161.
69 *Hansard,* II ii 806, 808, 821.
70 A literal translation of 'non mi ricordo' in modern Italian is 'I do not remember'.
71 *Hansard,* II ii 853–854, 872, 881.
72 Recorded in *The Important and Eventful Trial of Queen Caroline, Consort of George IV, for "Adulterous Intercourse" with Bartolomo Bergami,* 2 vols. (London, 1820), I 75. The exchange is given in brief at *Hansard* II ii 845.
73 *The Important and Eventful Trial of Queen Caroline,* I 75. The term 'tramontane' is also used in a footnote to *Beppo,* st. 37.
74 Lord Hampden and The Earl of Roseberry, *Hansard* II 845, 873–874.
75 *Hansard,* II iii 140.
76 See the aquatint, 'Address to her Majesty Queen Caroline Presented at Brandenburgh House 30 October 1820' (London, 1821), *Bodleian,* John Johnson QC Folder (12).
77 Anon., *The Italian Witness: A New Song* (London, 1820).
78 Both poems appeared in *Examiner* (27 August 1820): 558, 661. 'Memory and Want of Memory or Rather No Than Yes' and 'Non Mi Ricordo' in *LHSW*

V. 271–274. There are eight such satires written by Hunt. See Ibid., V 271–284. Hereafter referred to by line number in parenthesis in the text.

79 'Memory and Want of Memory' is the fifth of the eleven songs in the *The Non Mi Ricordo Song Book* (London: J. Bailey, 1820?).

80 *OED,* definition 2 a) for 'shabby'.

81 William Shakespeare, *The Merry Wives of Windsor*, ed. T. W. Craik (Oxford: Clarendon Press, 1989), I iii 3.

82 See Leigh Hunt, 'The Destruction of the Cenci Family', *Indicator* (26 July 1820): 329–336, Leigh Hunt, 'The Stories of Lamia, The Pot of Basil, The Eve of St. Agnes &c', *Indicator* (2 August 1820): 341.

83 Leigh Hunt, 'Meeting of the House of Lords, and the Queen', *Examiner* (20 August 1820): 530.

84 *LMWS* I 156.

85 Ibid.

86 'Neapolitan Revolution', *Examiner* (30 July 1820): 481.

87 Ibid.

88 Shelley, 'Lines written among the Euganean Hills', l. 168.

89 Richard Keppel Craven notes that Naples was illuminated on the 7, 8, 9 July, in *A Tour through the Southern Provinces of the Kingdom of Naples, to Which Is Subjoined a Sketch of the Immediate Circumstances Attending the Late Revolution* (London, 1821), 444.

90 *Hobhouse*, 20 July 1820.

91 *Hobhouse*, 22 July 1820.

92 For Naples in Panoramas, see John Feltham, *The Picture of London for 1806* (London, 1806), 290, and for of the use of Naples at Dr. Monro's 'Academy', see John Gage, *J.M.W. Turner 'A Wonderful Range of Mind'* (New Haven, CT: Yale University Press, 1987), 28.

93 For a brilliant account of these events, see Camillo Albanese, *Cronache di una rivoluzione: Napoli 1799* (Milano: FrancoAngeli, 1998).

94 See Vincenzo Cuoco, *Saggio storico sulla rivoluzione di Napoli* (Milan, 1801). and Foscolo's article, 'An Account of the Revolution of Naples during the Years 1798, 1799', *New Monthly Magazine* (January 1821): 33–64. Fox's speech to Parliament occurred on 3 February 1800.

95 John A. Davis, *Naples and Napoleon* (Oxford: Oxford University Press, 2006), 267–268.

96 'Diary of William Gell, 1814 Aug 9–1815 May 31'. *Beinecke* MS Osborn d293 f. 129^{r}.

97 For the wider effects of Neapolitan and Italian Anglophilia on the *Risorgimento*, see Isabella, *Risorgimento in Exile*, 111–150.

98 Bentinck quoted in John Rosselli, *Lord William Bentinck & the British Occupation of Sicily 1811–1814* (Cambridge: Cambridge University Press, 1956), 152.

99 Rossini had a motive for favouring English influence over possible Austrian control; his own father had been imprisoned and interrogated by

Austro-Prussian forces in 1799. See Richard Osborne, *Rossini*, 2nd ed. (Oxford: Oxford University Press, 2007), 5.

100 'Hail Elizabeth, the heroine, and the splendour of her age', Rossini (music) and Schmidt (libretto), *Elisabetta regina d'Inghilterra* (1815), II iii.

101 Osborne, *Rossini*, 223.

102 Davis, *Naples and Napoleon*, 288, 304.

103 Rosselli, *Lord William Bentinck & the British Occupation of Sicily*, 151.

104 Comtesse de Boigne, *Memoirs of the Comtesse de Boigne*, ed. Muhlstein, 2 vols. (New York: Helen Marx, 2003), I 177.

105 Ibid.

106 *Hansard*, II iii 120.

107 *Hansard*, II ii 1114–1115.

108 *Hansard*, II ii 1119.

109 *Hansard*, II ii 1117; for further examples of reports back to England concerning Caroline's manner of dress at Naples, see the letters of Ompteda quoted in Fraser, *Unruly Queen*, 266–268.

110 *Hansard*, II iii 328. Cp. the comment on how common it was for females 'to receive visitors when in bed' in Nicholas Brooke, *Observations on the Manners and Customs of Italy* (Bath, 1798), 55.

111 *Hansard*, II iii 409.

112 *Hansard*, II iii 121–122.

113 *Hansard*, II iii 358.

114 *Hansard*, II iii 121.

115 *The British Press* (21 August 1820).

116 *Statement of Facts Concerning the Conduct of Her Majesty Queen Caroline in Italy* (London, 1820), 5, 11. Fairburn published a number of pro-Caroline pamphlets, but also more general radical material, such as John Wade, *The Black Book; or, Corruption unmasked!* (London, 1820); and Augustus Montague Toplady, *English Constitutional Liberty Proved to be Compromised in Magna Carta! the Petition of Right! the Bill of Rights! and the Coronation Oath!!!* (London, 1820?).

117 Anon., *The Royal Martyr; or Life & Death of Queen Caroline* (Sunderland, 1821).

118 *Hansard*, II iii 253–254, other interruptions at *Hansard*, II iv 116–8; II iv 838.

119 See, Lucio Sponza, *Italian Immigrants in Nineteenth-Century Britain* (Leicester: Leicester University Press, 1988), 130; Pepe played an important role in Italian nationalist movements in London; see for example his pamphlet, 'The Non-Establishment of Liberty in Spain, Naples, Portugal, and Piedmont, Explained', *Pamphleteer* 24 (1824): 238. See also Appendix I. B of Margaret Wicks, *The Italian Exiles in London 1816–1848* (Manchester: Manchester University Press, 1937).

120 Keppel Craven, *A Tour through the Southern Provinces of the Kingdom of Naples*, 428, 438.

121 George T. Romani, *The Neapolitan Revolution of 1820–1821* (Evanston, IL: Northwestern University Press, 1950), 95; Davis, *Naples and Napoleon,* 295–296.
122 Anon., *To S. Nicholson, Mayor of Rochester Who Refused to Call a Meeting to Address the Queen* (London, n.d.).
123 *Weekly Intelligencer and British Luminary* (8 October 1820), 1.
124 *The Substance of the Speech of John George Lambton esq. MP at the Durham County Meeting, December 13, 1820* (London, 1820?), 11.
125 *Hansard,* II iv 1039.
126 Matthew Bevis, *The Art of Eloquence* (Oxford: Oxford University Press, 2007), 24, 26.
127 *Hansard,* II iv 1046.
128 *Hansard,* II iv 745, II iv 838.
129 For a longer reflection on this process, see Gramsci, *Quaderni del Carcere,* 1269–1267.
130 The Congress of Troppau was a meeting of the Quintuple Alliance in which the Powers (apart from Britain) agreed to supresss the Neapolitans, and signed the Troppau Protocol that meant similar action would be taken against future continental insurgencies. At Laibach, the occupation of Naples by the Austrians was confirmed and sanctioned, as was the Austrian occupation of Piedmont (which was also in revolt).
131 Hook was the editor of the *John Bull* from its inception in 1820. He got the job due to his anti-Caroline satire *Tentamen, or, An Essay towards the History of Whittington* (London, 1820).
132 *LMWS* I 156.
133 *Hansard,* II iii 1468.
134 'Theatrical Inquisition', *The Drama: or, Theatrical Pocket Magazine* (May 1821): 36.

6 Pisa 1820–1822

1 Pietro Gamba and a number of the Guiccioli family were expelled; see *BLJ* VIII 103–104.
2 *LPBS* II 442.
3 Margaret Mason to Percy Shelley, not dated, *Bodleian* MS. Abinger c. 67, ff. 46^{r-v}.
4 The following anonymous manuscript diaries show no entry for Pisa: *Beinecke* MS Osborn d408, MS Osborn d417, MS Osborn d324, MS Osborn d416, and Gen MS 132. *Beinecke* MS Osborn d424 mentions a visit there and *Beinecke* MS Osborn d190, (ff. 12^{v}–14^{r}), shows a day spent at Pisa (4 October 1822). Henry Best, *Italy as it is* (London, 1828), 250, only devotes 'one short summer's day' to Pisa.
5 Leigh Hunt, 'Letters from Abroad', *The Liberal: Verse and Prose from the South* (London, 1822), I 99.

6 See *LBCPW* IV 248. For a discussion of this translation, see Alan Rawes, '"From the Italian": Byron's Translation of Pulci's *Morgante Maggiore*', *Litteraria Prangensia* 23, no. 46 (2013): 6–22.
7 'The Bonfire of the Vanities'.
8 See Lindsay Waters, 'The Desultory Rhyme of Don Juan: Byron, Pulci and the Improvisatory Style', *English Literary History* 45 (1978): 429–442; and *Byron, The Italian Literary Influence*, 140–159.
9 *Risorgimento della Poesia Italiana dopo il Petrarca*, ed. Serafino Buonaiuti (London, 1813).
10 Ibid., iii. 'fallen back into its old primitiveness'.
11 Ginguené, *Histoire,* IV 233. 'those familiar words that Tuscan has in abundance'.
12 *LBCPW* IV 248.
13 A critique of this coarseness is given in John Herman Merivale, 'Account of the Morgante of Luigi Fulci' [*sic*], *Monthly Magazine* (May 1806): 304–308.
14 Samuel Taylor Coleridge, 'A Course of Lectures, Lecture III' [1818], *Lectures on Literature 1808–1819*, 2 vols., ed. Kathleen Coburn (London: Routledge and Keegan Paul, 1987), II 96.
15 *BLJ* VII 42.
16 *BLJ* VII 35.
17 *DJ* XIV 19.
18 'Letters of Timothy Tickler, esq. to Eminent Literary Characters no. VII', *Blackwood's* (July 1823): 90.
19 *LPBS* II 42.
20 For Byron's rhyming as an influence on Shelley, see Richard Cronin, *Shelley's Poetic Thoughts* (London: Macmillan, 1981), 73. For the connection between Shelley and Byron's ottava rima, see Christopher Goulding 'An Unpublished Shelley Letter', *Review of English Studies* 52 (2001): 233–237. The letter is from Shelley to Ollier on 27 August 1820, and in it he claims: 'This summer I have not been idle; I have written a fanciful thing in ottava rima called the 'Witch of Atlas'. I have translated also in ottava rima the Homeric hymn to Mercury, in about 100 stanzas: the effect is very droll. I have rendered also into choice English, with a subtle preface, the Symposium of Plato, &c, as Beppo says "other things that may be had for asking"'. For the *Ricciardetto,* see *MSJ* I 324–327.
21 Anon. (John Herman Merivale), *The Two First Cantos of Richardetto* (London: John Murray, 1820), x–xi.
22 See Richard Holmes, *Shelley: The Pursuit* (London: Harper Collins, 1994), 414–519.
23 *LPBS* II 339.
24 Michael O'Neill, 'Realms without a Name: Shelley and Italy's Intenser Day', *Dante and Italy in British Romanticism*, 77–78.
25 'Sonnet. From the Italian of Dante Alighieri to Guido Cavalcanti', [1816] *LongmanPS* I 451, ll. 7–8. The original is Dante, 'Guido, i'vorrei che tu e Lapo ed io', *Rime* VIII.

26 *OED*, 'strict', adj. 5a.
27 A good outline of this group is given in C. L. Cline, *Byron, Shelley and Their Pisan Circle* (London: John Murray, 1952).
28 *LMWS* I 163. 'The only Italian that has heart and soul'.
29 See Roderick Beaton, *Byron's War* (Cambridge: Cambridge University Press, 2013), 74–75.
30 *MSJ* I 341. For a longer discussion of the Shelleys' Greek studies in the period, see Will Bowers, 'On First Looking into Mary Shelley's Homer', *Review of English Studies* 69 (2018): 519–531.
31 A shooting party featuring Byron, Shelley, Taaffe, Gamba, and Trelawny was involved in a violent skirmish with a dragoon, who almost died. For the ways that the event caused the end of the coterie, see Holmes, *Shelley*, 708–709.
32 Timothy Webb, *The Violet in the Crucible* (Oxford: Clarendon Press, 1976), 312.
33 For this fragment, see *Bodleian* MS. Shelley adds. c. 4, f. 61[r]; and for Mary Shelley's reaction to Taaffe, see *LPBS* II 296.
34 *LPBS* II 310; *BLJ* IX 63; Hunt, 'Letters from Abroad', *Liberal*, I 111.
35 *BLJ* IX 90.
36 Pite, *Circle of Our Vision*, 44.
37 John Taaffe, *A Comment on the Divine Comedy of Dante Aligheri* (London, 1822), v.
38 Ibid., xii.
39 Ibid., xii–xiii.
40 Ugo Foscolo, 'Dante 2', 323; *SPP*, 'A Defence of Poetry', 526.
41 On Mason, see Edward McAleer, *The Sensitive Plant* (Chapel Hill: University of North Carolina Press, 1958).
42 See the diary of Mason's travelling companion: *The Grand Tours of Katherine Wilmot*, ed. Elizabeth Mayor (London: Weidenfeld & Nicholson, 1992).
43 William Godwin's diary contains multiple entries for Lady Mount Cashell in 1800–1803, 1807, 1810–1812, and 1814. See http://godwindiary.bodleian.ox.ac.uk/. Godwin published Mason's *The Stories of Old Daniel* (London, 1813).
44 Mason to Mary Shelley, 14 January 1820, quoted in McAleer, *The Sensitive Plant*, 142.
45 *MSJ* II 309; *The Journals of Claire Clairmont*, ed. Marion Kingston Stocking (Cambridge, MA: Harvard University Press, 1968), 119, 120.
46 See *LMWS* I 136; for more on Vaccà, see Caterina Del Vivo, *La 'Bella Vaccà' Leopoldo e Andrea* (Pisa: Edizioni ETS, 2009).
47 *LPBS* II 170.
48 Shelley, 'Julian and Maddalo', ll. 57–60.
49 *LPBS* II 176; *BLJ* VIII 104.
50 Rose, *Letters from the North of Italy*, II 116.
51 'Ode to Liberty' [1820], *LongmanPS* III 378–418, ll. 181–184.
52 G. M. Matthews, 'A Volcano's Voice in Shelley', *English Literary History* 24 (1957): 222.

53 'Neapolitan Revolution', *Examiner,* (30 July 1820): 481.
54 H. W. Williams, *Travels in Italy, Greece, and the Ionian Islands* (Edinburgh, 1820), 73.
55 William Feaver, *The Art of John Martin* (Oxford: Clarendon Press, 1975), 56.
56 See the series of paintings of Vesuvius in eruption by Joseph Wright of Derby (1773–1775); J. M. W. Turner's 'Vesuvius in Eruption' (1817); John Martin's 'The Eruption of Vesuvius' (1822) and 'The Destruction of Pompeii and Herculaneum' (1822).
57 Ralph Pite 'Shelley in Italy', *The Yearbook of English Studies* 34 (2004): 52.
58 Percy Bysshe Shelley, 'The Triumph of Life' [1822], ll. 206–207, 269–270. My text of this poem is based on the only surviving manuscript (*Bodleian* MS. Shelley adds. c. 4 ff. 19^{r}–53^{r}). The text is edited by Michael Rossington and Will Bowers, and will appear in the forthcoming *LongmanPS* V.
59 *LPBS* II 356.
60 *PL* V 708–10.
61 *PL,* 'Introduction', 16.
62 W. B. Yeats, 'The Philosophy of Shelley's Poetry' [1900], *Essays and Introductions* (New York: Macmillan, 1961), 88.
63 'A Defence of Poetry', *SPP* 526. All further references are given by page number in the body of the text.
64 *LPBS* II 335.
65 See *MSJ* I 205, I 248, I 294, I 295, I 333.
66 Orrin Wang, *Fantastic Modernity* (Baltimore, MD: Johns Hopkins University Press, 1996), 47. The poem can be divided into four parts – the narrator's description of the landscape at sunrise (ll. 1–40), the fall into the vision and the description of the triumph of Life (ll. 41–179), the conversation between the narrator and Rousseau about the triumph (ll. 180–308), and Rousseau's narrative of his vision (ll. 308–546) – all of which are discussed in the following reading.
67 Sismondi, *De la Littérature du Midi de l'Europe*, I 420–421.
68 See for example, 'Ode to the West Wind', *LongmanPS* III 208, ll. 29–32:

> Thou who didst waken from his summer dreams
> The blue Mediterranean, where he lay,
> Lulled by the coil of his crystalline streams,
> Beside a pumice isle in Baiae's bay,

The word-order of the first clause is awkward, with the meaning further delayed by the strong rhyme on 'dreams'. The slow progress of the tercet is halted by the medial caesurae following the polysyllabic 'Mediterranean', to again causes a stumbling cadence. These lines also display, in the quantity of adjectives used, verbosity not typically found in Italian terza rima poetry.
69 See 'The Tower of Famine', *LongmanPS* IV 35–43.
70 Taaffe, *Comment,* xxi, xx.
71 Hallam, *View of the State of Europe during the Middle Ages*, II 596.
72 'Dante 1', 460.

73 *Paradiso,* XXXIII 145. 'The love which moves the sun and the other stars'; *Purgatorio,* II 112. 'Love that discourses in my mind'.
74 *Inferno* IV 130–132. *Bodleian* MS. Shelley adds. c. 4, f. 33r shows that an earlier cancelled version of the line 'See the great bards of old who inly quelled' (l. 274) read 'See Homer and his brethren, – men who quelled', in what appears to be a reference to the figures of *Inferno* IV 70–151.
75 Thomas M. Greene, *The Light in Troy* (New Haven, CT: Yale University Press, 1982), 31.
76 A famous example of an enjambed tercet occurs in Ulysses' speech at *Inferno,* XXVI 81–82.
77 William Keach, *Shelley's Style* (New York: Meuthen, 1984), 194.
78 *Bodleian* MS. Shelley adds. c. 4 f. 48r. Dante only rhymes on 'rime' once, when describing the birdsong of Eden in *Purgatorio* XXVIII 18.
79 *PL* III 712–3, 714–5.
80 *Purgatorio,* I 115–117. 'The dawn was vanquishing the matin hour which fled before it, so that I recognized from afar the trembling of the sea'.
81 Paul de Man, 'Shelley Transfigured', *Deconstruction and Criticism,* ed. Bloom et al. (New York: Continuum, 1979), 63.
82 The enriching power of the sun is clear in earlier drafts too. See *Bodleian* MS. Shelley adds. c. 4 f. 55r , in which the sun comes 'out of the gloom / Of daily life' and gives the world 'The beauty of the presence which makes bright / Its desarts'.
83 Pite, *Circle of Our Vision,* 162; *LMWS* II 283; the passage is referred to as 'the approach of the boat with souls from earth to Purgatory', presumably *Purgatorio* II 22–51.
84 *MSJ* I 293–294. Mary Shelley does not note which *Purgatorio* cantos they read, but it is plausible that, as Percy Shelley had read the entire *Purgatorio* in April 1818 (I 204), they began from the beginning.
85 *Purgatorio,* I 32–33, 'worthy in his looks of so great reverence that no son owes more to his father'.
86 Mary Shelley, *Valperga* [1823], *The Novels and Selected Works of Mary Shelley,* ed. Nora Crook, 8 vols. (London: Pickering, 1996), III 84.
87 *Purgatorio,* I 43–45. '"Who has guided you, or what was a lamp to your issuing forth from the deep night that ever makes the infernal valley black?"'.
88 *Pforzheimer* PBS0283, f. 1r.
89 A concise history of the Roman triumph is given in Margaret Zaho, *Imago Triumphalis* (New York: Peter Lang, 2004), 13–25.
90 I take my text for 'Arch of Titus' from the edition published in Nora Crook and Tatsuo Tokoo, 'Shelley's Jewish "Orations"', *Keats–Shelley Journal* 59 (2010): 43–64, 58.
91 Edward Gibbon, *Miscellaneous Works,* ed. Lord Sheffield, 4 vols. (London, 1814) IV 359–399; 359. For PBS's reading of this work, see *MSJ* I 62–63.
92 For more on Shelley and Napoleon, see Cian Duffy, '"The Child of a Fierce Hour": Shelley and Napoleon Bonaparte', *Studies in Romanticism* 43 (2004): 399–416.

93 Anon., *Boadicea, Queen of Britain, Overthrowing Her Enemies* (London, 1820); P. and P. Gally, *Queen Caroline's Triumph over Her Enemies* (London, 1821).
94 See the fresco *Il Trionfo della Morte* at the Palazzo Scalfani, Palermo, and the depiction of Fame on the *desco da parto* of Lorenzo de' Medici at the Metropolitan Museum of Art, New York.
95 The distinction between the Northern and Italian tradition is explored in George Kernodle, *From Art to Theatre* (Chicago, IL: Chicago University Press, 1944), 52–110.
96 Greene, *Light in Troy*, 19.
97 A number of critics have made connections between the two works: Charles Robinson claims the 'Triumph' is, 'the seventh and probably final triumphal procession in the series begun by Petrarch', *Shelley and Byron: The Snake and Eagle Wreathed in Fight* (Baltimore, MD: Johns Hopkins University Press, 1976), 22; Weinberg has argued for the structural similarities between the works in *Shelley's Italian Experience*, 211–218.
98 Francesco Petrarca, *Triumphi*, ed. Marco Ariani (Milan: Mursia, 1988), all Italian quotations are from this edition; capitolo, book, and line are referred in the footnote and each quotation is given a translation from *The Triumphs of Petrarch*, trans. E. H. Wilkins (Chicago, IL: Chicago University Press, 1962).
99 *Eternitatis* I 5. 'covenant with one who trusts in him'.
100 *Mortis* I 31–33. 'a woman shrouded in a dress of black,/ With fury such as had perchance been seen/ When giants raged on the Phlegraean vale'.
101 *Fame* I 29–30. 'Triumphs that in Olden days / Proceeded through the sacred ways of Rome'.
102 *Fame* III 2–3. 'to the other side'.
103 *Fame* II 139–145.
104 See for example, *Mortis* II 1–3, II 139–141; *Fame* III 31–35, I 134.
105 *Fame* I 52–3. 'With him, two Catos, and two Fabii,/ Two Pauli, Bruti two, and two Marcelli'. See also, *Fame* II 10, I 41–143.
106 Alastair Fowler, *Triumphal Forms* (Cambridge: Cambridge University Press, 1970), 39.
107 *PL* II 666–673.
108 The drafts of the lines occur at *Bodleian* MS. Shelley adds. c. 4 ff. 29$^{r–v}$, some of the roughest lines in the MS. In an earlier draft, Rousseau replies immediately 'That is Napoleon', and there is further attempt to identify the speaker in the middle of his speech, which is struck through.
109 *LMWS* I 249.
110 Gibbon, *Miscellaneous Works* (1814), IV 394.
111 *Bodleian* MS. Shelley adds. c. 4 f. 24^{r}. Crook and Tokoo, 'Shelley's Jewish "Orations"', 58.
112 *Eternitatis*, I 28–29. 'And the three parts [Past, Present, Future] these I saw combined into one'.
113 *Mortis*, I 40–41. 'I who brought the Grecians to their fate, / And Troy, and then the Romans last of all'.

114 *Mortis,* I 79–84. 'Here now were they who were called fortunate, / Popes, emperors, and others who had ruled; / Now are they naked, poor, of all bereft. / Where now their riches? Where their honors now? / Where now their gems and sceptres, and their crowns, / Their mitres, and the purple they had worn?'.
115 De Man, 'Shelley Transfigured', 64, 45.
116 *LPBS* I 504.
117 The speech is to the Commons on 18 February 1800. See S. T. Coleridge, *Essays on his Times,* ed. David V. Erdman, *The Collected Works of Samuel Taylor Coleridge* III, 3 vols. (Princeton, NJ: Princeton University Press, 1978) i 185.
118 Marx, 'The Eighteenth Brumaire of Louis Bonaparte', *Collected Works,* XI 104.
119 'Feelings of a Republican on the Fall of Bonaparte' [1816], *LongmanPS* I 455–456, l. 6.
120 Ibid., l. 4.
121 *LPBS* II 156.
122 Lucan, *Pharsalia,* trans. J. D. Duff (London: Heinemann, 1977), I 128. 'if the victor had the gods on his side, the vanquished had Cato'.
123 Robert Southey, 'Letter to the Editor', *Courier* (11 January 1822): 2–3.
124 *Bodleian* MS. Shelley adds. c. 4 ff. 26^{v}, 29^{r}, 34^{r} 34^{v}, 39^{v}, 40^{v}, 43^{v}, 45^{r}, 45^{v}, 48^{v} rev., 49^{v}, 53^{v}.
125 *Courier* (5 August 1822): 3.
126 John Hay to Byron, 2 September 1822, *NLS* Ms. 43437 f. 1^{r}.
127 *BLJ* IX 189–190.
128 *Morgante* I iv 'It was then that I launched my little ship'; *Morgante* III i 'You who launched my wooden boat / and pledged to help me return it to port'. See also *Morgante,* II i, XIV i, XXI i, XXIV i, XXVIII i.
129 *DJ* III 98. See the description of Wordsworth's *Excursion* as 'the vasty version / of his new system to perplex the Sages', *DJ,* 'Dedication', 4; also 'Coleridge, too, has lately taken wing, / But, like a hawk encumbered with his hood, / Explaining Metaphysics to the Nation', *DJ*, 'Dedication', 2.
130 *Adonais* [1821], *LongmanPS* IV 235–330, l. 264.

Coda

1 Hunt, *Autobiography,* 376.
2 *Beinecke* Leigh Hunt Collection GEN MS 65, Box 1 Folder 18, Notebook. The diary begins at f. 5^{v}. Roe quotes from the diary, in *Fiery Heart,* 337–338.
3 Washington Irving, *The Sketch-Book of Geoffrey Crayon, Gent.* [1820–1821], ed. Susan Manning (Oxford: Oxford University Press, 1996), 15.
4 *Beinecke* GEN MS 65, f. 6^{v}.
5 Ibid., f. 7^{r}.
6 'Ode to the West Wind', ll. 29–30, *LongmanPS* III 208.
7 Hunt, *Autobiography,* 414.

8 *Pforzheimer* LH89, Leigh Hunt to Elizabeth Kent, Genoa, 7 November 1822, f. 1[v].
9 *Pforzheimer* LH92, Leigh Hunt to Elizabeth Kent, 11 January 1823, f. 1[v].
10 *Beinecke* GEN MS 65, f. 10[r.]
11 *Pforzheimer* LH92, Leigh Hunt to Elizabeth Kent, 11 January 1823, f. 2[r].
12 *PL* I 303.
13 Visitors included Beckford, the Brownings, Henry Crabb-Robinson, and Wordsworth. The abbey was also the subject of sentimental verse. See, Will Bowers, 'Vallombrosa Visited, 1638–1851', *Modern Philology*, forthcoming.
14 *LPBS* II 442.
15 *Beinecke* GEN MS 65 f. 1[v].
16 Cox, *Poetry and Politics in the Cockney School*, 223.
17 'The Brothers' [1800], *WWMW*, 159, l. 143. See also, Matthew 24:40.
18 *Beinecke* GEN MS 65, rear pastedown.
19 Leigh Hunt, 'Preface', *Liberal*, 2nd ed. (London, 1823), xi. All further references are to this edition, which is the second edition of the first issue bound with the first edition of the second issue. It contains the Preface to 'The Vision of Judgment' that was excluded from the first edition. Further references will be as *Liberal* followed by issue number and page number.
20 *BLJ* IX 190.
21 Byron, 'Preface to The Vision of Judgment', *Liberal* I ii.
22 Byron, 'The Vision of Judgment', st. 42, *Liberal* I 17. The line is an imitation of the opening line of Shelley's 'England in 1819' [1819?].
23 William H. Marshall, *Byron, Shelley, Hunt, and The Liberal* (Philadelphia: University of Pennsylvania Press, 1960), 58–62, 67–69. This reading is based on the account given in Thomas Medwin, *Conversations of Lord Byron* (London, 1824), 382–404.
24 See Marshall, *Byron, Shelley, Hunt, and The Liberal*, viii.
25 Letter from Leigh Hunt to Lord Byron, 22 January 1822, f. 2[v]. The Henry W. and Albert A. Berg Collection of English and American Literature, New York Public Library.
26 Of the sixty articles across four issues Hunt wrote thirty-four, Byron nine, and Hazlitt five. See Appendix III of Marshall, *Byron, Shelley, Hunt, and The Liberal*, 238–239.
27 Hunt, 'Letters from Abroad', *Liberal* I 103.
28 *Beinecke* GEN MS 65, rear pastedown.
29 See 15n.
30 Hunt, 'Letters from Abroad', *Liberal* I 100.
31 Ibid., I 102, 120, 99.
32 Schoina, *Romantic 'Anglo-Italians'*, 154.
33 Hunt, 'Letters from Abroad', *Liberal*, I 101, 105, 109.
34 H. W. Williams, *Travels in Italy, Greece, and the Ionian Islands*, 2 vols. (Edinburgh, 1820), I 51.
35 Chloe Chard, *Pleasure and Guilt on the Grand Tour* (Manchester: Manchester University Press, 1999), 2.

36 Hunt, *Autobiography*, 376.
37 William Wordsworth to Walter Savage Landor, 20 April 1822, *The Letters of William and Dorothy Wordsworth: the Later Years, Part 1*, ed. Ernest de Selincourt, rev. Alan Hill (Oxford: Clarendon Press, 1978), 124.
38 Ibid.
39 'The Liberal', *John Bull* (28 August 1822): 780.
40 William Hazlitt, 'On Jealousy and the Spleen of Party', *The Plain Speaker*, 2 vols. (London, 1826), II 439.
41 'The Letters of Timothy Tickler Esq. No. VII', *Blackwood's* (July 1823): 92.
42 *The Illiberal! Verse and Prose from the North* (London: 1822). It is not the only publication designed as a satire of *The Liberal.* For a further example, see *The London Liberal, an Antidote to 'Verse and Prose from the South'* (London, 1823).
43 Thomas Wise, *The Ashley Library*, 11 vols. (London: Private Circulation, 1922–1936), XI 167, 120; Marshall, *Byron, Shelley, Hunt, and the Liberal*, 120.
44 *Beinecke* call number A88 L33A. The quotations that follow are from this edition.
45 *Illiberal*, 5.
46 *Illiberal*, 7. Leigh Hunt, *Foliage* (London: 1818), cxvi.
47 Ibid., 18.
48 Ibid, 1; 'English Bards and Scotch Reviewers', [1809], *LBCPW* I 227–264, ll. 177–182.
49 'English Bards and Scotch Reviewers', l. 94.
50 See Foscolo, 'Dante 2', 340; Foscolo, 'Narrative Poems', 505.
51 Ugo Foscolo, *Essays on Petrarch* (London, 1823); Ugo Foscolo, *Discorso sul testo della 'Commedia' di Dante* (London, 1825). For an example of Foscolo's journalism in this later period, see 'The Italian Poets – Michel Angelo', *The New Monthly Magazine* (January 1822): 339–347.
52 The *Essays on Petrarch* were linked to Lady Dacre's 'Translations from Petrarch' contained in the same volume, and the *Discorso* was intended to be the introduction to an edition of the *Commedia* by Foscolo and published by Pickering, of which only the first part was printed in 1825.
53 'Letters of Timothy Tickler esq. XV', *Blackwood's* (May 1824): 564–565.
54 For Foscolo's final years, see Carlo Franzero, *A Life in Exile*, 93–127.
55 A comprehensive archival study of Binda's time in America, and later at Leghorn, is given in Arnold Blumberg, 'The Strange Career of Joseph Binda', *The South Carolina Historical Magazine* 67 (1966): 155–166.
56 The best archival and documentary research on Panizzi's time in England is the chapter in Margaret Wicks, *The Italian Exiles in London,* 124–162, and Constance Brooks, *Antonio Panizzi: Scholar & Patriot* (Manchester: Manchester University Press, 1931).
57 For reports of the lectures, see *The Liverpool Mercury* reports on 18 March 1825 and 11 November 1825. Panizzi wrote three articles for the *Foreign Review and Continental Miscellany* in 1828, and one for the *Westminster*

Review on Foscolo's *Discorso* (January 1827). Panizzi's first longer work *Orlando furioso di Ariosto with an Essay on the Romantic Narrative Poetry of the Italians* was not published until 1830.

58 Foscolo to Panizzi, 27 July 1826, *Lettere ad Antonio Panizzi*, ed. Luigi Fagan, 2 vols. (Florence, 1880), I 36. The lines are a slight alteration to Ludovico Arisoto *Orlando Furioso,* XXIII 128. 'I am not, indeed am not what I appear to be, He who was at one time Orlando is now under the earth'.

59 The first five volumes of the *Foreign Quarterly* are July 1827, November 1827, February 1828, June 1828, and September 1828.

60 Beste, *Italy As It Is*, 65.

61 *BL* Add MS 51643, f. 43^{r}.

62 For a view of this period from the Royal side, see E. A. Smith, *George IV* (New Haven, CT: Yale University Press, 1999), 205–225; and for the Whig side, see Anthony Hay, *The Whig Revival, 1808–1830* (London: Palgrave Macmillan, 2005), 111–137.

63 For more on this transformation, see James Buzard, *The Beaten Track* (Oxford: Clarendon Press, 1993), 41.

64 'Diary of Visit, 1826–7', *Bodleian* MS. Eng. Misc. e. 993, f. 77^{r}.

65 Ibid., f. 17^{r}; Ibid., f. 21^{r}.

66 Beste, *Italy As It Is*, 166.

67 Mary Shelley's three contributions to *The Liberal* are 'A Tale of the Passions' (II 289–326), 'Madame D' Houtetot' (III 67–85), and 'Giovanni Villani' (IV 281–297).

68 Mary Shelley, 'The English in Italy', *Westminster Review* (October 1826): 326–327.

69 For another reference to Hallam and Italy, and one which also concerns sensual escape, see Alfred Lord Tennyson, 'In Memoriam A. H. H.' [1849], lxxxix, *Tennyson,* ed. Christopher Ricks (London: Longman, 1989), 431–433.

70 Arthur Henry Hallam, 'Lady I bid Thee to a Sunny Dome', *Remains, in Verse and Prose* (London, 1834), 79.

71 Antonio Gallenga, *Episodes of My Second Life*, 2 vols. (London, 1884), II 92.

72 '*Horae Germanicae*', *Blackwood's* (November 1819): 136.

73 For the growth of German literature in the periodical culture of the 1820s and 1830, see Ashton, *The German Idea,* 68–70.

74 Ibid., 26.

75 Hunt, 'Preface', *Liberal,* I vii.

Bibliography

1 Manuscripts

The James Marshall and Marie-Louise Osborn Collection, Beinecke Rare Book and Manuscript Library, Yale University, New Haven, Connecticut, MS Osborn d190.
MS Osborn d324.
MS Osborn d408.
MS Osborn d416.
MS Osborn d417.
MS Osborn d424.
The Bodleian Library, Oxford University, Oxford, John Johnson Collection of Printed Ephemera, Queen Caroline Folder.
MS. Abinger c. 67.
MS. Eng. c. 7052.
MS. Eng. misc. e. 253.
MS. Eng. misc. e. 993.
MS. Eng. misc. e. 1376.
MS. Finch e. 9.
MS. Shelley adds. e. 10.
MS. Shelley adds. c. 4.
British Library. London, Ashley MS 906.
Add MS 36457.
Add MS 47571.
Add MS 51514.
Add MS 51569.
Add MS 51637.
Add MS 51643.
Add MS 51650.
Add MS 51894.
Add MS 51950–51957.
Add MS 52010.
Add MS 52181.
Harold Acton Library, British Institute, Florence, JLM diary MAQ 8.
Keats–Shelley House, Rome, Gay Papers Box 36A.

Lewis Walpole Library, Yale University, Farmington, Connecticut, LWL Ms. vol. 51.
National Library of Scotland, Edinburgh, Ms. 42288.
Ms. 43437.
Ms. 43448.
Ms. 43449.
Carl H. Pforzheimer Collection of Shelley and His Circle, New York Public Library, Astor, Lenox, and Tilden Foundations, New York, New York, LH. 89
LH. 92
MS Shelleyana 1082.
PBS. 0283.
LH. 89
The Henry W. and Albert A. Berg Collection of English and American Literature, New York Public Library, New York, New York, Letter from Leigh Hunt to Lord Byron, 22 January 1822.

2 Book Catalogues

'A catalogue of the remaining part of the library of M. de Mauregard, gone abroad; comprising a good collection of books, chiefly in the French language, many of them elegantly bound [. . .] sold by auction by Mr. King, junr. at his auction room, No. 36, Tavistock Street, Covent Garden, on Wednesday, February 25, 1801, and following day, at twelve o'clock.'. London, 1801.
'Catalogue of the valuable splendid and fine Collection of BOOKS, Consisting of almost every Author in the Italian Language many of which are the greatest rarity [. . .] THE GENUINE PROPERTY OF MR. L. DAPONTE, BOOKSELLER'. London, 1804.
'A catalogue of a valuable collection of rare and curious books, consigned from Italy, including many early editions of the classics, and choice Italian literature, [. . .] the property of an Italian gentleman, dec. which will be sold by auction, by Mr. Stanley, at his great room, no. 29, St. James's Street, on Tuesday the 9th of July, and following day'. London, 1816.

3 Primary

[Anon.]. *A Letter to the People of England.* London: 1820.
[Anon.]. *A Poetical Epistle from Alma Mater to Lord Byron.* Cambridge: Deighton and Sons, 1819.
[Anon.] *A summer voyage to the Gulph of Venice, in the Southwell frigate, Captain Manley junr. commander; an irregular ode* . London: 1750.
[Anon.]. *A Warning to Noble Lords Previous to the Trial of Queen Caroline: By a Loyal Subject.* London: John Fairburn, 1820.

[Anon.]. *Address to Her Majesty Queen Caroline Presented at Brandenburgh House 30 October 1820*. London: G. Humphrey, 1821.
[Anon.]. *Arrival of the Italian Wretches*. Dover: Broadsheet, 1820.
[Anon.]. *Beppo in London: A Metropolitan Story*. London: Duncombe, 1819.
[Anon.]. *Boadicea, Queen of Britain, Overthrowing her Enemies*. London: John Fairburn, 1820.
[Anon.]. *Glorious Arrival of the Friends of the Queen*. London: Catnach, n.d.
[Anon.]. *John Bull Peppering the Italian Rascals – or a Kick from Harwich to Holland*. London, 1820.
[Anon.]. *More News from Venice, By Beppo*. Oxford: J. Vincent, 1818.
[Anon.]. *Plenipo and the Devil! or, the Upshot of the Plot*. London: J. Johnston, 1820.
[Anon.]. *Promnelli Castle; or, the Fate of Melina de Lucelli, A Venetian Tale*. London: J. Lee, 1815.
[Anon.]. *Statement of Facts Concerning the Conduct of Her Majesty Queen Caroline in Italy; Particularizing Her Appearance and the Characters She Sustained at the Masquerade at San Carlo, in Naples; Her Reception at the Theatre, &c., &c., by an Eye-Witness*. London: John Fairburn, 1820.
[Anon.]. *The Album of the Cambridge Garrick Club*. Cambridge, 1836.
[Anon.]. *The Important and Eventful Trial of Queen Caroline, Consort of George IV, for "Adulterous Intercourse" with Bartolomo Bergami*. London: George Smeeton, 1820.
[Anon.]. *The Italian Witness: A New Song*. London: George Smeeton, 1820.
[Anon.]. *The Kettle Abusing the Pot. A Satirical Poem*. London: J. Johnston, 1820.
[Anon.]. *The Picture of London for 1806*. London: John Feltham, 1806.
[Anon.]. *The Royal Martyr; or Life & Death of Queen Caroline*. Sunderland: G. Summers, 1821.
[Anon.]. *The Substance of the Speech of John George Lambton esq. MP at the Durham County Meeting, December 13, 1820*. London: J. Ridgway, 1820.
[Anon.]. *The Unusual Industry Exerted to Impress on the Public Mind a Persuasion That Mr. Pitt Found the Country in a Flourishing, and Left it in a Ruinous State*. London, 1806.
[Anon.]. *To S. Nicholson, Mayor of Rochester Who Refused to Call a Meeting to Address the Queen*. London: W. Benbow, 1820.
Addison, Joseph. *A Letter from Italy[...]to which is added the Despairing Lover*. London: H. Hills, 1709.
Akenside, Mark. *Poetical Works*, edited by Robin Dix. Madison, NJ: Fairleigh Dickinson University Press, 1996.
Alfieri, Vittorio. *Del principe e delle lettere*. Kehl: Co'caratteri di Baskerville, 1795.
Della tirannide. Kehl: Co'caratteri di Baskerville, 1795.
Il Misogallo. London, 1799.
Quindici Tragedie di Vittorio Alfieri da Asti in tre Volume, edited by A. Montucci. Edinburgh: Longman, Hurst, Rees, and Orme,1806.
Rime. Kehl: Co'caratteri di Baskerville, 1789.
The Tragedies of Vittorio Alfieri, translated by Charles Lloyd. London: Longman and Co., 1815.
Vita di Vittorio Alfieri. London: [Piatti] 1804 [i.e. 1806].

Alighieri, Dante. *Inferno, The Divine Comedy*, volume I, part 1, edited and translated by Charles Singlelton. Princeton, NJ: Princeton University Press, 1977.

Paradiso, The Divine Comedy, volume III, part 1, edited and translated by Charles Singleton. Princeton, NJ: Princeton University Press, 1977.

Purgatorio, Dante Alighieri, The Divine Comedy, volume II, part 1, edited and translated by Charles Singleton. Princeton, NJ: Princeton University Press, 1977.

The Anti-Jacobin, or, Weekly Examiner. London. 1797–1798.

The Anti-Jacobin Review and Magazine. London, 1798–1821.

Ariosto, Ludovico. *Orlando Furioso*, edited by *Cesare Segre*. Milano: Mondadori, 1976.

Arnold, Sir Joseph. *Memoir of Thomas, First Lord Denman*. London: Longmans, Green and Co., 1873.

The Argus, 1789–1900.

Austen, Jane. *Northanger Abbey and Persuasion*. London: John Murray, 1818.

Baretti, Guiseppe. *An Account of the Manners and Customs of Italy*. London: T. Davies, 1768.

An Appendix to the Account of Italy. London: T. Davies, 1768.

Remarks on the Italian Language and Writers. London: R. Dodsley, 1753.

Belsham, Thomas. *A Review of Mr. Wilberforce's Treatise*. London: John Johnson, 1798.

Beste, Henry. *Italy As It Is; Or Narrative of an English Family's Residence for Three Years in That Country*. London: Henry Colburn, 1828.

Beyle, Marie-Henri (Stendhal). *Vie de Rossini*. Paris, 1929.

Black Dwarf. London: 1817–1824.

Blackwood's Edinburgh Magazine, Edinburgh: 1817–1902.

Blessington, Marguerite Gardiner, Countess of. *Conversations with Lord Byron*, edited by Ernest J. Lovell Jr. Princeton, NJ: Princeton University Press, 1969.

The Idler in Italy. London: Henry Colburn, 1839.

Boigne, Comtesse de. *Memoirs of the Comtesse de Boigne*, edited by Anka Muhlstein. New York: Helen Marx, 2003.

Boileau, Nicolas. *Œuvres poétiques*. Paris, 1872.

Boyd, Henry. *Poems Chiefly Dramatic and Lyric*. Dublin: Graisberry & Campbell, 1793.

Bozzi, Augustus, and Filippo Pananti. *A Letter to the Right Hon. W. Huskisson [. . .]on the Quarantine Bill*. London, 1825.

Appeal to Alexander, Emperor and Autocrat of All the Russians on Behalf of the Italians by the Editor of L'Italico. London: Richard Rees, 1814.

Autobiography. London, 1874.

L'Italico, ossia giornale politico, letterario e miscellaneo; da un società d'Italiani. London, 1813–1814.

Brooke, Nicholas. *Observations on the Manners and Customs of Italy*. Bath: R. Cruttwell, 1798.

The British Critic. London: 1793–1826.

The British Review and London Critical Journal. London: 1811–1825.

Brougham, Henry. *Speeches of Henry Lord Brougham*. Edinburgh: Adam and Charles Black, 1838.

The Life and Times of Henry Lord Brougham. Edinburgh: Blackwood, 1871.

Brown, William. *The Spirit of the Times*. Nottingham: W. Brown, 1822.

Browning, Elizabeth Barrett. *Casa Guidi Windows*. London: Chapman and Hall, 1851.

Browning, Robert. *Selected Poems*, edited by John Woolford et al. London: Longman, 2010.

Bruno, Cesare. *Studio italiano: poesie di più celebri autori, di vario metro e genere diverso*. London: Cesare Bruno, 1815, 2nd edition, 1818.

Buonaiuti, Serafino, ed. *Risorgimento della Poesia Italiana dopo Il Petrarca*. London: Giovanni Brettell, 1813.

Buonaiuti, Serafino, and James Godby. *Italian Scenery; Representing the Manners, Customs, and Amusements of the Different States of Italy*. London: Edward Orme, 1806.

Buratti, Pietro. *Poesie*. Venice: Naratovich, 1864–1867.

Elefanteide, edited by Tiziano Rizzo. Venice: Fillipi, 1988.

Burke, Edmund. *Reflections on the Revolution in France*, edited by L. G. Mitchell, Oxford: Oxford University Press, 1999.

Bury, Lady Charlotte Campbell. *The Murdered Queen*. London: W. Emans, 1838.

Cary, Henry. *The Vision, or, Hell, Purgatory, and Paradise, of Dante Alighieri*. London: Taylor and Hessey, 1814; 2nd edition, 1819.

Casti, Giovanni Battista. *Gli animali parlanti*. London: L. Da Ponte, 1803.

Gli animali parlanti, edited by Gabrielle Muresu. Ravenna: A. Longo, 1978.

Novelle galanti. London, 1793.

Cavendish, Georgina, and Gaetano Polidori. *The Passage of the Saint Gothard*. London: Gameau and Co., 1803.

Clairmont, Claire. *The Journals of Claire Clairmont*, edited by Marion Stocking. Cambridge, MA: Harvard University Press, 1968.

Cobbett, William, ed. *Cobbett's Parliamentary Debates Series 1*. London: 1803–1820.

Cobbett's Parliamentary Debates Series 2. London, 1820–1828.

Cobbett's Political Register. London, 1804–1816, 1819–1821.

Cobbett's Parliamentary History. London, 1806–1819.

Coleridge, Samuel Taylor. *The Friend*. London: Gale and Curtis, 1812.

Biographia Literaria. London: Rest Fenner, 1817.

Lectures on Literature 1808–1819, edited by Kathleen Coburn. London: Routledge and Keegan Paul, 1987.

The Courier. London, 1804–1842.

Cowden Clarke, Charles. *An Address to that Quarterly Reviewer Who Touched upon Mr. Leigh Hunt's 'Story of Rimini'*. London, 1816.

Cowper, William. *Poems*. London: J. Johnson, 1782.

The Task. London: J. Johnson, 1785.

The Task, edited by James Sambrook. London: Longman, 1994.

Critical Review, or Annals of Literature. London: 1756–1817.

Cruikshank, George, *The Spa Fields Orator Hunt-ing for Popularity to Do-good!!*. London: J. Sidebotham, 1817.

Cuoco, Vincenzo, *Saggio storico sulla rivoluzione di Napoli*. Milan, 1801.

Da Ponte, Lorenzo, trans. *La Profezia di Dante*. New York, 1821.

Memorie, edited by G. Gambarin and F. Nicolini. Bari, 1918.

Memoirs, translated by Elizabeth Abbott. New York: New York Review of Books, 2000.

Dalrymple, Sir Hew Whiteford. *The Whole Proceedings of the Court of Enquiry upon the Conduct of Sir Hew Dalrymple*. London: Sherwood, Neely, and Jones, 1808.

Dibdin, Charles. *Collection of Songs*. London: R. Lea, 1814.

The Professional Life of Mr. Dibdin. London, 1803.

The Songs of Charles Dibdin. London: G. H. Davidson, 1848.

Dorset, Catherine Ann. *The Lion's Masquerade*. London: J. Harris, 1808.

The Drama: or, Theatrical Pocket Magazine. London, 1821–1825.

The Edinburgh Review. Edinburgh, 1802–1910.

Egerton, Samuel, Baronet Bridges, *Letters on the Character and Poetical Genius of Lord Byron*. London: Longman & Co., 1824.

Eliot, George. *The Mill on the Floss*. Edinburgh: William Blackwood and Sons, 1860.

The English Review. London, 1783–1795.

Eustace, John Chetwode. *A Classical Tour Through Italy*, 3rd edition. London: Mawman, 1815.

Examiner. London, 1808–1881.

Fagan, Luigi, ed. *Lettere ad Antonio Panizzi*. Florence, 1880.

Fane, John, Lord Burgesh. *Correspondence of Lord Burgesh*. London: John Murray, 1912.

Farington, Joseph, *The Farington Diary*, edited by James Greig. London: Hutchinson, 1922–1928.

Faulkner, Thomas, *History and Antiquities of Kensington*. London: T. Egerton, 1820.

The Foreign Quarterly Review. London, 1827–1846.

Foscolo, Ugo. *Dell'Origine E Dell'Ufficio Della Letteratura, Orazione*, edited by Enzo Neppi. Florence: Leo Olschki, 2005.

Discorsi nel Parlamento in Morte di Francesco Horner tradotti dall' Inglese. London: Schhulze and Dean, 1817.

Discorso sul testo della 'Commedia' di Dante. London: William Pickering, 1825.

Edizione Nazionale delle Opere di Ugo Foscolo, edited by Mario Scotti et al. Florence: Le Monnier, 1933–1985.

Essays on Petrarch. London: John Murray, 1823.

Letters of Ortis. translated by 'F.B.'. London: Henry Colburn, 1814.

Letters of Ortis, translated by 'F.B.',London: Henry Colburn, 1818.

'Narrative and Romantic Poems of the Italians'. *Quarterly Review* (April 1819): 486–556.

Ultime Lettere di Jacopo Ortis. London: R. Zotti, 1811.
Ultime Lettere di Jacopo Ortis, w. Alcuni capitoli dell' Viaggio Sentimentale di Yorick. London: R. Zotti, 1817.
Ultime Lettere di Jacopo Ortis, w. Alcuni capitoli dell' Viaggio Sentimentale di Yorick. London: John Murray, 1817.
Ultime lettere di Jacopo Ortis. London, 1818.
Frere, John Hookham. *Prospectus and Specimen of an Intended National Work, by William and Robert Whistlecraft*. London: John Murray, 1817.
Memoir of J. H. Frere. London: B. M. Pickering, 1846.
Galiffe, Jacques Augustin. *Italy and Its Inhabitants; An Account of a Tour in That Country*. London, 1820.
Galignani, J. A. *Twenty-Four Lectures on the Italian Language by Mr. Galignani*. Edinburgh: Boosey, 1806.
Galignani's Messenger. Paris, 1814–1885.
Gallenga, Antonio. *Episodes of My Second Life*. London: Chapman & Hall, 1884.
Gally, P., and P. *Queen Caroline's Triumph over Her Enemies*. London, 1821.
Gazzetta Privilegiata di Venezia. Venice, 1816–1848.
Gibbon, Edward. *Memoirs of My Life*, edited by Georges L. Bonnard. London: Thomas Nelson, 1966.
The Miscellaneous Works of Edward Gibbon, edited by John Lord Sheffield. Dublin, 1796.
The Miscellaneous Works of Edward Gibbon, edited by John Lord Sheffield. London: John Murray, 1814.
Gifford, William. *The Baviad*. London, 1793.
The Baviad, and the Mæviad, revised edn. London: J. Wright, 1797.
Ginguené, Pierre-Louis. *Histoire Littéraire d'Italie*. Paris, 1811–1835.
Goede, Christian August Gottlieb. *A Foreigner's Opinion of England*. London: C. Taylor, 1821.
Goldsmith, Oliver, Thomas Gray, and William Collins. *The Poems of Gray, Collins, and Goldsmith*, edited by Roger Lonsdale. London: Longman, 1969.
Gordon, George, Lord Byron. *Byron's Letters and Journals*, edited by Leslie Marchand. London: John Murray, 1973–1994.
Lord Byron the Complete Poetical Works, edited by Jerome J. McGann and Barry Weller. Oxford: Clarendon 1980–1993.
The Miscellaneous Prose, edited by Andrew Nicholson. Oxford: Clarendon Press, 1991.
Granville, Harriet. *Letters of Harriet, Countess Granville Edited by Her Son*. London: Longmans and Co., 1894.
Hallam, Arthur Henry. *Remains, in Verse and Prose*. London: W. Nicol, 1834.
Hallam, Henry. *View of the State of Europe during the Middle Ages*. London: John Murray, 1818.
Harrington, James. *The Common-Wealth of Oceana*. London: Livwell Chapman, 1656.
Hazlitt, William, 'Christabel: Kubla Khan, a Vision'. *Edinburgh Review* (September 1816): 67.

Lectures on the English Poets. London: Taylor and Hessey, 1818.
The Letters of William Hazlitt, edited by Herschel M. Sikes. New York: New York University Press, 1978.
The Plain Speaker. London: Henry Colburn, 1826.
The Selected Writings of William Hazlitt, edited by Duncan Wu et al. London: Pickering, 1998.
Hemans, Felicia. *Modern Greece*. London: John Murray, 1817.
The Restoration of the Works of Art to Italy. Oxford: W. Baxter, 1816.
Hobhouse, John Cam. *Historical Illustrations of the Fourth Canto of Childe Harold*. London: John Murray, 1818.
Holland, Lady. *Elizabeth, Lady Holland to Her Son,* edited by Lord Ilchester. London: John Murray, 1946.
Holland, Lord. *Letter to a Neapolitan from an Englishman*. London: Thomas Davidson, 1818.
Hone, William, and George Cruikshank. *The Green Bag: A Dainty Dish to Set before a King*. London: J. Robins and Co., 1820.
Hook, Theodore. *Tentamen, or, An Essay towards the History of Whittington*. London: William Wright, 1820.
Horner, Francis. *The Horner Papers*, edited by Kenneth Bourne and William Taylor. Edinburgh: Edinburgh University Press, 1994.
Hunt, Leigh. *Amyntas: A Tale of the Woods*. London: T. and J. Allman, 1820.
Autobiography, edited by J. E. Morpurgo. London: Cresset Press, 1949.
Correspondence, edited by Thornton Hunt. London: Smith, Elder, and co., 1862.
The Feast of the Poets. London: James Cawthorn, 1814.
Foliage; or Poems Original and Translated. London: C. and J. Ollier, 1818.
Leigh Hunt: A Life in Letters, edited by Eleanor M. Gates. Essex, CT: Falls River Publications, 1998.
Leigh Hunt's Dramatic Criticism: 1808–1831, edited by Lawrence Huston Houtchens et al. London: Oxford University Press, 1950.
The Literary Pocket Book; or, Companion for the Lover of Nature and Art, 1819. London: C. and J. Ollier, 1818.
Lord Byron and Some of His Contemporaries, 2nd edition. London: Colburn, 1828.
The Old Court Suburb; or, Memorials of Kensington. London: Hurst and Blackett, 1855.
The Selected Writings of Leigh Hunt, edited by Robert Morrison, Michael Eberle-Sinatra, Jeffrey N. Cox, Greg Kucich, Charles Mahoney, and John Strachan. London: Pickering and Chatto, 2003.
The Story of Rimini. London: John Murray, 1816.
The Story of Rimini, Woodstock, NY: Woodstock Press, 2001.
The Illiberal! Verse and Prose from the North. London: 1822.
Irving, Washington. *The Sketch-Book of Geoffray Crayon, Gent*, edited by Susan Manning. Oxford: Oxford University Press, 1996.
John Bull. London: 1820–1893.

Johnson, Samuel. *Lives of the Poets,* edited by Rogers Lonsdale. Oxford: Oxford University Press, 2006.

Juvenal and Persius. *Satires,* edited and translated by Susanna Braund. Cambridge, MA: Harvard University Press, 2004.

Keats, John. *Poems of John Keats,* edited by Jack Stillinger. Cambridge, MA: Harvard University Press, 1978.

Keppel-Craven, Richard. *A Tour through the Southern Provinces of the Kingdom of Naples, to Which Is Subjoined a Sketch of the Immediate Circumstances Attending the Late Revolution.* London: Rodwell and Martin, 1821.

Lamb, Lady Caroline. *Glenarvon.* London: Henry Colburn, 1816.

Leoni, Michele, trans. *L'Italia, Canto IV, Del Pellegrinaggio di Childe Harold.* Italy, 1819.

Leopardi, Giacomo. *Discorso sopra lo stato presente dei costumi degl'italiani,* edited by Marco Dondero. Milan: Biblioteca Universale Rizzioli, 1998.

The Liberal: Verse and Prose from the South. London: John Hunt, 1822–1823.

The Literary Gazette: a Weekly Journal of Literature, Science, and the Fine Arts. London: 1817–1862.

The Literary Magazine, or Monthly Epitome of British Literature. London: 1797–1806.

The London Liberal, an Antidote to "Verse and Prose from the South". London: 1823.

Lucan. *Pharsalia,* translated by J. D. Duff. London: Heinemann, 1977.

Mason, Margaret Jane. *The Stories of Old Daniel.* London: M. J. Godwin, 1813.

Mathias, Thomas. *Aggiunta ai componimenti lirici de'più illustri poeti d'Italia,* London, 1808.

Canzone Toscane. London: 1806.

Canzone Toscane. London, 1816.

Componimenti lirici de' piu illustri poeti dItalia. London, 1802.

Componimenti lirici de'più illustri poeti d'Italia. Naples, 1819.

The Pursuits of Literature. 14th edition. London, 1808.

The Shade of Alexander Pope. London: T. Becket, 1799.

Medwin, Thomas. *Conversations of Lord Byron: Noted During a Residence with His Lordship at Pisa.* London: Henry Colburn, 1824.

Merivale, John Herman. "Account of the Morgante of Luigi Fulci" (*sic*). *Monthly Magazine* (May 1806): 304–308.

"Remarks on the Morgante Maggiore of Luigi Pulci." *Monthly Magazine* (June 1806): 510–513.

The Two First Cantos of Richardetto. London: John Murray, 1820.

Merry, Robert, Hester Thrale Piozzi, Bertie Greatheed, William Parsons et al. *The Florence Miscellany.* Florence: G. Cam, 1785.

Milton, John. *Paradise Lost,* edited by Alistair Fowler. London: Longman, 1988.

Poems of Mr. John Milton, Both English and Latin, Compos'd at Several Times. London: Humphrey Moseley, 1645.

Montucci, Antonio, *Italian Extracts; Being an Extensive Selection from Italian Authors*. Edinburgh: Boosey, 1806. 2nd edition. London: Boosey and Sons, 1818.

Montucci, Antonio, ed. *Quindici Tragedie di Vittorio Alfieri da Asti in tre Volume*. Edinburgh: Tommaso Boosey, 1806.

The Monthly Review. London: 1749–1844.

The Morning Chronicle. London: 1801–1865.

Murat, Joachim. *Italiani. L'ora è venuta*. Rimini, 1815.

Murray, John. *The Letters of John Murray to Lord Byron*, edited by Andrew Nicholson. Liverpool: Liverpool University Press, 2007.

Naldi, Giuseppe. *The Alien; or an Answer to Mr. Greville's Statement with Respect to Mr. Naldi's Action for Arrears of Salary*. London, 1811.

The New Annual Register, or General Repository of History, Politics, Arts, Sciences, and Literature. London: 1780–1825.

The New Monthly Magazine and Literary Journal. London: 1821–1834.

Nietzsche, Friedrich. *Der Fall Wagner*. Leipzig: 1888.

The Pamphleteer. London: 1813–1828.

Panizzi, Antonio. *Orlando furioso di Ariosto with an Essay on the Romantic Narrative Poetry of the Italians*. London: William Pickering, 1830.

Parini, Giuseepe. *Opere*, edited by Ettore Bonore. Milan: Ugo Mursia, 1969.

Peacock, Thomas Love. *Nightmare Abbey*. London: T. Hookham, 1818.

Pecchio, Giuseppe. *Semi-Serious Observations of an Italian Exile during His Residence in England*. London: 1833.

Petrarca, Francesco. *Rime sparse*, edited and translated by Robert M. Durling. Cambridge, MA: Harvard University Press, 1976.

Triumphi, edited by Marco Ariani. Milan: Mursia, 1988.

The Triumphs of Petrarch, translated by E. H. Wilkins. Chicago, IL: Chicago University Press, 1962.

Phillips, Charles. *The Queen's Case Stated*. London: William Hone, 1820.

Plutarch. *Moralia*. London: Loeb, 1959.

Polidori, Gaetano. *Poesi varie*. London: 1805.

Polidori, Gaetano, trans. *Il Como, Favola boschereccia*. London: 1812.

Il Licida, L'Allegro, ed Il Penseroso, translated by Gaetano Polidori. London, 1814.

Il Penseroso. London: 1809.

Polidori, John. *The Diary of Dr. John William Polidori, 1816*, edited by William Michael Rossetti. London: Elkin Matthews, 1916.

Pope, Alexander. *The Poems of Alexander Pope*, edited by John Butt. London: Routledge, 1989.

Pulci, Luigi. *Morgante*, edited by Franca Ageno. Milan: R. Ricciardi, 1955.

The Quarterly Review. London: 1809–1906.

Radcliffe, Ann. *A Sicilian Romance*. London: G. G. and J. Robinson, 1790.

The Italian. 2nd edition. London: G. G. and J. Robinson, 1797.

The Mysteries of Udolpho. 2nd edition. London: G. G. and J. Robinson, 1794.

Ring, John. *The Beauties of the Edinburgh Review*. London, 1807.

Robertson, William. *The History of the Reign of the Emperor Charles V.* London: A. Strahan, 1769.
Rogers, Samuel. *Italy, a Poem, Part the First.* London: John Murray, 1822.
Romilly, Samuel. *Romilly's Cambridge Diary, 1832–42.* Cambridge: Cambridge University Press, 1967.
Rosco (pseud.). *Horrida Bella, Pains and Penalties versus Truth and Justice.* London: G. Humphrey, 1820.
Roscoe, William. *The Life of Lorenzo de' Medici, Called the Magnificent.* 2nd edition. London: A. Strahan, 1796.
Rose, William Stewart. *The Court of the Beasts.* London: W. Bulmer and Co., 1816.
Letters from the North of Italy. London: John Murray, 1819.
trans. *Orlando Innamorato.* Edinburgh: W. Blackwood, 1823.
Rossini, Gioachino. *Elisabetta, Regina d'Inghilterra. Dramma Serio, in Two Acts.* London: W. Winchester and Son, 1818.
La Gazza ladra, The Thieving Magpie, A Semi-Serio Opera in Two Acts. London: John Ebers, 1821.
Rubbi, Andrea, ed. *Elogi Italiani.* Venice, 1782–1783.
Il giornale poetico. Venice, 1789.
Parnaso Italiano. Venice, 1784–1791.
Ruffhead, Owen. *The Life of Alexander Pope.* London, 1769.
Russell, Lord John. *A Letter to Mr. Wilberforce and a Petition to the King.* London: James Ridgway, 1820.
The Satirist, or, Monthly Meteor. London: 1807–1814.
Schelling, Friedrich. *Werke*, edited by M. Schroter, Munich: Beck, 1927–1928.
Scott, Walter. *Ivanhoe*, 2nd edn. Edinburgh: Longman, Hurst, Rees, Orme, and Brown, 1820.
The Journal of Sir Walter Scott. Edinburgh: D. Douglas, 1890.
The Letters of Sir Walter Scott, edited by H. C. J. Grierson. London: Constable, 1932–1937.
Poetical Works, edited by J. Logie Robertson. Oxford: Oxford University Press, 1913.
Waverley. Edinburgh: Longman, Hurst, Rees, Orme, and Brown, 1814.
Shakespeare, William. *As You Like It*, edited by Juliet Dunisberre. Walton: Arden, 2006.
Merry Wives of Windsor, edited by T. W. Craik. Oxford: Clarendon Press, 1989.
Othello, edited by E. A. J. Honigmann. Walton: Arden, 1997.
Shelley, Percy Bysshe. *A Philosophical View of Reform*, edited by Humphrey Milford. Oxford: Oxford University Press, 1920.
The Letters of Percy Bysshe Shelley, edited by Frederick L. Jones. Oxford: Clarendon Press, 1964.
The Poems of Shelley, edited by Kelvin Everest, G. M. Matthews et al. London: Longman, 1989–2013.
Poetical Works of Percy Bysshe Shelley, edited by Mary Shelley. London: E. Moxon, 1839. Single-volume edition.

Poetical Works of Percy Bysshe Shelley, edited by Mary Shelley. London: E. Moxon, 1839. Four-volume edition.

Rosalind and Helen. London: C. and J. Ollier, 1819.

Shelley and His Circle, 1773–1822, edited by Kenneth Neill Cameron, Donald H. Reiman et al. Cambridge, MA: Harvard University Press, 1961–2002.

Shelley's Poetry and Prose, edited by Donald Reiman and Neil Fraisat. New York: Norton, 2002.

Shelley's Prose Works, edited by Harry Buxton Forman. London: Reeves and Turner, 1880.

Shelley, Mary. *The Journal of Mary Shelley*, edited by Paula Feldman and Diana Scott-Kilvert. Oxford: Clarendon, 1987.

The Letters of Mary Wollstonecraft Shelley, edited by Betty T. Bennett. Baltimore, MD: Johns Hopkins University Press, 1980–1988.

Valperga: or the Life and Adventures of Castruccio, Prince of Lucca, edited by Nora Crook. London: Pickering, 1996.

Sheridan, Richard Brinsley. *The Letters of Richard Brinsley Sheridan*, edited by Cecil Price. Oxford: Clarendon Press, 1966.

The Ridotto of Bath. Bath: R. Crutwell, 1771.

Sismondi, Jean Charles Léonard de. *Histoire des républiques italiennes du Moyen Âge*. Paris, 1807–1818.

De la Littérature du Midi de l'Europe. Paris, 1813.

Smollett, Tobias. *The Adventures of Peregrine Pickle*. London: W. Owen, 1751.

Miscellaneous Works of Smollett, edited by Robert Anderson. London: Otridge and Rackham, 1796.

Travels through France and Italy. London: R. Baldwin, 1766.

Southey, Robert. *A Vision of Judgement*. London: William Dugdale, 1821.

'An Inquiry into the Causes of the General Poverty and Dependence of Mankind'. *Quarterly Review* (October 1816): 226.

The Correspondence of Robert Southey, edited by Charles Cuthbert Southey. London: Longman, Brown, Green, and Longmans, 1850.

Specimens of the Later English Poets, with Preliminary Notices. London: Longman & Co., 1807.

Sterne, Laurence, *A Sentimental Journey through France and Italy*. London: T. Becket, 1768.

Stevens, Wallace. *Collected Poems*. London: Faber and Faber, 1984.

Strongoli, Francesco Pignatell. *Memorie di Un Generale*, edited by Nino Cortese. Bari: Laterza, 1927.

Memorie intorno alla storia del Regno di Napoli dall' anno 1805 al 1815, Naples: 1820.

Sydney, Lady Morgan. *Italy*. London: H. Colburn, 1821.

Taaffe, John. *A Comment on the Divine Comedy of Dante Aligheri*. London: John Murray, 1822.

Tasso, Torquato. *Aminta*. London, 1800.

Tennyson, Alfred Lord. *Poems of Tennyson*, edited by Christopher Ricks. London: Longman, 1989.

The Times. London: 1785–present.

Tommaseo, Niccolò. *Dizionario estetico*. Florence, 1867.

Toplady, Augustus Montague. *English Constitutional Liberty Proved to be Comprised in Magna Charta! the Petition of Right! the Bill of Rights! and the Coronation Oath!!!* London: John Fairburn, n.d.

Torti, Francesco. *Prospetto del Parnaso Italiano*. Milan, 1806.

Vico, Giambattista. *New Science*, translated by Marsh. London: Penguin, 2000.

Voltaire, Francois-Marie Arouet de. *Oeuvres completes de Voltaire*. Paris, 1877–1885.

Wade, John. *The Black Book; or, Corruption Unmasked!* London: John Fairburn, 1820.

Walpole, Horace. *The Castle of Otranto*. 3rd edition. London: William Bathoe, 1764.

Warton, Joseph. *An Essay on the Writings and Genius of Pope*. London, 1756.

Warton, Thomas. *The History of English Poetry*. London, 1774–1781.

The Poetical Works of the Late Thomas Warton, 2 vols. Oxford: Oxford University Press 1802.

The Weekly Intelligencer, and British Luminary. London: 1818–1823.

Whishaw, John. *The "Pope" of Holland House. Selections from the Correspondence of John Whishaw*. London: T. Fisher Unwin, 1906.

The White Dwarf. London: 1817–1818.

Wilberforce, William. *A Practical View of the Prevailing Religious System*. 6th edition. London: T. Cadell, 1797.

Williams, H. W. *Travels in Italy, Greece, and the Ionian Islands*. Edinburgh: Constable, 1820.

Wilkinson, Sarah. *The Spectre; or, the Ruins of Belfont Priory*. London: J. Ker, 1806.

Wilmot, Katherine. *The Grand Tours of Katherine Wilmot*, edited by Elizabeth Mayor. London: Weidenfeld & Nicholson, 1992.

Wordsworth, William. *The Excursion*, edited by Sally Bushell, James Butler, and Michael Jaye. Ithaca, NY: Cornell University Press, 2007.

The Major Works, edited by Stephen Gill. Oxford: Oxford University Press, 1984.

Poems in Two Volumes. London: Longman, Hurst, Rees, and Orme, 1807.

Wordsworth, William, and Dorothy Wordsworth. *The Letters of William and Dorothy Wordsworth: the Later Years, part 1*, edited by E. de Selincourt, revised by Alan Hill. Oxford: Clarendon Press, 1978.

Yeats, W. B. *Essays and Introductions*. New York: Macmillan, 1961.

Young, Arthur. *An Enquiry into the State of the Public Mind*. Dublin, 1798.

Zenobio, Count Alvise. *An Address to the People of England*. London: J. Ridgway, 1792.

4 Secondary

Acton, Harold. *The Bourbons of Naples 1734–1825*. London: Prion, 1998.

Albert, William. *The Turnpike Road System in England 1663–1840*. Cambridge: Cambridge University Press, 1972.

Amarasinghe, Upali. *Dryden and Pope in the Early Nineteenth Century, A Study of Changing Literary Taste, 1800–1830*. Cambridge: Cambridge University Press, 1962.

Anderson, Benedict. *Imagined Communities*. 2nd edition. London: Verso, 2004.

Aquilecchia, Giovanni et al., eds. *Collected Essays on Italian Language and Literature Presented to Kathleen Speight*. Manchester: Manchester University Press, 1971.

Arthos, John. *Milton and the Italian Cities*. New York: Barnes and Noble, 1968.

Ashton, Rosemary. *The German Idea, Four English Writers and the Reception of German Thought, 1800–1860*. Cambridge: Cambridge University Press, 1980. Reprinted London: Libris, 1994.

Avitabile, Grazia. *The Controversy on Romanticism in Italy. First Phase, 1816–1823*. New York: Vanni, 1959.

Bahktin, Mikhail. *Rabelais and His World*, translated by Helen Iswolsky. London: MIT Press, 1968.

Bainbridge, Simon. *British Poetry and the Revolutionary and Napoleonic Wars: Visions of Conflict*. Oxford: Oxford University Press, 2003.

Baker, John Jay. 'Myth, Subjectivity and the Problem of Historical Time in Shelley's "Lines written among the Euganean Hills"'. *English Literary History* 56 (1989): 149–172.

Bandiera, Laura and Diego Saglia, eds. *British Romanticism and Italian Literature: Translating, Reviewing, Rewriting*. Amsterdam: Rodopi, 2005.

Barber, Cesar Lombardi. *Shakespeare's Festive Comedy: A Study of Dramatic Form and Its Relation to Social Custom*. Princeton, NJ: Princeton University Press, 1959.

Barthes, Roland. *The Eiffel Tower and Other Mythologies*, translated by Richard Howard. Berkeley, CA: University of California Press, 1997.

Bate, Walter Jackson. *The Burden of the Past and the English Poet*. London: Chatto and Windus, 1971.

Beaton, Roderick. *Byron's War: Romantic Rebellion, Greek Revolution*. Cambridge: Cambridge University Press, 2013.

Beatty, Bernard, and Vincent Newey, eds. *Byron and the Limits of Ficiton*. Liverpool: Liverpool University Press, 2006.

Beatty, Frederick L. 'Byron and the Story of Francesca da Rimini'. *PMLA* 75 (1960): 395–401.

Bellorini, Egido, ed. *Discussioni e Polemiche sul Romanticismo, 1816–1826*. Bari: Laterza, 1943.

Benchimol, Alex. *Intellectual Politics and Cultural Conflict in the Romantic Period: Scottish Whigs, English Radicals and the Making of the British Public Sphere*. Farnham: Ashgate, 2010.

Bertelli, Stefania. *Il Carnevale di Venezia nel Settecento*. Roma: Jouvence, 1992.
Bevan, Vaughan. *The Development of British Immigration Law*. London: Croom Helm, 1986.
Bevis, Matthew. *The Art of Eloquence: Byron, Dickens, Tennyson, Joyce*. Oxford: Oxford University Press, 2007.
Blanning, T .C. W. *The Culture of Power and the Power of Culture: Old Regime Europe 1660–1789*. Oxford: Oxford University Press, 2002.
Bloom, Harold, ed. *Deconstruction and Criticism*. New York: Continuum, 1979.
Blumberg, Arnold, 'The Strange Career of Joseph Binda', *The South Carolina Historical Magazine* 67 (1966): 155–166.
Bollati, Giulio. *L'italiano: il carattere nazionale come storia e come invenzione*. Torino: Einaudi, 1996.
Bolt, Rodney. *Lorenzo Da Ponte: The Adventures of Mozart's Librettist in the Old and New Worlds*. London: Bloomsbury, 2006.
Bowers, Will. 'Byron's Rhyming Clime', *Essays in Criticism* 69 (2019): 157–177.
'The Dilemma of a "Romantic" Anthology'. *Publishing History* 67 (2010): 65–89.
'The Many Rooms of Holland House'. *Re-evaluating the Literary Coterie*, edited by Will Bowers and H. L. Crumme. London: Palgrave, 2016.
'On First Looking into Mary Shelley's Homer'. *Review of English Studies* 69, no. 290 (2018): 519–531.
'Vallombrosa Visited, 1638–1851', *Modern Philology*, forthcoming.
Boyd, Hilton. *A Mad, Bad and Dangerous People?: England 1783–1846*. Oxford: Clarendon Press, 2006.
Braida, Antonella. *Dante and the Romantics*. Basingstoke: Palgrave Macmillan, 2004.
Brand, Charles. *Italy and the English Romantics. The Italianate Fashion in Early Nineteenth-Century England*. Cambridge: Cambridge University Press, 1957.
Bryne, Michael. *Britain and the European Powers, 1815–65*. London: Hodder & Stoughton, 1998.
Burrow, J. W. *Whigs and Liberals: Continuity and Change in British Political Thought*. Oxford: Clarendon Press, 1988.
Burwick, Fred and Paul Douglass, eds. *Dante and Italy in British Romanticism*. Basingstoke: Palgrave Macmillan, 2011.
Butler, Marilyn. *Romantics, Rebels and Reactionaries: English Literature and Its Background 1760–1830*. Oxford: Oxford University Press, 1981.
Buzard, James. *The Beaten Track: European Tourism, Literature, and the Ways to 'Culture' 1800–1918*. Oxford: Clarendon Press, 1993.
Caesar, Michael. *Dante: The Critical Heritage*. London: Routledge, 1989.
Calè, Luisa. *Fuseli's Milton Gallery: 'Turning Readers into Spectators'*. Oxford: Oxford University Press, 2006.
Cambon, Glauco. *Ugo Foscolo – Poet of Exile*. Princeton, NJ: Princeton University Press, 1980.
Camilletti, Fabio. *Classicism and Romanticism in Italian Literature*. London: Pickering and Chatto, 2013.

Caponigri, Robert. *Time and Idea: The Theory of History in Giambattista Vico*. Chicago, IL: Henry Regnery, 1953.

Casanova, Pascale. 'Combative Literatures'. *New Left Review* 72 (2011): 123–134.

Castle, Terry. *Masquerade and Civilization: The Carnivalesque in Eighteenth-Century English Culture and Fiction*. London: Meuthen, 1986.

Cattaneo, Carlo. *Ugo Foscolo e L'Italia*. Milan, 1861.

Cavaliero, Roderick. *Italia Romantica: English Writers and Romantic Freedom*. London: Macmillan, 2005.

Chandler, James. *England in 1819: The Politics of Literary Culture and the Case of Romantic Historicism*. Chicago, IL: Chicago University Press, 1998.

'The Pope Controversy: Romantic Poetics and the English Canon'. *Critical Enquiry* 10 (1984): 481–509.

Chard, Chloe. *Pleasure and Guilt on the Grand Tour: Travel Writing and Imaginative Geography, 1600–1830*. Manchester: Manchester University Press, 1999.

Cheeke, Stephen. *Byron and Place*. London: Palgrave, 2003.

Christie, William. *The Edinburgh Review in the Literary Culture of Romantic Britain: Mammoth and Megalonyx*. London: Pickering and Chatto, 2009.

'Francis Jeffrey in Recent Whig Interpretations of Romantic Literary History'. *English Literary History* 76 (2009): 577–597.

Claggett, William J. M., and Byron E. Shafer, eds. *The American Public Mind: The Issues and Structure of Politics in the Post-War United States*. Cambridge: Cambridge University Press, 2010.

Cline, C. L. *Byron, Shelley and Their Pisan Circle*. London: John Murray, 1952.

Cochran, Peter. *Byron and Italy*. Newcastle: Cambridge Scholars Press, 2012.

'Romanticism' – and Byron. Newcastle: Cambridge Scholars Press, 2009.

Cockburn, Henry. *Life of Lord Jeffrey: With a Selection from His Correspondence*. Edinburgh, 1852.

Colley, Linda. *Britons: Forging the Nation 1707–1837*. New Haven, CT: Yale University Press, 2005.

Cox, Jeffrey N. 'Keats in the Cockney School'. *Romanticism* 2 (1996): 27–39.

Poetry and Politics in the Cockney School: Keats, Shelley, Hunt, and Their Circle. Cambridge: Cambridge University Press, 1998.

Romanticism in the Shadow of War: Literary Culture in the Napoleonic War Years. Cambridge: Cambridge University Press, 2014.

Crisafulli, Lilla Maria, ed. *Immaginando L'Italia – Itinerari letterari del Romanticismo Inglese*. Bologna: Clueb, 2002.

Croce, Benedetto. *Filosofia, Poesia, Storia*. Milan: Ricciardi, 1955.

Cronin, Richard. *Paper Pellets: British Literary Culture After Waterloo*. Oxford: Oxford University Press, 2010.

The Politics of Romantic Poetry: in Search of the Pure Commonwealth. London: Macmillan, 2000.

Shelley's Poetic Thoughts. London: Macmillan, 1981.

Crook, Nora, and Tatsuo Tokoo. 'Shelley's Jewish "Orations"'. *Keats-Shelley Journal* 59 (2010): 43–64.

Crouzet-Pavan, Elizabeth. *Venice Triumphant*, translated by Lydia Cochrane. Baltimore, MD: Johns Hopkins University Press, 2002.

Culler, Jonathan. *Framing the Sign: Criticism and Its Institutions*. Oxford: Basil Blackwell, 1988.

Curran, Stuart. *Poetic Form and British Romanticism*. New York: Oxford University Press, 1986.

Dart, Gregory. *Rousseau, Robespierre and English Romanticism*. Cambridge: Cambridge University Press, 1999.

Davis, John A. *Naples and Napoleon: Southern Italy and the European Revolutions, 1780–1860*. Oxford: Oxford University Press, 2006.

De Bolla, Peter. *The Education of the Eye: Painting, Landscape, and Architecture in Eighteenth-Century Britain*. Palo Alto, CA: Stanford University Press, 2003.

De Man, Paul. *The Rhetoric of Romanticism*. New York: Columbia University Press, 1984.

De Maria, Blake. *Becoming Venetian: Immigrants and the Arts in Early Modern Venice*. New Haven, CT: Yale University Press, 2010.

De Montluzin, Emily Lorraine. *The Anti-Jacobins, 1798–1800: The Early Contributors to the Anti-Jacobin Review*. Basingstoke: Macmillan, 1988.

De Sanctis, Francesco. *Storia della Letteratura Italiana*, edited by Morano. Naples: 1879.

Deleuze, Glies, and Felix Guttari. *Kafka: Toward a Minor Literature*, translated by Dana Polan. Minneapolis, MN: University of Minnesota Press, 1986.

Del Vivo, Caterina. *La 'Bella Vaccà' Leopoldo e Andrea*. Pisa: Edizioni ETS, 2009.

Dinwiddy, J. R. 'The Use of the Crown's Power of Deportation under the Aliens Act, 1793–1826'. *Historical Research* 41, no. 104 (November 1968): 193–211.

Dionisotti, Carlo. *Appunti sui moderni: Foscolo, Leopardi, Manzoni e altri*, Bologna: Mulino, 1988.

Dobson, Michael. *The Making of the National Poet: Shakespeare, Adaptation, and Authorship, 1660–1769*. Oxford: Oxford University Press, 1992.

Duff, David. *Romance and Revolution: Shelley and the Politics of a Genre*. Cambridge: Cambridge University Press, 1994.

Duffy, Cian. '"The Child of a Fierce Hour": Shelley and Napoleon Bonaparte'. *Studies in Romanticism* 43 (2004): 399–416.

Duffy, Michael. *The Englishman and the Foreigner*. London: Chadwyck-Healey, 1986.

Dyer, Gary. *British Satire and the Politics of Style 1789–1832*. Cambridge: Cambridge University Press, 1997.

Eagleton, Terry. *The Function of Criticism: From 'The Spectator' to Post-Structuralism*. London: Verso, 1984.

Heathcliff and the Great Hunger: Studies in Irish Culture. London: Verso, 1995.

Eberle-Sinatra, Michael. *Leigh Hunt and the London Literary Scene: A Reception History of his Major Works, 1805–1828*. London: Routledge, 2005.

Eglin, John. *Venice Transfigured: The Myth of Venice in British Culture 1660–1797*. New York: Palgrave, 2001.

Eichler, Albert. *John Hookham Frere. Sein Leben und seine Werke. Sein Einfluss auf Lord Byron*. Vienna: W. Braumüller, 1905.

Ellis, Steve. *Dante and English Poetry: Shelley to T. S. Eliot*, Cambridge: Cambridge University Press, 1983.

Empson, William. *Some Versions of Pastoral: A Study of the Pastoral Form in Literature*. London: Penguin, 1995.

Epstein, James. *Radical Expression: Political Language, Ritual, and Symbol in England, 1790–1850*. Oxford: Oxford University Press, 1994.

Everest, Kelvin, ed. *Shelley Revalued: Essays from the Gregynog Conference*. Leicester: Leicester University Press, 1983.

Fahrmeir, Andreas. *Citizens and Aliens: Foreigners and the Law in Britain and the German States, 1789–1870*. New York: Bergahn Books, 2000.

Fairclough, Mary. *The Romantic Crowd: Sympathy, Controversy and Print Culture*. Cambridge: Cambridge University Press, 2013.

Feaver, William. *The Art of John Martin*. Oxford: Clarendon Press, 1975.

Firpo, Luigi. 'Le origini dell'antimachiavellismo'. *Il Pensiero Politico* 2 (1969): 337–367.

Foot, Paul. *Red Shelley*. Witham: Sedgwick and Jackson, 1980.

Fowler, Alastair. *Triumphal Forms: Structural Patterns in Elizabethan Poetry*. Cambridge: Cambridge University Press, 1970.

France, Peter and Kenneth Haynes, eds. *The Oxford History of Literary Translation in English*. Oxford: Oxford University Press, 2006.

Franzero, Carlo Maria. *A Life in Exile: Ugo Foscolo in London, 1816–1827*. London: W. H. Allen, 1977.

Fraser, Flora. *The Unruly Queen, The Life of Queen Caroline*. Berkeley, CA.: University of California Press, 1997.

Freidman, Michael H. *The Making of a Tory Humanist: William Wordsworth and the Idea of Community*. New York: Columbia University Press, 1979.

Frey, Anna. *British State Romanticism: Authorship, Agency, and Bureaucratic Nationalism*. Palo Alto, CA: Stanford University Press, 2010.

Fubini, Mario. *Ugo Foscolo. Saggio critico*. Florence: La Nuova Italia, 1962.

Ugo Foscolo : Saggi, studi, note. Florence: La Nuova Italia, 1978.

Gamer, Michael. *Romanticism, Self-Canonization, and the Business of Poetry*. Cambridge: Cambridge University Press, 2017.

Gage, John. *J. M. W. Turner 'A Wonderful Range of Mind'*. New Haven, CT: Yale University Press, 1987.

Gardner, John. *Poetry and Popular Protest: Peterloo, Cato Street and the Queen Caroline Controversy*. Basingstoke: Palgrave Macmillan, 2011.

Gaull, Marilyn. *English Romanticism: The Human Context*. New York: W. W. Norton, 1988.

George, M. Dorothy. *English Political Caricature*. Oxford: Clarendon Press, 1959.

Gill, Stephen. *William Wordsworth: A Life*. Oxford: Clarendon Press, 1989.

Gilmartin, Kevin. *Writing against Revolution: Literary Conservatism in Britain 1790–1832*. Cambridge: Cambridge University Press, 2007.

Glass, Loren. 'Blood and Affection: The Poetics of Incest in *Manfred* and *Parisina*'. *Studies In Romanticism* 34 (1995): 211–226.

Gleckner, Robert F. *Byron and the Ruins of Paradise*. Baltimore, MD: Johns Hopkins Press, 1967.

Gleckner, Robert F., and Enscoe Gerald. *Romanticism, Points of View*. Detroit, MI: Wayne State University Press, 1964.

Goodman, Dena. *The Republic of Letters: A Cultural History of the French Enlightenment*. Ithaca, NY: Cornell University Press, 1994.

Goulding, Christopher. 'An Unpublished Shelley Letter'. *Review of English Studies* 52 (2001): 233–237.

Graf, Arturo. *L'anglomania e l'influsso inglese in Italia nel secolo xviii*. Turin: Ermanno Loescher, 1911.

Graham, Peter. *Don Juan and Regency England*. Charlottesville: University Press of Virgina, 1990.

Gramsci, Antonio. *Quaderni del carcere*, edited by Valentino Gerratana. Turin: Einaudi, 1975.

Green, Matthew, and Piya Pal-Lapinski, eds. *Byron and the Politics of Freedom and Terror*. London: Palgrave Macmillan, 2011.

Greene, Thomas M. *The Light in Troy: Imitation and Discovery in Renaissance Poetry*. New Haven, CT: Yale University Press, 1982.

Gregory, Alan P. *Coleridge and the Conservative Imagination*. Macon, GA: Mercer University Press, 2002.

Gregory, Desmond. *Napoleon's Italy*. Madison, NJ: Farleigh Dickinson, 2001.

Griffin, Robert. *Wordsworth's Pope: A Study in Literary Historiography*. Cambridge: Cambridge University Press, 1995.

Grossi, Paolo. *Pierre-Louis Ginguené, historien de la littérature italienne*. Oxford: Peter Lang, 2006.

Halmi, Nicholas. *The Genealogy of the Romantic Symbol*. Oxford: Oxford University Press, 2007.

Hamilton, Paul. *Realpoetik: European Romanticism and Literary Politics*. Oxford: Oxford University Press, 2013.

Hargreaves-Mawdsley, W. N. *The English Della Cruscans and Their Time, 1783–1828*. The Hague: Martin Nijhoff, 1967.

Harling, Philip. *The Waning of 'Old Corruption': The Politics of Economical Reform in Britain, 1779–1846*. Oxford: Clarendon Press, 1996.

Havely, Nick. *Dante's British Public, from the Fourteenth Century to the Present*. Oxford: Oxford University Press, 2014.

Dante in the Nineteenth Century: Reception, Canonicity, and Popularization. Oxford: Peter Lang, 2011.

Hay, Anthony. *The Whig Revival, 1808–1830*. London: Palgrave Macmillan, 2005.

Haycroft, T. W. 'Alien Legislation and the Prerogative of the Crown'. *Law Quarterly Review* 50 (1897): 165–186.

Herman, Peter C., ed. *Historicizing Theory*. Albany, NY: State University of New York Press, 2004.

Hibbert, Christopher. *Highwaymen*. London: Weidenfeld and Nicolson, 1967.

Hill, Christopher. *A Nation of Change and Novelty*. London: Routledge, 1990.
Hill, Geoffrey. *Collected Writings*. Oxford: Oxford University Press, 2009.
Hodges, Sheila. *Lorenzo Da Ponte: The Life and Times of Mozart's Librettist*. London: Granada, 1985.
Holden, Anthony. *The Man Who Wrote Mozart: The Extraordinary Life of Lorenzo Da Ponte*. London: Phoenix, 2006.
Holmes, Richard. *Shelley: The Pursuit*. 2nd edition. London: Harper Collins, 1994.
Hone, J. Ann. *For the Cause of Truth: Radicalism in London 1796–1821*. Oxford: Oxford University Press, 1982.
Hume, Robert D. *The Economics of Culture in London, 1660–1820*. Oxford: Oxford University Press, 2017.
Ilchester, Lord Giles. *The Home of the Hollands, 1605–1820*. London: John Murray, 1937.
Jacoff, Rachel, ed. *The Cambridge Companion to Dante*. Cambridge: Cambridge University Press, 1993.
Jones, Steven E. *Shelley's Satire: Violence, Exhortation, and Authority*. DeKalb, IL: Northern Illinois University Press, 1994.
Kassler, Michael, ed. *Music Entries at Stationer's Hall 1710–1818*. Aldershot: Ashgate, 2004.
Keach, William. *Arbitrary Power: Romanticism, Language, Politics*. Princeton, NJ: Princeton University Press, 2004.
Shelley's Style. New York: Meuthen, 1984.
Kelsall, Malcolm. *Byron's Politics*. Brighton: Harvester, 1987.
Kernodle, George. *From Art to Theatre. Form and Convention in the Renaissance*. Chicago, IL: Chicago University Press, 1944.
Klancher, Jon P. *The Making of English Reading Audiences, 1790–1832*. Madison, WI: University of Wisconsin Press, 1987.
Kroeber, Karl. *The Artifice of Reality: Poetic Style in Wordsworth, Foscolo, Keats, and Leopardi*. Madison, WI: University of Wisconsin Press, 1964.
Kucich, Greg. '"The Wit in the Dungeon": Leigh Hunt and the Insolent Politics of Cockney Coteries', *Romanticism on Net* 14 (1999).
Laven, David. Sex, 'Self-Fashioning and Spelling: (Auto)biographical Distortion, Prostitution, and Byron's Venetian Residence'. *Literaria Pragensia* 23, no. 46 (2013): 38–52.
Venice and the Venetia Under the Hapsburgs 1815–1835. Oxford: Oxford University Press, 2002.
Lazzarini, Antonio. *Patrizi, ussari, alboranti: il bosco del Cansiglio fra Venezia, Napoleone e l'Austria*. Veneto: D. De Bastiani, 2002.
Leask, Nigel. *Curiosity and the Aesthetics of Travel-Writing, 1770–1840: 'From an Antique Land'*. Oxford: Oxford University Press, 2002.
Lelli-Mami, Giorgio. *Francesco Mami, Cesenate Amico di Ugo Foscolo*. Cesena: Sintini, 1984.
Lemmi, Francesco. *La Restaurazione austriaca e Milano nel 1814*. Bologna, 1902.
Lennard, John. *But I Digress: The Exploitation of Parentheses in English Printed Verse*. Oxford: Clarendon Press, 1991.

Lévi-Strauss, Claude. *La Pensée sauvage*. London: Weidenfeld and Nicholson, 1966.
Lindenberger, Herbert. *Opera: The Extravagant Art*. Ithaca, NY: Cornell University Press, 1984.
Lindon, John. *Englishing Foscolo's Sepolcri*. Reading: Department of Italian Studies, 2008.
'Italy, 1799'. *Romance Studies* 18 (2000).
Studi sul Foscolo 'inglese'. Pisa: Giardini, 1987.
Links, J. G. *Canaletto and His Patrons*. London: Paul Elek, 1977.
Lister, Warwick. *Amico: The Life of Giovanni Battista Viotti*. Oxford: Oxford University Press, 2009.
Liu, Alan. 'The Power of Formalism: The New Historicism'. *English Literary History* 56 (1989): 721–771.
Lockhart, John Gibson. *Memoirs of the Life of Sir W. Scott*. Edinburgh: R. Cadell, 1839.
Lovejoy, Arthur. *The Great Chain of Being*. Cambridge, MA: Harvard University Press, 1936.
Luzzi, Joseph. *Romantic Europe and the Ghost of Italy*. New Haven, CT: Yale University Press, 2008.
Matthews, G. M. 'A Volcano's Voice in Shelley'. *English Literary History* 24 (1957): 191–228.
McAleer, Edward. *The Sensitive Plant: A Life of Lady Mount Cashell*. Chapel Hill, NC: University of North Carolina Press, 1958.
McCalman, Iain. *Radical Underworld: Prophets, Revolutionaries and Pornographers in London, 1795–1840*. Cambridge: Cambridge University Press, 1988.
MacCarthy, Fiona. *Byron: Life and Legend*. London: John Murray, 2002.
McCue, Maureen. *British Romanticism and the Reception of Old Master Art, 1793–1840*. Aldershot: Ashgate, 2014.
MacDonald, Peter Lorne. *Poor Polidori: A Critical Biography of the Author of the Vampyre*. Toronto: University of Toronto Press, 1991.
McFarlane, Cameron. *The Sodomite in Fiction and Satire, 1660–1750*. New York: Columbia University Press, 1997.
McGann, Jerome. *A Critique of Modern Textual Criticism*. Chicago, IL: Chicago University Press, 1983.
Fiery Dust: Byron's Poetic Development. Chicago, IL: Chicago University Press, 1968.
The Poetics of Sensibility: A Revolution in Literary Style. Oxford: Oxford University Press, 1996.
McNeil, Peter. *Pretty Gentlemen: Macaroni Men and the Eighteenth-Century Fashion World*. New Haven, CT: Yale University Press, 2018.
Mainardi, Patricia. *The End of the Salon: Art and the State in the Early Third Republic*. Cambridge: Cambridge University Press, 1993.
Manning, Peter. *Reading Romantics: Texts and Contexts*. Oxford: Oxford University Press, 1990.
Marshall, Roderick. *Italy in English Literature, 1755–1815. Origins of the Romantic Interest in Italy*. New York: Columbia University Press, 1934.

Marshall, William H. *Byron, Shelley, Hunt, and The Liberal*. Philadelphia: University of Pennsylvania Press, 1960.

Martin, Philip W. *Byron: A Poet Before His Public*. Cambridge: Cambridge University Press, 1982.

Marx, Karl. *A Contribution to the Critique from Hegel's Philosophy of Right*. London: 1844.

Marx, Karl, and Frederick Engels, *Collected Works*, translated by Richard Dixon et al. London: Lawrence and Wishart, 1975–2004.

Matzneff, Gabriel. *La diététique de Lord Byron*. Paris: La Table Ronde, 1984.

Maurizio, Isabella. *Risorgimento in Exile: Italian Émigrés and the Liberal International in the Post-Napoleonic Era*. Oxford: Oxford University Press, 2009.

Mayer, David. *Harlequin in His Element: The English Pantomime, 1806–1836*. Cambridge, MA: Harvard University Press, 1969.

Mitchell, Leslie. *Holland House*. London: Duckworth, 1980.

Molmenti, Pompeo Gherardo. *La storia di Venezia nella vita privata dalle origini alla caduta della Repubblica*. Bergamo: 1905.

Mori, Jennifer. *The Culture of Diplomacy: Britain in Europe, c. 1750–1830*. Manchester: Manchester University Press, 2010.

Mulhern, Francis. *Culture/Metaculture*. London: Routledge, 2000.

Mulvihill, James. 'Character and Culture in Hazlitt's Spirit of the Age'. *Nineteenth-Century Literature* 45 (1990): 281–299.

Nagari, Mario. *Pietro Rolandi da Quarona Valsesia*. Novara: 1959.

Nicholson, Andrew, ed. *The Manuscripts of the Younger Romantics: Lord Byron XII*. New York: Garland, 1998.

Norwich, John Julius. *Venice: The Greatness and The Fall*. London: Penguin, 1981.

Paradise of Cities. London: Viking, 2003.

O'Connor, Maura. *The Romance of Italy and the English Political Imagination*. London: Macmillan, 1998.

O'Neill, Michael. *Romanticism and the Self-Conscious Poem*. Oxford: Clarendon Press, 1997.

O'Neill, Michael, and Anthony Howe, eds., with the assistance of Madeleine Callaghan. *The Oxford Handbook of Percy Bysshe Shelley*. Oxford: Oxford University Press, 2013.

O'Neill, Michael, and Mark Sandy, eds. *Romanticism*. London: Routledge, 2006.

O'Neill, Michael, Mark Sandy, and Sarah Wooton. *Venice and the Cultural Imagination*. London: Pickering and Chatto, 2012.

O'Neill, Tom. 'The Figure of Alfieri in "Dei Sepolcri"'. *Italica* 55 (1978): 321–337.

Oliver, Susan. 'Crossing "Dark Barriers": Intertextuality and Dialogue between Lord Byron and Sir Walter Scott'. *Studies in Romanticism* 47 (2008): 15–35.

Osborne, Richard. *Rossni*. 2nd edition. Oxford: Oxford University Press, 2007.

Pagnini, Cesare. *Bibliografia dapontiana*. Trieste, 1960.

Parks, George B. 'The First Italianate Englishman'. *Studies in the Renaissance* VIII (1961): 197–216.

Parmegiani, Sandra. *Ugo Foscolo and English Culture*. London: Maney, 2010.

Pemble, John. *Venice Rediscovered.* Oxford: Oxford University Press, 1995.

Peterfreund, Stuart. 'Shelley, Monboddo, Vico, and the Language of Poetry'. *Style* 15 (1981): 382–400.

Pfau, Thomas, and Robert F. Gleckner, eds. *Lessons of Romanticism.* Durham, NC: Duke University Press, 1998.

Piper, William Bowman. *The Heroic Couplet.* Cleveland, OH: Case Western University Press, 1969.

Pite, Ralph. *The Circle of Our Vision: Dante's Presence in English Romantic Poetry.* Oxford: Oxford University Press, 1994.

'Shelley in Italy'. *The Yearbook of English Studies* 34 (2004): 46–61.

Pocock, J. G. A. *The Machiavellian Moment: Florentine Political Thought and the Atlantic Republican Tradition.* Princeton, NJ: Princeton University Press, 1975.

'The Machiavellian Moment Revisited: A Study in History and Ideology'. *Journal of Modern History* 53 (1981): 49–72.

Virtue, Commerce, and History: Essays on Political Thought and History, Chiefly in the Eighteenth Century. Cambridge: Cambridge University Press, 1976.

Pratt, Lynda, ed. *Robert Southey and the Contexts of English Romanticism.* Aldershot: Ashgate, 2006.

Praz, Mario. *The Flaming Heart: Essays on Crashaw, Macchiavelli, and Other Studies in the Relations between Italian and English Literature from Chaucer to T. S. Eliot.* Gloucester, MA: Peter Smith, 1966.

Quennell, Peter. *Genius in the Drawing-Room: The Literary Salon in the Nineteenth and Twentieth Centuries.* London: Weidenfeld and Nicolson, 1980.

Rath, Reuben John. *The Provisional Austrian Regime in the Lombardy-Venetia, 1814–1815.* Austin, TX: University Texas Press, 1969.

Rawes, Alan. *Byron's Poetic Experimentation.* Aldershot: Ashgate, 2000.

'"From the Italian": Byron's Translation of Pulci's Morgante Maggiore'. *Litteraria Prangensia* 23, no. 46 (2013): 6–22.

Rawes, Alan, and Diego Saglia eds. *Byron and Italy.* Manchester: Manchester University Press, 2017.

Reiman, Donald H. *Shelley's "The Triumph of Life": A Critical Study.* Urbana, IL: University of Illinois Press, 1965.

'Structure, Symbol, and Theme in 'Lines Written among the "Euganean Hills"'. *PMLA* 77 (1962): 404–413.

Ricks, Christopher. *Essays in Appreciation.* Oxford: Oxford University Press, 1996.

Roberts, Richard Ellis. *Samuel Rogers and His Circle.* London: Methuen & Co., 1910.

Robinson, Charles E. *Shelley and Byron: The Snake and Eagle Wreathed in Fight.* Baltimore, MD: Johns Hopkins University Press, 1976.

Roe, Nicholas. *Fiery Heart: The First Life of Leigh Hunt.* London: Pimlico, 2005.

John Keats and the Culture of Dissent. Oxford: Oxford University Press, 1997.

The Politics of Nature: Wordsworth and Some Contemporaries. Basingstoke: Macmillan, 1992.

Wordsworth and Coleridge: The Radical Years. Oxford: Oxford University Press, 1988.

Roe, Nicholas, ed. *Leigh Hunt: Life, Poetics, Politics*. London: Routledge, 2003.

Romani, George T. *The Neapolitan Revolution of 1820–1821*. Evanston, IL: Northwestern University Press, 1950.

Rosselli, John. *Lord William Bentinck and the British Occupation of Sicily 1811–1814*. Cambridge: Cambridge University Press, 1956.

Lord William Bentinck: The Making of a Liberal Imperialist, 1774–1839. Delhi: Thomson, 1974.

The Opera Industry in Italy from Cimarosa to Verdi: The Role of the Impresario. Cambridge: Cambridge University Press, 1984.

Rudé, George F. E. 'The Gordon Riots: A Study of the Rioters and Their Victims'. *Transactions of the Royal Historical Society* 6 (1956): 93–114.

Rutherford, Andrew. *Byron: A Critical Study*. Palo Alto, CA: Stanford University Press, 1961.

Sack, James J. *From Jacobite to Conservative: Reaction and Orthodoxy in Britain, c.1760–1832*. Cambridge: Cambridge University Press, 1993.

Saglia, Diego. *European Literatures in Britain, 1815–1832: Romantic Translations*. Cambridge: Cambridge University Press, 2018.

Poetic Castles in Spain: British Romanticism and Figurations of Iberia. Amsterdam: Rodopi, 2000.

Said, Edward W. *Reflections on Exile*. Cambridge, MA: Harvard University Press, 2000.

Sangiorgi, Roberto. 'Giambattista Casti's "Novelle Galanti" and Lord Byron's "Beppo"'. *Italica* 28 (December 1951): 261–269.

Schmidt, Arnold. *Byron and the Rhetoric of Italian Nationalism*, New York: Palgrave Macmillan, 2010.

Schoenfield, Mark. *British Periodicals and Romantic Identity: The 'Literary Lower Empire'*. London: Palgrave, 2009.

Schoina, Maria. *Romantic 'Anglo-Italians': Configurations of Identity in Byron, the Shelleys, and the Pisan Circle*. Aldershot: Ashgate, 2009.

Scrivener, Michael. *The Cosmopolitan Ideal in the Age of Revolution and Reaction*. London: Pickering & Chatto, 2007.

Serpelloni, Christian. *In difesa di Napoleone: Bonaparte, la Serenissima e il processo di Venezia*. Verona: Cierre, 2006.

Seymour, Elizabeth Mary Romilly, Lady, ed. *The "Pope" of Holland House: Selections from the Correspondence of John Whishaw and His Friends 1813–1840*. London: 1906.

Sinfield, Alan. *Faultlines. Cultural Materialism and the Politics of Dissident Reading*. Oxford: Clarendon Press, 1992.

Smiles, Samuel. *A Publisher and His Friends: Memoirs and Correspondence of John Murray*. London: John Murray, 1891.

Smith, E. A. *George IV*. New Haven, CT: Yale University Press, 1999.

Sóriga, Renato. 'Augustus Bozzi Granville e la Rivista 'L'Italico''. *Bollettino della Società pavese di storia patria* 14 (1914): 265–301.

Speight, Kathleen. 'An English Writer of Italian Verse'. *Studies in Philology* 43 (1946): 70–80.

Sponza, Lucio. *Italian Immigrants in Nineteenth Century Britain*. Leicester: Leicester University Press, 1988.

St. Clair, William. *The Reading Nation in the Romantic Period.* Cambridge: Cambridge University Press, 2004.

Stabler, Jane. *The Artistry of Exile: Romantic and Victorian Writers in Italy*. Oxford: Oxford University Press, 2013.

Byron, Poetics, and History. Cambridge: Cambridge University Press, 2002.

Stabler, Jane, ed. *Byron*. London: Longman, 1998.

Sternberger, Dolf. *Panorama of the Nineteenth Century*, translated by Joachim Neugroschel. Oxford: Basil Blackwell, 1977.

Stevenson, John, ed. *London in the Age of Reform*. Oxford: Blackwell, 1977.

Stewart, David. *Romantic Magazines and Metropolitan Literary Culture*. Basingstoke: Palgrave Macmillan, 2011.

Stevenson, Lionel. '"My Last Duchess" and Parisina'. *Modern Language Notes* 74 (1959): 489–492.

Succi, Dario, ed. *Capricci veneziani del Settecento*. Turin: Allemandi, 1988.

Swinburne, Algernon Charles. *Essays and Studies*. London, 1876.

Tanner, Tony. *Venice Desired*. Cambridge, MA: Harvard University Press, 1992.

Thompson, E. P. *Making History: Writings on History and Culture*. New York: The New Press, 1994.

The Making of the English Working Class. London: Penguin 1968.

'Patrician Society, Plebeian Culture'. *Journal of Social History* (1974): 382–405.

The Romantics. Rendelsham: Merlin Press, 1997.

Took, John and Prue Shaw, eds. *Reflexivity: Critical Themes in the Italian Cultural Tradition*. Ravenna: A. Longo, 2000.

Trinchero, Cristina. *Pierre-Louis Ginguené e l'identità nazionale italiana nel contesto vultural europeo*. Rome: Bulzoni, 2004.

Urry, John. *The Tourist Gaze: Leisure and Travel in Contemporary Societies*. London: SAGE, 2011.

Van Rennes, J. J. *Bowles, Byron, and the Pope Controversy*. Amsterdam: H. J. Paris, 1927.

Vassallo, Peter. *Byron, The Italian Literary Influence*. London: Macmillan, 1984.

Vincent, E. R. *Byron, Hobhouse and Foscolo*. Cambridge: Cambridge University Press, 1949.

Ugo Foscolo. Cambridge: Cambridge University Press, 1953.

Walford Davies, Damian, ed. *Romaticism, History, Historicism*. London: Routledge, 2009.

Wang, Orrin. *Fantastic Modernity: Dialectical Readings in Romanticism and Theory*. Baltimore, MD: Johns Hopkins University Press, 1996.

Wasserman, Earl. 'The Return of the Enjambed Couplet'. *English Literary History* 7 (1940): 239–252.

Shelley: A Critical Reading. Baltimore, MD: Johns Hopkins University Press, 1971.

Waters, Lindsay. 'The 'Desultory Rhyme of Don Juan: Byron, Pulci and the Improvisatory Style'. *English Literary History* 45 (1978): 429–442.

Webb, Timothy. 'After Horsemonger Lane: Leigh Hunt's London Letters to Byron (1815–1816)'. *Romanticism* 16 (2010): 233–266.

'Leigh Hunt's Letters to Byron from Horsemonger Lane Gaol: A Commentary'. *The Byron Journal* 37 (2009): 21–32.

'Leigh Hunt to Lord Byron: Eight Letters from Horsemonger Lane Gaol'. *The Byron Journal* 36 (2008): 131–142.

The Violet in the Crucible: Shelley and Translation. Oxford: Clarendon Press, 1976.

Webster, Sir Charles. *The Foreign Policy of Castlereagh 1815–1822*. London: George Bell, 1934.

Weinberg, Alan. *Shelley's Italian Experience*. London: Macmillan, 1991.

Wheatley, Kim. 'The Blackwood's Attacks on Leigh Hunt'. *Nineteenth-Century Literature* 47 (1992): 1–31.

Wicks, Margaret. *The Italian Exiles in London 1816–1848*. Manchester: Manchester University Press, 1937.

Williams, Raymond. *Marxism and Literature*. Oxford: Oxford University Press, 1977.

Wilson, Cheryl, ed. *Byron: Heritage and Legacy*. London: Palgrave, 2009.

Wise, Thomas J. *The Ashley Library. A Catalogue of Printed Books, Manuscripts and Autograph Letters Collected by T. J. Wise*. London: Private Circulation, 1922–1936.

Wolfson, Susan. *Formal Charges: The Shaping of Poetry in British Romanticism*. Princeton, NJ: Princeton University Press, 1997.

Wood, Gillen D'Arcy. *Romanticism and Music Culture in Britain, 1770–1840: Virtue and Virtuosity*. Cambridge: Cambridge University Press, 2010.

Wood, Marcus. *Radical Satire and Print Culture, 1790–1822*. Oxford: Clarendon Press, 1994.

Worley, Sharon. *Women's Literary Salons and Political Propaganda During the Napoleonic Era: The Cradle of Patriotic Nationalism*. Lewiston, NY: Edwin Mellen Press, 2009.

Worrall, David. *The Politics of Romantic Theatricality, 1787–1832: The Road to the Stage*. Basingstoke: Palgrave Macmillan 2007.

Wright, Herbert G. *Boccaccio in England from Chaucer to Tennyson*. London: Athlone Press, 1957.

Zaho, Margaret. *Imago Triumphalis: The Function and Significance of Triumphal Imagery for Italian Renaissance Rulers*. New York: Peter Lang, 2004.

Zorzi, Alvise. *Venezia Austriaca 1798–1866*. Rome: Laterza, 1985.

Zuccato, Edoardo. *Petrarch in Romantic England*. Basingstoke: Palgrave Macmillan, 2008.

5 Online Resources and Other Media

Curtis, Richard, and Ben Elton. *Blackadder the Third*. BBC. First aired 1987.

Godwin, William. *The Diary of William Godwin*, edited by Victoria Myers, David O'Shaughnessy, and Mark Philp. Oxford: Oxford Digital Library, 2010. http://godwindiary.bodleian.ox.ac.uk/people/ZEN01.html

Hobhouse, John Cam. *Diary*, edited by Peter Cochran, 2009. http://petercochran.wordpress.com/hobhouses-diary/

Hunt, Leigh. *Leigh Hunt Online: The Letters*. Digitised by University of Iowa at http://digital.lib.uiowa.edu/leighhunt/ (2014).

Oxford English Dictionary Online. Oxford: Oxford University Press, 2014. http://oed.com

Index

CAMBRIDGE STUDIES IN ROMANTICISM

General Editor
JAMES CHANDLER, *University of Chicago*

1. *Romantic Correspondence: Women, Politics and the Fiction of Letters*
MARY A. FAVRET

2. *British Romantic Writers and the East: Anxieties of Empire*
NIGEL LEASK

3. *Poetry as an Occupation and an Art in Britain, 1760–1830*
PETER MURPHY

4. *Edmund Burke's Aesthetic Ideology: Language, Gender and Political Economy in Revolution*
TOM FURNISS

5. *In the Theatre of Romanticism: Coleridge, Nationalism, Women*
JULIE A. CARLSON

6. *Keats, Narrative and Audience*
ANDREW BENNETT

7. *Romance and Revolution: Shelley and the Politics of a Genre*
DAVID DUFF

8. *Literature, Education, and Romanticism: Reading as Social Practice, 1780–1832*
ALAN RICHARDSON

9. *Women Writing about Money: Women's Fiction in England, 1790–1820*
EDWARD COPELAND

10. *Shelley and the Revolution in Taste: The Body and the Natural World*
TIMOTHY MORTON

11. *William Cobbett: The Politics of Style*
LEONORA NATTRASS

12. *The Rise of Supernatural Fiction, 1762–1800*
E. J. CLERY

13. *Women Travel Writers and the Language of Aesthetics, 1716–1818*
ELIZABETH A. BOHLS

14. *Napoleon and English Romanticism*
SIMON BAINBRIDGE

15. *Romantic Vagrancy: Wordsworth and the Simulation of Freedom*
CELESTE LANGAN

16. *Wordsworth and the Geologists*
JOHN WYATT

17. *Wordsworth's Pope: A Study in Literary Historiography*
ROBERT J. GRIFFIN

18. *The Politics of Sensibility: Race, Gender and Commerce in the Sentimental Novel*
MARKMAN ELLIS

19. *Reading Daughters' Fictions, 1709–1834: Novels and Society from Manley to Edgeworth*
CAROLINE GONDA

20. *Romantic Identities: Varieties of Subjectivity, 1774–1830*
ANDREA K. HENDERSON

21. *Print Politics: The Press and Radical Opposition in Early Nineteenth-Century England*
KEVIN GILMARTIN

22. *Reinventing Allegory*
THERESA M. KELLEY

23. *British Satire and the Politics of Style, 1789–1832*
GARY DYER

24. *The Romantic Reformation: Religious Politics in English Literature, 1789–1824*
ROBERT M. RYAN

25. *De Quincey's Romanticism: Canonical Minority and the Forms of Transmission*
MARGARET RUSSETT

26. *Coleridge on Dreaming: Romanticism, Dreams and the Medical Imagination*
JENNIFER FORD

27. *Romantic Imperialism: Universal Empire and the Culture of Modernity*
SAREE MAKDISI

28. *Ideology and Utopia in the Poetry of William Blake*
NICHOLAS M. WILLIAMS

29. *Sexual Politics and the Romantic Author*
SONIA HOFKOSH

30. *Lyric and Labour in the Romantic Tradition*
ANNE JANOWITZ

31. *Poetry and Politics in the Cockney School: Keats, Shelley, Hunt and Their Circle*
JEFFREY N. COX

32. *Rousseau, Robespierre and English Romanticism*
GREGORY DART

33. *Contesting the Gothic: Fiction, Genre and Cultural Conflict, 1764–1832*
JAMES WATT

34. *Romanticism, Aesthetics, and Nationalism*
DAVID ARAM KAISER

35. *Romantic Poets and the Culture of Posterity*
ANDREW BENNETT

36. *The Crisis of Literature in the 1790s: Print Culture and the Public Sphere*
PAUL KEEN

37. *Romantic Atheism: Poetry and Freethought, 1780–1830*
MARTIN PRIESTMAN

38. *Romanticism and Slave Narratives: Transatlantic Testimonies*
HELEN THOMAS

39. *Imagination under Pressure, 1789–1832: Aesthetics, Politics, and Utility*
JOHN WHALE

40. *Romanticism and the Gothic: Genre, Reception, and Canon Formation, 1790–1820*
MICHAEL GAMER

41. *Romanticism and the Human Sciences: Poetry, Population, and the Discourse of the Species*
MAUREEN N. MCLANE

42. *The Poetics of Spice: Romantic Consumerism and the Exotic*
TIMOTHY MORTON

43. *British Fiction and the Production of Social Order, 1740–1830*
MIRANDA J. BURGESS

44. *Women Writers and the English Nation in the 1790s*
ANGELA KEANE

45. *Literary Magazines and British Romanticism*
MARK PARKER

46. *Women, Nationalism and the Romantic Stage: Theatre and Politics in Britain, 1780–1800*
BETSY BOLTON

47. *British Romanticism and the Science of the Mind*
ALAN RICHARDSON

48. *The Anti-Jacobin Novel: British Conservatism and the French Revolution*
M. O. GRENBY

49. *Romantic Austen: Sexual Politics and the Literary Canon*
CLARA TUITE

50. *Byron and Romanticism*
JEROME MCGANN and JAMES SODERHOLM

51. *The Romantic National Tale and the Question of Ireland*
INA FERRIS

52. *Byron, Poetics and History*
JANE STABLER

53. *Religion, Toleration, and British Writing, 1790–1830*
MARK CANUEL

54. *Fatal Women of Romanticism*
ADRIANA CRACIUN

55. *Knowledge and Indifference in English Romantic Prose*
TIM MILNES

56. *Mary Wollstonecraft and the Feminist Imagination*
BARBARA TAYLOR

57. *Romanticism, Maternity and the Body Politic*
JULIE KIPP

58. *Romanticism and Animal Rights*
DAVID PERKINS

59. *Georgic Modernity and British Romanticism: Poetry and the Mediation of History*
KEVIS GOODMAN

60. *Literature, Science and Exploration in the Romantic Era: Bodies of Knowledge*
TIMOTHY FULFORD, DEBBIE LEE, and PETER J. KITSON

61. *Romantic Colonization and British Anti-Slavery*
DEIRDRE COLEMAN

62. *Anger, Revolution, and Romanticism*
ANDREW M. STAUFFER

63. *Shelley and the Revolutionary Sublime*
CIAN DUFFY

64. *Fictions and Fakes: Forging Romantic Authenticity, 1760–1845*
MARGARET RUSSETT

65. *Early Romanticism and Religious Dissent*
DANIEL E. WHITE

66. *The Invention of Evening: Perception and Time in Romantic Poetry*
CHRISTOPHER R. MILLER

67. *Wordsworth's Philosophic Song*
SIMON JARVIS

68. *Romanticism and the Rise of the Mass Public*
ANDREW FRANTA

69. *Writing against Revolution: Literary Conservatism in Britain, 1790–1832*
KEVIN GILMARTIN

70. *Women, Sociability and Theatre in Georgian London*
GILLIAN RUSSELL

71. *The Lake Poets and Professional Identity*
BRIAN GOLDBERG

72. *Wordsworth Writing*
ANDREW BENNETT

73. *Science and Sensation in Romantic Poetry*
NOEL JACKSON

74. *Advertising and Satirical Culture in the Romantic Period*
JOHN STRACHAN

75. *Romanticism and the Painful Pleasures of Modern Life*
ANDREA K. HENDERSON

76. *Balladeering, Minstrelsy, and the Making of British Romantic Poetry*
MAUREEN N. MCLANE

77. *Romanticism and Improvisation, 1750–1850*
ANGELA ESTERHAMMER

78. *Scotland and the Fictions of Geography: North Britain, 1760–1830*
PENNY FIELDING

79. *Wordsworth, Commodification and Social Concern: The Poetics of Modernity*
DAVID SIMPSON

80. *Sentimental Masculinity and the Rise of History, 1790–1890*
MIKE GOODE

81. *Fracture and Fragmentation in British Romanticism*
ALEXANDER REGIER

82. *Romanticism and Music Culture in Britain, 1770–1840: Virtue and Virtuosity*
GILLEN D'ARCY WOOD

83. *The Truth about Romanticism: Pragmatism and Idealism in Keats, Shelley, Coleridge*
TIM MILNES

84. *Blake's Gifts: Poetry and the Politics of Exchange*
SARAH HAGGARTY

85. *Real Money and Romanticism*
MATTHEW ROWLINSON

86. *Sentimental Literature and Anglo-Scottish Identity, 1745–1820*
JULIET SHIELDS

87. *Romantic Tragedies: The Dark Employments of Wordsworth, Coleridge, and Shelley*
REEVE PARKER

88. *Blake, Sexuality and Bourgeois Politeness*
SUSAN MATTHEWS

89. *Idleness, Contemplation and the Aesthetic*
RICHARD ADELMAN

90. *Shelley's Visual Imagination*
NANCY MOORE GOSLEE

91. *A Cultural History of the Irish Novel, 1790–1829*
CLAIRE CONNOLLY

92. *Literature, Commerce, and the Spectacle of Modernity, 1750–1800*
PAUL KEEN

93. *Romanticism and Childhood: The Infantilization of British Literary Culture*
ANN WEIRDA ROWLAND

94. *Metropolitan Art and Literature, 1810–1840: Cockney Adventures*
GREGORY DART

95. *Wordsworth and the Enlightenment Idea of Pleasure*
ROWAN BOYSON

96. *John Clare and Community*
JOHN GOODRIDGE

97. *The Romantic Crowd*
MARY FAIRCLOUGH

98. *Romantic Women Writers, Revolution and Prophecy*
ORIANNE SMITH

99. *Britain, France and the Gothic, 1764–1820*
ANGELA WRIGHT

100. *Transfiguring the Arts and Sciences*
JON KLANCHER

101. *Shelley and the Apprehension of Life*
ROSS WILSON

102. *Poetics of Character: Transatlantic Encounters 1700–1900*
SUSAN MANNING

103. *Romanticism and Caricature*
IAN HAYWOOD

104. *The Late Poetry of the Lake Poets: Romanticism Revised*
TIM FULFORD

105. *Forging Romantic China: Sino-British Cultural Exchange 1760–1840*
PETER J. KITSON

106. *Coleridge and the Philosophy of Poetic Form*
EWAN JAMES JONES

107. *Romanticism in the Shadow of War: Literary Culture in the Napoleonic War Years*
JEFFREY N. COX

108. *Slavery and the Politics of Place: Representing the Colonial Caribbean, 1770–1833*
ELIZABETH A. BOHLS

109. *The Orient and the Young Romantics*
ANDREW WARREN

110. *Lord Byron and Scandalous Celebrity*
CLARA TUITE

111. *Radical Orientalism: Rights, Reform, and Romanticism*
GERARD COHEN-VRIGNAUD

112. *Print, Publicity, and Popular Radicalism in the 1790s*
JON MEE

113. *Wordsworth and the Art of Philosophical Travel*
MARK OFFORD

114. *Romanticism, Self-Canonization, and the Business of Poetry*
MICHAEL GAMER

115. *Women Wanderers and the Writing of Mobility, 1784–1814*
INGRID HORROCKS

116. *Eighteen Hundred and Eleven: Poetry, Protest and Economic Crisis*
E. J. CLERY

117. *Urbanization and English Romantic Poetry*
STEPHEN TEDESCHI

118. *The Poetics of Decline in British Romanticism*
JONATHAN SACHS

119. *The Caribbean and the Medical Imagination, 1764–1834: Slavery, Disease and Colonial Modernity*
EMILY SENIOR

120. *Science, Form, and the Problem of Induction in British Romanticism*
DAHLIA PORTER

121. *Wordsworth and the Poetics of Air*
THOMAS H. FORD

122. *Romantic Art in Practice: Cultural Work and the Sister Arts, 1760–1820*
THORA BRYLOWE

123. *European Literatures in Britain, 1815-1832: Romantic Translations*
IEGO SIGALIA

124. *Romanticism and theatrical experience: Kean, Hazlitt and Keats in the Age of Theatrical News*
JONATHAN MULROONEY

125. *The Romantic Tavern: Literature and Conviviality in the Age of Revolution*
IAN NEWMAN

126. *British Orientalisms, 1759–1835*
JAMES WATT

127. *Print and Performance in the 1820s*
ANGELA ESTERHAMMER

128. *The Italian Idea*
WILL BOWERS

129. *The Ephemeral Eighteenth Century*
GILLIAN RUSSELL